How to
Read
Better
and Faster

Other Books by Norman Lewis

How to Read Better and Faster

Fourth Edition

NORMAN LEWIS

Rio Hondo College

GOYL SaaB

BINNY PUBLISHING HOUSE

A Subsidiary of
W.R. Goyal Publishers & Distributors
86, UB Jawahar Nagar, Delhi - 110 007
Tel: 23858362, 23852986, e-mail:goyal@vsnl.com

How to Read Better and Faster, Fourth Edition

Copyright © 1978 by Norman Lewis.
        © Binny Publishing House, for the Indian Edtion

This Indian Edition 2005

First Indian Edition 1980, Published by arrangement
with HARPER & ROW Publishers. Inc. New York.

Binny Publishing House Books are distributed
by GENERAL BOOK DEPOT, 1691, NAI SARAK
DELHI-110 006, INDIA; Tel: 2326 3695, 2325 0635
e-mail:goyal@vsnl.com

Published by Ravinder Goyal, Binny Publishing House,
Delhi-110 007, India

Printed in India at
Meenakshi Art Printers, Delhi - 110006

Acknowledgements

Grateful acknowledgment is made for permission to use the following material. Page 5: "A Happy Anniversary Lunch, and Then...," by Richard Amerian, from the *Los Angeles Times*, August 6, 1976. Reprinted by permission of the author. Page 9: "Moral: Money Is as Slippery as a $3 Eel," by Carly Mary Cady, from the *Los Angeles Times*, August 9, 1976. Reprinted by permission of the author. All selections and tests in the ten exercises in Chapter 2: from Norman Lewis, *Reading, Spelling, Vocabulary, Pronunciation* (Books 1, 2, 3). Copyright 1967 by Amsco School Publications, New York. Reprinted by permission. Page 22: "Learning in School," from *Learning: A Survey of Psychological Interpretations*, Intext Publishers Group, New York (formerly Chandler). Reprinted by permission of the publisher. Page 24: "The Sacred Cows of India," from *Culture, People, Nature: An Introduction to General Anthropology*, by Marvin Harris, Thomas Y. Crowell Company, New York, 1975. Page 27: "Driver Applicants Drive Some Testers Up or Through Wall," by Ron Cooper. Reprinted by permission of *The Wall Street Journal*, © Dow Jones & Company Inc., March 28, 1975. All rights reserved. Page 33: from *Streamline Your Mind*, by James L. Mursell, J. B. Lippincott Company, Philadelphia. Page 34: "Who, Me? Chop Off the Worm's Head?" by Douglas Cox, from the *Los Angeles Times*, August 19, 1976. Reprinted by permission of the author. Page 36: "A Stutterer Writes to a Former Teacher," by Irving S. Shaw. Reprinted by permission from the *National Education Journal*. Page 38: "Johnny, a Rejected Child," by Bertha Padouk. Reprinted by permission from *Understanding the Child*. Page 41: "The Bandit Had Brown Hair—I Think," by Jeff Bunzel, from the *Los Angeles Times*, March 15, 1976. Reprinted by permission. Page 48: from *The Air University Reading Improvement Program*, The Air University, Maxwell Air Force Base, Montgomery, Alabama, June 1948. Reprinted by permission. Page 61: "Professors Learn to Read," by Esther J. McConihe, from *Adult Education*. Page 65–66: from *Silent Reading*, by J. A. O'Brien, Macmillan, New York. Pages 68–69: from *Improvement in Reading*, by Louella Cole, Holt, Rinehart and Winston, New York.

Reprinted by permission. Page 72: "Some Editors Overcensortive," by Jack Smith, from the *Los Angeles Times*, April 18, 1976. Reprinted by permission. Page 75: "The Class Menagerie," by Jack Smith, from the *Los Angeles Times*, April 18, 1976. Reprinted by permission. Page 80: "College Enrollment on Rise," from *The Register*, February 12, 1976, Santa Ana, California. Reprinted by permission of the Associated Press. Page 80: "Fried Foods," by Irving S. Cutter, M. D., from *Your Life*. Reprinted by permission. Page 81: "Your Diary," from *Your Life*. Reprinted by permission. Page 81: "The Best Learning," by Cyril O. Houle, from *Classroom Techniques in Improving Reading*, compiled and edited by William S. Gray, University of Chicago Press, Chicago. Reprinted by permission. Page 82: "Thought and Language," from *Language: An Introduction to the Study of Speech*, by Edward Sapir, Harcourt, Brace, Jovanovich, New York, 1949. Reprinted by permission. Page 82: "Oh My God! My Name's Not on Any of Those Lists!" by Emil Draitser, from the *Los Angeles Times*, June 25, 1976. Reprinted by permission. Page 84: "BA '75: The Hapless Odyssey of a Young Classicist Cum Clerk," by Michael Christie, from the *Los Angeles Times*, March 30, 1976. Reprinted by permission of the author. Page 88: from a piece by Delwyn G. Schubert in the *Clearing House*. Reprinted by permission. Page 88, Exercise 9: from *Man Against Himself*, by Karl Menninger, Harcourt, Brace, Jovanovich, New York. Page 89, Exercise 10: from a piece by Mandel Sherman in *Clinical Studies in Reading*. Copyright 1949 by the University of Chicago Press. Reprinted by permission. Page 89, Exercise 11: from the *Reader's Digest*. Copyright 1956 by the Reader's Digest Association, Inc. Reprinted by permission. Pages 89-90, Exercise 12: from a piece by Fred W. Jobe in *Clinical Studies in Reading*. Copyright 1953 by the University of Chicago Press. Reprinted by permission. Page 90, Exercise 13: from a piece by Frank Laycock in the *Journal of Experimental Education*. Page 90, Exercise 14: from a piece by Peter L. Spencer in *The Yearbook of the Claremont College Reading Conference*. Pages 103-104, Exercises 17 and 18: from *Reading, Spelling, Vocabulary, Pronunciation* (Books 1, 2, 3), by Norman Lewis, Copyright 1967 by Amsco School Publications, Inc., New York. Reprinted by special permission. Page 106: "The Sudden Handicap," by Kate Holliday, from the *Los Angeles Times*, February 5, 1975. Reprinted by permission. Page 109: "For June Graduates, a Few Words About Work," by Peter P. Bruno, Jr., from the *Los Angeles Times*, May 13, 1976. Reprinted by permission. Page 114: "Make Me a Child Again, Just for Tonight," by Milton R. Stern, from *Pleasures in Learning*, published by the Division of General Education, New York University. Reprinted by permission. Page 117: "Take It Easy to Learn Better," by Donald A. Laird, from *Your Life*. Reprinted by permission. Pages 127-128: "A Child of Flower Children Withers Away," by Bill Weinstein, from the *Los Angeles Times*, June 11, 1976. Reprinted by permission of the author. Pages 129-130: "The Mark of a Society That No Longer Trusts," by Paul Chitlik, from the *Los Angeles Times*, March 25, 1976. Reprinted by permission of the author. Page 131: "Efficiency," by Paul F. Watkins, from the *Herald Progress*, Ashland, Virginia. Reprinted by permission. Page 131: "A Child's Vocabulary," from "Jimmy John," by Anna Perrott Rose, from the *Ladies' Home Journal*. Reprinted by permission of the author. Pages 132-134: "Rock 'n' Eggroll, With a Side of Coke," by C. Y. Lee, from the *Los Angeles Times*, March 6, 1976. Reprinted by permission of the author. Pages 136-138: "Bangling the Language," by Norman Cousins, from the *Saturday Review*. Reprinted by permission. Pages 138-139: "It Ain't the Length, It's the Obscurity," an editorial in the *New York News.* Reprinted by permission. Pages 140–141: "Green Light Means Danger," by William S. Dutton, from *Collier's.* Copyright 1949 by the Crowell-Collier Publishing Co. Reprinted by permission. Pages 142–143: "Is Traffic-Court Justice Blind?," by Albert Q. Maisel, from *Reader's Digest.* Reprinted by permission of the author and of *Reader's Digest.* Pages 145–146, Exercise 32: from *Publisher's Weekly.* Reprinted by permission. Pages 146–149: "The Improvement of Eye Movements," by Ruth Strang, from *Study Type of Reading Exercises.* Reprinted by permission. Pages 149–151: "On a Magazine Cover," by Bennett Cerf, from *Shake Well Before Using,* Simon & Schuster, Inc., New York. Reprinted by permission. Pages 151–152: "What? You a Quiz Clansman?" by Murray Robinson, from the New York *World-Telegram and Sun.* Reprinted by permission. Page 161: " 'Benefits' for Big Boys," by Sylvia F. Porter, from the *New York Post.* Copyright 1956, The Hall Syndicate, Inc. Reprinted by permission. Page 162: "How to Concentrate Better," by T. E. Cochran. Ph.D., from *Your Life.* Copyright 1957 by the Kingsway Press, Inc. Reprinted by permission. Pages 164–167: "How to Make a Million," by Joseph T. Nolan, from *The New York Times Magazine.* Reprinted by permission. Pages 171–172: "The Interval in Learning," by Bruno Furst, from *Stop Forgetting,* Greenberg: Publisher, New York. Reprinted by permission of the author. Pages 173–174, Exercise 39: from "Improving Rate of Comprehension," by Lester R. Wheeler and Viola D. Wheeler, in the *High School Journal.* Reprinted by permission. Pages 176–177: "Self-Respect and Self-Confidence," by Douglas Remsen, M.D., from *Talk.* Reprinted by permission. Page 177: "Speech Patterns," from the *New York Times.* Reprinted by permission. Page 178: "Retaliation Reaction," by James Sonnett Greene, M.D., from *Talk.* Reprinted by permission. Pages 178–179: "Chinese, Japanese, and Polynesian," by Bjorn Karlsen, from a lecture delivered at the Claremont College Reading Conference, Claremont, California, 1955. Reprinted by permission. Page 181: "Lengthening Longevity," by William C. FitzGibbon, from *The New York Times Magazine.* Reprinted by permission. Pages 181–182: "Lightning and Safety," by Dr. Theodore R. Van Dellen, from the *New York Sunday News.* Reprinted by permission of the author and the Chicago-Tribune—New York News Syndicate, Inc. Pages 182–183: "Quiz Kid," by Katherine V. Bishop, from an address delivered at Claremont, California. Reprinted by permission of *The Yearbook of the Claremont College Reading Conference.* Pages 183–184: "At Times I Think My Daughter Hates Me . . . ," by Ruth Englund Forrest, from the *Los Angeles Times,* July 1, 1976. Reprinted by permission of the author. Page 186: "The Best Time for Learning," from *You* Can *Remember: A Home Study Course in Memory and Concentration,* by Dr. Bruno Furst and Lotte Furst. Reprinted by permission. Pages 189–190: "Bobby Returns to the Scene of the Crime," by Leon Lasken, from the *Los Angeles Times,* June 22, 1976. Reprinted by permission of the author. Pages 194–198: " 'Cures' for the Common Cold," by Harold S. Diehl, M.D., from *The American Mercury.* Reprinted by permission. Pages 199–201: "Inflation Hits the Campuses," by Milton M. Pressley. Reprinted by permission of the *Wall Street Journal,* © Dow Jones & Company, Inc., January 21, 1976. All rights reserved. Pages 203–206: "Diet and Die," by Carlton Fredericks, from *Coronet.* Copyright 1947 by Esquire, Inc. Reprinted by permission of *Coronet* and of the author. Pages 207–208: "Coexisting with Teen-Agers," by Eda J. LeShan, from *The New York Times Magazine.* Reprinted by permission. Pages 210–211, Exercise 45: from *Mind, Medicine, and Man,* by Gregory Zilboorg,

M.D., Harcourt, Brace, Jovanovich, New York. Reprinted by permission of the publishers. Page 211, Exercise 46: *from Remedial Reading at the College and Adult Levels,* by G. T. Buswell, Copyright 1939 by the University of Chicago Press. Pages 211-212, Exercise 47: from "Measurement and Improvement in Reading," in the *Baltimore Bulletin of Education,* by Arthur E. Traxler. Reprinted by permission. Pages 212-214: "The Gull Who Came to Dinner—and Stayed On," by Nick B. Williams, from the *Los Angeles Times,* February 9, 1976. Reprinted by permission of the author. Page 217: from *Teaching Every Child to Read,* by Kathleen B. Hester, Harper & Row, 1955. Reprinted by permission. Page 218: from the *Saturday Review.* Reprinted by permission. Pages 224-225: "Beware the Psychos," by Fred Dickenson, from the *New York Mirror.* Copyright 1956, King Features Syndicate, Inc. Reprinted by permission. Pages 226-229: "Why Do Accidents Happen?" from *Consumer Reports,* published by Consumers Union, Mt. Vernon, New York. Reprinted by permission.

Dedication

No writer exists in a vacuum; no author's work is untouched, in one way or another, by family, friends, and associates.

The following warm people have given me so much of themselves—personally, professionally, or both—that this book is far better than it could possibly have been without them:

Mary; Margie, Hart, and Holly; Debbie and Allen; Rhoda and Ralph; Milton; Max; Myrtle and Ace; Donny and Estelle; Helen and Ben; Sharon; Danny and Mary; Judy and Bob; Doris; Muriel—

Karen and Bob Kopfstein; Bob Finnerty; Janice and David Potts; Leonard Vogel, one of America's great painters, and Shirley; Doris Garcia; Ruth and Leo; Dave and Jan Hopkins; Seymour and Nan; Marvin and Carol Colter; Robert and Eleanor Poitou; Walter Garcia; Ted and Margaret Snyder; Sally Landsburg; George and Phyllis Juric; Robert L. Crowell; Albert Beller; Aaron Breitbart—

Marty and Roz Chodos; Leon and Kay East; Jim and Edna Olsen; Chuck Nichamon; Sue Sullivan, Rosemary and Debbie Greenman, Alice Hessing, Dave and Lynn Bisset; Tony and Kathy Garcia; Marijane and Paul Paulsen; Mahlon and Gwen Woirhay; Bob and Monica Myers; Susan Obler; Elior and Sally Kinarthy; Helen and Russ Hurford; Danny Hernandez; Walter and Fran Becker; Jean Bryan; Mary El and Dick Gayman—

All my students and the staff at Rio Hondo College, including:

Jean Kachaturian, Lorin Warner, Carolyn Russell, Rod Sciborski, Vera Laushkin, John Hahn, Liz Johnson, Leonora Davila, Jim Hawley—

Joan Nay, Mary Ann Pacheco, Mary Lewis, Bill Burns, Mary Post, George Char, Norm Peters, Paula Matos—

Jerry Lenington, Jay Loughran, Barbara Ginader, Tom Huffman, Mack Parks, Mary Treser—

Len Grandy, Don Jenkins, Alex Pantaleoni, Jim Albanese, Joe Michaels, Marilyn Houseman, Rita Scott, Chris Hamilton, Larry Scher, Peter Ruth, Andy Howard, Tom Miller, Roger Nedry—

Yosh Nakamura, Don Cornelsen, Kay Little, Jim Dillon, Bob Becker, Louise Hilker, Hildegard Platzer, Frances Peterson, John Kim, Jean Korf, Hazel Haas, Pat Boyle—

Margie Lopez, Jo Watson, Kay Arth, Geneva Comstock, Jackie Olson, Sandy Lesser Sylvia Mitchell, Louise Prado, Melinda Dixon, Elsie Davidson, Alfred Garcia—

My editor at Harper & Row, Phillip Leininger, who so helpfully, patiently, and perceptively guided this revision; and Karen Kopfstein and Peggy Chulack who so cheerfully and caringly typed the manuscript.

Seymour Prog, Director of the Reading and Study Skills Center at Rio Hondo College, member of the Board of Directors of the Western College Reading Association, and Past President of the Rio Hondo Council of the California Reading Association, I.R.A., has given me invaluable guidance as I worked on this Fourth Edition; I wish to express my deep gratitude to him.

Contents

1

How to Read Better and Faster
Than You Now Do   1

(Sessions 1 and 2, in which you discover that you are capable of
reading 50 to 60 percent faster and with better comprehension)

2

How to Develop a Sense of Urgency
When You Read   13

(Sessions 3 and 4, in which you attempt to sharpen your concentration
and comprehension by learning to read with a sense of urgency)

How to Vary Your Rate According to Your Purpose 21

(Sessions 5 and 6, in which you learn to control your rate depending on what you wish to accomplish)

How to Read for Main Ideas 31

(Sessions 7, 8, and 9, in which you aggressively pursue the gist of material, distinguish subordinate details from main ideas, and sense the structure of a piece of writing)

All About Perception 45

(Sessions 10–13, in which you learn about peripheral vision, span of recognition, fixations, and afterimage; and in which you start your training on rapid perception so that eventually you will be able to interpret more of what you see in less time)

Inner Speech, Lip Movements, Vocalization, and Regressions 65

(Sessions 14, 15, and 16, in which you learn how to give up
three habits that drastically reduce comprehension speed)

How to Get the Gist Quickly   77

(Sessions 17–21, in which you practice rapid grasp of main ideas,
continue to improve your perception, and learn how to read
a complete novel in a single evening)

Test Your Reading Vocabulary   97

(Sessions 22–24, in which you test the range of your reading vocabulary;
face a second challenge to your reding habits;
and learn to distinguish "theme" from "variations")

How to Read with Aggressive Comprehension 113

(Sessions 25–27, in which you become more adept at recognizing an author's
pattern of thinking; continue your practice in speeding up comprehension;
learn a new technique for increasing the usability of your peripheral vision;
and make a detailed evaluation of your progress thus far)

How to X-Ray Material   135

(Sessions 28–31, in which you continue developing habits
of thinking along with an author as you read; of driving rapidly and urgently
to grasp the structure of an author's thinking;
and of sweeping down columns of print with good comprehension)

How to Skim   157

(Sessions 32–34, in which you get intensive instruction in skimming,
learning how, when, and why to use the technique; and are challenged
to read a complete issue of your favorite magazine in a single evening)

More Practice in Driving for the Gist 175

(Sessions 35–37, in which you increase your skill and speed
in driving through details to get the main ideas)

How to Whip Through Material
with Good Comprehension 193

(Sessions 38–40, in which you get added training in aggressive
and rapid comprehension)

How to Read with a Questioning Mind 215

(Session 41, in which you learn about the importance
of reading critically, and of traveling widely among books
that deal with many fields of human knowledge)

Final Training in Rapid Comprehension 223

(Session 42, in which you tackle two fairly complex selections,
continuing to respond aggressively to the structure of writing.
You evaluate your total progress)

Tables

Timed Selections

Accurate Response Exercises

Rapid Comprehension Exercises

Rapid Perception Exercises

Selections for Skimming

Perception Training Exercises

Work Sessions

Preface
to the Fourth Edition

Anyone who can read can learn to read better and faster!

Consider: The most effective method for mastering any skill is continuous practice under professional instruction.

Therefore: The royal road to better and faster comprehension in reading is simply—

Reading, more reading, and still more and more reading—under expert guidance.

The fourth edition of *How to Read Better and Faster*, which has been completely revised and updated to reflect the present state of the art of reading instruction, offers just such expert guidance.

As a glance through the table of contents will immediately indicate, the book now places particular emphasis on *five indispensable techniques* that will:

- Sharpen your comprehension
- Build your self-assurance and skill in dominating a page of print
- Permanently increase your reading efficiency and speed.

These five techniques are:

1. *Reading more, and for longer periods of time.*

Methods of reading an entire novel or a complete magazine in a single evening are discussed, taught, and encouraged.

A greatly expanded list of current books in many areas of knowledge. including novels, mysteries, and science fiction, is provided.

Frequent challenges (which, with determination, you can meet) are set for you to read more, more widely, and more continuously.

2. *Reading always, and everything, with a calm, sure, confident "sense of urgency."*

Chapter after chapter, session after session, exercise after exercise, you will learn how to avoid dawdling and daydreaming as you read.

You will thus conquer, once and for all, any slightest tendency you may now have to mind-wander through pages of print with little or no comprehension.

3. *Reading with a keen awareness of the structure of a piece of writing.*

Selections from magazines, newspapers, and textbooks are thoroughly analyzed.

You quickly become familiar with how a writer structures material.

You learn how to look for, and how to find, "comprehension clues" to a writer's pattern of thinking.

You gain ever-increasing skill in distinguishing main ideas from supporting details.

You discover the difference between the "theme" of a selection and the "variations on the theme."

You become adept at skimming what can be profitably skimmed; at scanning what requires no more than superficial scanning; and at paying close attention to what is *important* and *central* in a page of print.

4. *Reading flexibly.*

You practice adjusting your rate and style of reading to *what* you read and to your *purpose* in reading it.

You gain skill in suiting your technique to the type of material you read.

You learn the *efficient* way to study textbook material, if such study is necessary.

You learn the *efficient* way to whip through light novels.

You learn the *efficient* way to skim technical material for the essential facts.

You learn the *efficient* way to drive through a magazine article, a newspaper column, or a chapter in a book for immediate comprehension of the *gist* of what a writer is saying.

And as you practice varying your techniques according to *what* you are reading and to *your reason for reading it*, you will find that your own efficiency as a reader (in short, your comprehension and speed) will improve spectacularly.

5. *Reading so that you interpret more of what you see in less time.*

New perception exercises have been added that will increase your span of recognition and permit you to make greater use of your peripheral vision.

Repeated practice with such exercises will help you respond more quickly, more smoothly, and more dynamically to the *meaning* of a longer portion of a line of print.

This fourth edition has been thoroughly rewritten, revised, and expanded.

New material, new techniques, new exercises, and new selections have been added.

Outdated matter has been eliminated.

As a result, *How to Read Better and Faster* is now a complete handbook that will, if you work with it seriously, consistently, and methodically, go very far toward revolutionizing your reading skill.*

NORMAN LEWIS

* Please note, as a matter purely of convenience, and *not* male chauvinism, the words "he," "him," and "his" are used to denote a person of either sex. Women read as much as men — possibly more — and it would, I suppose, be equally logical to use "she" and "her" for a person — equally logical, but since untraditional and therefore unusual, likely to be conspicuous and to interfere with a reader's concentration. Where possible, I have used the plurals "readers", "people", "they", "them", "their". In any case, in the text of this book, "he" always means "he/she" or "she/he"; "him" and "his" include "her", etc.

How to Read Better and Faster Than You Now Do

PREVIEW

In Chapter 1 you will discover that you are capable of reading up to 50 percent faster than you now read.

If you are the average untrained reader, there is one central fact you must face at the outset.

And that is—*you read altogether too slowly.*

At this very moment, on this very page, you are reading more slowly than you should read—more slowly than you need to read for good comprehension—and, most important of all, *much more slowly than you are actually capable of reading.*

Your lack of speed—still assuming that you are the average untrained reader—results chiefly from three factors:

1. *Bad habits* that you have built up through years of the wrong kind of practice

2. *Unaggressive techniques of comprehension* that interfere with total concentration and stand in the way of your responding to a page of print as rapidly and as actively as your potential ability makes possible

3. *Poor techniques of perception* that cause an unnecessary time lag between the *act of seeing* and the *mental interpretation* of what you see

You read slowly, in short, not because you're a poor reader, but because you're an inefficient reader.

In this chapter you will learn:

• What a short period of intensive training in efficient reading techniques can do for your speed and comprehension

• How similar training at adult and college reading centers has increased the reading speed of thousands of students

• What your *present* reading rate is on material of average difficulty

• What your *potential* rate is on such material

• How to apply six important rules for realizing your *potential* rate in all your reading

---

SESSION 1

WHAT TRAINING CAN DO FOR YOU

Look at it this way:

—If, within a short period of time, you could boost your general reading rate by 50 or 60 percent

—If, with continued and earnest application, you could eventually double or even triple your *permanent* speed

—If you could learn to strip a page down to its essentials without wasted time or effort

—If you could build up efficient habits of knifing cleanly and quickly through the words and details of material, straight to the main ideas and important points

—If you could accomplish all this after only a few months of stimulating practice

—*Would it be worth trying?*

Or look at it this way:

You are a college student who has somehow never made a comfortable adjustment to books, especially textbooks, and you now find yourself overwhelmed, possibly even intimidated, by the amount of reading required in your courses. In fact, you are finding yourself falling further and further behind as each week passes.

—If you could develop a mind-set in which you realize that *you*—not the *book*—are the master

—If you could learn to look forward wtih self-assurance and eagerness to tackling your reading assignments because you know how to whip through a chapter efficiently and with accurate comprehension

—If you could discover techniques for quickly extracting the *essence,* the *meat,* of a page, of a chapter, of a whole book—with total concentration, without wasted effort, without sweat

—*Would that be worth your while?*

Or look at still one more way:

You now read, let us say for the sake of argument, ten or fewer books a year:

—If you could finish 20 or more without spending one extra minute on your reading

—If, through more aggressive comprehension and greater perception skill, you could learn to cover a book of average length in an evening or two of solid concentration

—If, through the same means, you could learn to sail through your daily newspaper or favorite magazine in half the time you now take without missing anything of importance

—If you could develop the power of responding more actively to *everything* you read

—And if, as a result, you discovered such new or heightened pleasures in the printed page that you found yourself turning more and more frequently to reading, not only as a rewarding leisure-time activity but also as a productive learning experience

—*Would all that be a rich enough reward for some months of systematic (and enjoyable) training?*

Take some other possibilities:

You are a business executive; and scores of papers come to your desk each day: reports, trade journals, minutes of meetings, clippings pertinent to the affairs of your firm. Each must be read, quickly but accurately; it is important, perhaps crucial, that you be able to glance through a page for a few seconds and pull out the essential points, the main ideas. You can't go slowly; in a busy day there simply isn't time to examine every word, to ponder every detail. You know that you must develop the ability to push through material at top speed.

Or you are a lawyer, an accountant, a tax expert, an engineer, a scientist, an editor, a proofreader. During your professional day you must read slowly, carefully, word by word in some instances, because every syllable, every punctuation mark, every subtle implication has to be studied and examined. And so you have built up habits of careful, minutely analytical, snail-paced reading, with infinite attention to minor details. The result? Your reading at the office or plant is efficient enough—efficient for the type of reading you are required to do professionally. But when you try to do reading of another sort, light, general reading purely for enjoyment and relaxation, you find (naturally enough) that your office habits have spread over into your personal life, and it takes you an hour to cover a long magazine article, a month or more to finish a novel. You note this phenomenon first with surprise, then with increasing annoyance, for you are getting practically no reading done after working hours.

Or you are a high school or college student, and in the same time it takes you to absorb a few pages in a textbook, your classmates are able to cover a whole chapter. Despite the hours of study you devote to your courses, you realize, with dismay, that you're not hacking it. And you begin to suspect the reasons:

Your reading is too slow, too poky, too time-consuming, too inefficient.

Your mind tends to wander, for, in truth, you'd rather be doing something else.

Your comprehension is not as immediate nor as accurate as you would like it to be.

And your ability to *retain what you've read* somehow, mysteriously, falls short, even though your memory is otherwise just as good as anyone else's.

(Once you get well into your training you will see for yourself the interconnectedness, the cause-and-effect relationship, between reading efficiency, speed and accuracy of comprehension, and retention ability.)

Now—

Whether the circumstances of your life—because you are an executive, a professional person, or a student—require you to get *more* reading done in *less* time

Or whether you have become aware that many of your classmates, friends, or associates read much faster than you do, and with equally good—or often better—comprehension and retention

Or whether you have simply begun to feel an uneasy sense of inadequacy in your day-to-day performance, and are disturbed by a growing realization that you are reading less than you used to, or less than you would like to, or less than you ought to

If you were convinced that a few months of intensive training could materially increase the efficiency and speed of your reading, would you consider it time well spent?

You are now holding in your hands a book that aims to help you achieve all the goals catalogued above—a book that offers you the step-by-step training and practice that can make you a far better, far more efficient, far more rapid reader than you are today.

But merely *reading* this book is not enough.

You must *use* it, you must *work* with it—intensively, faithfully, honestly.

You must not skip one single page.

You must not let anything stop you from enthusiastically and methodically completing your job from beginning to end.

And most important, you must be willing to devote time and effort.

If you go through this book conscientiously, you have weeks and months of hard work ahead of you. Hard, but stimulating and encouraging from the start—for every small skill you master will effect a noticeable change in your reading performance. *And when you have completed the last session of your training, you will find that you have learned to cruise through print at a rate of speed, and with an effortless efficiency, that you might once have thought hardly possible.*

WHAT TRAINING HAS DONE FOR OTHERS

Is there any reason for feeling confident that efficiency, skill, and speed can be increased in a comparatively short time?

There are many reasons—and all of them are backed up by scientific findings, by laboratory results. That a person of normal intelligence can learn to read better and faster is not a theory; it is a fact.

It is a fact that has been established in the reading centers of hundreds of colleges and universities throughout the country. Here are a few random but representative examples:

At the University of Florida, as reported by John A. Broxson in the *Peabody Journal of Education,* 175 adults took a three-month reading course, meeting once a week for a four-hour session. The group was composed of business men and women, teachers, lawyers, ministers, a newspaper reporter, homemakers, club-women, and two superintendents of schools. At the start of the course, 111 students were reading at the rate of 115 to 210 words per minute, or no better than seventh-grade elementary school level. Twelve weeks later almost all had shown spectacular improvement, 52 out of these 111 slowest readers sailing along at a rate of 295 to 325 words per minute—high school senior and college level. While only 20 percent of the 175 adults had been able to read at college speed before training, over 40 percent could do so before the course was over.

Another example: Dr. Robert M. Bear, director of the reading clinic at Dartmouth College, reported:

In the ten years that we have been helping Dartmouth students improve their reading, I have seen few freshmen who read nearly as rapidly and efficiently as they should—and could—after a little training. Year after year, our reading classes start off at an average of around 230 words per minute, and finish up a few weeks later at around 500 words per minute.

A third and fourth example: at Purdue University, a pilot training program was offered to 307 entering freshmen, and by the fifteenth week, as reported by Professors Russell Cosper and Barriss Mills in the *Journal of Higher Education,* members of this group had increased their speed by 62 percent. Another group of 282 freshmen, similar in general and reading abilities to those enrolled in training, but pursuing only the regular course of study, made a gain of but 9 percent over the same period. Professors Cosper and Mills drew these very significant conclusions from a comparison between training and nontraining:

In general, results seemed to show that reading ability improves very slowly, if at all, in the conventional course of study. . . . By working directly on reading skill, it is possible to increase decidedly the rate at which a student can grasp the content of the printed page.

Through its Extension Center, Purdue offered a training course to industrial executives whose plants were located in the area. One group, ranging in age from 31-41, increased in average speed from 245 to 470 words per minute—a gain of over 90 percent. A class of older executives, in the 46-58 age group, started at 256 words per minute and completed training with a speed of 414 words per minute—a gain of approximately 60 percent.

Age may play some part in slowing down the *rate* of improvement after the middle years are reached, but is apparently no bar to healthy gains—notice that the adults well beyond their prime came within 2 percent of the achievement made by the Purdue freshmen. Professor Ernest W. Kinne, to whose article in *College English* I am indebted for the above statistics, remarks:

> . . . one may conclude that the older adults responded somewhat more slowly in gains in speed, but had a slight advantage in comprehension. . . . On the whole, the adults compare very favorably with the average performance of the younger students, belying the old saw about teaching an old dog new tricks.

And a final example: at the Adult Reading Laboratory of the City College of New York, a group of 14 students, at the end of a 12-week training period in faster reading, recorded an average arithmetic gain in speed of 69.1 percent. Notice some of the radical improvements in rate in the chart below.

	Start of Course		End of Course	
Student	Rate (WPM)	Comprehension (%)	Rate (WPM)	Comprehension (%)
A	237	100	360	100
B	400	100	675	100
C	325	100	540	100
D	289	85	540	100
E	237	92	540	90
F	217	95	337	95
G	260	100	386	100
H	237	95	540	100
I	217	80	337	90
J	434	100	600	100
K	325	100	514	100
L	237	90	416	100
M	237	60	360	80
N	306	100	540	100

Reports from college reading centers throughout the country underline two facts:

• Most untrained students read unnecessarily slowly and inefficiently.

• After a comparatively short period of intensive training, these students can sharpen their comprehension skill, can increase their overall efficiency, and can, as a result, add considerably to their speed.

WHAT LIES AHEAD?

Day by day, as your training progresses, you will be on the alert to detect the changes in your reading performance. Individually, these changes may be slight, but they will be perceptible; they may be gradual, but they will be cumulative. And eventually they will add up to broad and sweeping alterations in your basic habits, in your approach, in the techniques you use to master a page of print.

For, to repeat a principle that is the keystone of all the training this book offers you:

You—not the book, not the page, not the paragraph—*are the master.*

You are the master—and the book, the page, etc., can become your willing servant.

You will be in unending competition, as you move through your work, not with others, but with yourself, with your previous self as a reader.

In what ways are you reading better today than you did yesterday?

How much faster do you now cruise through print than you did last week?

With how much more skill and assurance do you attack your twentieth reading selection than you did your first, or fifth, or tenth, or fifteenth?

With how much greater speed and efficiency do you now tackle and successfully complete your assigned reading than you did last week, or last month?

How many more books do you now find yourself reading in a given period of time than previously?

And, especially, how much more *pleasure* are you getting from your reading by learning how to make a closer, friendlier, more dominant contact with a page of print, *by learning to become the master?*

In order to make these comparisons, you will keep continuous statistics on the rate of your reading and on the efficiency of your comprehension.

You will set up for yourself, one after another, specific goals to reach, and you will measure, session by session, how successfully you have reached them.

And throughout, as you gradually perfect your technique, as you increase your skill, and as you build up your speed, you will set new personal records of performance—and then you will immediately attempt to beat these records.

HOW FAST DO YOU NOW READ?

A Test of Your Present Reading Speed

Your first step, now, is to test your present performance so that you may establish a yardstick with which to measure your improvement, a criterion by which to judge your progress.

In taking this test, function as you normally do, reading

for the kind of comprehension you are accustomed to, and in the same manner in which you generally cover any material of similar type—*avoid, as much as possible, any consciousness of a test situation.*

If possible, have someone time you, in minutes and seconds, from the start of your reading at the first arrow, until you finish at the concluding arrow.

Or use a stopwatch or other mechanical timer if you have one, starting the timer at the first arrow as you begin to read, stopping it when you reach the concluding arrow.

If neither assistant, stop watch, or other timer is available, time yourself by (1) noting, in the space below, the exact time before you start (allow 10 additional seconds for writing down the time), and (2) the exact time when you finish. The table for computing your present rate will be found on page 7 directly after the comprehension test.

SELECTION 1

A Happy Anniversary Lunch, and Then . . .
by Richard Amerian

Time at start: _____ minutes _____ seconds

Start timing ➡ I won't soon forget my fourth wedding anniversary. Four years earlier, a woman had entered my life and changed it. On that fourth anniversary day, another woman entered my life—and my courtroom—and changed my perceptions a bit.

That day for me blended the ingredients of successful marriage with something that is usually unrelated—contempt of court. Much has been written of the first; the second tends to be briefly noted in the newspaper and then consigned to the law books.

Judges' contempt powers are awesome. When these powers must be used, the judicial officer becomes not only judge, jury and executioner, but also witness because, in most instances, the courtroom is where the contemptuous act occurs. It is the judge who, based on his standards of seemly conduct, determines what a contemptuous act is, and it is the judge who, based on the facts, decides if a contemptuous act has been committed. If he so rules, it is the judge who punishes by imposing sentence.

Because he has such powers, a judge must be slow to anger and quick to forgive; otherwise he may risk abusing these powers.

But to return to the events of my fourth anniversary:

On this special day I planned to lunch at home with my wife. But before I could leave the courthouse I had to deal with three cases—all scheduled to begin at 11:30. I hoped to get one set up for trial in the afternoon, then postpone the others. It was 11:45, however, before all three defendants were in the courtroom and I was studying the complaints against them: One was charged with assault, another with driving under the influence, and the third with theft.

I had to decide which to hear first, and that day my choice was not so much conscious as random. I simply picked up one of the three pink complaint slips and called the name typed on it. Up stepped a woman in her 40s, a lawyer at her side.

"You, ma'am," I told the woman, "are charged with violating Section 23102a of the Vehicle Code—operating a motor vehicle while under the influence of intoxicating liquor and while under the combined influence of intoxicating liquor and a drug. The offense is alleged to have occurred on or about...."

"Drugs?" she shrieked. "What are you trying to pull?"

"Ma'am, I am only telling you what the complaint sets out as the charge; I don't know anything at all about the facts of the case."

"What kind of kangaroo court is this?" she screamed.

"Please stop talking," I said. "Not one more word. I expect each male who comes to the courtroom to act like a gentleman and each female to act like a lady. Leave now. You are ordered to come back at 1:30 P.M. I will expect you to act like a lady at that time or you will face problems totally unrelated to the charge which brought you to court."

Defendants and witnesses in the remaining cases bristled. I bristled. The courtroom personnel bristled. The other cases, however, went routinely. It was a few minutes past noon when I gaveled the session to a close.

On the 15-minute drive home, I was preoccupied with pleasant reveries about my wedding day four years earlier and the lunch I would soon have with my wife. The baby would already have been fed, so there would be just my wife and me to share memories.

Our time together, however, was much too brief. At 1 P.M. it was time to leave, for a pressing court calendar awaited me. Worse yet, I would have to deal with the bitter-tongued woman of my morning session whose case I'd held over. Driving back to the courthouse, I ran through a scenario in my head: I'll start by explaining that I, as a judge, had nothing to do with filing the original charge against her—its content (which had prompted her outburst) is strictly the prosecutor's responsibility.

Back in court, the spectators settled in their seats as I asked the woman to step forward. For 10 minutes I drove home my point, taking care to be fair and thorough. The woman smiled and nodded, so I thought things were going smoothly.

Then I asked: "Do you understand the nature of the charges lodged against you?"

"When do I genuflect?" she said sarcastically.

My response was immediate. "For making that statement you are held in contempt of court. The sentence is three days in jail. Take her away."

I stepped down quickly from the bench. It was now 1:45 P.M. and there was no time to lose. Preparation of a contempt commitment, fully describing what had transpired, was needed to explain why the woman should be jailed. Should my contempt order be tested in a higher court, my action would stand or fall on its content.

When my secretary arrived, I rushed through a first draft. Time was of the essence: Until that paper was prepared in its final form and signed by me, all female prisoners in the court complex faced delays in being transported to the County Jail.

After dictating the draft, I realized I had done nothing about the charges that had brought the woman into my court. All I had done was react with anger on hearing the word "genuflect." Now it was too late—she was gone. There was no way to rectify my error, and after the incident I knew I shouldn't try. I returned her case to the calendar court for reassignment to another judge.

By 4 P.M. I had signed the final contempt order in accordance with the California Code of Civil Procedure. Then, after presiding at another trial, I headed home with some relief.

At the wheel, I reflected on the day's meaning. It was not the first time in six years as a judge that I had encountered erratic behavior, nor will it be the last. Almost always I give the offenders a chance to think things over, to retract their statements or retreat from their positions. Almost always they do.

Why was today different? One lesson it taught was that judges, just like defendants, are individuals with complex hopes, aspirations, and expectations. Judges are human. They live in communities. They have wedding anniversaries. They react to events both within and without the courtroom.

On occasion, people overreact—on both sides of the bench. On occasion these facts of life are forgotten by judges and non-judges alike. Surely, from time to time, it is a good thing for judges to be reminded of their frailties, the better to wield their enormous power over those in trouble.

My reflective mood was broken when, on arriving home, I entered the kitchen to my wife's greeting, "Hi, dear," she said. "Happy anniversary—again. Did you have a good afternoon?" ◄ **End timing**

Record here the time required on this selection: _____ minutes _____ seconds

Test Your Comprehension

Which *one* of the following statements most accurately summarizes the *main idea* of the selection you have just finished?

1. Judge Amerian's fourth wedding anniversary was a combination of a successful marriage and a contempt-of-court citation.

2. A judge should be slow to anger and quick to forgive.

3. The first defendant that morning was a very discourteous woman.

4. The judge's wedding anniversary was spoiled by the extra work demanded by the contempt citation.

5. There are times when judges, like other people, may overreact, and judges should remind themselves of their weaknesses in order to exercise their enormous power more judiciously.

6. Judges, like other humans, have complex hopes and expectations.

Key The answer is given in somewhat cryptic form so that you will not inadvertently discover the correct response before making your own choice. The number of the statement that best summarizes the main idea can be found by subtracting six from seven and adding four.

(If you checked the incorrect response, reread the selection to discover why you erred in thinking one of the *details* or one of the *contributing ideas* was the *main message* of the selection. Much of your training in this book will help you understand the *structure* of writing so that you can more accurately and more quickly grasp main ideas and see details and supporting points in their proper perspective.)

Compute Your Rate
(Approximate Number of Words: 1100)

(If you have a calculator, divide 1100 by the minutes and seconds expressed as a whole number and a decimal.

Thus, for 1 minute 15 seconds, 1100 is divided by 1.25; for 1 minute 30 seconds, 1100 is divided by 1.50; and so on. If you are not using a calculator, read your rate to the closest time from the following table.)

Time	WPM	Time	WPM
1 min.	1100	3 min. 45 sec.	293
1 min. 10 sec.	943	4 min.	275
1 min. 15 sec.	880	4 min. 15 sec.	259
1 min. 20 sec.	825	4 min. 30 sec.	244
1 min. 30 sec.	733	4 min. 45 sec.	238
1 min. 45 sec.	629	5 min.	220
2 min.	550	5 min. 15 sec.	210
2 min. 15 sec.	489	5 min. 30 sec.	200
2 min. 30 sec.	440	5 min. 45 sec.	191
2 min. 45 sec.	400	6 min.	183
3 min.	367	6 min. 15 sec.	176
3 min. 15 sec.	338	6 min. 30 sec.	169
3 min. 30 sec.	314	6 min. 45 sec.	163
		7 min.	157

Your present rate of Reading: _____ WPM

Record Your Statistics

You now have a base figure by which to gauge your improvement as you gradually build up your speed chapter by chapter. Record this figure on the chart for phase 1 on page 234. On the graph below the chart, plot your first statistic by marking a heavy dot in the appropriate place on the line for selection 1.

As you glance at page 234, you will notice that it contains room for information on selections 1-9 only. When filled in, this first chart and graph will give you a quick pictorial representation of your progress during the preliminary period of training—a period in which you will be doing a good deal of new learning; in which you will be wrestling with and attempting to use a variety of new and perhaps unfamiliar techniques. You will be making a start at breaking down comfortable, old, less efficient habits, and replacing them with new, much more efficient, and much more dynamic methods of attacking a page of print.

At this point you are probably curious about how your present rate measures up to the average. Average untrained readers, or the typical students beginning work at any of the college reading centers spread throughout the country, invariably cover material pitched on the level of Judge Amerian's article at a rate of 175-225 words per minute (WPM). They would require anywhere from 5 to 6¼ minutes to read this selection with what they consider adequate comprehension. On the other hand, if our theoretical readers are somewhat above average, if they have learned to perform at or close to college level, they would go considerably faster, in the neighborhood of 325-350 WPM, so that they would have finished in about 3-3½ minutes. (Both rates, of course, merely indicate what

certain types of readers *do,* not by any means what they are *capable of doing*.)

Your rate may be, probably is, somewhere between average and college speed. Or it may possibly be slower, even very much slower than average; or, on the contrary, it may be considerably faster than college level.

Actually, while such comparisons are interesting, they are of no great moment. You read as you read Good, bad, or indifferent, your present rate is roughly whatever this test has indicated. What will be far more interesting, and of far greater significance, as you go on, will be how much your comprehension sharpens, how much your concentration improves, and how much your rate increases as compared to your initial performance.

The *extent* of your progress will indicate:

• Whether you are capitalizing on your latent abilities

• Whether you are learning to sharpen and speed up your comprehension

• Whether you are mastering the technique of aggressively attacking a page of print, rather than passively reading words

• Whether you are mobilizing your concentration by knowing *not only what you are looking for* in your reading, but also *how to find it most quickly and accurately*

• Whether you are developing a clear awareness that a book (page, paragraph, etc.) is *not your enemy* but your willing servant—an awareness that will come as soon as you make the firm decision that *you,* not the book, etc., *are the master!*

The comparisons that will interest you most, bear in mind, are those between your later and your earlier performances, between how you function at any given time and how you functioned days or weeks or months previously.

SESSION 2

PROOF THAT YOU CAN READ FASTER

I have said that *average untrained people read much more slowly than they are actually capable of reading.*

Semester after semester, during the years that I supervised the courses at the Adult Reading Laboratory of City College, I would demonstrate the truth of this statement to my students.

Let me ask you to imagine yourself taking part in a typical first meeting of one of these courses. So that you can get the full flavor of what invariably occurred, I shall use the present tense in explaining the procedure we followed and in describing the general reactions of the students.

I start by testing the class on material of about the same length and level of difficulty as the article on which you timed yourself in the previous section.

"Read this selection," I say, "exactly as you always read. Pretend you are at home in your favorite easy chair. Just read."

Then I time the performance with a stop watch, noting the passage of every 5, 10, or 15 seconds on the blackboard.

The great bulk of the class reads at approximately 200-250 WPM. Three or four read at college level (325-350 WPM) or better; one or two, abnormally slow, bumble along at 125-175 WPM.

These students have taken the course because they are troubled and unhappy about their reading. Slow reading, they realize, is awkward, unsatisfying reading. They know that trained readers can cover material in less time, with more enjoyment and better comprehension.

After my students have examined their first statistics, they invariably ask the obvious question: "Can we increase our speed by the end of the course?"

"You can do better than that," I answer. "You can increase your speed today—before this session is over."

I then hand out a second selection of about the same length and difficulty as the first one on which they have been tested.

"Now," I say, "understand this about yourselves. The probability is very great that you are reading slowly partly because you have developed lazy habits. You are unwilling to jog your minds. You find that you can *comfortably* react to the message of print at a certain speed—a comparatively low speed, as you've discovered today. You have got into the habit of sauntering leisurely along a mental countryside when you should push along briskly and with a purpose—the purpose of finding the *meat* of an author's ideas in the quickest possible time. You occasionally stop to admire the intellectual scenery, or you sometimes retrace your steps to make sure you've seen *everything*, instead of pushing ahead with the exclusive desire of getting an overall view. The result? You read at an unnecessarily slow rate.

"I am going to let you prove to yourselves that you can do better—much better.

"When the signal is given, jump right into this new selection. Follow the main thread of the ideas, keep going at a *consciously* fast pace. Feel that you're going *fast,* but not so fast, of course, that comprehension is lost. You may miss the full flavor or meaning of certain words, or of occasional sentences. No matter. Keep right on pushing. Try it as an experiment, and see what happens. Remember—the idea is to get the *main thought* of the selection *quickly.*"

I then give the signal and they start to read. If you could watch these people now, you would see an actual *physical* change in them. They are visibly alert—they have mobilized themselves for reading—and it is apparent that they are now concentrating far better than at their first attempt, when they were reading comfortably, overrelaxed. Now they are *working* at reading. You can see that they are immersed—totally immersed—in the material; there is an air of concentration about them that was conspicuously absent a few minutes before. As you will shortly discover for yourself when you train to speed up your own reading, it is impossible *not* to have sharper concentration when you consciously read for faster understanding of main ideas, when you purposefully sweep through material looking for the essential points of an author's thinking.

After the second test is over, we again gather statistics. When I say to you that my students are astonished, I am making an understatement. Some of them find their new results almost unbelievable.

Those students who read the first selection at 200–250 WPM get through the second piece in the neighborhood of 300 WPM—an immediate improvement of 20–50 percent. The few faster readers also show marked improvements; to use the words of one of these students some years back, it is as if "we have suddenly dropped our shackles." These 325–350 WPM readers discover that they are able, if they really try, to attain a rate of close to 450 WPM, a good, efficient, cruising speed. And the one or two very slow readers have also caught fire—they have stopped reading *words* and have begun to look for *ideas,* and the change is clearly reflected in their increased rate.

My students are now convinced that they have the *ability* to perform faster. All they need to do from that point on is practice reading in such a way that the *ability to perform* becomes *habitual performance.*

You, too, have the ability to read much faster than you now read.

The next few pages will convince you.

On page 9 you will find a piece of approximately the same difficulty as, but somewhat shorter than, the one on which you have determined your present reading speed. (The difference of approximately 225 words is not significant.)

While the *material* will be similar, your *attitude* must be very different as you read. Aim to understand the ideas more quickly by mobilizing yourself for quick reading. Get the thoughts *fast;* do not get bogged down in details; just follow the main thread. If occasionally a word eludes you, or if a thought is somewhat fuzzy, keep plowing right through nonetheless. Read under slight speed pressure and with a purpose—the purpose of getting *the main thought* quickly. *Get in, get the thought, and get out.* Do not *read words;* rather, *absorb thoughts, ideas.* Move along rapidly, but of course do not lose comprehension, for your primary purpose in all reading is understanding, not speed. But you will be attempting to discover whether you are able, eventually, to become a much faster reader than you are today. As before, have someone time you, use a stop watch, or note the time in minutes and seconds when you are ready to start. (In the latter instance, again allow ten extra seconds for writing in the time.)

A Test of Your Potential Reading Speed

Read the following selection through rapidly, aiming at a quick understanding of the main idea.

SELECTION 2

Moral: Money Is as Slippery as a $3 Eel
by Carly Mary Cady

Time at start: _____ minutes _____ seconds

Start timing ➡ Last year I won $18,200 in cash and $800 in prizes as a contestant on a now-defunct CBS-TV game show called "Now You See It." I was a "good" contestant: tearful, swooning and avarice-driven.

But now, 15 months later, I have flunked out as a bookkeeper. I can't figure what happened to the winnings I eked out during eight shows, the bulk of which came when I answered this esoteric question: "Who was Popeye's hamburger-eating friend?"

All I know for sure is that it's gone, and I'm back to living paycheck to paycheck. That's why, it seems to me, the show would have been more aptly named, "Now You See It . . . Now You Don't"—since the moolah that came my way has vanished much like magicians' rabbits.

Hard though I've tried, I can't unravel the mystery of my missing loot. Not most of it, anyway. Uncle Sam, of course, got his share: $4,200. Then I paid off my car and helped my mother get two new caps for her front teeth (at least *she's* got something to smile about). I also treated myself to an $850 typewriter and a weekend in Las Vegas. But once you subtract these sums, that still leaves $11,000 to account for.

Oh yes, there was that self-indulgent clothes-buying spree I went on one weekend—there went another $600—and the time I took my mother on her first outing to Disneyland (we stayed two nights in a nearby hotel). And I visited Palm Springs, purchased a wall hanging for my living room and signed on an answering service.

Come to think of it, everything's starting to add up.

As I leaf through my tell-tale checkbook, my trail of spending gets warmer: $50 for an aquarium and $85 for dermatology. Also, for the first time, I dined out a lot without fear of bank overdrawals. In fact, I've never been more relaxed about spending money than during those halcyon days.

Still, just where *did* all the rest go?

Well, I took a karate course and learned just enough to antagonize anyone who might attack me. I moved into a more expensive apartment—but not that much more expensive. I hired a cleaning lady who comes in twice a month and is now indispensable.

I had my couch recovered (aha! $450), bought two new living-room chairs (aha again! $550), plus a lamp and a bookshelf. These were fairly major expenses, but now, on closer thought, I recall incurring a good many smaller outlays—high-style haircuts, for instance, and porcelain fingernails—all of which helped nickel-and-dime my little fortune away.

What else? I gave three or four good-sized dinner parties. I probably spent $400 on books. I also bought a *ficus benjamina* for my apartment. Okay, but that still leaves me with $8,000.

Oh yes, did I mention the aquarium? What I didn't mention was that I stocked it with three Siamese fighting fish, at $2.99 each. Nor did I skimp on gifts for friends and relatives. As an example, my mother got a new color TV set. No, hold on . . . the TV set doesn't count: I purchased it *after* the game show money went—well, wherever it went. Is there a black hole in space somewhere that sucks up money like stardust?

Come back to earth, baby. On my mother's birthday, didn't I take her to a surprise party for eight at one of her favorite restaurants? Another time, I rented a limousine for the evening to pick up my date, and it transported us to one of the 100 or so movies, plays and operas that I attended during this protracted spree. But perhaps my greatest extravagance was sending Christmas cards to all my cats' animal friends.

I must also confess that, when it came to working last year, I didn't exactly knock myself out at the typewriter. Actually, I took off about four months, if you add up all the time between magazine-writing assignments. Unfortunately, day-to-day living expenses do add up, so when all is said and done, the mystery isn't so mysterious anymore.

Maybe you'll criticize me for not having invested the $14,000 I had left after taxes. Well, I *did* look for a house (God, how I looked!) but I couldn't find anything in my price range that was even the size of my apartment. My doctor recommended Puerto Rican telephone bonds at 6% (tax free), and my mother kept plugging for the security of a savings and loan deposit. But instead of doing any of those things, I spent the money, pure and simple. After all, I hadn't exactly broken my back earning it, or even wracked my brain—"Wimpy" simply leaped out from my memory bank.

Naming Popeye's hamburger-eating friend was a pushover, actually, for anyone who has spent time in England: there are "Wimpyburger" stands all over London.

So thanks, Popeye, Wimpy, Olive Oyl and all the old gang. It was great while it lasted, and so what if I can't dip into my savings to pay the rent? Come to think of it, maybe I can help make ends meet by selling an article somewhere about Carly the Big Spender... ◄ **End timing**

Record here the time required on this selection: _____minutes _____seconds

Test Your Comprehension

Check the main idea:

1. The author won over $18,000 on a quiz show and spent it all foolishly

2. People who come into sudden riches become reckless spenders and soon find themselves in debt.

3. Ms. Cady had trouble recalling how she spent more than $18,000 that she won on a quiz show, and finally took consolation from the fact that she hadn't worked very hard for the money.

4. The author, not used to having a great deal of money, found herself uncomfortable until she spent it all.

5. People who win a sizable amount of money will stop working and devote their time to pleasure.

Key Subtract four from six and add one to determine the number of the correct answer.

Compute Your Rate
(Approximate Number of Words: 875)

As in selection 1, use your calculator to determine your rate (divide 875 by your time expressed as minutes and a decimal), or read your rate from the table below.

Time	WPM	Time	WPM
1 min.	875	3 min.	292
1 min. 15 sec.	700	3 min. 15 sec.	269
1 min. 30 sec.	583	3 min. 30 sec.	250
1 min. 45 sec.	500	3 min. 45 sec.	233
2 min.	438	4 min.	219
2 min. 15 sec.	389	4 min. 15 sec.	206
2 min. 30 sec.	350	4 min. 30 sec.	194
2 min. 45 sec.	318		

Your potential reading rate: _____WPM

(Record this statistic on the chart and graph on page 234)

You have probably proved to yourself, as a result of these tests' that you can read faster—at least 20 to 50 percent faster

But, you may be thinking, "It was far from comfortable,

and I was not quite as sure of my comprehension as I usually am."

You're right, completely—on both counts. An average, slow reader cannot become a rapid, efficient reader overnight—even though a start in the right direction can be made within five minutes, as you have already discovered for yourself. Your training and practice, from this point on, will aim to help you develop your innate capacity for:

• Quicker, more accurate, comprehension

• Sharper, more immediate, concentration

• More active participation in thinking along with an author

• Deeper involvement in, and therefore greater mastery over, a page of print

If you practice faithfully and intelligently, your training will be successful, and a much faster *habitual* rate of reading (which, in essence, is *a faster rate of comprehension*) will be as natural for you as your previous rate was.

And—very much to the point—you will feel self-assured about your *comprehension*, you will be aware of your *reading efficiency*, and you will discover (again the important theme) *that a book (page, etc.) is not your master, but your willing servant.*

SIX RULES FOR FASTER COMPREHENSION

One of the important goals of your training is to transform your *potential* speed into a normal, habitual speed. To achieve this goal, you will, throughout this book, be constantly and repeatedly asked, encouraged, urged, and expected to follow—you will be prodded, cajoled, and at times even shamed into following—these important rules for improving your reading:

1. READ MORE

You will have to read much, much more than you are now in the habit of reading. If you're a slow reader, you very likely do little more than go through the daily papers and a few light magazines. You read whenever you happen to have a few spare minutes, you read merely to pass time. Or perhaps you hardly ever read at all unless you absolutely have to.

From now on, *you must make time for reading.* My students always allocated, during their training, at least three evenings every week, and at least two full, continuous hours during those evenings, to the reading of books. Speed can be developed into a permanent habit only if you do what naturally fast and skillful readers have always done, from childhood on: read a lot. That means at least a full book every week; that means several evenings of concentrated reading every week. Unless you develop the habit of reading for two hours or more at a stretch, several stretches every week, do not expect ever to become an efficient or a rapid reader. (But as reading becomes gradually more rewarding and more meaningful and less like a chore, this requirement will turn out to be a lot easier and considerably less taxing than it may sound to you at this moment.)

2. LEARN TO READ FOR MAIN IDEAS

Stop wasting time and effort on details. When you read an article, push through efficiently for a quick recognition of the main idea that the details support and illustrate; be more interested in the writer's basic thinking than in his minor points.

When you read a volume of nonfiction, be intent on getting the theme, the broad ideas, the framework on which the author has built the book. Don't let an occasionally perplexing paragraph, page, or chapter slow you up. Keep speeding through. As the complete picture is filled in by rapid overall reading, the few puzzling details will either turn out to have been inconsequential or will be cleared up as you move along.

When you read a short story or novel, follow the thread of the plot, consciously look for and find the "conflict," skim whenever you feel impelled to—don't meander in poky fashion from word to word and sentence to sentence.

3. CHALLENGE YOUR COMPREHENSION

Fast readers are good readers. They're fast because they have learned to understand print quickly, and they understand quickly because they give themselves constant practice in understanding. To this end, they read challenging material; and you must do the same. Does a novel sound deep? Does a book of nonfiction seem difficult? Does an article in a magazine look as if it will require more thinking than you feel prepared to do? Then that's the type of reading that will give you the most valuable training.

You will never become a better reader by limiting yourself to easy reading—you cannot grow intellectually by pampering yourself. Ask yourself: "Do I know more about myself and the rest of the world, as a result of my reading, than I did five years ago?" If your honest answer is *no,*

then you'd better get started, today, on a more challenging type of reading than you've been accustomed to in the past.

4. BUDGET YOUR TIME

Say to yourself: "I have five chapters in sociology, anthropology, psychology (or whatever) to read by next week."

And then give yourself a limited, specific time in which to complete the assignment; for example, three chapters tonight, *in two hours* (allowing time for underlining, writing in the margin, taking notes, etc.), and two chapters tomorrow night, *in an hour and a half.*

Set the exact time when you will *start*—6 P.M., 7 P.M., etc., and, with an eye on the clock, so to speak, determine to finish by 8 P.M., 9 P.M., etc.

You may be amazed to discover that setting *a specific time* and a *definite* (but reasonable) *time limit* will mobilize your concentration and will be one small, but important, step in improving your comprehension.

Or say to yourself:

"I have this book and I want to finish it by tomorrow night."

And then get into it. If you know that you must finish half the book tonight and the other half by tomorrow, you'll speed up, because you'll have to. You'll develop tricks of getting ahead, of skimming parts that are less essential, of looking for main ideas, of reading at your top potential rate.

Good readers always have a feeling of going fast, for they have developed fast habits. Indeed, adults and college students who have trained themselves to read rapidly would *find their original slow pace uncomfortable and unpleasant.*

Or say to yourself: "I am going to finish this magazine, complete, getting what I want out of it, in two hours." And, such is the adaptability of the human mind under pressure, you *will* finish it in two hours. It is amazing what people can do if they really try. Why not put yourself to the test?

While you are training with this book, give yourself a time limit on whatever you read—and live up to that time limit. In this way you will mobilize yourself for reading as an intellectual pursuit, and only in this way will you train yourself to understand at your highest potential rate.

5. PACE YOURSELF

When you start a new book, read for quick understanding for 15 minutes. Count the number of pages you've finished in that time, multiply by 4, and you have your potential speed for that book in pages per hour. (Of course, some books are slower reading than others—it takes more time to cover 50 pages in a college text than in a light novel. The more solidly packed the ideas are on a page, the more time it will take to cover that page. But throughout a given book, all the material will likely be on the same level.)

Keep to the rate you've set for yourself in pages per hour. In this way, you will learn to devise personal tricks that will speed you up and that will, at the same time, sharpen your comprehension skill. But you must practice every day, or nearly every day, if you wish to make high speed natural and automatic, if you wish to become efficient in rapid comprehension.

6. DEVELOP HABITS OF IMMEDIATE CONCENTRATION

Nothing makes concentration so easy, so immediate, as the technique of sweeping through material purposefully looking for main ideas and broad concepts.

All people of normal intelligence can concentrate when they read, but slow readers put themselves at a disadvantage.

If, through laziness, you read at a slower rate than the rate at which you are able to comprehend, there is great temptation for your mind to wander.

The brightest persons in a class are not always the best students. If the work is too easy for them, they become bored, they think of more interesting things, they daydream, they stop paying attention. This analogy explains why a slow reader picks up a book or magazine, goes through a few pages, and finding that attention is wandering, puts it down and turns to something else.

By reading always at your top comprehension speed, you constantly challenge your understanding, you stimulate your mind, you get involved in the author's thoughts without half trying.

And, as an added dividend, you soon find that the increased concentration you get from fast, aggressive reading sharpens your understanding and enjoyment, for every distracting thought is pushed out of your mind.

But reading *about* the principles of efficient and rapid comprehension is not going to make you a faster or better reader.

Only putting those principles *into practice,* over a period of time, can do that for you.

How long will it take? That depends on what sort of person you are and how assiduously you apply yourself Under prime conditions, habits of speed and aggressive comprehension can become automatic after a few months of daily, or almost daily, practice. This is not just theory—students in adult and college reading centers prove it a fact year after year.

And when, as a result of your training, you find yourself not only doing much more reading than ever before, but also getting much more *out* of your reading, you will agree that it was time and effort well spent.

The important thing is that you now know, from actual self-testing, that you have the ability to read faster than you generally do.

The training that lies ahead will show you how to capitalize on this ability, will help you make habitual and normal the rapid rate, the quick and self-assured grasp of main ideas, that characterize the efficient reader. Exercise by exercise, drill by drill, selection after selection, you will learn to eliminate the faulty habits and inefficient techniques that interfere with total concentration, that slow up your comprehension, that keep your rate of reading down to a much lower level than you are potentially capable of achieving.

How to Develop
a Sense of Urgency
When You Read

PREVIEW

In Chapter 2 you test your capacity for total concentration when you operate under a sense of urgency; you then discover whether such concentration improves your overall comprehension.

• Become totally immersed in your reading and thus sharpen your powers of concentration when you operate under slight time pressure

Now that you have discovered both your present reading rate and your potential for reading much faster, try an experiment on ten simple and very brief selections.

Determine, as a result of this experiment, whether you can

• Develop a sense of urgency when you read

• Overcome any habits of dawdling you may have built up over years of inefficient reading

URGENCY IS THE NAME OF THE GAME

If you have discovered, from your experiences with the two selections in Chapter 1, that you are not now as fast or as efficient a reader as your potential ability makes possible, then there is a strong likelihood that you have developed, over a period of years, the habit of *dawdling while you read.*

If you read selection 1 in the previous chapter at a rate between 175–250 WPM, you may have formed habits of wandering through print in a random, purposeless way, letting words and ideas wash over you, making no demands on what you are reading—whether the material is light or heavy, recreational or study, fiction or non-fiction.

It is possible, if you have built up such habits, that you permit yourself the costly luxury of being distracted by your surroundings; you are in no hurry to get anywhere because you have no awareness of where you wish to go; and you often passively—even blankly—follow words, your mind only partially engaged, instead of *aggressively asking questions and demanding answers.*

You are, in brief, uncommitted and overrelaxed when you read.

As a result, you rarely stay with a book for more than half an hour or an hour at a time, for passivity leads to boredom, and boredom is so singularly unpleasant that it is only natural to avoid it whenever possible.

I ask you, in this chapter, to take the first step toward learning to attack all your reading, of whatever kind or for whatever purpose, with *a sense of urgency.*

Urgency is the name of the game if you wish to be a rapid, skillful, responsive reader:

An urgency to understand quickly

An urgency to respond accurately and intelligently

An urgency to get thoroughly involved and to concentrate completely

A CHALLENGE TO URGENCY

I challenge you to develop this *sense of urgency* to such a high degree that your entire being is immediately keyed up, and your adrenalin instantly starts to flow, when you confront a page of print.

I offer you, as preliminary practice, five very short and very simple reading selections.

And I ask you to *read,* to *understand,* and to *respond* to each selection in *no more than 1½ minutes.*

You will be reading under time pressure.

Your aim, as you practice, is to get immediately involved in the material, to rip out the essential facts, and to respond to a comprehension test—*all in 90 seconds or less!*

And so versatile is the human mind—so versatile and capable is your own mind—that a task which at first may seem formidable—not to say almost impossible—will eventually, with enough practice and determination, become child's play!

Human determination has made it possible for mountain climbers to reach the top of Everest.

Human determination has made it possible to place astronauts on the moon.

Human determination makes it possible to reach the unreachable stars, to realize the impossible dreams.

Your determination will make it possible for you to *read,* to *understand quickly,* and to *respond accurately* to a page of print *in a minimum of time!*

And the practice you will get in the *Accurate Response Exercises* in this chapter will make it possible for you to develop so clear and sharp a *sense of urgency* when you read that habits of dawdling and passivity will be gradually and permanently discarded.

Bear in mind that in the acquisition and refinement of any new skill the going will at first be rough. As I will say to you again and again in these pages—*persevere!*

EXERCISES IN ACCURATE RESPONSE

Have a pen or pencil at hand for checking off answers.

Have someone time you, or time yourself, or set your stopwatch or timer, for *exactly 1½ minutes!* In the short period of 90 seconds, not a moment more, you are to read each selection and then mark five statements about it *true* or *false.*

Do the *true-false* test without referring again to what you have read.

Do not guess. If you cannot decide whether a statement is *true* or *false,* leave the answer blank. Note that you are to try to finish *both the selection and the test* in 90 seconds or less.

ACCURATE RESPONSE EXERCISE 1

In 90 seconds or less, read the following material and circle T or F for each statement.

Set your timer for, or have someone call time in, exactly 90 seconds.

Stop when time is over, finished or not.

Dry Ice

Read!

Can you imagine ice that does not melt and is not wet? Then you can imagine dry ice. Dry ice is made by freezing a gas called carbon dioxide. Dry ice is quite different from ordinary ice, which is simply frozen water.

Dry ice was first manufactured in 1925. It has since fulfilled the fondest hopes of its inventor. It can be used for making artificial fog in the movies (when steam is passed over dry ice, a very dense vapor rises), and for destroying insects in grain supplies. It is more practical than ordinary ice because it takes up less space and is 142 degrees colder. Since it evaporates instead of melting, it is cleaner to use. For these reasons it is extremely popular, and many people prefer it to ordinary ice.

Dry ice is so cold that, if you touch it with your bare fingers, it will burn you!

Respond!

1. Dry ice is made from water, but because it is specially treated it does not melt. T. F.

2. The first dry ice was manufactured in the 1950's. T. F.

3. Dry ice has more uses than ordinary ice. T. F.

4. Dry ice is not as cold as ordinary ice. T. F.

5. Artificial fog can be made by passing steam over dry ice. T. F.

Did you make it in 90 seconds? Feel no anxiety if you did not—you are at the very start of your practice in reading quickly and responding accurately. Your aim, as always, is *to improve gradually and surely,* not to become an expert at once.

Correct answers to the first five exercises will be found in the key on page 17. Do not check until you have completed all five exercises.

ACCURATE RESPONSE EXERCISE 2

Set your timer for, or have someone call time in, *exactly 90 seconds.*

The Gold Rush

Read!

Over one hundred years ago, the news that gold had been discovered in California electrified the entire country. Immediately, thousands of men rushed West with but one concern—to get to California before the next fellow. Everyone was confident that he would find gold and become wealthy. Little did the travelers know about the hardships and inconveniences they would have to endure: desert heat, mountain cold, miles of mud, raging rivers. Besides, they would be menaced by hostile Indians, ferocious beasts, starvation, and disease.

How many people died in the "Gold Rush" nobody knows; what is known is that thousands of the more self-reliant travelers did get to their destination, did find gold, and did become wealthy. In five years, the population of California rose from 5,000 to 100,000.

Respond!

1. The discovery of gold in California caused a tremendous increase in the population of that state. T. F.

2. Thousands of people tried to get to California as quickly as possible T. F.

3. It was not well known that the journey to California would be full of difficulties and danger. T. F.

4. The route to California lay through deserts, over mountains, and across rivers. T. F.

5. Fortunately, the Indians along the way were all friendly and helpful to the travelers. T. F.

ACCURATE RESPONSE EXERCISE 3

Continue as before.

Victims of the Dust Storms

Read!

After the dust storms had swept over the Midwest in 1935 and 1936, thousands of families left their useless farms and began traveling by automobile to California, where, they had heard, there was enough work for everybody. When they reached their destination, they discovered that workers were needed only a few weeks a year. You can easily imagine how disappointed they were. On frequent occasions they found themselves without money or food. Life was extremely inconvenient for them. Often they slept in tents or shacks, got their water from ditches, and, when night came, were without lights (for of course they had no electricity). The federal government, impressed by their misery, endeavored to help these unfortunate farmers by setting up large camps for them to live in while they looked for work.

Respond!

1. Dust storms ruined many midwest farms in the 1930's. T. F.
2. Farmers who were victims of the dust storms moved to California to look for work. T. F.
3. When they reached California, they discovered there was a demand for workers for only a short time each year. T. F.
4. Nevertheless, they found life in California very pleasant and easy. T. F.
5. The federal government built camps for the refugees. T. F.

ACCURATE RESPONSE EXERCISE 4

Continue as before.

Elephant Keeper

Read!

In an interview recently with a newspaper reporter, the elephant keeper at a large circus revealed some interesting facts about the care and feeding of his 46 animals. An individual elephant drinks 100 gallons of water every day. Together, the 46 elephants daily eat 2 tons of hay, 25 bushels of oats, and 300 pounds of bran.

Occasionally, the keeper has to shave each elephant. Do you suppose he uses a razor? The only instrument that can be used on the tough elephant hair is a blowtorch! The hot flame, moved quickly over the skin of the elephant, burns the whiskers off painlessly.

To keep the elephants in good physical condition, the keeper trims their tusks with a hacksaw every three years and oils their hides once a year so that their skin won't crack.

Elephants are shrewd animals. "They'll outsmart you every move you make unless you watch them," comments their keeper.

Respond!

1. Elephants do not drink much water. T. F.
2. The chief foods in an elephant's diet are grains, cereals, fruits, and vegetables. T. F.
3. Sometimes an elephant has to be shaved with a very sharp razor. T. F.
4. Once a week an elephant's tusk has to be oiled to avoid cracking. T. F.
5. Elephants are smart, tricky animals T. F.

ACCURATE RESPONSE EXERCISE 5

Continue as before.

Are Monkeys Like People?

Read!

Well, as a matter of fact, they are! When certain kinds of monkeys are domesticated, they act just like human beings. They smoke cigars, drink beer, and look almost human when dressed in children's clothing. If you invite them to dinner, they can sit quite comfortably in real chairs and use a knife and fork exactly as you do.

As with people, some monkeys are lazy, like those who sleep all day in the zoo, and some are industrious, like the little fellows who collect pen-

nies for the organ-grinder.

In speaking of monkeys which act like human beings, mention should be made of the Brazilian monkey which often balances himself on the top of a tree and makes a speech to the monkeys below him. Sometimes he even leads them in singing, first howling some weird notes, then signaling his companions to join in the chorus. And you can bet they join in, enjoying it just as much as any boy or girl would!

Respond!

1. Some monkeys smoke cigars and drink beer.   T.   F.

2. Even the smartest monkeys cannot be taught to use a knife and fork when they eat.   T.   F.

3. Monkeys are just like people in that some are lazy and some work hard.   T.   F.

4. Some monkeys, without any training, remind you of human beings.   T.   F.

5. The Brazilian monkey sings in a sweet, pleasant voice.   T.   F.

How Are You Doing?

First, check your answers to the comprehension tests for exercises 1-5.

Key

	Ex. 1	Ex. 2	Ex. 3	Ex. 4	Ex. 5
1.	F	1. T	1. T	1. F	1. T
2.	F	2. T	2. T	2. F	2. T
3.	T	3. T	3. T	3. F	3. T
4.	F	4. T	4. F	4. F	4. T
5.	T	5. F	5. T	5. T	5. F

Score: _____ %   _____ %   _____ %   _____ %   _____ %

Allowing 20% for a correct choice on each test, score yourself in the spaces provided above from 0–100%. No credit is allowed for blank answers.

Now average your scores on the five tests by adding the totals and dividing by five.

Average response score for Ex. 1-5: _____ %

This was your first trial run in reading accurately under time pressure and with a *sense of urgency*.

Think about your experiences, and then answer the following questions:

1. Did you finish *all* selections and tests in the time allotted? ☐ yes ☐ no

2. If not, how many out of the five did you complete? _____

3. Judging by your comprehension scores, was your ability to understand quickly and respond accurately: ☐ excellent ☐ good ☐ fair ☐ poor

4. Were you feeling greater assurance as you did the last one or two exercises than when you started with exercise 1? ☐ yes ☐ no

5. Are you beginning, in your opinion, to develop some skill in reading with a *sense of urgency* while responding accurately to meaning? ☐ yes ☐ no

SESSION 4

That was a trial run. Ready to try again and see whether you can gradually build your skill and self-assurance?

Do five more *Accurate Response Exercises,* of the same level of difficulty. You will perhaps discover, to your delight, that practice *does* help, that success *does* come with effort and determination and a positive mind-set.

As before, the time limit in each exercise is *90 seconds* for completing both the selection and the *true-false* test. Do all five exercises before checking your answers with the key on page 20.

ACCURATE RESPONSE EXERCISE 6   Their Ears Help Them See!

Read!

A professor at an eastern college believes that the special sense blind people depend on is connected in some way with their hearing.

The professor recently described 1500 tests in which blind people and people with normal sight, but blindfolded, attempted to avoid walking into walls. The blind passed the tests with greater ease than those who could see!

The blind would stride forward confidently, sensing the wall when they were as much as fifteen feet from it. They claimed that their ears sent them a warning message that the wall was near. This seems quite possible, for when their ears were covered so that they could not hear, they often ran right into the wall.

You can imagine how valuable this strange power must be to the blind. Do you think that it is Nature's way of making up to them for their lost sight?

Respond!

1. Blind people seem to have a special sense not possessed by those who can see.   T.   F.

2. When people with normal sight are blindfolded, their hearing becomes sharper.   T.   F.

3. In the tests conducted by the college professor, those who could see did much better than those who were blind.   T.   F.

4. The blind people claimed that they received signals that warned them of nearby objects.   T.   F.

5. Covering the ears of the blind people did not stop them from receiving these signals.   T.   F.

ACCURATE RESPONSE EXERCISE 7   Monkeys Are No Fools

Read!

The management of a North Carolina zoo recently issued a notice to visitors not to give the monkeys lighted cigarettes. What was the necessity for this startling request? Were the monkeys smoking? Were the little fellows acquiring the tobacco habit?

No, the explanation is simpler—and funnier. The rascals were using the cigarettes—and with considerable success—to rid themselves of fleas. They would hold the lighted ends to their fur until the fleas became so uncomfortably hot that they jumped right out of their skins—that is, the monkeys' skins.

Now, as you doubtless know, monkeys have a reputation for being very smart; so you will not be surprised that they adopted this appropriate means of freeing themselves of their tormentors. The only trouble was that a few of the less intelligent monkeys seriously burned themselves handling the cigarettes! As a consequence, the zoo authorities had to put an end to the practice in order to save some of the creatures from going up in flames.

Respond!

1. Monkeys in a North Carolina zoo were learning to smoke tobacco.   T.   F.

2. They were ridding themselves of fleas by using lighted cigarettes.   T.   F.

3. They got these cigarettes from the zookeepers.   T.   F.

4. Monkeys are considered intelligent animals.   T.   F.

5. Some monkeys are stupid enough to burn themselves with lighted cigarettes.   T.   F.

ACCURATE RESPONSE EXERCISE 8   An Indian Letter Carrier

Read!

Delivering mail to small villages in India was once a difficult, perilous, and exciting job. The postman traveled on foot, often wading through swamps or crawling through jungles in order to reach the many villages on his route.

The Indian mailman might sometimes encounter a fierce tiger or panther along the way, yet the only weapon he carried was a sharp spear. He never went to work without his bells, which he would shake in order (so he said) to ward off evil spirits. Wild animals or evil spirits, nothing ever interrupted his work.

The Indian letter carrier was an honored and respected person; he was treated with great courtesy. So wise was he thought to be that he was frequently called upon to settle village disputes.

It is certainly evident that only a very brave man would take a job that compelled him to fight off wild animals in order to get his work done. You can understand why everyone in India looked upon the man who delivered mail as a true national hero.

Respond!

1. An Indian mailman used to carry a gun as protection against wild animals.   T. F.
2. He would also take along a set of bells to frighten off tigers and panthers.   T. F.
3. The letter carrier was often asked to settle arguments in the villages that he visited.   T. F.
4. Mailmen in India were considered heroes.   T. F
5. Some people in India used to believe in evil spirits.   T. F.

ACCURATE RESPONSE EXERCISE 9   The Tiger At Work

Read!

A tiger spends most of his life looking for food. For nights on end he prowls through the forest, hunting for a trail that will lead to his dinner. He may follow the scent of a jackal for a mile or more, and yet never catch up with it, for tigers have bursts of speed for brief distances only. Most of the animals a tiger normally attacks can run much faster than the big cat.

The tiger may find a herd of deer, but before he can leap into action a doe becomes aware of his presence, barks a warning message, and the herd escapes, scattering in all directions. A tiger is hungry much of the time, and may have to hunt for many nights before he is successful.

Finally he comes upon a group of grazing buffalo, chooses one that looks fat and delicious, and pounces like lightning. He will then force the buffalo to the ground, sink his teeth and claws into its throat, and spend the next two or three days eating his fill, for he never knows where his next meal is coming from.

Respond!

1. Tigers are often hungry.   T. F.
2. A tiger is one of the fastest animals in the forest.   T. F.
3. Tigers do not spend much time hunting.   T. F.
4. An animal that is aware of a tiger's presence can usually escape.   T. F.
5. A tiger kills an animal with his teeth and claws.   T. F.

ACCURATE RESPONSE EXERCISE 10   Radium

Read!

Radium is one of the most amazing things in the world. It is continuously changing to form other elements. Finally, after many hundreds of years, what once was radium has become a form of lead.

As radium changes, it gives off intense invisible rays, and light and heat. Because radium gives off light, it glows in the dark. In one hour it produces enough heat to melt one and one-half times its own weight in ice.

Most of the radium in the world is prepared from pitchblende, a dark, bluish-black mineral.

Pitchblende is very rare, and it takes thousands of tons of the mineral to produce only a few ounces of radium. You can understand, then, why radium is so expensive and difficult to obtain. Radium is so scarce, and the price for it is so high, that you could be a millionaire if you owned only half a pound of it!

The rays given off by radium are able to destroy certain kinds of dangerous growths in the body. For this reason, the main use of radium has been by doctors in an attempt to heal some kinds of cancer and skin diseases.

Respond!

1. Radium becomes a form of lead after many hundreds of years.   T.   F.
2. Radium produces enough heat in an hour to melt half its own weight in ice.   T.   F.
3. Pitchblende, a light brown mineral, is found in many places.   T.   F.
4. Radium is very rare and very expensive.   T.   F.
5. Doctors have used radium in treating some diseases.   T.   F.

How Are You Doing?

First, check your answers to the comprehension tests for exercises 6-10.

Key

	Ex. 6	Ex. 7	Ex. 8	Ex. 9	Ex. 10
	1. T	1. F	1. F	1. T	1. T
	2. F	2. T	2. F	2. F	2. F
	3. F	3. F	3. T	3. F	3. F
	4. T	4. T	4. T	4. T	4. T
	5. F	5. T	5. T	5. T	5. T
Score:	_____%	_____%	_____%	_____%	_____%

Allowing 20% for a correct choice on each test, score yourself in the spaces provided above from 0-100%. No credit is allowed for blank answers.

Now average your scores on the five tests by adding the totals and dividing by five.

Average response score for Ex. 6-10: _____%

Think about your second experience with these *Accurate Response Exercises*.

Here are the same questions you answered earlier about exercises 1-5. Answer them once more, but in reference to the second batch of exercises, and then compare your responses to the two questionnaires. (The first questionnaire is on page 17).

1. Did you finish all selections and tests in the time allotted? ☐ yes ☐ no
2. If not, how many out of the five did you complete? _____
3. Judging by your comprehension scores, was your ability to understand quickly and respond accurately: ☐ excellent ☐ good ☐ fair ☐ poor
4. Were you feeling greater assurance and comfort as you did the last one or two exercises than when you started with exercise 6? ☐ yes ☐ no
5. Are you beginning, in your opinion, to develop some skill in reading with a "sense of urgency" while responding accurately to meaning? ☐ yes ☐ no

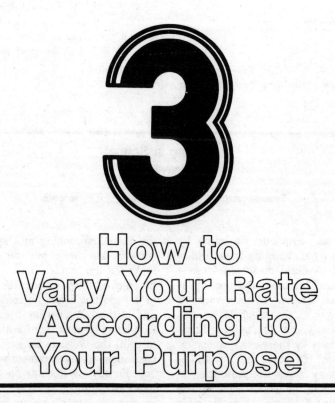

How to
Vary Your Rate
According to
Your Purpose

PREVIEW

In Chapter 3 you deliberately adopt a specific mind-set when you tackle a reading selection. You learn how to control your rate according to what you wish to accomplish.

You have discovered that you are capable of reading faster if you learn to *push yourself*—gently but firmly.

Now let us conduct an experiment, with you as the subject, to discover what happens if you decide on your purpose *before you start to read*.

YOU ARE THE SUBJECT
OF A PSYCHOLOGICAL EXPERIMENT

Are you willing to make some (perhaps surprising!) discoveries about yourself by taking part in an experiment?

The experiment will be concerned with your *reading performance,* but in truth the experiment is *psychological,* for your aim will be to find out how you react, *mentally* and/or *emotionally* (if there is any actual separation between mind and emotion, which is doubtful), when you read under varying instructions and differing stimuli.

To gain accurate information about your reading habits, follow the instructions carefully and exactly. Assume, for the sake of the experiment, that you are preparing to cope with real-life situations, and attempt to cooperate as fully as you can.

THE EXPERIMENT—PART I

Instructions

Assume that you are taking a college course in the *psychology of learning*, and that you have been given an assignment to *study* the following material for an important test that will cover any or all of the *details* of the information contained in the selection.

Your aim is to score as high as possible on the test.

However, read the material *once only,* and do not take notes.

Write the time in minutes and seconds when you start, then read through to the end, writing the time when you finish, as well as the total time elapsed.

(Allow, as before, ten extra seconds for noting·down the time. If someone is timing you, have that person make a note of the time at start and finish, and also the total elapsed time.)

SELECTION 3

Learning in School
by Winfred F. Hill

Time at start: _____ minutes _____ seconds

Start timing ➡ Let us begin our discussion by looking at a setting in which learning is the primary focus: the school. A child in school faces a bewilderingly complex learning situation. It is complex from his point of view; it is even more so from the point of view of the psychologist who bravely attempts to analyze it. The child is influenced in countless ways by the varied aspects of the classroom situation. He learns much from the teacher, including many things not prescribed in the curriculum and some things of which neither teacher nor pupil is aware. He also learns from his books, from his fellow students, and from the physical arrangements of the school. Part of what he learns is measurable as specific knowledge and skills, while another part involves changes, some very subtle but a few quite dramatic, in attitudes, emotions, social behavior, and a variety of other reactions. The psychologist's job is to analyze such complex situations into their component parts and to try to understand the principles of learning and motivation involved.

Let us consider some incidents in the school day of a particular sixth-grader, Alex B. We meet Alex first as he is studying a vocabulary list in his reading book. His teacher (a trifle old-fashioned) has instructed the class to learn to spell these words. He is thus confronted with a list of twelve words for which he must learn to give the correct written form when presented with the spoken form. However, in studying from his book he faces a slightly different task, since only the written form is before him and he must provide the spoken version (subvocally) himself. He goes through the list, pronouncing and spelling the words to himself, but finds his attention wandering. He looks out the window and remembers how much he enjoyed the previous weekend. Snapping back to the spelling book, he continues dutifully to the end of the list. Then he tries covering all but the first letter of each word with his hand and trying to spell the word to himself. At "r" he proceeds cautiously, trying to remember the rule for "i" and "e." Finally he decides on "receive," moves his hand away, and relaxes a bit as he finds his guess confirmed. At "s" he spells to himself without hesitation, "seperate," then frowns as he sees his mistake. He stares for a moment at the "ar," trying to fix it in his memory, then continues through the list. Half way through, he finds himself unable to remember a word from the first letter.

Annoyed, he looks at the word and then concentrates heavily on trying to remember it. Two words later, the same thing happens again. He looks at the word, wonders why it should be hard to remember, and begins to feel discouraged. He stares at the picture on the wall of Washington crossing the Delaware, and imagines himself leading such an expedition. Catching the teacher's eye, he returns quickly to his book and finishes the list. He spells the last word confidently, "cematary," only to find "cemetery," staring back at him from the page. Puzzled, he looks back and forth from "separate" to "cemetery" and thinks, "I hate spelling."

We see Alex next at recess running excitedly out to join a softball game. He begins the game in the outfield. As the batter hits a ground ball in his direction, he starts running, his speed and direction adjusted to make his path intercept that of the ball. As he nears the ball he bends over, puts his hands in front of it, and closes them at just the right moment to catch the ball. He then looks up, notes the position of the runner, and throws the ball in the direction of first base, his arm motion just forceful enough to carry the ball to the first baseman. This whole sequence of coordinated, purposeful behavior occurs rapidly, almost automatically, with no evidence of thought or verbal self-instruction. Watching him, the teacher is impressed by how much Alex has improved at softball since she has known him.

During the game, Alex calls frequently, "Wait'll I get to bat!" and "When'm I up?" Finally his turn comes. He pounds the plate and shouts, "Put it over!" When the pitcher throws the ball, Alex takes a mighty swing at it, and misses. He looks chagrined, but shouts, "Let's have another!" Again he swings and misses. This time he frowns and says nothing. He stands more rigidly at the plate, his teeth clenched. His swing at the third pitch is more tense, less free, and again he misses. He throws the bat down and stalks away. At his next turn in the outfield, he does no shouting, and his fielding is less coordinated. When recess ends, he returns quietly to the classroom, ignoring the chatter around him. He seems relieved that recess is over.

Later we see Alex during his math lesson. The class has been learning how to find the areas of rectangles. Now the teacher raises the problem of how to find the area of a triangle. She draws a right triangle with a 4″ and a 3″ side on the blackboard and asks the students what the area is. Alex likes math and enjoys learning how to solve new problems, so he eagerly tries to figure this one out. He tries to apply the rule for rectangles, but can't see how to do it. Then the teacher draws two more lines, making a rectangle with the hypotenuse of the triangle as its diagonal. Alex stares at this for a moment, then grins and excitedly holds up his hand. "The area is six. The whole rectangle is 12, and there are two triangles, and each triangle is half of the rectangle!" The teacher smiles. "Very good. The area is half of 4 times 3. Math makes a lot of sense when you figure it out like that." Alex basks in his success, pleased both with the teacher's approval and with his triumph over the impersonal challenge of the problem.

We leave Alex now, happy that a rather frustrating day for him has ended with success. ◀ Stop!

Time at finish: _____ minutes _____ seconds

Total time elapsed: _____ minutes _____ seconds

Test Your Comprehension

Mark each statement as *True, False,* or *Not Covered* by circling T, F, or N. *Do not refer to the material while taking this test.*

If you find you are unable to answer any question, simply omit it; do *not* guess.

1. A learning situation in school is puzzling and complicated for a child. T. F. N.
2. A learning situation is more complex for the child than for the psychologist who analyzes it. T. F. N.
3. A child's learning is influenced by the classroom situation. T. F. N.
4. A child learns things from an instructor that the instructor is not aware of teaching. T. F. N.
5. In the classroom, a child learns only what is prescribed by the curriculum. T. F. N.
6. Whatever a child learns, whether from books, fellow students, or teachers, is measurable as specific knowledge or skills. T. F. N.
7. A child's learning will depend in part on background and intelligence. T. F. N.
8. It is the psychologist's job to help students increase their learning ability. T. F. N.
9. Alex B.'s English teacher uses modern methods of instruction. T. F. N.
10. Alex's teacher pronounces each word that Alex must learn to spell. T. F. N.
11. Alex has to learn to spell ten words. T. F. N.
12. Alex spells *receive* and *separate* correctly, but misspells *cemetery*. T. F. N.
13. Alex's teacher is annoyed with him when Alex looks at the wall to stare at a picture of Washington crossing the Delaware. T. F. N.
14. Alex feels discouraged about learning spelling, and thinks to himself, "I hate spelling." T. F. N.
15. Alex impresses his teacher with his improvement at softball. T. F. N.
16. Alex plays an excellent game of softball during recess. T. F. N.
17. Alex seems unhappy when recess is over, and returns to the classroom reluctantly. T. F. N.

18. Alex is more successful in math than in spelling.   T. F. N.

19. Although Alex gets no expression of approval from his math teacher, he is pleased at his triumph in figuring out the area of a right triangle. T. F. N.

20. Alex's day in school has been rather frustrating.   T. F. N.

Compute Your Rate
(Approximate Number of Words: 1125)

Time	WPM	Time	WPM
1 min.	1125	3 min. 15 sec.	346
1 min. 15 sec.	938	3 min. 30 sec.	321
1 min. 30 sec.	750	3 min. 45 sec.	300
1 min. 45 sec.	643	4 min.	281
2 min.	563	4 min. 15 sec.	265
2 min. 15 sec.	500	4 min. 30 sec.	250
2 min. 30 sec.	450	4 min. 45 sec.	237
2 min. 45 sec.	409	5 min.	225
3 min.	375	5 min. 15 sec.	214
		5 min. 30 sec.	205

Your rate on selection 3: _____WPM

(Record this statistic on the chart and graph on page 234)

Check Your Answers

1. T; 2. F, 3. T; 4. T; 5. F; 6. F; 7. N; 8. N; 9. F; 10. F; 11. F; 12. F; 13. N; 14. T; 15. T; 16. T; 17. F; 18. T; 19. F; 20. T.

Your score on the comprehension test: _____%

(Each correct answer, 5%; no credit for a blank answer)

Statistics and Reactions:
Part I of the Experiment

Check the appropriate box or fill in the blank, according either to your subjective reactions or to the statistics you gathered.

1. Your rate on selection 3: _____WPM

2. This is ☐ higher than ☐ lower than, ☐ the same as, your rate on selection 1 (page 7).

3. Your comprehension score: _____%

4. Considering your usual scores on tests, do you consider this score: ☐ good ☐ average ☐ poor?

5. Did you feel under stress, believing there would be a difficult test on details following your reading? ☐ yes ☐ no

6. How was your concentration? ☐ poor ☐ scattered ☐ good ☐ excellent

7. Were you aware of reading ☐ fast and smoothly, or ☐ slowly and carefully?

8. Did you read this selection in the same way that you usually read for tests? ☐ yes ☐ no

9. If your answer to question 8 was *no*, what, briefly, was the difference? _____

_____

_____

_____

10. Did you consider the test a good measure of your reading ability? ☐ yes ☐ no

THE EXPERIMENT—PART II

Instructions

1. Assume that you are taking a college course in anthropology, and that your assignment for the next class session is to be prepared on the material in the next reading selection.

2. Read the selection so that you understand it thoroughly, but be particularly interested in the central point or points the author is making—*do not get bogged down in details; rather, be aware of the details as clarifying or reinforcing the author's ideas.*

3. Read with a *sense of urgency* and speed, but do not go so fast that all comprehension is lost.

4. Move along rapidly, thinking *with* the author; try to lose awareness of *individual* words, skimming unimportant words, phrases, or details if these get in the way of your search for central meaning.

SELECTION 4

The Sacred Cows of India
by Marvin Harris

Time at start: _____minutes _____seconds

Start timing. Go! ➡ The most puzzling religious beliefs and rituals are those that seem to work against the maximization of productive capacity under conditions of severe population pressure and food shortage. Sometimes it appears as if a whole population is deliberately limiting its chances of survival in order to observe some religious custom or taboo.

A classic example is that of the Hindu treatment of cattle. Everyone agrees that the human population of India subsists on inadequate calorie and protein rations. Yet the Hindu religion bans the slaughter of cattle and taboos the eating of beef. These taboos are often held responsible for the creation of large numbers of aged, decrepit, barren, and useless cattle. Such animals are depicted as roaming aimlessly across the Indian countryside, clogging the roads, stopping the trains, stealing food from the marketplace, and blocking city streets. A closer look at some of the details of the ecosystem of the Indian subcontinent, however, suggests that the taboo in question increases rather than decreases the capacity of the present Indian system of food production to support human life.

The basis of traditional Indian agriculture is the ox-drawn plow. Each peasant farmer needs at least two oxen to plow the fields at the proper time of year. To replace these oxen a farmer also needs at least one cow. Despite the impression of surplus cattle, the central fact of Indian rural life is that there is a shortage of oxen, since one-third of the peasant households own less than the minimum pair. Obviously, therefore, the cows must be too old, decrepit, and sick to do a proper job of reproducing. At this point the ban on slaughter and beef consumption is thought to exert its deleterious effect. For rather than kill dry, barren, and aged cows, the Hindu farmer is depicted as ritually obsessed with preserving the life of each sacred beast, no matter how useless it may become. From the point of view of the farmer, however, these relatively undesirable creatures may be quite essential and useful. The farmer would prefer to have more vigorous cows, but is prevented from achieving this goal not by the taboos against slaughter but by the shortage of land and pasture.

Even barren cows, however, are by no means a total loss. Their dung makes an essential contribution to the energy system as fertilizer and as cooking fuel. Millions of tons of artificial fertilizer at prices beyond the reach of the small farmer would be required to make up for the loss of dung if substantial numbers of cows were sent to slaughter. Since cow dung is a major source of cooking fuel, the slaughter of substantial numbers of animals would also require the purchase of expensive dung substitutes, such as wood, coal, or kerosene. Cow dung is cheap because the cows do not eat foods that can be eaten by people. Instead they eat the stubble left in the fields and the marginal patches of grass on steep hillsides, roadside ditches, railroad embankments, and other nonarable lands. This constant scavenging gives the impression that they are roaming around aimlessly devouring everything in sight. But most cows have an owner, and in the cities, after poking about in the market refuse and nibbling on neighbors' lawns, each animal returns to its stall at the end of the day.

In a study of the bioenergetic balance involved in the cattle complex of villages in West Bengal, Stewart Odend'hal (1972) found that "basically, the cattle convert items of little direct human value into products of immediate human utility." Their gross energetic efficiency in supplying useful products was several times greater than that characteristic of agro-industrial beef production. He concludes that "judging the productive value of Indian cattle based on western standards is inappropriate."

Although it might be possible to maintain or exceed the present level of production of oxen and dung with substantially fewer cows of larger and better breeds, the question arises as to how these cows would be distributed among the poor farmers. Are the farmers who have only one or two decrepit animals to be driven from the land?

Aside from the problem of whether present levels of population and productivity could be maintained with fewer cows, there is the theoretically more crucial question of whether it is the taboo on slaughter that accounts for the observed ratio of cattle to people. This seems highly unlikely. Despite the ban on slaughter, the Hindu farmers cull their herds and adjust sex ratios to crops, weather, and regional conditions. The cattle are killed by various indirect means equivalent to ... benign and malign neglect.... The effectiveness of this form of control may be judged from the following fact. In the Gangetic plain, one of the most religiously orthodox regions of India, there are 213 oxen for every 100 cows.

Stepping away from the point of view of the individual farmer, there are a number of additional reasons for concluding that the Hindu taboos have a positive rather than negative effect upon the carrying capacity of the ecosystem. The ban on slaughter, whatever its consequences for culling the herds, discourages the development of a meat-packing industry. For reasons previously suggested, such an industry would be ecologically disastrous in a land as densely populated as India. In this connection it should be pointed out that the protein output of the existing system is not unimportant. Although the Indian cows are very poor milkers by Western standards, they nonetheless contribute critical if small quantities of protein to the diets of millions of people. Moreover, a considerable amount of beef does get eaten during the course of the year since the animals that die a natural death are consumed by carrion-eating outcastes. Finally, the critical function of the ban on slaughter during famines should be noted. When hunger stalks the Indian countryside the slaughter taboo helps the peasants to resist the temptation to eat their cattle. If this temptation were to win out over religious scruples, it would be impossible for them to plant new crops when the rains began. Thus the intense resistance among Hindu saints to the slaughter and consumption of beef takes on a new meaning in the context of the Indian ecosystem. In the words of Mahatma Gandhi:

Why the cow was selected for apotheosis is obvious to me. The cow was in India the best companion. She was the giver of plenty. Not only did she give milk but she also made agriculture possible.

Time at finish: _____ minutes _____ seconds

Total time elapsed: _____ minutes _____ seconds

Test Your Comprehension

I. The material contains *one* overriding, central point. Without referring to the selection, can you complete the following sentence, expressing this central idea in your own words?

The Hindu ban against the slaughter of cattle and the eating of beef _____

_____

_____

rather than _____

_____

_____

II. Mark the following statements as *true* or *false*, *according to the material.*

1. Barren cows are a total loss to the Indian system of food production.　　T.　F.

2. Cow dung is essential as fertilizer and cooking fuel.　　T.　F.

3. Wood, coal, kerosene, and chemicals would be a cheaper form of fuel and fertilizer than cow dung for the Indian farmer.　　T.　F.

4. Cows eat food that humans need, thus depriving Indians of nourishment.　　T.　F.

5. It is inappropriate to judge the productive value of Indian cattle by Western standards.　　T.　F.

6. It is the ban against cattle slaughter that accounts for the ratio of cows to people.　　T.　F.

7. The Hindu taboos have a positive effect on the Indian ecosystem.　　T.　F.

8. The cows provide some protein to the diet of millions of Indians.　　T.　F.

9. Some Indians do eat cattle meat.　　T.　F.

10. If Hindu Indians slaughtered and ate their cattle during a famine, better conditions would prevail for the planting of new crops when the rains began.　　T.　F.

Compute Your Rate
(Approximate Number of Words: 1100)

Time	WPM	Time	WPM
1 min.	1100	3 min. 15 sec.	338
1 min. 15 sec.	880	3 min. 30 sec.	314
1 min. 30 sec.	733	3 min. 45 sec.	293
1 min. 45 sec.	629	4 min.	275
2 min.	550	4 min. 15 sec.	259
2 min. 15 sec.	489	4 min. 30 sec.	244
2 min. 30 sec.	440	4 min. 45 sec.	232
2 min. 45 sec.	400	5 min.	220
3 min.	367	5 min. 15 sec.	210
		5 min. 30 sec.	200

Your rate on selection 4: _____ WPM

(Record this statistic on the chart and graph on page 234)

Check Your Answers

I. (50%) The Hindu ban against the slaughter of cattle and the eating of beef *increases the capacity of the system of food production to support human life* rather than *decreasing this capacity.*

(Your answer will doubtless differ in language, but if it essentially makes the point above, give yourself full credit.)

II. (5% for each correct choice; total 50%) 1. F; 2. T; 3. F; 4. F; 5. T; 6. F; 7. T; 8. T; 9. T; 10. F.

Your comprehension score: _____ %

Statistics and Reactions: Part II of the Experiment

Check the appropriate box, or fill in the blank, according either to your subjective reactions or to the statistics you gathered.

1. Your rate on selection 4: _____ WPM
2. Your rate on selection 3: _____ WPM (see page 24)
3. Your rate on selection 4 is ☐ higher than, ☐ lower than, ☐ approximately the same as, your rate on selection 3.
4. Did you *feel* that you were going faster on selection 4 than on selection 3 (disregarding the statistics)? ☐ yes ☐ no
5. If your answer was *yes,* think about the reasons or motivation, and say more: _____

_____

_____

6. Similarly, if your answer was *no,* say more: _____

_____

_____

7. Compare your level of concentration on selection 4 with that of selection 3: ☐ better ☐ poorer ☐ the same
8. Were you aware that the level of sentence structure and vocabulary was more difficult in selection 4 than in selection 3? ☐ yes ☐ no

9. Compare your comprehension score on selection 4 with that of selection 3: ☐ higher ☐ lower ☐ the same
10. In which selection did you feel *more* the master? ☐ selection 3 ☐ selection 4
11. Explain, if possible, your answer to question 10: __

_____

_____

SESSION 6

THE EXPERIMENT—PART III

Instructions

1. Assume you are reading the material in the next selection purely for recreation and because the title caught your eye in a newspaper and you felt interested.
2. Read rapidly, aware of an *urgency* to finish, but *aiming at understanding and enjoying,* and while pushing your speed, do *not* sacrifice comprehension.

SELECTION 5

Driver Applicants Drive Some Testers Up or Through Wall
by Ron Cooper

Time at start: _____ minutes _____ seconds

Start timing. ➡ The applicant, petrified by anxiety, sat in the car while the driving examiner spieled his standard soothing pitch ("Good afternoon. Please relax, this won't take long").

It didn't take long. The driver started up the car, put it in gear—and sent it hurtling, in a cascade of bricks and plaster, right through the wall of the motor vehicles department building and into the men's room. The examiner shakily marked down another failure in the books of the California Department of Motor Vehicles.

Although all states test first-time driver applicants, it's especially in mass-transit-short, auto-crazy California that the testing agency has become a driving force in the lives of its citizens. For California has almost 12% of all the registered vehicles in the U.S., and in much of the state the only way to get around is to drive. And to drive legally you have to steer past the tests—both on paper and on the road with an examiner aboard—given by the DMV, as the agency's called.

About 20% of the 1.2 million road tests given annually by California's examiners result in fail-

ure. Sometimes it's spectacular failure: Autos driven by panicked applicants not only have attacked DMV buildings but have charged through hedges, walls, fences, show windows and other targets.

Cross Country Jaunt

One auto lunged into a restaurant, neatly queuing up in the salad-bar line. A woman, told to back into a parking place, froze solid as her car jumped the curb, crossed the sidewalk, breached a chain-link fence, slid down a grassy slope, plowed up a garden ("beautifully landscaped," observed the examiner in passing), and finally, appropriately, ended it all by resting against a cemetery headstone.

Such maneuvers strain the nerves of California's 500 examiners. W.C. (Woody) Wilson, chief of the DMV's license division, says, "We've had some uptight examiners quit on the advice of their doctors." But he claims that, all considered, it isn't a bad job. Most examiners, who make $9,500 to $11,500 a year, agree.

At least it isn't boring. There are about 30 accidents a month during tests (no examiners have been killed, the DMV notes gratefully), and practically all examiners have logged some close calls.

"You know it's got to happen," says Ann Duncan, one of about 70 women examiners in the state. "What you don't know is how you're going to react to your first close call. Mine happened when a lady pulled in front of a bus. I calmed her down, got us back in one piece, and headed for the restroom. I was sick for a half-hour."

Many examiners don't stall when bailing out of the car if their applicant is dangerously incompetent. "As we started out of the parking lot this lady started singing, 'Nearer My God to Thee,' " recalls Examiner Vincent Jones of Long Beach. "Before we'd gone far I was singing louder than she was. I walked back."

Dangerous Words

Some of the perils are partly semantic. David Hammero, now an examiner-instructor in Sacramento, was testing a young woman and told her to prepare to turn left at an upcoming intersection. Just as she was about to swing into the turn, she looked at him and asked, "Left?" "Right," he replied. And right she went, right across three lanes of traffic for a right turn. Mr. Hammero says he apologized for his vagueness and "we both had a good laugh." And then he flunked her.

The news that they've failed revs up the tempers of some drivers, who offer to crash-test the examiner. Others turn to scorn. One well-dressed matron, who had failed by regally cruising through almost every red light and stop sign on the test route, drew herself up to full grandeur, peered at the offending examiner over pince-nez glasses, and laid on the frost: "Young man, the trouble with you is that you have never driven a Cadillac."

To avoid the possibility of failure, some applicants offer bribes (generally, the would-be briber is simply told to put the money away and pass the test legally, but the cops aren't called). Other once-licensed applicants try to brainwash the examiner by showing him all sorts of safe-driving citations they've won, many of them issued by insurance companies. Examiner Robert Jones of Los Angeles claims to know of an insurer that denies its award to a policyholder for only one failing—dying suddenly.

A few lasses try to pass by making passes—at the examiner. Bob Hunter of Los Angeles recalls one bombshell who kept stroking her leg and hiking her filmy dress higher and higher as the test progressed. "I had to clear my throat when I told her she failed," he says. "Boy, that dress came back down in a hurry."

Some applicants never even make it out of the DMV parking lot—fortunately. These include people who "take a couple of belts" to relax before the test and wind up so relaxed they can barely stand, according to a DMV spokesman. Others either don't know anything about driving, or panic freezes their thought processes. Examiner Isabel Woods of Sacramento remembers one driver who didn't get her into the car. Asked to show his hand signals, he gave the left hand signal correctly. To do the right, he slid across the front seat, cranked down the right-hand window and stuck out his arm. End of test.

The testers try never to prejudge an applicant on the basis of age, sex or physique. "I've seen folks in their 80s pass just fine, along with nervous teenagers who just finished their driver's training courses," says Maro Sasaki of Los Angeles. "Recently I tested an amputee with special equipment in his vehicle. He was an excellent driver. You just can't develop prejudices. You'd be proving yourself wrong constantly."

Though examiners try to dispense equal justice, sometimes they bend over backwards to try to fill a special need. A bizarre case occurred in San Diego, where a student needed a license so he could drive to college. But he had a nervous affliction that prevented him from making good left turns. The DMV gave him a license with a special restriction saying he couldn't turn left, and helped him work out home-to-school-and-back routes that called only for rights. ◄ **End Timing**

Time at finish: _____ minutes _____ seconds

Total time elapsed: _____ minutes _____ seconds

Comprehension Test
Complete this sentence to give *briefly* the main point of the article: Examiners for the California Department of Motor Vehicles _____

_____

_____

Compute Your Rate
(Approximate Number of Words: 1080)

Use your calculator, or read your rate from the following table.

Time	WPM	Time	WPM
1 min.	1080	3 min.	360
1 min. 10 sec.	926	3 min. 15 sec.	332
1 min. 15 sec.	864	3 min. 30 sec.	309
1 min. 20 sec.	810	3 min. 45 sec.	288
1 min. 30 sec.	720	4 min.	270
1 min. 45 sec.	617	4 min. 15 sec.	254
2 min.	540	4 min. 30 sec.	240
2 min. 15 sec.	480	4 min. 45 sec.	227
2 min. 30 sec.	432	5 min.	216
2 min. 45 sec.	393		

Your Rate on Selection 5: _____WPM

(Record this statistic on the chart and graph on page 234)

Check Your Answer

Examiners from the California Department of Motor Vehicles *have had some strange (bizarre, ridiculous, dangerous, etc.) experiences in giving road tests to the millions of people who apply annually for drivers' licenses.*

Your own answer will be expressed in different language and may possibly have additional information, but you have probably written something essentially similar to the point made above.

Statistics and Reactions:
Part III of the Experiment

Check the appropriate box, or fill in the blank, according either to your subjective reactions or to the statistics you have gathered.

1. Your rate on selection 5: _____WPM
2. Compared to selections 3 and 4, this rate is: ☐ higher ☐ lower ☐ approximately the same
3. Were you aware of reading *faster* on selection 5 than on the two previous selections? ☐ yes ☐ no
4. Say more about your *feeling* of speed on this selection, explaining, if possible, your *yes* or *no* answer to question 3. _____

_____

_____

5. Compare your level of concentration on selection 5 with that on selections 3 and 4: ☐ better ☐ poorer ☐ the same
6. Say more about your answer to question 5: _____

_____

_____

7. Did you feel that you were the *master* of selection 5? ☐ yes ☐ no
8. Say more about your answer to question 7: ____

_____

_____

9. Do you consider selection 5 *easier reading* than selections 3 or 4? ☐ yes ☐ no
10. Say *why* you think it was, or was not, easier: ____

_____

_____

DRAWING CONCLUSIONS FROM THE EXPERIMENT

As you no doubt realize, you were asked to read each of the three selections in this chapter with a different purpose in mind. Therefore, if you attempted to follow the instructions carefully, you approached each reading selection with a different *psychological attitude.*

In the first of the three selections (*Learning in School*), you paid attention to details—perhaps even to totally unimportant details. When this type of reading is *required* (and, except in special instances, it rarely is), rate of reading will, of course, be slower. Frequently, if readers have developed habits of concentrating on details, they may lose the central point, the main idea, of the material they read in such a way that the *content dominates them.*

Efficient readers have learned to dominate content—no matter whether their purpose is: (1) to remember details, (2) to understand and respond to key ideas, or (3) to read for relaxation, recreation, and enjoyment.

In the second of the three selections (*The Sacred Cows of India*), you were reading for the key idea. Perhaps you found it quickly at the start of the selection— *that the Hindu taboos are useful in the system of food production*—and perhaps you realized that all the rest of the material was no more than *support* and *explanation* of this key idea.

If so, you were in command of the material; you knew not only *what* the author was saying, but also *why he was saying it.*

And so, since you were now *actively involved in following and analyzing the content,* both your concentration and speed might have increased.

In the last selection (*Driver Applicants . . .*), if, as instructed, you read the breezy article for enjoyment, you might still have realized *what the author was doing and how he was doing it.*

If so, you enjoyed the material, but still as *master,* not *servant*—and your rate and concentration might have increased still further!

What You Can Learn About Yourself from the Experiment

Reread now, if you will, the three questionnaires you filled out, examining your reactions to each selection and your statistics on rate and comprehension.

There are no right or wrong answers to these questionnaires.

Your answers will tell you:

• Whether you are capable of suiting your rate and style of reading to your *purpose*

• Whether you go faster on easier material, or whether you are stuck in one *rigid, unchanging,* rate no matter *what* or *why* you are reading

• Whether you can begin to *dominate* material by first deciding on your *purpose,* and thus both speed up your comprehension and increase your enjoyment—or whether, *at this point,* you still find a page of print your enemy, and still need to be convinced, *by actual experience,* that reading can be both productive and enjoyable once you have trained yourself in the techniques of *rapid, accurate, aggressive* comprehension

This experiment tells you where you are now.

In the pages that follow, you will discover that it is possible to *move*—to *progress*—to *change*—to become efficient and aggressive in *all* your reading of *any* kind: study-type reading for class discussion or tests (if you are a student, or if you are preparing for an examination of some sort); informational reading for your business, your profession, or your personal intellectual growth; purely recreational reading for pleasure and relaxation; or reading that helps you keep up with what's happening in the world.

How to Read
for Main Ideas*

PREVIEW

In Chapter 4 you practice intensively on four selections, learning to apply aggressive techniques that will speed up your comprehension.

You have discovered that you are capable of reading faster if you make a real effort, and if you concentrate on looking for main ideas.

You have experimented with varying your rate, and with determining your mind-set, according to your *purpose* in reading.

Now your training moves into high gear, and in this chapter you will learn:

• How to rate your reading efficiency

* Throughout the book, the terms, *main idea, central theme, central thought, main point*, etc. will be used interchangeably and with identical meaning.

• How to push through a selection briskly, aggressively pursuing the gist of an author's communication
• How to distinguish subordinate details from main ideas
• How to sense the structure of a piece of writing
• How to remember what you read

SESSION 7

HOW EFFICIENT IS YOUR READING?

The distinction between an efficient and an inefficient reader is so definite and clear-cut that we can graphically chart the differences in two contrasting columns. Think of your own reading habits and techniques as you examine the following chart. In which column do you most frequently see yourself mirrored? Take a pencil or pen and check off your characteristics as you meet them.

You Are an Inefficient Reader if:

1. You read slowly, generally 175–250 WPM or less. ☐
2. You read all material, of whatever type or difficulty, at an unvarying rate. ☐
3. You read word by word or, in extreme cases, syllable by syllable. ☐
4. You make many "regressions"—that is, you *reread* syllables, words, or phrases to assure yourself that you have seen and understood them correctly.☐
5. You move your eyes eight to a dozen times or more to cover the average line of print. ☐
6. You "vocalize," that is, you *sound words out* with you lips, tongue, or vocal cords, thus keeping your speed down to your rate of oral reading and, as a consequence, seriously interfering with smooth comprehension; or you may be excessively dependent on "inner speech," that is, on *hearing the sound* of the words you are reading. ☐
7. You often get bogged down in details and subordinate elements at the sacrifice of a clear awareness of salient concepts and important overall ideas. ☐
8. You read passively, sentence after sentence, without any understanding of either the material as a whole or of the relationship of the parts. ☐
9. You concentrate imperfectly. Because you are not deeply and actively involved in what you are reading, you are easily distracted by irrelevant thoughts, by external noises, or by the happenings around you. As a result, your retention and recall are poor. ☐

You Are an Efficient Reader if:

1. You have a cruising rate of at least 400–500 WPM. ☐
2. You vary your rate according to the type of material—you go faster on easier material, on narrative stretches, on paragraphs of supporting details, etc.; you suit your speed to what you want to get out of the material. ☐
3. You read for ideas, are rarely conscious of individual words; you skim or skip unimportant words, paragraphs, sections, or even whole chapters. ☐
4. You have few, if any, "regressions"—your perception is accurate, fast, dependable, and so nearly unconscious that you can concentrate on meaning rather than on separate words. ☐
5. You cover the average line of print in three or four eye movements. ☐
6. You read *silently* in the literal sense of the word—your lips, tongue, and vocal cords are motionless, and you are far more aware of meaning than of sound. ☐
7. You push briskly through details to grasp main ideas; you are more interested in the basic thinking that shapes an author's writing than in minor points. ☐
8. You read with aggressive comprehension, thinking along with the author, interpreting the purpose and function of the broad sections of material, and searching always for the central meaning of any piece of writing. ☐
9. You concentrate immediately and perfectly. You become so involved with the ideas on a page that you temporarily lose contact with the outside world. In consequence, you have excellent retention and recall. ☐

10. You fatigue easily because reading is—for you—a slow, unrewarding, even a tedious process; you spend only as much time with books as is absolutely necessary. ☐

10. You read for hours at a time without becoming tired; you can—and usually do—complete an entire novel or magazine in a single sitting. ☐

What has brought inefficient readers to their sorry state? How account for the effortless skill of efficient readers? Part (but only a minor part) of the answer to these questions can be given in the phrase *perception speed*. Inefficient readers have built up and thoroughly refined a set of incorrect eye habits, and by continuous repetition have developed these habits to such a point that they act as an impediment to smooth and rapid reading.

But perception, keep in mind, is only part of the answer.

A much more important part of the answer can be given in the phrase *intellectual habits*.

Inefficient readers are often *overconscientious,* to use the term in a special sense. They methodically read every word in a selection, giving equal weight and time to *all* words, to every single word, no matter how relatively unimportant, instead of using words as a means of grasping the author's ideas.

Inefficient readers do not quite trust the adequacy of their comprehension. They read meticulously, digesting and redigesting every sentence, every paragraph. Paradoxically enough, not only their speed suffers as a result of such extreme care, but their comprehension also, for they get so involved in details and relatively unimportant minor points that they often miss the main theme of the writing. They are an excellent example of not seeing the forest because of the thickness of the trees. If they are reading a book, they may struggle mightily to master every page, down to the last comma and semicolon, and may nevertheless fail to understand the overall ideas and implications of a chapter. In short, inefficient readers strive too hard to be perfect in their grasp of every word, every phrase, every detail, instead of pushing through swiftly to follow the basic concepts.

Therefore, they often regress. Having no confidence in their comprehension, they go back to check on figures, minor points, statistics, bits of description whose only purpose is to lend atmosphere—and the regressions cut their train of thought, make them overconscious of words, ruin their concentration, break the smoothness of their absorption of ideas, and, of course, radically reduce their speed. They have never trained themselves to plow straight ahead as fast as their understanding makes possible. They have simply never learned to develop the habit of moving along rapidly, of reading with "a sense of urgency."

There are additional factors that are relevant to reading efficiency:

Efficient readers have so large a vocabulary that the words they meet are quick conveyors of thought. The vocabulary of inefficient readers, on the other hand, is so limited that many of the words they encounter represent a mystery to be puzzled out before ideas can be fully grasped and appreciated.

Efficient readers have already read so much that they can constantly compare and contrast their present reading with their previous reading experiences; they have a background on which to build. Inefficient readers too often have to approach every little bit of reading as a new and unrelated experience.

Efficient readers have developed strong intellectual curiosity; and all the reading they do helps in some measure to satisfy that curiosity. The inefficient reader's intellectual curiosity has gradually grown weaker because reading has never been a sufficiently comfortable or rapid process to make the satisfaction of their curiosity worth the effort.

If you suspect that you are not normally as efficient, as rapid, or as responsive a reader as you would like to be, let me tell you this—without qualification. The good habits needed for fast and skillful reading can be developed in a comparatively short time. You can train the speed and accuracy of your visual perception. You can learn to attack material with the kind of aggressiveness that will sharpen your concentration and increase your rate of comprehension. You can learn to eliminate regressions, to by-pass your vocal apparatus, to decrease an overdependency on "hearing" the words you read. You can learn to stop paying poky attention to minor details. You can, with the proper practice and guidance, learn to plow ahead reading always with "a sense of urgency," speedily absorbing the main ideas, getting the overall picture. You can start building your vocabulary and stimulating your intellectual curiosity. *And as a result, you will, in all likelihood, make tremendous gains in speed.* Not the kind of forced gain you discovered from your work in Chapter I, but permanent, habitual gains that will come from radically improved habits and techniques of reading.

You can do all this if you actively *will* it instead of merely *wishing* for it. What is the difference between *willing* and *wishing* in learning? As Dr. James L. Mursell, professor of education at Teachers College, Columbia University, explains it:

The *wish* to learn is diffuse and general. The *will* to learn is concentrated and specific. The wish to learn means that we repeat a thing again and again hoping for something to happen. The will to learn means that we dig down and analyze, that we try to find out exactly what is wrong and exactly how to put it right. Let us take an analogy. A man may have a wish for better physical health and strength. His wish for health becomes a will to health only when he finds out what he must do to become more healthy, and then does it. So the will to learn means an intelligent and persistent search for the conditions of improvement and an intelligent and persistent concentration upon them.

Canny words, those, and important words—words that should condition your entire attitude toward increasing your reading efficiency. And every page in this book aims to help you "dig down and analyze"; aims to help you "find out exactly what is wrong and exactly how to put it right" aims to show you how you can succeed in your "intelligent and persistent search for the conditions of improvement" of which Dr. Mursell speaks.

SESSION 8

MAIN IDEAS AND SUPPORTING DETAILS

But enough of theory—let's get down to work.

I offer you now four practice selections, and I ask you to read each one with a *sense of urgency,* and with somewhat greater speed than is completely comfortable. Read with one dominating purpose—*to find the main idea and to find it quickly.* Push through briskly in a single-minded pursuit of the *gist* of the author's communication—do not concentrate on individual words or on supporting details, and, especially, *do not go back if you think you missed something.*

This is a big order, and you may or may not be immediately successful, but a conscious and sincere attempt to move along at a rapid clip, looking for main ideas, is more important at this point than success or failure.

As in previous selections, keep a strict time check, or have someone time you accurately.

1. First read the title and author of each selection (these are not included in the word count).

2. Then note the time in writing in the blanks preceding the text of the selection. (Allow ten seconds for writing in the time.)

3. Start reading (urgently! rapidly!) at the first arrow.

4. Lose all consciousness of time, concentrating only on the reading and on a speedy grasp of main ideas.

5. When you come to the terminating arrow, note the new time, subtract, and record, in the blank provided for that purpose, the number of minutes and seconds that your reading required.

6. Take the comprehension test.

7. Then determine your rate from the table that follows the test, and record this statistic on the chart and graph on page 234.

8. Next study carefully the discussion of each selection, and compare your reactions and comprehension with those that a trained and skillful reader would have. You will thus discover where your technique was good and where it was faulty; selection by selection, you will learn what errors

you make, why you make them, and how to avoid making them in the future; you will "find out exactly what is wrong and exactly how to put it right." In this way you will effect gradual changes in your comprehension patterns and also in your method of attack on reading material; and you will pave the way for the acquisition of habits that make fast, efficient, and aggressive reading normal and natural for you.

I want to state again, even at the risk of being tediously repetitious, that your dominating aim in reading these selections is to *cut rapidly through the words, sentences, and details to find and follow the author's main idea.*

This is not as hard as it may at first sound—it is not a bit hard if you will make an honest attempt to alter some of the comfortable and probably inefficient reading patterns you have grown too used to, that you have become too fond of, that it may be unpleasant, even painful, to give up.

Perhaps you have got into the habit of sauntering leisurely, too leisurely, when it's just as easy to run. Perhaps you get bogged down in details instead of con-

centrating purposefully on finding and understanding the main idea. Perhaps you think that every word has to be chewed and digested before you can go on to the next one, that every sentence has to be mulled over, that every thought has to be studied before you can really understand it; believe me, this is not so. All the words, all the sentences, all the thoughts in any selection add up to a final point, a final effect, a dominant and central idea. *Get into the selection, get that central idea, and get out.* If you have any success in putting these instructions into practice, both your overall understanding and your increase in rate will surprise you.

Ready for your first try?

Remember the instructions: *read at a consciously accelerated rate, intent on extracting the essence of the piece quickly and with no lost motion.*

Your purpose, in these four selections, is to think along with the writer and to discover, as quickly as possible, the central idea around which the selection is built.

SELECTION 6

Who, Me? Chop Off the Worm's Head?
by Douglas Cox

Time at start: _____minutes _____seconds

Start timing ➡ [1] Just about everybody is tearing into this year's Peck's bad boy of U.S. education—so-called "grade inflation," which is what happens when teachers give students far higher grades than they did in years past for comparable or even better work. The practice was cited this week in a series of *Times* articles as one reason for a disturbing decline in student achievement levels.

[2] As a former college instructor myself, I have come face to face with the kind of delicate human dilemma which can heighten "grade inflation." My severest test occurred while I was teaching English at USC—and I still have qualms about whether I responded appropriately.

[3] The challenge came from a young student of mine I shall call "Eddie," who began his college career in the fall of 1974. He was hardly the bright-eyed freshman of legend. Indeed, Eddie's inability to express himself—either verbally or in writing—seemed to imply that he had trouble thinking coherently. By anyone's standards, Eddie was an academic catastrophe.

[4] By some quirk, however, Eddie had made it into USC. Soon he was among 25 freshmen who came to sit and stare back at me from the other side of a battered wooden podium, their futures in the balance.

[5] Freshman composition instructors like myself

were, apparently, the university's first-string hatchetmen. From the beginning, we had been told to ferret out new students who couldn't come up to snuff and then deliver the *coup de grace*.

[6] But English scholars are notoriously squeamish about lopping off students' heads, and so many of us had to be reassured that we would deliver our death blows for the students' *own good*. I quickly concluded that one freshman who deserved the ax—certainly for his own good—was Eddie, by far the most inept student in my class.

[7] Having read several of his numbing essays, I was ready to bring down the ax when Eddie, perhaps out of sheer frustration with his own incompetence, created "The Worm."

[8] The Worm was the persona Eddie adopted when writing his "composition journal," a standard exercise in which students are encouraged to put down something—anything—in the name of "free expression."

[9] Eddie, as The Worm, was a shadowy figure who haunted the alleys behind the conventions of freshman composition, rummaging through garbage heaps of formulas and techniques discarded by the more adept and eloquent.

[10] But The Worm also was a boldy incisive writer. He'd found, all by himself, that he had some things he wanted to say, and that the medi-

um of a journal suited him. The Worm didn't write; rather, he raved—with many obscenities—about countless things that confused and overwhelmed him: pretty girls, beer, cars and, not least of all, his own ugliness. The Worm put his thoughts into bluebooks—ruled notebooks with blue paper covers—transforming them into unique if chaotic confessionals.

[11] As the weeks went by, Eddie as The Worm caught fire with a succession of hideously phrased entries which, nevertheless, were lucid and moving. But the real Eddie—the one who submitted formal essays in his own name rather than as The Worm—was still batting pretty close to zero. Since formal compositions counted far more heavily than journal entries, the two Eddies came to the end of the term with a near-failing grade.

[12] Eddie found that out in a note I clipped to what was, ironically, an especially brilliant journal installment. I explained in precise pedagogical language that he probably wouldn't pass freshman comp because, regrettably, The Worm had exerted little influence on Eddie's more "substantial" compositions.

[13] Soon afterward it was time to choose each student's final mark and record it on the official computer grading sheet. I did so by reading final journal entries and then reviewing the grades I had given on formal essays.

[14] Eddie's now familiar bluebook lay at the bottom of the stack. When at last I came to it, I found that he had concluded with a note addressed to me. In surprisingly perfect, though simple, English, he said: "Thank you for letting me say things. You've given me more confidence than anyone and I can write now. I'm not doing very much, but thank you, anyway." He signed it, "Eddie, The Worm."

[15] That stopped me. I knew Eddie well enough to realize this wasn't an 11th hour move to soften me up for a better grade. And it happened that, although I was a fashionably cynical young instructor, I finally began to waver.

[16] Why should I be the one to lop off Eddie's head for his own good? After all, I thought, grabbing at a straw, Eddie *had* eloquently raged and suffered in those bluebooks. So I squinted at my grading sheet, pondered long and hard, and then, *damnit,* wrote an "A" beside Eddie's name.

[17] My act of encouragement—a reprieve, really—must have only prolonged Eddie's academic misery, for I learned later that Eddie The Worm did not make it through the next semester. More stringent standards than my own ultimately prevailed.

[18] Clearly, Eddie deserved to have his head lopped off, if not for his sake (as I had been told), then for the sake of academia. But even now, long after the decapitation, I am glad someone other than I administered the blow. Had I been the executioner, I would have rewarded him cruelly for what, after all, had been a good college try.

[19] All of which helps explain, I suppose, why I have followed Eddie and his alter ego, The Worm, right out the classroom door and have now taken up an entirely new line of work. ◀ **Stop timing!**

Record here the time required on this selection:_____ minutes_____seconds

Test Your Comprehension

Check the statement that most accurately reflects the central message of this selection.

1. Grade inflation removes the incentive to achieve; students are now getting far higher grades than they did in the past for comparable or even better work.

2. Instructors of freshman composition at the University of Southern California were supposed to eliminate students who were unqualified to do college work—for the students' own good.

3. Eddie had two personalities—himself and "The Worm."

4. Both of Eddie's personalities did poor work in freshman composition.

5. The author is still not sure whether he did the right thing in giving Eddie an "A," and his ambivalence and doubts influenced his decision to give up teaching.

6. It does not pay for an instructor to be kind; the stringent standards of academic grading must prevail if students are to be trained to cope with life.

Compute Your Rate
(Approximate Number of Words: 935)

Time	WPM	Time	WPM
1 min.	935	2 min. 15 sec.	416
1 min. 10 sec.	806	2 min. 30 sec.	374
1 min. 15 sec.	748	2 min. 45 sec.	340
1 min. 20 sec.	701	3 min.	312
1 min. 30 sec.	623	3 min. 15 sec.	288
1 min. 45 sec.	534	3 min. 30 sec.	267
2 min.	467	3 min. 45 sec.	249

Your rate on Selection 6: _____WPM

(Record this statistic on the chart and graph on page 234)

Gain over Selection 1 (page 7): _____WPM

Discussion of the Selection

Key The number of the correct answer to the comprehension test can be found by subtracting three from eight.

Paragraph 1 is introductory, setting the scene for Mr. Cox's dilemma and how he resolved it, as described in detail in paragraphs 2–16.

The final three paragraphs contain the whole point of the article: Mr. Cox is still not sure whether he did or did not do the right thing, and rather than continue wrestling with such problems he left the profession.

SELECTION 7

A Stutterer Writes to a Former Teacher
by Irving S. Shaw

Time at start: _____ minutes _____ seconds

Start timing ➡ [1] Remember me? I came into your classroom more timid than the rest. My first thoughts were: When would I be called upon to recite? How would you react to my hesitance in speech? Would my classmates ridicule me? I hoped you could help me.

[2] As the long days passed without my being called on, my anxiety intensified. My back ached, because I was constantly sitting on the edge of my chair.

[3] At last you asked me a simple question. Do you remember how I blushed, how everybody in class turned to gaze?

[4] The silence of the room, the impatient look on your face, and the stares of my classmates brought on the worst blockage I had ever experienced. My facial contortion brought an uproarious laugh from the class and a puzzled look to your face.

[5] Do you remember what you did then? You reprimanded the class and moved me to a side seat—to be forgotten for the rest of the year.

[6] You did not know that my stuttering was not caused by a physical defect, but by a personality impediment. You did not understand my problem, and your reaction only aggravated my condition.

[7] Because of your attitude of taking my stuttering as a serious and troublesome problem, I became more self-conscious. Had you taken a lighter attitude, encouraged me to speak, and accepted me as one of the class, you would have helped instead of hurt me.

[8] I was never encouraged to enter social activities. How I craved for companionship; how I needed self-expression! Except for my stuttering I was like any other pupil, but you made me feel different.

[9] How frequently I wanted to speak to you informally, as the others did. Did you perhaps feel that I didn't care to chat? How wrong you were! The teacher who accepts the stutterer and who understands his make-up, can make it easier for him to develop a proper attitude about his problem.

[10] I never stuttered when I sang, so singing gave me an opportunity to feel on equal terms with others. Yet even when you discovered I had a good voice, you did not choose me to sing a song in the class play. If only you had capitalized on my simple musical talent!

[11] Do you remember one particular instance when I requested a pass? I threw in a block, a spasm, which bewildered you as usual. You looked away, believing I would find it easier to speak. This only made things worse, for I felt that you were not paying attention or that you couldn't "take" the speech block. For days after this experience I was depressed, my speech difficulty worse than ever.

[12] By the way, is Mrs. Ray still around? I wish she had been my teacher throughout the years. Her way of asking questions was so unusual that even I was able to speak up. She frequently asked for volunteers, and never cared if anyone answered without recognition. By not having to be the center of attraction, and by not thinking of speech, I frequently answered with no regard to my impediment.

[13] Talking to Mrs. Ray after class was easy, too. When I did have a block, she just said, "Slow, easy." The fact that she didn't turn away and the realization that she understood gave me a great deal of encouragement.

[14] If only you had sensed, as Mrs. Ray did, that the aim in guiding the personality development of the stutterer should be the same as the aim for any other child: to help him acquire a feeling of personal security so that he can face the future with confidence.

[15] When I got to high school, my stuttering grew worse than ever, and I became more withdrawn. The confidence given me by Mrs. Ray could not withstand the treatment I received from others who had no understanding of my problem.

[16] Then another teacher came into my life who was interested in me and helped me. He advised me to improve myself by seeking outlets through school activities.

[17] After one or two trial efforts at other things, I took up handball. A few pointers from the coach,

and in no time at all I was on the team.

[18] At last I had something other than myself to think about. I was accepted as one of the group, and my speech was of little concern. I let the ball do all of the talking, and how it did roar! Did you read that I won the city high school championship for two successive years?

[19] That teacher's kindly interest changed my life. No longer did I eat alone in the school lunchroom. People gradually became my friends, and I used to tell them that my speech impediment was because of tight shoes. I found that joking about the defect made it less important.

[20] My confidence increased, anxiety lessened, and slowly but surely better speech resulted.

[21] I hesitate to think what might have happened if I had not encountered some teachers who understood my problem and were able to help me! ◄ End timing

Time at finish: _____ minutes _____ seconds

Record here the time required on this selection: _____ minutes _____ seconds

Test Your Comprehension

Central Thought of Selection 7:

Think about what you have just read, and then briefly complete the following sentence.

Stutterers need _____

_____

—only from this will they gain _____

_____

_____

Compute Your Rate
(Approximate Number of Words: 840)

Time	WPM	Time	WPM
1 min.	840	2 min. 15 sec.	362
1 min. 15 sec.	672	2 min. 30 sec.	334
1 min. 30 sec.	558	2 min. 45 sec.	304
1 min. 45 sec.	480	3 min.	280
2 min.	420	3 min. 30 sec.	240

Your rate on Selection 7: _____ WPM

(Record this statistic on the chart and graph on page 234)

Gain over Selection 1 (page 7): _____ WPM

The central thought of selection 7 might be phrased somewhat as follows:

Stutterers need *and crave acceptance*—only from this will they gain *the feeling of confidence and personal security that will help them improve their speech.*

Compare what you have written to the statement above. Your wording may be quite different, but the idea should be similar.

Discussion of the Selection

Here, as you no doubt realized while you were reading, is a piece in which a mass of details and narrative incidents is presented in combination with interpretation—and it is the interpretation, of course, which gradually builds up into a strong and inescapable central theme.

The first bit of interpretation occurs in the last sentence of paragraph 7 (*"Had you taken a lighter attitude . . ."*) and the key phrase in this sentence is *"accepted me as one of the class. . . ."* The author has used over 25 percent of his material to prepare you for his main idea, *that a stutterer craves and needs acceptance*—and then continues with an even larger block of material, right through paragraph 13, elaborating on and pounding home this same central point.

In paragraph 14, the writer restates the theme (*". . . that the aim in guiding the personality development of the stutterer should be the same [i.e., acceptance] as the aim for any other child . . ."*); and then, in another key sentence of the piece, he broadens his theme to include the idea that *acceptance* results in *"a feeling of personal security. . . ."*

Paragraphs 15 through 17 add more details to support the theme, with paragraph 20 (*"My confidence increased . . . and better speech resulted"*) restating, in different words, the idea of *personal security*.

You are not, of course, expected to go through this conscious and elaborate type of analysis as you read. But accurate comprehension of the central meaning of any piece of writing is based on a recognition, perhaps largely subverbal, of how the author has organized the material, knit together the various strands of the fabric, combined the parts to produce a total effect. And efficient readers, intent on extracting the essence of a page as quickly as possible, always have some feeling, whether or not they verbalize it, of how the broad sections of material are related, and of how the important concepts are supported, explained, clarified, or illustrated by subordinate details.

My purpose in asking you to go back over each selection as you study the analysis is to sharpen your sense of the structure of material, to develop your skill in differentiating subordinate elements from main ideas. The more practiced you become in recognizing how details are used to introduce, bolster, pound home, clarify, or illustrate main ideas, the more rapidly and successfully will you be able to pull these ideas out of your reading, and the clearer will be your grasp of the final meaning of what a writer is saying to you.

SESSION 9

So let us continue this valuable practice on the next two selections. Push through the details rapidly, be aware of a *sense of urgency* as you read, keep on the alert for the main idea, and come out of your reading of each selection with an awareness of what *all the words add up to*.

SELECTION 8

Johnny, a Rejected Child
by Bertha Padouk

Time at start: _____ minutes _____ seconds

Start timing ➡ [1] This is the story of Johnny, who is ten years of age and is now in the fifth grade. In September 1951 he was referred to the school nurse because of poor bladder control. He would constantly wet and soil his trousers. He was shy and withdrawn. He was shunned by other children because of his bad odor. He was unresponsive in class and he would never smile.

[2] When the school nurse visited Johnny's house, she discovered a "shack without a bathroom." A barber chair served as the living room furniture. Johnny's father, who is highly emotional, is a strict disciplinarian. Johnny is afraid of his father, who feels that his boy is never serious about anything.

[3] In addition to Johnny, there are two other children—an older son in the service and a daughter now in the first term of high school. Both parents work.

[4] Shortly after the nurse's visit the school guidance counselor interviewed Johnny's father, who refused to get any help from any guidance source—either the Bureau of Child Guidance or some other agency.

[5] The school psychologist gave Johnny a Stanford Binet L Test in October 1951. This revealed that the youngster had an I.Q. of 116, had a higher potential for learning than was indicated in his functioning, and had a definite reading disability because of an emotional block. Use of primer materials in reading on a remedial instructional basis was recommended. These were put into effect by his classroom teacher. Only a slight improvement was noted by June 1952.

[6] In September of the same year Johnny was assigned to an Opportunity Class (small register) with a most sympathetic teacher. Two months later he became a member of the Reading Club (a remedial reading class was granted to the school at this time).

[7] On November 17, 1952, the results of two reading tests (Project Oral Reading and Project Silent Reading) revealed:

Johnny s Reading Age		7.6
" Reading Grade		2.6
" Retardation		3.4

Confusions and Substitutions
their brother for they brought

wild	"	wide	
bed	"	band	
fry	"	fire	
ounce	"	inch	
Rover	"	river	etc.

Phonetic Attack on New Words
Johnny could not blend, sound out or figure out by phonetic or contextual clues.

Omissions
He left out several words at a time—as "it began, I know, like ours." These omissions happened most frequently at the beginning and in the middle of a sentence.

Comprehension
When he was asked what he had read, the answer was, "I don't know."

Voice
Monotonous—vocalized—did not stop at a period.

Picture Clues
He did not notice them.

Reading Habits
He pointed during oral reading and vocalized during silent reading.

[8] Johnny, who was afraid to express himself, and who handled his conflicts by withdrawal and depressive reactions, had to be reintroduced to reading in a relaxed atmosphere that would promote interest, self-respect, understanding, and achievement.

[9] At the beginning of each lesson in the Reading Club ten minutes were given to oral language.

The group, consisting of six children, would rhyme funny words, discuss ways of helping other children, tell about experiences over the weekend, and engage in oral picture reading. Statements made by the children were written on experiential charts with the name of the individual child who contributed to the story. At this point Johnny began to show a marked interest. It was necessary to ask Johnny several questions before one sentence could be formed:

Teacher—"What did you do on Sunday?"
Johnny—"I went fishing."
Teacher—"With whom did you go?"
Johnny—"With my father."
Teacher—"What did you catch?"
Johnny—"Carp."
Teacher—"What's that?"
Johnny—"A brown fish."
Teacher—"Are they good to eat?"
Johnny—"Yes."
Teacher—"Johnny, please put all this information in a story so that I can print it on this chart. The other children will then be able to enjoy this wonderful story of yours."

Johnny—"I went fishing with my father on Sunday. We caught six carp. They are a brown fish and are good to eat."

[10] Thus, by direct questioning, Johnny became interested in expressing himself and in reading his answers. Furthermore, his status among the other children in the Reading Club improved considerably. A feeling of self-respect and achievement gradually became his.

[11] One of the activities in the Reading Club is finger painting, which is correlated with poetry, music enjoyment, and expressional and creative writing. On one occasion rain poems were read to the group. The children were encouraged to express their reactions to these poems. Johnny contributed to "rain sounds." After a stimulating discussion in which each member of the Reading Club participated, finger painting was introduced. Johnny had never finger-painted before. He started to talk to the boy next to him:

Johnny—"I have never finger-painted."
Richard—"Neither have I."
Paul—"In finger painting you do not use a brush."
Matty—"I think finger painting must be messy."
Paul—"Let's find out."

[12] At last Johnny had found some interest—some activity in common with other boys. This was the beginning of his becoming friendly with others.

[13] During this period of adjustment for Johnny, who was beginning to enjoy reading and related activities (finger painting, expressional writing in the form of individual and group dictation to the teacher, picture reading, working with Dixie mesh, group discussion, clay work, etc.), the guidance counselor constantly kept the father informed of his boy's progress in school. A very strong plea was made that the rigid discipline at home should be relaxed. The father finally decided to cooperate with the request. He began to notice the changes in his son. Within a short time the odor emanating from Johnny's clothing ceased.

[14] Within a period of seven months Johnny, from a reading grade of 2.5, made a year and a half progress in reading with a score of 4.1 in May 1953.

[15] On November 19, 1953, Johnny was given a silent and an oral reading test. He made these scores.

Gray Oral—5.9

Stanford Achievement Test D—4.3

[16] It is expected that Johnny will do even better in the near future.

[17] On Johnny's birthday, the Remedial Reading Teacher phoned Johnny's father. She told the father what fine progress the boy was making in reading and that Johnny was a bright boy. Over the phone she heard the father say to his son: "My boy, that's wonderful. I am very proud of you."

[18] Then he asked his son to play a clarinet solo to celebrate the event. This proved to be a turning point in Johnny's social and intellectual development.

[19] Utilizing to good advantage the services of the school nurse, the psychologist, the guidance counselor, and the classroom teacher, the remedial reading teacher was able to add her services to stem a severe case of enuresis (a manifestation of Johnny's anxiety over his paternal relationship). The reading club room established an atmosphere of learning conducive to academic achievement and social recognition.

[20] Thanks to coordinated efforts on the part of the school personnel, a problem which originated in the home is being currently solved. From rejection to acceptance by father and classmates epitomized the story of Johnny. ◄ End timing

Time at finish: _____ minutes _____ seconds

Record here the time required on this selection: _____ minutes _____ seconds

Test Your Comprehension

Central Thought of Selection 8:

Think about what you have just read, and then briefly complete the following sentence.

Johnny's reading and other problems were solved because _____

_____

_____

Compute Your Rate
(Approximate Number of Words: 1200)

Time	WPM	Time	WPM
1 min.	1200	3 min.	400
1 min. 15 sec.	960	3 min. 15 sec.	368
1 min. 30 sec.	800	3 min. 30 sec.	342
1 min. 45 sec.	686	3 min. 45 sec.	320
2 min.	600	4 min.	300
2 min. 15 sec.	532	4 min. 15 sec.	282
2 min. 30 sec.	480	4 min. 30 sec.	266
2 min. 45 sec.	436	5 min.	240

Your rate on Selection 8: _____ WPM

(Record this statistic on the chart and graph on page 234)

Gain over selection 1 (page 7): _____ WPM

I am now going to ask you to take a more active part in analyzing the structure of material. Referring to the numbered paragraphs in Ms. Padouk's article, answer the following questions:

1. Paragraphs 1 through 4 constitute the first major part of this piece. What is the purpose, very briefly, of this section? _____

_____

2. Paragraphs 5, 6, and 7 make up a second section—what is the author doing here? _____

_____

3. Paragraphs 8 through 13 form the third section—what is this about? _____

_____

4. What is the author presenting in the next section, paragraphs 14 through 18? _____

_____

5. Finally, in the last two paragraphs, 19 and 20, what is the author doing? _____

_____

_____

Discussion of the Selection

The article we are working on is full of the kind of statistics and specialized explanations that might well slow down the rate of the untrained reader—minutes can be wasted, and concentration interfered with, by an attempt to wrestle with the technical terminology often found in this type of writing.

Skillful readers, on the other hand, would recognize almost from the first few sentences that they are dealing with a *problem-solution* piece—and would be interested at once in discovering quickly what the problem is and how it was solved. To this end, they would avoid getting enmeshed in statistics and would skim through the conversation and narrative details, extracting only the flavor; and since they know from the start what they are looking for (the solution to Johnny's difficulties), they would whiz through the piece at high speed. (*Skilled reading always involves suiting your pace to the type of material and to what you are trying to get out of it.*)

This article has a simple, clear-cut structure that contributes strongly to rapid comprehension. In paragraphs 1 through 4, the problem is described and the background filled in (answer to question 1); in paragraphs 5 through 7, the author is tabulating the statistics on Johnny's reading performance and elaborating on his reading disabilities—she is still discussing the problem (answer to question 2); in paragraphs 8 through 13 she describes the therapy used with Johnny (answer to question 3), and if you were at all alert to structure as you read you realized that at this point the central theme of the article was beginning. In paragraphs 14 through 18, the results of the therapy are presented (answer to question 4), and the important point you should have come away with is that these results were good.

And then, in the last two paragraphs, 19 and 20, the author sums up what has been accomplished with Johnny, and by what means (answer to question 5). In the very final paragraph the total meaning of all the facts and details of the piece is explicitly stated.

You might have completed the central thought of Selection 8 somewhat as follows (see page 40): . . . *active steps were taken to change rejection to acceptance, both at home and in school.*

Compare what you have written to the statement above. Your wording may be different, but the idea should be similar.

The Bandit Had Brown Hair—I Think
by Jeff Bunzel

Time at start: _____ minutes _____ seconds

Start timing ➡ [1] I wish that guy had not chosen me to rob. It would have spared me a difficult dilemma.

[2] I had been working part-time at a service station here since it opened earlier this winter. This particular day I had the late afternoon and early evening shift all to myself. At 7:30 I began to close up by dropping most of the receipts into a safe, then locking the pumps.

[3] Next I went into the garage to get the long dipstick that measures exactly how many inches of gasoline are left in each tank. As I came out of the garage, I looked back toward the small office and saw a man standing inside, his back to the large windows.

[4] I put down the stick, walked over to the office and pushed the door open. "What do you need?" I said, or something like it.

[5] He turned slowly around. His sallow face was clean-shaven, and he wore a small knitted cap on the back of his head. Scraggly brown hair curled from under the cap, barely hitting the collar of his well-worn leather jacket. The man limply handed me a dollar bill and asked for change.

[6] Giving him the coins, I noticed his face never changed expression: a complete blank.

[7] "You don't have a pay phone, huh?" he said. "Where's the nearest one?"

[8] I turned around toward the open door and pointed down the street where, several blocks away, a pay phone was located. When I glanced back at the man, he had his right hand inside his jacket.

[9] "All right, get back in here," he ordered. "Let's go. Put all the money in a bag."

[10] Curiously, I was not all that startled or afraid. The man was so very calm. He acted like an old hand at stickups, so I decided not to test whether he was actually packing a gun.

[11] A money box—not the hidden safe—was visible on the other side of the office, and I shuffled across to it. In doing so. I studied the bulge in his jacket and could not tell if it was his finger, an empty bottle or the real thing. But there was something I could tell about his face, and I did not like what I saw: His vacant expression had turned into a mean scowl.

[12] I put my key in the lock and opened the box. The money bag was underneath a top drawer, and as I reached for it, the man said: "Don't move your hand another inch or I'll blow your goddam brains out!"

[13] I jumped back and threw my hands in the air. "Hey, man," I pleaded, "I was only going for the bag. Just leave me alone, okay?"

[14] He pushed me aside and grabbed the bills out of the box. In those few seconds I studied him carefully. He reminded me of a little kid selfishly snatching candy on Halloween—his eyes were that intent.

[15] "All right," he said. "Now give me the money you got on you." He emphasized this demand by poking and jabbing from within his zipped-up jacket, as a speaker might use a stunted hand to help make his point. I had a wad of bills in my shirt pocket and threw it onto a desk. The man used his other hand to stuff the bills inside his jacket.

[16] "The truck," he said, "—let's get you in the truck."

[17] He meant my 1963 Datsun pickup, which was parked in the garage. As I started walking there, twinges of fright ran down my back, like pinpricks.

[18] "Now get on the floor of that thing," the robber said, all business.

[19] "Hey, just don't hurt me, man! All right! Just leave me alone!"

[20] "Don't get excited," he said. "No one's getting hurt. Get in the truck."

[21] I climbed onto the front seat and lay on my back, watching. I half expected a bullet to come blasting through the window.

[22] Suddenly he jerked the door all the way open. "I said get on the floor. *Now move!*"

[23] I rolled over and landed face down. "Okay," he said, "Give me five minutes."

[24] That was it. He was gone—but my dilemma had just begun.

[25] His total haul was around $160. The police arrived in five minutes. They took fingerprints, showed me mugshots and wanted to know everything I could remember. That made me rehash the whole incident in my mind for several days, over and over again but hard though I tried, the bandit never came into sharp focus.

[26] I began to wonder if I would ever see him clearly. A friend said: "Don't worry—if you see him again, *you'll know.*"

[27] I am not a detached observer who believes that society bears the sole blame for the nation's proliferating crime rate. It seems clear the only long-term solution is social reform. This is neither a rebellious thought nor a cry to throw open the

jail doors. It is, rather, a realization of what has to be done in the years ahead.

[28] Still, we must somehow deal today with crime as it affects us individually. In the process of becoming a victim, I came to want short-term action to prevent this particular perpetrator from further harming society.

[29] That, at least, is how I felt after the holdup, and so I was more than willing to cooperate when the Berkeley police showed me mugshots.

[30] One of them looked like the guy, so I marked him as a likely suspect on the back of the photo. It was then the police told me he had a record of two previous armed robberies. Once they picked him up, they hoped I could make a positive identification.

[31] I hoped so, too. Surely society has the right to protect itself from criminals, even if it played a role in shaping them. Should the search fail for this bandit, others might suffer far worse than I did.

[32] Later that week a detective took me to the county jail. They had a suspect in custody, and I agreed to try picking him out of a lineup. A public defender was present to make sure the procedure was conducted fairly. Of the six men facing me, I indicated the one they were holding as the suspect, then had second thoughts.

[33] He looked very much like the man who robbed me—same build, same face. But somehow his hair looked different, not so scraggly now. I could not make a positive identification, but the detective was not disgruntled. He almost surprised me by agreeing it was imperative to be absolutely certain.

[34] The police say they have found additional evidence, and the case will hinge on whether the trial judge will admit it. They will not tell me what the evidence is, for that might prejudice my own testimony.

[35] How much easier it would be if I had been 100% sure. But to convict an innocent man in the name of protecting society—that would be the worst crime of all. ◀ **End timing**

Record here the time required on this selection: _____ minutes _____ seconds

Test Your Comprehension

Central Thought of Selection 9:

Think about what you have just read, and then briefly complete the following sentence.

The author believes that the only long-term solution to crime is _____

_____

_____ ,

but that we must also deal with crime as _____

_____

_____

Nevertheless, since Mr. Bunzel was not 100 percent sure of his identification of the bandit, he realizes that _____

_____

_____

Compute Your Rate
(Approximate Number of Words: 1125)

Time	WPM	Time	WPM
1 min.	1125	1 min. 40 sec.	675
1 min. 5 sec.	1042	1 min. 45 sec.	643
1 min. 10 sec.	970	2 min.	563
1 min. 15 sec.	900	2 min. 15 sec.	500
1 min. 20 sec.	844	2 min. 30 sec.	450
1 min. 30 sec.	750	2 min. 45 sec.	409

Time	WPM	Time	WPM
3 min.	375	3 min. 45 sec.	300
3 min. 15 sec.	346	4 min.	281
3 min. 30 sec.	321	4 min. 15 sec.	264
		4 min. 30 sec.	250

Your Rate On Selection 9: _____ WPM

(Record this statistic on the chart and graph on pages 234)

Gain Over Selection 1 (page 7): _____ WPM

Discussion of the Selection

Paragraphs 1–26 are narrative—Mr. Bunzel relates an experience he had. Recognizing the narrative style, you read very rapidly, following the story line but aware that the author will use his experience to make a point.

Knowing that you are looking for the point of the story, you recognize it in paragraphs 27 and 28—"The long term solution is social reform. . . . still we must somehow deal today with crime as it affects us individually."

Paragraphs 29 and 30 continue the story and paragraph 31 reiterates a point made previously.

There is more of the story in paragraphs 32–34, with the final part of the central thought expressed in the last paragraph of the selection—"But to convict an innocent man . . . that would be the worst crime of all."

Mr. Bunzel wrote his piece to express a three-horned dilemma he faced after being held up by a bandit.

Social reform is the long-term solution to crime.

Yet, we must deal with crime today.

And another yet, how could he convict an innocent man?

Your answer, in your own language, should have included these three points—and if you read the material with a full awareness that the author faced a dilemma, you were alert to how the piece was constructed.

Reflect, for a moment, on what this type of training aims to help you accomplish. You are learning, by actual practice, to look at material not as a conglomeration of words or phrases or sentences, not as a parade of unrelated facts or details or ideas—but rather as an integrated whole with a dominant and overall meaning. You are learning to move along more rapidly, to push through the details and extract a final meaning, to sense the broad structure of an author's thinking—in short, you are learning to read aggressively, not just take in words.

This ends one phase of your training, and with the next chapter a new phase will begin. And so we are ready, now, to examine the statistics you have been keeping and to see whether we can spot a trend.

Suppose you copy down, from the chart on page 234, your rates on selections 1–9. Examine this chart. Your rates may show great variation from selection to selection. If so, this is a good sign—you are suiting your speed to the changes in complexity and style of the material.

Selection	WPM	Selection	WPM
1	_____	6	_____
2	_____	7	_____
3	_____	8	_____
4	_____	9	_____
5	_____		

Do your rates on the last four selections show a definite gain over your rates on selections 1 and 2? This is an even better sign.

Your rates may possibly be fairly constant, after a significant jump over your performance on the first selection. If this is so, there is cause for rejoicing. You have demonstrated your capacity for accelerating your normal and habitual speed of comprehension—you have climbed to a higher plateau where you may remain for a while as you integrate the new techniques you are learning.

Let us do a little arithmetic. Add up your statistics on selections 2–9, and divide by 8 to find an average rate during this early phase of your training. How much higher is it than your rate on selection 1? And what is the percentage of increase? To find this last figure, divide the average gain by your initial rate, and carry the answer to two decimal places. For example, if your starting rate was 213 WPM, and your average rate on selections 2–9 was 295

WPM, you subtract 213 from 295, and then divide this answer, 82, by 213, giving you approximately 0.38, or 38%. Record these statistics below and also in the appropriate spaces on page 234.

Average gain in rate: _____ WPM

Percentage gain in rate: _____ %

A TEST OF YOUR RETENTION AND RECALL

And now let us try an interesting experiment. One of the significant dividends that training promises is an increase in *retention and recall*—and learning to seek out main ideas is one of the chief means of earning such a dividend. Without further reference to the selections you have read in this chapter, how successfully can you recall the gist of each one?

Retention Test

Once again, write out, *very briefly,* the gist of each of the following articles.

Selection 6: "Who, Me,? Chop Off the Worm's Head?" _____

_____

_____

_____

_____

_____

_____

Selection 7: "A Stutterer Writes to a Former Teacher"

_____

_____

Selection 8: "Johnny, a Rejected Child" _____

_____

_____

Selection 9: "The Bandit Had Brown Hair—I Think" __

_____

_____

_____

_____

_____

_____

_____

Key
Selection 6: see page 35 choice 5
Selection 7: see page 37
Selection 8: see page 40
Selection 9: see page 43

All About
Perception

PREVIEW

Chapter 5 explains how it is possible to interpret *more* of what you see—and in *less* time.

So far you have learned:

How to read with a *sense of urgency*

How to increase your rate by deliberately going faster

How to tailor your speed according to the material and your purpose in reading it

How to avoid poky and time-consuming attention to minor details

How to sweep briskly through material, speedily following main ideas, sensing the broad structure of the author's thinking, and getting an accurate, overall, understanding of the *gist* of a selection

In this chapter you will deal with the anatomy of perception:

- Peripheral vision
- Span of recognition
- Fixations and interfixation movements
- Afterimage

You will start your training on rapid perception, using isolated words and phrases.

Finally, you will read another long selection, under time pressure, looking first for the author's central idea, and then rereading to grasp the essential supporting details.

SESSION 10

READING AS A VISUAL PROCESS

You do not read with your eyes at all, but with your mind. Your eyes are only a vehicle of transmission—they flash the visual impulses that your brain interprets and your mind reacts to. Such interpretation and reaction may be instantaneous or halting, accurate or erroneous, easy or full of effort, depending not on the sharpness of your vision but on the clearness and richness of your understanding, and on the reflexive perception habits under which you operate.

The eyes are the camera of the mind. Like a camera, they do no more than snap the photograph. From that point on, the brain does all the work—it develops the negative, prints the picture, and stores away the result.

Like a camera, the eyes must focus on the subject before a photograph can be taken. They may focus and refocus three to a dozen times on a single line of print, up to a hundred times or more on an average page, in order to continue feeding successive images to the brain for interpretation.

Sit in front of a reader and peer up into his★ eyes as they move across a page of print. It is a fascinating process to watch, especially if you have never observed it before. You will see his eyes focus at a point somewhere near the beginning of a line and remain there for a very brief period of time, generally a fraction of a second. It is during this momentary pause that he is reading—depending on his skill, his eyes are photographing a phrase unit, a couple of words, a single word, or maybe only a portion of a word. Then his eyes jerk sharply to the right, focus for a second time, snap a second photograph, and jerk again to the right. These alternating jerks and pauses go on until the end of the line is reached, at which point his eyes sweep back to the left, focus on the following line, and the movement-pause, movement-pause process starts all over again, continuing line by line, paragraph by paragraph, page by page.

Go on watching for a while. Soon you will be able to count the number of pauses made on each line. If the reader you are observing is fairly skillful you may see only three to five pauses. If he is awkward and inexperienced you may be able to count ten to a dozen or more, and on many lines, if not on practically every line, you may see his eyes suddenly reverse and jerk to the left. He is making *regressions*—he is going back to check on the camera. The picture that his mind developed failed to make sense,

★ See Disclaimer, page xix.

or in some way nis comprehension momentarily broke down.

Does all this seem vastly complicated? It is, of course. Nevertheless, these constantly alternating movements and pauses are completely reflexive and pretty nearly unconscious, controlled automatically by the ability and speed of the mind in absorbing and integrating what the eyes see.

They are as reflexive and automatic as the movements in eating, an activity in which, particularly when one is hungry, there is ordinarily little or no conscious control over, or even awareness of, the separate motions of opening and closing the mouth, raising and dropping the lower jaw, grinding the teeth, or swallowing. In a sense, such motions are directed and controlled by the stomach, which dictates the amount of food it wishes to receive and the rate at which it can comfortably receive it.

So also in reading—the mind dictates the portion of print it wishes to interpret at one time, and the rate at which the eyes should continue feeding it these portions.

Reading, then, is accomplished by a continuous alternation of ocular pauses and movements—or what we call *fixations* and *interfixation movements*.

Fixation is the technical term for the fractional second in which the eyes focus on a portion of a line of print. During a fixation the external movement of the eyes stops, an image is transmitted to the brain, and words are read. Then the eyes move slightly to the right, a new point of fixation is made, and another image is flashed to the brain.

In order to keep reading, the eyes must move; but *while reading*, the eyes are externally motionless. During the movement between two fixations (*interfixation movements*), there is a marked reduction in visual sharpness—vision is clear only when the eyes are stationary, or *fixated*. However, owing to the persistence of an *afterimage* in the brain, there is no sensation of loss of sight, no sensation even of a blur, as the eyes focus and refocus, moving from one fixation point to the next.

What is *afterimage?* Try staring at an object for 30 seconds, then quickly close your eyes. You can still see the object, can't you, for just the briefest fraction of a second? Or stare at this object again, very rapidly shutting and opening your eyes a half dozen times. Doesn't it seem as if your sight is continuous? It isn't, of course—the optical illusion results from the slight persistence of the afterimage. It is this afterimage during the interfixations that produces an illusion of smooth and continuous vision as you read, even though there are alternating periods of sight and partial blindness. In truth, it is not the vision, but rather the flow of visual impulses to the brain, that is smooth and continuous, for the mind, under conditions of normal comprehension, is fusing the impulses it receives into a steady stream of meaning.

Let us examine the process more closely. A reader, confronted with a page of print starts to read the first line:

The eye moves across a printed line and you read. The eye

To begin reading, his eyes fixate at a point somewhere at the beginning of the line and remain there, if he is the average reader, for about one-fourth to one-half a second. If we attempted to diagram the action, it would look something like this:

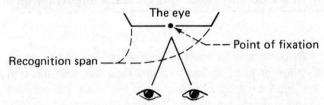

Having photographed the first two words (**the eye**) by fixating between them, his eyes then travel to the right and make a second point of fixation, then a third, a fourth, and so on until the end of the line is reached. Then they make a return sweep to the following line and start fixating all over again. For example:

The eye moves across a printed line and you read. The eye is a very special sense organ because it is a direct extension of the brain. Consequently reading is almost a direct mental process.

This pattern shows the unconscious eye movements of a reader of average efficiency. A line of type about four inches long is read in six or seven fixations. A skilled reader might cover such a line in three or four fixations—an extremely inefficient reader, on the other hand, would require nine to twelve fixations, or even more.

Now, oddly enough, the process of making fixations and of moving the eyes is so rapid, so reflexive, so unconscious that you might read eight hours a day and never realize what your eyes are doing. And this is exactly as it should be. *You are not supposed to feel your eyes fixating and moving. The more aware you are of these movements, the less skillfully you are reading.* Nevertheless, the movements go on—for without them, no reading could be done.

Let us now contrast the reading patterns of the efficient and the inefficient reader.

THE EFFICIENT READER

The eye moves across a printed line and you read. The eye is a very special sense organ because it is a direct extension of the brain. Consequently reading is almost a direct mental process.

THE INEFFICIENT READER

The eye moves across a printed line and you read. The eye is a very special sense organ because it is a direct extension of the brain. Consequently reading is almost a direct mental process.

By being able to cover a book-length line of type at an average of three to four fixations to a line, with three to four medium-sized words to each eye span, the efficient reader not only saves time; he also works less hard and has fewer periods of nonreading. The skillful reader does not take any longer to absorb three or four words than the inefficient reader needs for a single word. The former's fixations are certainly no longer in duration than the latter's, and generally are much shorter.

The inefficient reader whose patterns are illustrated above is the word-by-word reader. The reason his eye spans take in only a single word at a time is no fault of his vision: word-by-word reading is simply a habit he has perfected through constant practice. As a result, the meaning of the page comes to him choppily, and thinking is made difficult, for normal thought does not occur by words, but by phrases and pictures. A picture is much more quickly drawn in the mind by several combined words than by individual ones.

(The pattern we have just been studying does not by any means represent the worst possible reader. Many poor readers have such short eye spans that they cannot even take in a whole word at one fixation. Such undisciplined readers may even go so far as to attack a line of type syllable by syllable, or even letter by letter.)

You now understand the broad outlines of reading as a visual process, you now have an idea of how the eyes function in feeding images to the brain for translation into meaning. *What has all this to do with your own training to speed up comprehension?* The answer will be found in the following excerpt from *The Air University Reading Improvement Program:*

Nature of Reading

The eye moves across a printed line and you read. The eye is a very special sense organ because it is a direct extension of the brain. Consequently reading is almost a direct mental process. The eye, however, does not read while it moves. Decades ago physiologists learned that the eye sees only when it stops.

Reading, therefore, consists of a series of fixations which the eye makes while viewing a printed line. During these fixation pauses, the material viewed is translated into meanings by the brain. A good reader will make three to four fixations for an ordinary line of print: the poor reader eight to twelve or more. Ability to cover a wider span, to view a large field, is directly related to reading ability. The span is also related to speed of reading, since the eye travels about 6 percent of the time between fixations and spends about 94 percent of the time on the fixation pauses.

The good reader is also able to spend a shorter time on each fixation. He will stop only about a fifth of a second on each fixation; the poor reader will take twice as long.

Finally, the good reader makes fewer regressions per line or, in other words, his eye travels back over material less frequently. As a result, the rapid reader is able to read continuously and thus follow the meaning of the writer more easily.

To improve reading ability, it is necessary to have training to develop these characteristics: (1) a wide recognition span, (2) few fixation pauses per line, (3) short fixation pauses, and (4) few regressions.

AN EXPERIMENT IN FIXATIONS

Now, for just a few minutes, let us attempt to make the interdependence and interaction of your own eyes and mind a bit more conscious, so that you will thoroughly understand the basis and the reason for the training that will be offered to you in later sections of this chapter. I ask you to experiment personally with a single line of print in order to realize what is actually happening as you read.

This is the line of print on which you will work:

Our eyes move across the page in jerks and pauses as we read.

STEP 1

First, focus at the beginning of the line as you normally would in starting to read.

What did you see? Perhaps two words—**our eyes.** You made your initial fixation by focusing your eyes at a point approximately in the middle of the space occupied by the two words, and in a fraction of a second you read the print on both sides of that point. This was accomplished, you realize, not by sweeping from the **O** in **Our** through to the **s** in **eyes,** but by taking a single, instantaneous picture of the entire space.

STEP 2

Now start the line again. Make your initial fixation as you did before, then move your eyes to make a second fixation.

What did you see this time? Perhaps two more words—**move across.** After interpreting the first photograph snapped by your eyes, your mind called for more material, and your eyes automatically responded by feeding a second image to your brain.

STEP 3

Take your pen or pencil, and go back once again to the line of print.

This time read it through completely by making conscious and deliberate fixation after fixation until you have finished the last word. Mark off each of your recognition spans with a slanting line as you move from the beginning to the end of the line.

Did it work out somewhat as follows?

Our eyes/move across/the page/in jerks/and pauses/as we/read.

If so, you made seven fixations to the line—or perhaps you made more or fewer fixations. No matter. What is important is that as you increase your reading efficiency, your fixations will be fewer on a line of print, and your eye spans will be longer, not by conscious will but in response to the habits of faster and more self-confident comprehension.

You cannot deliberately control your eye-movements and read for meaning at the same time—but you can train yourself to see and understand more rapidly.

Let us now approach the culmination of our experiment by taking step 4.

STEP 4

The line has been broken up below into longer portions. Attempt to read each portion in one fixation by consciously focusing your eyes above the black dot in the center of the phrase.

Our eyes move

●

across the page

●

in jerks and pauses

●

as we read.

●

What did you discover? By consciously fixating at the black dot, were you able to read the entire phrase without moving your eyes? Probably so. Or were the outer edges of each phrase less clear than the center word or words? Or was it perhaps impossible to see anything but a few letters to the left and right of the fixation point? (Your answer will depend not on the efficiency of your eyes but on the mental habits you have built up through years of reading.)

No matter how successful or unsuccessful you may have been in interpreting the complete phrases above in single fixations, you can now understand one of the goals of your training: the building up of such strong and deep-seated habits that you will automatically and reflexively read with wide recognition spans, and your fixations will be made, without conscious control on your part, in *phrase units*, rather than in *one- or two-word units*.

STEP 5

Now read the entire boldface line on page 49 one final time. Read it rapidly and without any thought or awareness of fixations or of eye movements.

I have asked you to take this last step in order to close the experiment by disabusing you of the notion that you can learn to read more rapidly by consciously controlling your fixations. It is perhaps possible to "read" for a while with self-directed fixations—but at the end of half a page fatigue will set in and little if any comprehension will result.

Your fixations are automatically controlled by your comprehension, and the only kind of training that will work is the steady practice of habits that will condition your mind to do two things:

Accept more material from your eyes at each fixation

React more speedily to this material as it is fed in

A NOTE ON FIXATION TIME

Extremely poor readers may linger on an individual word for as long as a full second. They may fixate on the longer words syllable by syllable before they are able to interpret the total picture. And each of their fixations may take twice as long as a skilled reader requires for interpreting a *complete phrase*.

I want to give you an opportunity to identify momentarily with an extremely poor reader—I want you to experience personally a small degree of the laborious, the almost agonizing, effort involved when you have to extract meaning through exceedingly slow and awkward fixations and narrow recognition spans.

Without reversing the book, read the next two paragraphs, which, as you will notice, are printed upside down. Read from right to left across each line.

You are now fixating from right to left, rather than in the direction you are accustomed to, but this is not the reason for your difficulty and slow rate. (Left to right printing is merely a tradition—with a little experience one can read just as competently from right to left, as in Hebrew; or straight down, as in Chinese; or even, if material were so printed, straight up from the bottom of a page, or left-to-right and then right-to-left on alternating lines. Indeed some of these odd systems have much to recommend them as time-savers.)

You are having trouble, and probably also experiencing some discomfort, in extracting meaning from these paragraphs solely because the shapes and configurations of the words are so peculiar and unfamiliar to you that only a very short recognition span combined with a long fixation time permits your mind to interpret with any accuracy what your eyes are photographing.

The poor reader's fixation times may be comparatively long for another reason. In order to comprehend, he must move his tongue or lips or vocal cords, or even whisper audibly, for he has learned to understand meaning only by recognizing the shape or feel or sound of words. His speed, as a result, is limited to not much more than the rate at which he can read aloud. And this is far slower, of course, than the rate at which he could interpret meaning by completely bypassing the vocal apparatus—far slower and far, far less efficient.

You are not, of course, a pathologically slow and awkward reader. You do not have to puzzle out most words, your fixations probably last no more than two-fifths of a second, and your recognition span covers generally at least two words, sometimes more. You doubtless never whisper or move your lips or tongue when you read, and, if your rate is now over 250 WPM, you do not rely on your vocal cords to assist you in interpreting meaning.

But possibly you are a little overdependent on *thinking* the words as you read them, a little too conscious of *hearing* them in your mind's ear. (Such *inner hearing* or *inner speech* goes on to a certain extent in all readers, but with less and less consciousness of the individual words or phrases as speed increases and concentration deepens.) Possibly, also, there are some slight vestiges of vocalization still accompanying your reading performance—so slight that you are rarely if ever aware of them, but nevertheless serving to keep your fixations significantly longer, and your recognition spans significantly narrower, than necessary.

If these possibilities exist, as they do for most untrained readers, then the perception exercises that follow in the next sections will help you break a pattern of interpreting visual impulses less rapidly and less efficiently than you are capable of doing.

Practicing on rapid perception trains your mind to interpret accurately and instantaneously the photograph snapped by your eyes.

The type of exercises on which you will shortly start working is usually called "tachistoscopic (ta-kiss-ta-SKOP-ik) training," after the device known as a "tachistoscope" (ta-KISS-ta-skope), which flashes words and phrases on a screen at exposures varying from one full second down to as low as 1/100 of a second.

Individual tachistoscopes are used throughout the country in the reading centers of colleges and universities, to provide the kind of training in quick perception that is so valuable in increasing rate of reading. In a supplement to the *Keystone Tachistoscope Manual*, William B. Greet and John H. Eargle of the Keystone School and Guidance Center, San Antonio, Texas, explain the principle behind such training as follows:

Since we use but a fraction of our capacities, according to research psychologists, and since approximately 80 percent of our knowledge comes to us through our eyes, increasing usable vision and broadening spans of perception and recognition . . . [has as its purpose to] increase speed, comprehension, accuracy, and self-confidence in reading. . . .

By gradually increasing the speed of the flash and the amount of material to be perceived, unnecessary eye movements are eliminated and the spans of perception and recognition broadened. This technique drives vision impulses to lower reflex levels, where, as learning proceeds, the interval necessary between reception and interpretation is reduced.

A similar explanation is offered by *The Air University Reading Improvement Program* (cited earlier):

> The use of the tachistoscope in rapid recognition was developed by Dr. Samuel Renshaw at The Ohio State University. When the armed services realized the need for speed-up training in aircraft recognition, Army and Navy pilots used the tachistoscope with outstandingly successful results. Dr. Renshaw is one of our most prominent leaders in experimentation with visual problems and has tested the tachistoscope widely for reading benefits. . . .
>
> The tachistoscope helps the reader approach his limit of precision of vision and peripheral span. The untrained eye has a limited field of vision but with training on quick recognition this field of functional recognition expands.
>
> The tachistoscope has other values. It provides training in several visual processes simultaneously. Not only does it increase the eye span, it also decreases the length of eye fixation. The shutter of the Flashmeter can be controlled so that an interval as short as 1/100 of a second can be obtained. For purposes of training in the Reading Laboratory 1/100 second gives enough speed to provide practice in quickening the eye fixation, since the shortest recorded fixation during reading is several times as long as 1/100 second.
>
> Another value of the tachistoscope is that it forces the reader to grasp material as a form-field, seen as a whole. With such a quick flash he cannot vocalize or get side-tracked on elements of the visual pattern; he must take it in at once or it is gone as soon as the afterimage fades. . . .

ONE KEY TO RAPID READING

Actual reading, you recall, is done during the fractional seconds in which the eyes fixate. The efficient reader reacts to a number of words at a single fixation: his unit of comprehension is a complete phrase, a thought sequence. The inefficient reader responds to single words, one at a time; or, if his reading is very poor, parts of words, individual syllables.

Thus, to cover a line of print such as is used in this book, a highly skilled reader might make three or four fixations. After coming to rest at the first point on a new line, his eyes need move only twice or three times more before he is ready to make a return sweep to the beginning of the next line. After that first fixation, then, there are at most two or three moments of nonfocusing, only two or three fractional seconds in which his eyes are not reading. The unskilled reader, on the other hand, may have to move his eyes eight or nine or more times before he has read the whole line: there is a correspondingly greater number of moments of nonreading. This extra time allotted by the poor reader to nonreading accounts in part for his slowness.

But only in part.

Suppose there are two boxes in front of you, both nailed to the top of a table. Box A contains a thousand marbles. Box B is empty. It is your job to transfer the marbles from one box to the other. How would you do it?

You could, if you liked, pick up the marbles one by one, dropping each into the second box before you picked up another from the first one. That would take a long time. The muscles in your arm and hand would become tired long before you finished. You would be doing your task in as inefficient a way as possible.

Or you could pick up the marbles two at a time. That would double your speed. But to do the job as quickly and as efficiently as possible, you would grab up handful after handful. The more you grabbed each time, the sooner you'd be through, and the less you would be likely to tire.

This analogy is admirably applicable to reading. If your eyes photograph only one or two words at a time, the process must perforce be a slow and painful one. However, if your eyes grab up "handfuls" of words, you can read like the wind. *The more words you absorb in a single fixation, the faster you read.* That is the second part of the reason that increased efficiency in perception can so radically speed up your reading.

There is a third, and very significant, factor.

Reading is not actually done with the eyes, as I have pointed out; reading is a mental activity. It is done with the mind—the eyes acting as sensory extensions of the brain, as a transmitting belt carrying images of words to the brain. (Blind people, as you know, can read, even though they have lost, or never had, the use of their eyes. They can train their fingers to substitute for eyes; their fingers can become the sensory extensions of their brain.)

If your eyes feed your mind one word at a time, you grasp the thought of a printed page choppily, disconnectedly; for thought normally comes in phrases, not in single words. There is practically no meaning at all in the single word *one*. There is very little thought in the single word *bright*. The word *morning*, although it has a fuller significance by itself than either *one* or *bright*, contains a good deal less meaning than the complete phrase, *one bright morning*.

The word-by-word reader forces his mind to slow up because his eyes are continually feeding it words that are devoid, or nearly devoid, of meaning. His mind receives the impulse, *one*—and must wait patiently for the second impulse, *bright*—and must wait still again for the third impulse, *morning*—before it has something definite to work on.

The eyes of the efficient reader feed his mind, in a *single* impulse, a complete thought, *one bright morning.* No dead spots. No waiting. No interruption to the process of thinking. And no waste of time—for the idea, *one bright* morning, can be photographed by the eyes and registered in the mind *more quickly as a single unit* than can the three separate words, one after the other, that make up that thought.

In reading, the whole is more significant than the sum of its parts. The "whole" is a phrase, a thought; the parts are individual words which, by themselves, one by one, are often useless for comprehension.

The third factor, then, is that the reader who takes in *more* words in a single fixation understands more quickly; and, since the final purpose of reading is to understand, the more nearly instantaneously the thought of a printed line is grasped, and the more smoothly the eyes and mind co-operate, the more rapid and efficient the entire process becomes.

One key to rapid reading is the perception and interpretation of large numbers of words at each fixation.

Merely knowing this fact is not enough.

Expert as you may become at understanding the principles of rapid, efficient reading, you cannot become a fast reader until you are able, as a result of constant, hard practice, to apply these principles as a matter of automatic habit. You can say to yourself, "I am now going to use wide fixations; I am going to perceive quickly and accurately; and thus I am going to read faster," but you will have as little success as the person who has memorized the principles of expert swimming and then jumps into the water for a half-mile race. If he has never been in the water before, he will likely thrash around awkwardly and perhaps eventually drown, for his knowledge of the rules *intellectually* would not, by itself, make his body respond *physically*.

The person who intends to become an expert swimmer must practice one skill after another until the correct bodily movements become habitual and automatic; he must build up such an excellent set of co-ordinating reflexive habits that his body does the proper things without any conscious direction from his mind. In first learning how to swim, he must go through each part of the act consciously. Then, by practice, by more and more and more practice, by constantly and patiently refining his good habits and by ruthlessly weeding out his bad ones, he trains his body to function by itself.

Becoming a fast reader requires the same continuous, intelligent practice, the same single-minded diligence that are essential to the conquest of any high-order skill; it requires the building up and refinement of good habits to the point where instantaneous perception and wide fixations; lack of vocalization, regressions and lip movements; and rapid mental reaction to the *ideas* on the printed page become so nearly automatic that the mind can be left entirely free to concentrate on what an author is saying.

MACULAR AND PERIPHERAL IMAGE

In reading centers of colleges and universities, students are taught, through tachistoscopic training, to perceive and interpret more words in a single fixation and to reduce to a minimum the time spent on making that fixation. They are trained to make greater use of their peripheral vision, and thereby to increase the width of their interpretable eye spans while reading.

You can find out quickly what peripheral vision is by holding your forefinger up in front of your eyes at a comfortable distance—say ten to twelve inches.

When you do that, and stare at your finger, what do you see?

Your finger, of course. You see your finger clearly and sharply because your eyes are focusing on it. This image comes to you through the macula of the retina of your eyes, that portion of the optical equipment which sees objects in the direct line of vision. We might call your finger, in this instance, your macular image.

But do you see only your finger? Look again, and you will notice, though not so clearly, many things on all sides of your finger. Don't shift your gaze, keep focused directly on your finger, and yet you can see, though perhaps vaguely, many objects above and below the macular image and to the right or left of it, possible for quite a distance in all directions.

Everything you see in addition to your finger is being photographed by your peripheral vision; or we may say that the less distinct images you receive on all sides of your finger are the peripheral images.

Perception training with words and phrases is intended to help you react more accurately to the peripheral images you receive while reading.

Perception training is purely psychological—it has no effect whatever on the organic structure or on the efficiency of your eyes, but rather sharpens and accelerates your mental interpretations of the ocular images that are sent to your brain during each fixation. Sloppy, slow, or awkward seeing, in reading as in anything else, is the result of poor development of *mental images* and not necessarily a sign of poor vision. By means of perception exercises, you are attempting to teach your mind to interpret as quickly and completely as possible the image transmitted to it by an ocular fixation.*

Macular vision transmits the center of the phrase as a stimulus to the brain, and peripheral vision transmits those parts which are to the left and right of the center. A phrase

*Needless to say, I am taking for granted that your eyes are capable of good vision at reading distance or have been corrected through glasses or other means. If you feel that your vision is faulty, I strongly recommend a thorough checkup by a competent ophthalmologist or optometrist before you proceed with your training.

such as *in the reading centers* can be grasped as an entity if you have trained your peripheral vision; but actually there are two kinds of image, macular and peripheral, as shown below.

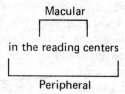

Macular

in the reading centers

Peripheral

It thus stands to reason that the sharper and more efficient your interpretation of peripheral vision becomes, the wider your usable eye spans will be, and the more material you will be able to interpret at each fixation.

SESSION 11

TRAINING IN WORD PERCEPTION

Perception Exercise 1

You know how a pianist may warm up by playing the scales?

I ask you to warm up to Perception Exercises by starting on "word recognition."

Take a pen or pencil, and working at efficient speed (Concentrate! No dawdling! Mobilize yourself to attack a page of print!), check off on each line *the word that is identical to the word in the key column on the left.*

Time yourself: however long it takes you to complete exercise 1, try to shave a few seconds off your time when you do exercise 2.

Once you have registered the *key word* in your mind, *do not think of the meaning of any of the words that follow.*

Simply snap a picture of the key word, then scan the rest of the line to find, *quickly,* an identical picture.

If you fail to find the *word that is the same as the key word* at your first scan, *do not go back.*

Simply go on to the next line and slow down a bit.

Do not check back until you have finished all 25 lines. After you have established your time spent on the exercise, then go back and compare *the words you checked* with the *key words,* and write the number of your correct responses in the blank at the end of exercise 1.

Your goal: 25 correct answers in 30 seconds or less.

Time at this moment: _____ minutes _____ seconds

Start timing!

Key Word

1. **gleeful** glad glee gleesome gleeful glum glower

2. **pall** pail play pale pleat pall pluck

3. **airy** fairy terry airy ashen airs aim

4. **zoo** zone zoo zebra zilch zenith zoom

5. **queen** king quiet queen quaver quid quay

6. **nourish** nuclear notice nurture nourishment notice nourish

7. **lottery** let love flattery large lover lottery

8. **barer** bearer blarer barrier barer glarer rarer

9. **crazy** cracked crazed daisy lazy crazy mazy

10. **bee** been bee bead bread breed broom

11. **broom** brain broad broom broth bring brook

12. **love** live love loved lived life wove

13. **speed** spend speed sprint spoon spear speak

14. **train** brain main stain tarn turn train

15. **wear** where wear wary wore wealth wry

16. **time** tire tine tone time took touch

17. **stain** store stain strain strike stack stand

18. **lightning** lightening frightening lighter looking liking lightning

19. **laughter** daughter laughing laughed lighter after laughter

20. **spry** dry spy cry fry spry try

21. **doing** going doing daring drying wooing gong

22. **floor** flare flair flaw floom flax floor

23. **eaten** eating eater beater eaten eat eats

24. **brush** brash blush flush brush brushing bush

25. **simple** simple simpler pimple sickle silly silent

Stop timing!

Time spent: _____seconds

Number correct: _____

Perception Exercise 2

Your training in this exercise will be somewhat more demanding. In *some* of the 25 lines (not all of them), the *key word* will appear *twice*. You will now have to scan the entire line in each instance, looking for a possible *second repetition of the key word*.

Follow these instructions:

Snap a picture of the *key word,* then scan the rest of the line to find, *quickly,* any identical picture *or pictures.*

If you fail to find the *key word* repeated at your first scan, *do not go back.*

Simply go on to the next line and slow down a bit.

Do not check back until you have finished all 25 lines. After you have established your time spent on the exercise, count the number of words you have checked and compare your results with the answer that follows the exercise.

Your goal: To complete the exercises in 40 seconds or less, finding all the repetitions that occur.

Time at this moment: _____minutes _____seconds

Start timing!

Key Word

1. **fries** fried frier friar flier fry fries

2. **greener** green grown greener greenest grower growler

3. **splash** splat dash flash slush splash squash

4. **trembled** tremble trembling trimmer trouble tremble trembled

5. **thrush** thrush thrash trust thrush trash trashed

6. **cough** could cramp cough cuff crown cow

7. **mixed** might waxed fixed foxed mixed axed

8. **yesses** yes you guesses foxes yesses misses

9. **grain** brain strain drain grain green train

10. **clearer** cleaner cleaver clever clear clearer clover

11. **marked** marked sparked market marred marked mashed

12. **mired** wired fired tired mired milled miler

13. **gnawed** gnaw gnat gnashed gnawed gnu gnarled

14. **sprawl** drawl sprawled sprawler sprawl spring spray

15. **lived** loved lives lived love lover lived

16. **king** kiss kale cool king wing thing

17. **bee** be been beet bee bleed blood

18. **sting** sting stung string sting stand stiff

19. **flow** feel flinch flake flow flash flow

20. **dried** dries drier dryer fries dried dried

21. **push** bush put pun punt push paint

22. **clothes** close closer closed clothes cloth clothing

23. **glows** grows gray glow glows gleam glean

24. **hunt** hint hand hot hunt hurt hunt

25. **pale** peel pull pill pale pole pale

Stop timing!

Number of repetitions: 33

Number you found: _____

Time spent: _____seconds

Analyze Your Perception Habits

Answer these questions in writing:

1. Were you comfortable doing exercises 1 and 2?___

2. Which exercise was more comfortable? _____

3. Did you stay at or under the time goal for each exercise? _____

4. Did your time *decrease* for exercise 2? _____

5. Did your score *increase* for exercise 2? _____

6. Were you becoming more skillful, as you went on, in not "hearing" the words in your mind? _____ _____

Similar perception exercises will occur later in your training, and it will be interesting for you to compare your answers to the questionnaire above with the answers you give at the end of later exercises.

TRAINING IN
INSTANTANEOUS WORD PERCEPTION

Let us try a new technique, now, in your training to perceive words instantaneously and accurately.

Perception Exercise 3

Instructions:

1. Place the Fixation Card (which you will find between the pages of the book)* in such a way that the *phrase arrow* is just above the first word in the list starting on this page, and the *word arrow* squarely meets the arrow on the page.

2. Pull the card down just far enough to expose the word *and immediately push the card back* so that the word is again hidden.

3. During the time the word is exposed, glance at it quickly, registering its appearance in your mind. *Try not to say or "hear" the word. Visualize* it only.

4. Proceed in the same way from word to word, column to column.

5. In the slight fraction of a second in which the word is exposed, it is up to you to *visualize it accurately* —and this will be no mean task, for each word will be somewhat similar, but not exactly identical, to one or more words that precede and/or follow it. If you have a little trouble at first, *do not slacken your speed of exposure and concealment;* the idea is not to decrease the speed of your arm movement until it coincides with the speed of your perception, but, on the contrary, to accelerate your speed of perception so that it will equal the swiftness of your arm.

---

* If the Fixation card is missing, use any 3 by 5 inch unlined index card. Simply draw an arrow to the *right* edge of the card, as illustrated below, approximately ¼ inch from the top. Label it *word arrow.* Draw another arrow to the *left* edge, again approximately ¼ inch from the top, labeling it *phrase arrow.*

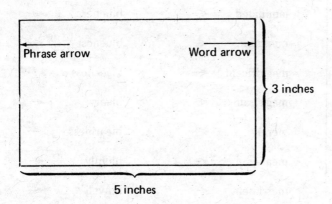

Your job, in other words, is to prove the falsity of the old adage that the hand is quicker than the eye.

6. If you perceive only a blur at the first exposure, try again. You cannot expect to become an Olympic swimmer the first time you jump into the water.

7. How well you do in this exercise is less important than the practice you are starting, less important than beginning to feel some comfort in perceiving words in instantaneous fixations. And as you go from one exercise to the next, your skill and speed will increase.

fits	←	flint	←
fists	←	fought	←
fights	←	flirt	←
flights	←	frets	←
flits	←	fasts	←
slats	←	fluster	←
slash	←	flutter	←
slams	←	flitter	←
slants	←	fritter	←
slow	←	battle	←
first	←	bitter	←
frost	←	black	←
slough	←	pain	←
slit	←	pane	←
slink	←	pram	←
slosh	←	prom	←
sash	←	prime	←
slips	←	prong	←
slaps	←	plant	←
slakes	←	plank	←
bright	←	brittle	←
bricks	←	bottle	←
breaks	←	blocks	←

brink	←	blinks	←
front	←	bleats	←

Perception Exercise 4

Continue as before, aiming at instantaneous perception; allow time for *only one fixation* at each exposure.

great	←	flowing	←
grate	←	flew	←
grace	←	flies	←
gracious	←	scotch	←
graceful	←	shimmer	←
grim	←	slowly	←
glimmer	←	tendency	←
glow	←	telephone	←
string	←	tenacious	←
strung	←	teller	←
stretch	←	toll	←
straw	←	toes	←
stretching	←	too	←
scratching	←	returns	←
glean	←	foolish	←
glints	←	riches	←
gloom	←	rashes	←
gloomy	←	rats	←
glum	←	rolling	←
glad	←	rate	←
spray	←	remember	←
strew	←	returning	←
fragrant	←	reason	←
flagrant	←	reasonable	←
flimsy	←	referring	←

Perception Exercise 5

At this point, progress may be erratic, but the *practice* will eventually pay dividends if it has not already done so.

You may have noticed that exercise 4 contained a number of two- and three-syllable words, rather than the exclusively one-syllable words found in exercise 3.

Learning takes place when each task is slightly more difficult than the previous one. And so the present exercise will contain two- and three-syllable words plus occasional four-syllable words.

Ready to reach a little higher than your comfortable grasp?

Continue as before.

lovely	←	allowing	←
lover	←	allergy	←
loveliness	←	allergist	←
living	←	altogether	←
lively	←	crowing	←
liveliness	←	crowning	←
luxury	←	treasure	←
luxurious	←	treasurer	←
trailer	←	measurement	←
trusting	←	maximum	←
truthfulness	←	crucify	←
truthfully	←	creases	←
loosely	←	creature	←
lonely	←	creatively	←
loneliness	←	blowing	←
laminated	←	blueness	←
minimum	←	bluenose	←
magnificent	←	blackness	←
magistrate	←	bleary	←
merely	←	bleariness	←
meatier	←	bluntly	←
merriment	←	bravely	←

allocation	←	bravery	←
allotment	←	transition	←
allowance	←	traveling	←

SESSION 12

TRAINING IN PHRASE PERCEPTION

Perception Exercise 6

Place the Fixation Card in such a way that the top *left* edge is just above the first phrase in the list below, and the *phrase arrow* squarely meets the arrow on the page. (Use you own card, illustrated on page 57, if the Fixation card is missing.)

The broad arrow marked "Fixate here" indicates the approximate center of each phrase, and through a combination of macular and peripheral images you will eventually, after some periods of training, be able to interpret the entire phrase. Rely on your vision, not your speech, in doing this exercise; *refrain, if possible, from repeating the phrase in your mind after you have seen it.* If necessary, allow yourself two or more exposures on a phrase if the first exposure is not successful. However, at each successive exposure, attempt to *see the entire phrase,* not just that portion you may have missed in the first exposure. Remember to keep the time of exposure so small that you will be able to make only *one* fixation on each phrase.

→ a basic need	→ two good ideas
→ a basic idea	→ some strange ideas
→ a third meaning	→ no good idea
→ a fourth meaning	→ no possible idea
→ type of learning	→ a cute idea
→ need of warming	→ a cure for all
→ my real purpose	→ a city of stone
→ his first purpose	→ a cure-all
→ a single woman	→ a sure cure
→ a single cup	→ a strange cure
→ a lonely woman	→ telephone connection
→ a lonely man	→ hold the line

→ an only son	→ hold it tight
→ gave her life	→ hold it taut
→ took his wife	→ come to naught
→ with a knife	→ came at night
→ unnecessary strife	→ do it right
→ not too unusual	→ right this way
→ hardly unusual	→ can you wait
→ most unusual	→ read the book
→ they tell me	→ fire the cook
→ he tells me	→ cook for two
→ I tell them	→ find the book
→ don't tell me	→ book the band
→ I may never	→ beat the band
→ I rarely do	→ boot the cook
→ I surely do	→ bake the cake
→ I certainly don't	→ take the cake
→ a great idea	→ took the cake
→ a foolish idea	→ hold a wake

Perception Exercise 7

Now that you have warmed up with the phrases in exercise 6, you are ready to be a little more demanding of your powers. You allowed yourself to make more than one exposure, if you found such multiple exposure necessary. From now on, consider your training successful only if you see the complete phrase *the first time;* if you do not, go directly to the next phrase and continue working, phrase by phrase, until increased success is achieved.

→ he won't marry	→ a fine car
→ we won't tarry	→ a complete lemon
→ can you carry	→ broken-down hack
→ you can carry	→ money can't buy
→ with whom I share	→ love and kisses
→ he'll get along	→ down the street

→ good to know

→ good to see

→ food for thought

→ he had thought

→ because of him

→ with all the contacts

→ with many contacts

→ with few contacts

→ try to relax

→ much more lonely

→ much less lonely

→ one cup only

→ one enchanted evening

→ one strange evening

→ this rare evening

→ a spare evening

→ spare an evening

→ spare a day

→ spare some time

→ take some time

→ an inconvenient time

→ too much time

→ full of lime

→ the salty brine

→ rare old wine

→ sparkling wine

→ very strong wine

→ this strong wine

→ a time of stress

→ a time to play

→ fine and dandy

→ not a treatment

→ not a reaction

→ a bad cold

→ good as gold

→ gold and silver

→ copper and bronze

→ wire and spit

→ a new ingredient

→ smoother performance

→ it really is

→ like a bank

→ like a baby

→ like a baby's bank

→ like a piggy bank

→ like a stuffed owl

→ like a stuffed pig

→ like a stuffy pig

→ like a wise owl

→ a wise old owl

→ a prize owl

→ air conditioning

→ Elgin watch

→ the night watch

→ the new watch

→ a few watches

→ truly yours

→ yours truly

→ a crowded car

→ the back seat

→ the time to go

→ continue the work

→ hard work to do

→ well-paid work

→ old work-horse

→ kind of work

→ rare old jerk

→ good old jerk

→ jerked his finger

→ made a ringer

→ took the ring

→ joined the army

→ old army game

→ an exciting game

→ big game hunter

→ hunted big game

→ smelled a rat

→ on a bat

→ weird old house

→ two-story house

→ Ford has everything

→ the window seat

→ filled with love

→ fat as a rail

→ thin as a bug

→ snug as a bug

→ thin as a rail

→ built like a house

→ gone and forgotten

→ permanently ruined

→ completely bereft

→ no single stone

→ had actually seen

→ blinked his eyes

→ you rich folks

→ we poor people

→ we the people

→ in order to get

→ twice a week

→ on first seeing

→ without real fun

→ What's wrong?

You have made a start, now, at training your perception—at learning to interpret quickly and accurately the pictures your eyes photograph, and at permitting your eyes to photograph a wider portion of print, during each fixation, for such interpretation.

This is, of course, only the beginning of such learning and training—to develop any degree of skill and accuracy in rapid perception, you must devote a great deal of practice to the numerous perception drills that you will find spread throughout the book.

Intensive and continuous practice on these drills will reduce, perhaps almost to the vanishing point, any *time lag* between your reception of, and your mental response to, the visual images offered by a line of print—will make your interpretation of the meaning of such images as immediate, indeed as nearly instantaneous, as possible.

So do all perception exercises religiously, unfailingly, whenever you come upon them. I cannot overemphasize their importance, I cannot overrate their value in your total training program; as you gradually build your skill, you yourself will realize from personal experience how effectively instantaneous responses, fewer fixations, and wider recognition spans can increase your reading speed.

Certain factors in the reading process may, singly or in various combinations, drastically interfere with the nearly instantaneous reaction to meaning that perception training aims at—may act as circuit breakers, so to speak, of the electrical impulses that the eyes flash to the brain. The most serious of such factors are (1) lip movements, (2) vocalization, (3) excessive reliance on inner speech, and (4) addiction to unnecessary regressions. How these factors operate to retard interpretation and thus slow up the rate of comprehension will be the subject of the next chapter.

SESSION 13

CUTTING THROUGH DETAILS TO GRASP THE CENTRAL IDEA

Read the following selection rapidly, moving along at a good brisk pace, with the dominating aim of extracting from the material *the gist, the central idea, the general point* (all ways of saying the same thing) that the author is making.

Mobilize yourself to *get into the material, thinking along with the author, sensing the author's organization of ideas, and demanding constantly from the selection:* "What does this all add up to?"

As before, start your timing at the first black arrow; when you reach the second arrow, note, in the appropriate blank, the exact number of minutes and seconds you required to finish the selection. Use your calculator to determine your rate, or read your rate from the table that follows the comprehension test.

SELECTION 10

Professors Learn to Read
by Esther J. McConihe

Time at start: _____minutes _____seconds

I

Start timing ➡ [1] When the headline, "Profs Learn to Read," appeared over a story in the campus paper at Western Reserve University, it marked the beginning of considerable interest in a training program to improve reading efficiency that had been inaugurated after repeated requests from an interested faculty to "give us a chance to brush up on our reading techniques."

II

[2] Early in the fall semester, 40 faculty members who had indicated an interest in reading training were organized into two sections on the basis of convenience in scheduling. The "students" included, among others, a dean of the liberal arts school and professor of English, author of many articles in professional journals, of two books, and of two workbooks on word study; a member of the Law School faculty; several research doctors in the School of Medicine; professors from the Frances Payne Bolton School of Nursing, some of whom have written extensively for publication; a university librarian; and a professor of geology and astronomy, also an author.

[3] The academic status of the group indicated considerable expertness with the written word from extensive experience in both reading and writing. Needless to say, the challenge from a group of this calibre was great.

III

[4] A 10-week program of weekly hour and a half sessions was started. At the opening session the members were introduced to the procedures. The "gadgets," i.e., the reading pacers, tachistoscope, and reading films, were demonstrated, and their purpose in training explained. The group decided upon testing to determine the status of each member's reading skills; consequently at the second session the Cooperative English Test, C2 Reading, Form T, and the Minnesota Speed of Reading Test, Form A, were administered. The zeal with which the groups applied themselves to this humdrum experience was inspiring to the writer and would have opened the eyes of many of the underclassmen of the university if they could have witnessed it.

[5] Results of the tests were given to each member individually in a personal report. Group data

on this testing will be discussed below under "Results."

[6] The following eight sessions were devoted to training. Tachistoscopic practice with digits and phrases was one of the most popular devices, and the group was very quickly reading phrases of from 21 to 25 typewriter units of space in 1/100 of a second. Digit reading for such groups rarely equals phrase reading because the practice periods are too short and infrequent to develop the requisite skill in reproducing such an exacting presentation as a seven-digit number shown in 1/100 of a second. A second mechanical technique was the Harvard Reading Films, Series B, which have been explained in detail in many places so need not be discussed further here. For this group the films were of less value than my experience has shown them to be with most adult groups.

[7] At each session a brief lecture-discussion period gave the instructor the opportunity to demonstrate something of the complex nature of reading and to present the various techniques which are useful to the able adult in bringing his reading skills up to the level of his reading needs. Since this was a group of very able readers, it was necessary only to stress various means of utilizing the already good language and logic skills of the members and to press for speed of comprehension. These orientation periods were also the time for individual members to air their problems. Many a "Yes, but—" put the leader to devising realistic suggestions for meeting the problems which were aired during these discussion periods. Frequently the group made its own suggestions, i.e., a problem by one member was met by a suggestion from another who had encountered the same problem.

[8] Each session concluded with a timed reading test. Results of this test were plotted on individual graphs so that each member could watch his progress from week to week. This is a good motivating device because it presents progress in graphic form. Many times a reader needs this tangible proof of progress because at first he may not be aware of improved speed in day-by-day reading.

[9] Between sessions each member came to the Center twice a week and read, using one of the several reading pacing devices with which many reading training centers are equipped. Each person was urged to bring a book of his own choosing but was advised to keep to easy-flowing prose at first in an attempt to develop a rapid pace with rhythmic eye movements. The emphasis in programs like this is at first on improving the mechanics. Fewer and shorter fixations, or pauses, per line, a good return sweep to the next line with rhythmic progression across the line and down the page are some of these. Easy fiction furnishes the best practice because it offers no obstacles from unfamiliar vocabulary, complex organization of ideas, or unfamiliar content.

[10] A third area of training was reading at home without benefit of coaching or machines. Selected articles, chosen for their suitability to the group's interests as well as for the particular techniques being developed, were given at every session. These were read at any time between sessions, timed, and the words per minute computed by the reader. The central thought of the article was written out, and this material was discussed at the sessions. Such discussion was fruitful in revealing to the group the reading experiences of the several members as they experimented with the techniques they were practicing. Members were urged to read an hour a day, attempting to reproduce, unaided, the same smooth-flowing, rhythmic, rapid rate they were developing with the pacing machines.

IV

[11] What were the results of such a course with such a group? As measured by standardized reading tests, the group as a whole made 76 percent improvement in speed, with comprehension held constant. The greatest gain by a reader was 135 percent, a gain of 285 words per minute over his entering speed. This reader had perfect attendance, used the reading pacing machine between sessions more times than any other member, and reported back on all intersessional material assigned. Another reader showed only 10 percent gain in speed and with it a 10 percent loss in comprehension. This member was, by observation, extremely ego-involved throughout the training, found the techniques disturbing, although challenging, and wrote at the close of the course, "... For a time during the course my pride suffered acutely and all kinds of blocks and distractions came between me and those timed readings you gave us. I am not yet over that, but I believe it is due to the fact that I do not yet feel the degree of security which I hope (and plan) to achieve." It may be expected that when this reader returns for a recheck in six months, more noticeable gains will be evident.

[12] So much for formal gain, but what about subjective report and observation? Here the results are varied and interesting. This being a group of persons for whom good reading is as essential as good intelligence, they were in dead earnest about benefiting from the training. Here are some of their comments:

[13] "... the ability to free oneself (an ongoing process still) from the feeling that *everything* must be read for complete and specific details."

[14] "... one reads with variations in speed as is necessary. I find myself doing that with less thought about it—skimming here, reading rapidly

now, then again more slowly as I may feel the need for meditating on some particular thought or enjoying some particular passage."

[15] "Improvement in my mental outlook on reading. When I sit down now to a piece of reading, I realize I must concentrate, get rid of distractions, look for the signposts of organization, such as topic sentences, transitional words and summaries, and read with a flexible speed that depends on what I want to get out of the piece."

[16] "Has given me a new method of attack on reading. I really ask myself, 'Why am I reading this?' I believe this has helped me increase my speed even in articles from which I need to get minute details."

[17] "Has increased my ability to skim medical and nursing literature. This has been proven to me many times over. I can get what I want from an article by skimming in the right way."

[18] "What I expected at the outset was to increase my speed, but what I have gained is an appreciation of how to read."

[19] "I remember . . . my feeling of resentment about having so little time to read. Now I know I can read much more if I do not try to read everything at the same rate with which I read difficult clinical material."

[20] "One technique that has been particularly useful to me has been the idea of getting a frame of reference for the material being read. Heretofore I think I had usually simply started at the beginning and read. I believe the 'previewing' aids in retention of the material read. It also eliminates unnecessary detail."

[21] Needless to say, this course was a lively and illuminating experience for both the participants and the leader. Most of the members discovered to their surprise that this skill, which had always been a vital part of their stock-in-trade, could be considerably improved. Several showed up in the instructor's office requesting additional training. All put the techniques to use throughout the course and took active part in the discussion.

[22] The "Yes, but—" responses mentioned above were the times when the instructor learned a good deal about how well-trained adults read. "Am I not insulting the author when I read at breakneck speed something which it took him days or weeks to write?" "What do I do when these transitional words don't really 'transish'?" (This from a Law School professor.) "Yes, but sometimes a specific word makes all the difference between understanding and not understanding, so am I not in danger of missing the meaning if I read by phrases?" "We've been trained to believe that every detail is absolutely essential. What if I read a patient's chart like this?" (This being rapid overviewing and the comment being made by a member of the nursing school faculty.) Each objection was legitimate and each had to be answered within its own framework. The result was a lively atmosphere of mutual respect, understanding, and learning between leader and group which resulted in an experience that was rich and rewarding to this author and, it is to be hoped, to the 20 persons who successfully completed the course. ◄ **End timing**

Time at finish _____ minutes _____ seconds

Record Here the Time Required on this Selection: _____ minutes _____ seconds

Test Your Comprehension

Complete the following statement, in your own words, to indicate the central idea of the selection:

A group of professors who had had extensive experience with the written word _____

_____

_____

_____

_____

_____

Compute Your Rate
(Approximate Number of Words: 1800)

Time	WPM	Time	WPM
2 min. 30 sec.	720	5 min. 15 sec.	345
2 min. 45 sec.	655	5 min. 30 sec.	325
3 min.	600	6 min.	300
3 min. 15 sec.	555	6 min. 30 sec.	275
3 min. 30 sec.	515	7 min.	260
3 min. 45 sec.	480	7 min. 30 sec.	240
4 min.	450	8 min.	225
4 min. 15 sec.	425	8 min. 30 sec.	210
4 min. 30 sec.	400	9 min.	200
4 min. 45 sec.	380	10 min.	180
5 min.	360	11 min.	165

Your Rate On Selection 10: _____ WPM

(Record this statistic on the chart and graph on page 235)

Discussion of the Selection

When this article is considered *in its entirety*, the organization is clear, simple, and completely logical:

Paragraph 1: Introduction
Paragraphs 2 and 3: Kind of students in the course
Paragraphs 4 through 10: Explanation of the training offered
Paragraphs 11 through 22: Results of the training

What parts of the selection you read carefully and what parts you skimmed depended on your purpose. As a student who is being trained to improve in skill and speed, you were no doubt particularly interested in paragraphs 6 through 10, in which the actual details of training are explained—the general reader might have skimmed through this part of the article. (Possibly, despite your interest, you skimmed nevertheless, since these details are by now so familiar to you.) Teachers of reading would also be interested in the specific methods that Ms. McConihe used, but would likely skim the section to discover whether it contained anything that was new to them. As teachers, they might be especially alert to the implications of the last two paragraphs, in which the author explains her reaction to her students. I think that skillful readers would have largely skimmed paragraphs 12 through 20 as soon as they recognized that these were repetitive details of the students' subjective reactions to the training—unless, for private reasons of their own, they had some personal interest in these details as *details,* rather than in their use as support for the central meaning.

What I am saying, then, is that the first purpose of reading any selection—a purpose common to all readers—is to get the central meaning of the *whole* and to recognize how the author organizes facts and information to make this central idea most clear, most convincing, most effective. Skillful readers, long habituated to concentrating on the *important* elements of material, would sense at once that paragraphs 2 and 3 of this selection begin to develop the main idea. *Aha!* they think to themselves, consciously or otherwise, *these professors should already be good readers, they've had so much experience.* Their minds are focused now on discovering whether there is still room for improvement, and so they are alert to the continued development of the main theme in paragraph 11 (*they increased their speed by 76 percent*) and again in paragraph 21 (*they learned with surprise, etc.*). Although reading for the main idea, they do not *ignore* the details. However, instead of getting lost in the details they fit them into their proper place in the framework of the piece and note how they contribute to the central theme—by this means they can skim through these details if they wish to.

Above and beyond this primary purpose of quickly finding the central meaning and general structure of writing, skillful readers will react to material according to any individual purpose they may have. They will skim or read thoroughly, go faster or slow up, push aside details once their function is understood, or concentrate on details carefully—all depending on what purpose they are reading for.

A possible way to summarize the main thought of the selection is as follows:

A group of professors who had had extensive experience with the written word *were trained in specified ways to improve their reading—as a result, they greatly increased their speed, and learned with surprise that their skill could be considerably sharpened.*

Check back to your own summary on page 63, and decide whether you understood the general meaning of the selection.

READING AND REREADING

You know, now, the general message the author of Selection 10 wished to convey to you; you read the material with the *clear purpose* in mind of extracting this message in the quickest and most efficient way possible. You have an overview of the material, and you understand the *structure* of the author's thinking.

But let us assume, for whatever reason, that it is important that you *study,* rather than *read,* this material—you need to know and retain the *details* as well as the *central meaning* of the selection

What do you do?

You read it *twice.*

In a *first, quick,* reading, you follow the author's *pattern of thinking and organization of ideas* and come away with the *general meaning.*

Then, knowing what the piece has to say in *general,* you read it again for *particular details.*

This is the main principle of successful studying, when studying is required: *Read quickly for an accurate overview; then reread for details, knowing what you are looking for.*

The details make more sense, are more efficiently understood and more easily remembered, when you are armed with a knowledge of the *central idea.*

Inner Speech, Lip Movements, Vocalization, and Regressions

PREVIEW

Chapter 6 explains in detail how to give up three bad habits that drastically reduce speed of comprehension.

• How to stop making frequent and unnecessary regressions

Training to become a rapid reader involves not only the constant practice of *efficient* techniques, but also the ruthless elimination of any *inefficient* habits that hold your comprehension down to a rate far lower than you are actually capable of.

And so, in this chapter, you will learn:

• How to reduce excessive dependency on inner speech

• How to read without lip movements or other forms of vocalization

SESSION 14

INNER SPEECH

According to J. A. O'Brien, an expert in the field of reading instruction, there are essentially three kinds of readers: *motor* readers, *auditory* readers, and *visual* readers.

Motor readers are lip movers, vocalizers. They accom-

65

pany their reading with various (and quite unnecessary) movements of the muscles of articulation. "In other words," as O'Brien explains it, "reading is not confined to the visualization of the printed symbols. Concomitant with this visualization there occur movements, more or less incipient in character, of the tongue, lips, vocal cords, larynx, inner palate, throat, and the general physiological mechanism that functions in oral speech. The reader goes through the form of saying the words to himself."

Auditory readers are excessively dependent on *"hearing"* a page of print—they are very much aware of *"saying"* words in their mind, although their speech organs are completely at rest.

Visual readers, in contrast, not only completely bypass their vocal apparatus in their response to meaning—they are also, for the most part, largely unaware of the individual words that combine to make up such meaning. They can, in short, understand words and phrases without first stopping either to *"say"* them or to *"hear"* their sound; they read with their eyes and mind, not with their mouths or ears.

These three types of readers—*motor, auditory,* and *visual*—are, as you can guess, listed in ascending order of skill. *Lip movers* or *vocalizers* are extremely slow readers, for they are artificially keeping their speed down to the rate at which they can pronounce words—and this is about one-fourth as fast as they could read silently. They tire quickly because there is so much muscular activity. They make frequent regressions, for their eyes tend to rush ahead and their voice stays behind. Often they use a finger to point, so that they can keep their eyes back where their voice is. They tend to be word-by-word readers, for the unit of pronunciation is a word, or even a syllable, although the unit of meaning is usually a phrase and sometimes a whole sentence. They make numerous fixations on a line, since their eyes must focus on every syllable or word that their lips pronounce. And, finally, their comprehension is poor, for their mind is as much involved with the mechanics of reading as it is with ideas—if not more so. In fine, the whole reading process is a chore, and the less they read the happier they are.

Auditory readers are much more skillful, much more rapid. Their speed need not be unduly hampered, for they are not actually pronouncing the words they *"hear,"* but only imagining the pronunciation. If their awareness of, and reliance on, the *sounds* of words is not very great, their rate of comprehension does not suffer to any alarming extent; however, if they cannot easily increase their speed to over 400 words per minute, they are undoubtedly much more dependent on inner speech than they need to be.

Inner speech probably occurs to some extent in *all* readers, even the fastest and most skillful—but visual readers do not have to *lean* on it before they can respond to meaning. Auditory readers often do—that is the significant difference between them.

Strong, excessive, dependence on inner speech is not necessary for understanding. When you listen with keen interest to people who are talking, when you become really involved in what they are saying, you are, as you know, almost totally unaware of the individual *words* they are using—for you are concentrating on the *ideas* that their words add up to. You respond to words not as *words,* but as conveyors of *meaning.* You think along with the ideas, you react intellectually and emotionally to the thoughts expressed, you agree or disagree, you may even interrupt at times to express the thoughts and reactions that the ideas stimulate in you. *But one thing you do not do is consciously repeat in your mind the words you hear before you understand what these words mean.* You don't do this because you obviously don't have to—in reading, *conscious, excessive* mental repetition of the words on a page is equally unnecessary.

Have you ever watched an expert stenographer taking rapid dictation? The pencil whizzes across the shorthand notebook at a rate that clearly rules out any possibility that the stenographer is repeating words before writing them down. The dictator's words stimulate impulses in the stenographer's brain that are instantaneously transmitted to flying fingers—there is no time for conscious repetition.

The interested listener and the expert stenographer respond to the meaning of *auditory* stimuli without conscious reliance on inner speech. Is it possible to react similarly to the meaning of purely *visual* stimuli?

Let us consider this question at some length.

Suppose that an experiment is set up in which you are asked to press one lever when a *red* light flashes, a different lever when a *green* light flashes. Imagine yourself sitting at a table with your right hand resting on the lever for red, your left hand on the one for green.

The light flashes. What do you do?

First, of course, you interpret the color. Is it red, or is it green? (If you are color-blind, this experiment is not for you.) Having made your decision, you next recall which hand is for which color. Then, finally, you press the correct lever.

How long a time interval elapses between the flashing of the light and your manual response? I think you know the answer. After a few warm-up tries (and the requirements of the experiment are so simple that these may not be necessary), you respond almost instantaneously—you are able to press the proper lever each time in no more than one-tenth of a second. (I have tried this experiment over and over with my students, and that's the longest it ever takes.)

Now, we may ask, how can you react so quickly if you first have to make all these conscious and verbalized decisions? (Just saying to yourself *Is it red or green?* takes almost a second.)

And again you know the answer. *You do not consciously verbalize your decisions.* Instantaneously after the flash, your brain interprets the color of the light, remembers that *red is right, green is left,* and transmits a pressure impulse to the proper hand—all this wordlessly and in one-tenth of a second or less!

Suppose, however, that you were in the habit of consciously verbalizing all your bodily responses to visual stimuli, something clearly improbable and abnormal. When the light flashed you might say to yourself, *red—right* or *green—left,* and then press. Would you still be able to react as quickly? Obviously not—you would take at least twice as long.

Most bodily responses to visual images occur, as you know, without consciously *verbalized* recognition or direction. When you raise your arm to ward off a blow, jump out of the path of an oncoming car, or stamp on the brake or twist the steering wheel of an automobile to avoid a sudden obstacle, your brain, reacting to the visual danger signals, instantaneously shoots impulses through the proper nerve pathways—and this, too, happens apparently wordlessly and in the merest fraction of a second. Indeed it is only if the perception of peril causes momentary muscular paralysis that inner speech may take the place of action. You see the danger, but for some reason you are frozen into petrified immobility; and yet you may be conscious, during such an awful moment, of thinking wildly to yourself, in actual words, *He's going to hit me!* or *I'm going to hit it!* And sure enough he does, or you do.

Let us get away, now, from physical responses and consider a form of thinking that more closely approximates the mental activity involved in silent reading.

Here, as an instance, is a simple example in addition for you to work out. As you figure the sum, pay close attention to the amount of conscious inner speech you use.

$$5+6+3+8+4+2=?$$

What did you say to yourself in order to get the correct answer? Did you say, *five and six are eleven, eleven and three are fourteen, fourteen and eight are twenty-two, twenty-two and four are twenty-six, twenty-six and two are twenty-eight?* If you did, you have never learned the quick and efficient way to do your sums.

Or did you, perhaps, cut down your inner speech to the following: *eleven, fourteen, twenty-two, twenty-six, twenty-eight?* If you did (and anyone can work this way with a little practice), you were responding to the visual impulses set up by the numbers 5, 6, 3, 8, 4, and 2 without once verbalizing what you saw.

As it happens, there is an even more rapid and more efficient way to add these six numbers, namely, *eleven, twenty-two, twenty-eight.* What have we done this time? To the sum of the first two numbers, *eleven,* we've added the sum of the next two to get *twenty-two,* then added the sum of the last two to get *twenty-eight*—even less conscious inner speech than before. (This method, too, can be made habitual with a little practice.)

Try a few addition problems on your own now, using either of the two efficient methods described above, so that you will clearly understand how *reduced reliance on inner speech and verbalization can speed up your responses to visual images.*

$$2+9+1+7+3+6=?$$
$$5+5+3+7+2+8=?$$
$$9+1+4+6+7+3=?$$
$$4+5+1+8+9+9=?$$
$$5+3+2+6+1+7=?$$

Reading a page of print is, admittedly, not exactly the same as pressing a lever when you see a light flash, moving your body to ward off perceived danger, or computing sums in arithmetic. But there are two important areas of similarity, namely: (1) reading, like these other activities, consists of responding to the *meaning* of visual images; and (2) the less inner speech or conscious verbalization, the quicker the response.

A certain amount of inner speech, as I have said, undoubtedly accompanies all silent reading. This may be so partly because, as children, we understood words as meaningful *sounds* long before we were able to read them as written or printed symbols. Children learn to read by connecting the picture of a word with some sound that they are familiar with—and all reading is dependent, in the earliest stages of learning, on sounds and on oral activity. When children become more experienced with words as visual symbols, they find that they can gain meaning without making audible sounds, although for a short time, as a kind of transitional stage, they will either whisper faintly or move their tongue and lips silently. (And this is a stage that some poor readers never manage to progress beyond.) As children's skill and experience increase, they give up their dependence on the vocal mechanism and rely solely on inner speech. Eventually, if they mature into efficient and rapid readers, they gradually lose a good deal of their awareness even of inner speech. They can now respond to the meaning of words without consciously depending on remembered sound. Indeed, as I have pointed out, efficient readers are largely unaware of the presence of the individual words that make up the meaning of a page of print.

The occurrence of at least some degree of inner speech in all silent reading may be partly due, also, to the fact that in most languages the written or printed symbols represent the actual spoken sounds of words—hence it may be impossible for readers to eliminate completely in their mind the connection between sound and meaning.

Obviously, then, you cannot *totally* eradicate the auditory reactions that may attend your own reading. However, you can considerably reduce your reliance on them; indeed, you can become almost completely unaware of them; and thus you can cut them down to a point where they no longer retard, even to the slightest amount, your immediate response to meaning.

How can you do this? Largely by intensive and frequent practice on instantaneous perception; and by consciously attempting, during your work on word and phrase drills, to verbalize less and less the visual image that you expose for a fraction of a second in the window of the Fixation Card.

If you are *excessively* dependent on inner speech as you read (and a rate of under 275 WPM would indicate that this may be so), increasing the speed of your mental responses to visual images by means of perception exercises will be of tremendous benefit to you.

However, let me issue a note of warning at this point: the conscious inhibition of auditory reactions, immensely valuable and profitable during perception practice, *is pointless and may even be dangerous when applied to actual reading.*

For when you read for meaning, your mind should be entirely occupied with the pursuit of ideas. If part of your mind is concerned with suppressing inner speech, comprehension will suffer and the enjoyment so vital to skillful reading will be lost. On the other hand, if you constantly read as fast as your comprehension permits, the perception training you are getting will be transferred, without conscious effort on your part, over into your general reading. The more involved you become in the *ideas* on a page, the less will you be aware of the individual *words* in which these ideas are expressed. As you increase your ability to grasp ideas quickly and to respond to them actively, you will gradually decrease your dependence on "*hearing*" the words and sounds that make up ideas.

LIP MOVEMENTS AND VOCALIZATION

If you are a motor reader, you have to attack your problem in a different way. *You must consciously inhibit every last vestige of movement in the vocal mechanism not only during perception practice but in all your reading.*

How can you tell whether a page of print elicits any degree of motor responses in you? To begin with, if your rate is 250 WPM or better, you may rest assured that you have given up the childhood crutch of saying or whispering words, or of forming them with your lips and tongue, in order to understand them. (And if this is so, the rest of this section will be of only academic interest to you.)

If, however, your rate is considerably below 250 WPM on material well within your comprehension, the chances are good that vocal movements of some sort are interfering with normal speed.

Pay close attention to your lips and tongue as you read the following italicized words: *tick, tack, toe; drip, drop, drape; sit, sat, set; limp, lump, lamp; pit, pat, pet; bass,*

base, bus; past, pressed, post; must, massed, mussed; fist, fast, fussed. Did you feel any motion at all in the vocal mechanism? Did your tongue move, even the least bit, to sound out the consonants *t* and *d?* Did your lips move, even ever so slightly, on the consonants *p, b, m,* and *f?* Did you make any sounds, however barely audible, or detect even the hint of whispering?

If the answer is *yes* to any of these questions, you are a lip mover or a vocalizer or both; and you will never be able to grasp the meaning of a page with even average speed until you completely eliminate every slight remnant and trace of vocal movement and sound from your silent reading.

This is not hard to do if you are willing to undergo a short period of discomfort. Louella Cole, in her book *Improvement of Reading,* makes two suggestions for teaching a child to read without vocalization. They are suggestions which are also adaptable to the adult. Here they are, in her own words:

The simplest method is to render the speech mechanism incapable of pronouncing words, even partially. A simple and effective means of bringing about this result is to have the child put two fingers into his mouth, using them to separate his upper and lower teeth and to hold down his tongue. Nobody can articulate words with his mouth hanging open. If the child, through force of habit, moves his jaws to articulate, he bites his fingers. With the tongue and the jaws both out of commission, there will be no pronunciation. Instead of his fingers a child may use his ruler or a large-sized eraser. The fingers are better than either wood or rubber, however, partly because the pupil is unwilling to bite them and partly because he always has them with him!

Another, if even less elegant, procedure is to let the child chew gum while he is reading. His speech mechanism is out of commission, not because it is at rest but because it is doing something else. No one can pronounce words and chew gum simultaneously. Naturally, a pupil should not persist in these techniques until they become habits. They should be used only until the tendency to pronounce words has been broken.

Dr. Cole cites this interesting case:

John was a loud vocalizer. Whatever else might be wrong with him, it was evident at once to the teacher of the remedial class that something must be done to stop the noise John made, if the other children were to get their work done. Without waiting to make any analysis, Miss A. promptly recommended the finger-in-the-mouth technique. There ensued a silence—but almost no comprehension of the reading matter. John seemed unable to recognize even the simplest words unless he could pronounce them. In order to find something that John could read without vocalizing, it was necessary to use a second-grade book. During the first week John had his doubts about the value of this method but agreed to give it a fair trial. Before the end of the second week he had begun to feel that his reading was much less labored than ever before. Instead of being work, the simple book he was using became play. At about this time the boy appeared one morning with a neatly whittled and sandpapered piece of wood, all wrapped up in a clean handkerchief. During the following six weeks John kept the piece of wood between his teeth whenever he was reading. No other treatment was used for this boy. Yet in two months' time he improved nearly three years in speed and over a year in comprehension. Moreover, he reported a great increase in the ease with which he read. After leaving the class, John continued to carry the wood around with him, but he used it less and less. At the end of the year he was reading without any artificial aid to keep him from vocalizing.

I have found, from my own experience with students who were motor readers, that maintaining a rigidity in the vocal apparatus while reading will eliminate lip movements and vocalization within two weeks. During *every bit* of reading in this two-week period, the jaws must be clamped shut, the tongue held rigid against the roof of the mouth, and the lips maintained absolutely motionless, even if, in difficult cases, the students must use thumb and forefinger to hold their lips in a viselike grip.

Vocalization is the one inefficient habit of reading that is the quickest to disappear when an inhibiting set of conditions is put into effect. At first the students are comically uncomfortable. Their eyes pop. They are the very picture of misery. Their whole being cries out to be allowed to relapse into the comfortable habit of accompanying their reading with muscular activity. But if their spirit is stronger than their flesh, they very shortly find nonvocalized reading decreasing in discomfort. Soon they need to exert less force to keep their vocal apparatus still, and they then discover what every good reader has long since learned and forgotten—that words can be understood without sounding them out, without whispering them, without even forming them silently with the lips and tongue. At this point comprehension becomes so much more efficient, so much faster, and so much easier, that they are ready to relinquish permanently an infantile pattern that has unnecessarily persisted into adulthood, a pattern that *compels* an extremely slow rate of reading, that, indeed, makes reading an awkward and unpleasant experience. They have, maturely, been willing to suffer some pain in the expectation of future rewards—and they are not disappointed.

If you are a lip-mover or vocalizer, you too must be prepared to undergo a short period of discomfort. Possibly, in the beginning, you will get little or no meaning from a page if you totally suppress your motor reactions. But *persevere.* If necessary, practice on the simplest kind of material you can find—even a child's second- or third-grade reader, or juvenile books written for seven- or eight-year-olds, or picture books with only the most elementary kind of text. *But read with your eyes only, not with any part of your mouth or vocal apparatus.* And eventually full comprehension will return. When it does, and with it far greater speed and ease, the rewards will more than compensate for the pain.

REGRESSIONS

Habitually or compulsively regressive readers do not fully **trust** their comprehension—perhaps they do not quite trust their ability in any area in which they function.

Let us look at an extreme case: X, a woman of 38, did well in many aspects of training at the Reading Laboratory, but always her progress was impeded by a compulsive need to regress. If a selection contained figures or statistics, she would have an incomplete feeling unless she went back, time and time again, and reread them, often breaking the trend of her comprehension in order to reassure herself that she had seen them correctly the first time. On any one line of print she would return several times to the first few words before she reached the last one. In the normal person, regressions are caused mainly by faulty comprehension or by an unfamiliarity with vocabulary, but with X they appeared to be an almost neurotic pattern.

Further discussions with her turned up the fascinating fact that she was a habitual "regressor" (if we may extend the term to non-reading acts) in everything she did. After she stepped out of her apartment, and locked the door behind her, she would open it again, and walk back to make sure the lights were turned out, her last cigarette extinguished, the radio shut off, and the windows closed. If she went to the ladies' room in a public place, she would no sooner pass the threshold than she would have to rush out in a panic to make sure that the door had, indeed, been marked "Ladies" and not "Men." After making a business phone call (she was the secretary to the vice-president of a bank), she would often put a call through a second time to the same person to ask him if she had remembered to tell him so-and-so (of course, she always had). She was a neat, methodical worker, but she lost an immense amount of time, energy, and efficiency by constantly checking up on herself.

And this pattern carried over, naturally, into her reading. Though her intelligence was considerably above average and her comprehension good, she never trusted either—so she was a slow reader, with poor concentration and four to six regressions on every line of print.

If you yourself are conscious of making only occasional regressions, pay no further attention to this aspect of the reading act. But if you feel that usually you cannot understand a page of print to your full satisfaction without frequently going back to verify your first impressions, then take warning: You may be regressing *because of habit and anxiety,* not because your comprehension was inadequate.

The most effective means of breaking a habit is to set up conditions that will encourage the contrary and opposing habit.

Thus, when we wish to teach children not to misspell a word, the most effective method is to have them practice on the correct spelling until the incorrect one fades from their memory. (What is habit but reflexive and automatic memory of previous acts?)

To teach aviators *not* to pull back the stick and attempt

to climb when they feel their plane going into a stall or a spin (for such an action, logical as it may seem, makes them lose control over their plane and in many cases results in a fatal crack-up), we must enable them to gain such complete mastery over the reverse habit—that is, pushing the stick forward and forcing the plane into a more rapid descent—that their muscles will react instantaneously, and the former habit will fade from their memory because a new habit is taking its place.

So with *regressions*. To inhibit and finally destroy the habit of reading backward—that is, letting the eyes return to words or phrases previously read in a line of print—you must set up the contrary and opposing habit of *constantly reading forward*.

Reading, like most other skills, is a whole complex of automatic habits. When the habits are good, reading is efficient and rapid; when the habits are bad, reading is slow, awkward, unsatisfying. The habit of frequent and unnecessary regressions not only reduces the speed of reading (obviously), but by disrupting the smooth and continuous flow of meaning it also interferes with comprehension—which is ironic, for severely regressive readers, by unceasingly checking up on their understanding, succeed only in ruining it.

Skillful readers may make occasional voluntary regressions, but solely out of actual and realistic need, never from habit or compulsion, or because they do not entirely trust their ability to comprehend. They go back to reread a word or phrase only if they are certain that it is utterly useless to go on without doing so; otherwise they keep pushing rapidly ahead, for they are far more interested in central meaning and in ideas than they are in individual words, phrases, or details.

Of course, if ideas are expressed ambiguously or confusingly, or in extremely complicated or involved language, meaning will be elusive, and rereading and still further rereading may be necessary—but then the fault lies with the writer, not with the reader. S. N. Behrman, in a short story that appeared in the *New Yorker*, touchingly describes the reaction of one of his characters to such elusive writing:

Reflecting on these miseries, yet struggling also to keep his mind on the words he was reading, Mr. Weintraub took off his glasses and polished them again. Because his formal education had been sketchy, he did not know that he had a right to demand clarity and simplicity from an author, or that the relationship between writer and reader was a reciprocal one and the responsibility for understanding divided equally between them. He cursed himself for being stupid, and he felt a certain pride that for [his son] Willard, presumably, these massive and coagulated paragraphs were hammock reading.

Regressions, then, are by no means forbidden—*if they are absolutely necessary*. When you have an impulse to regress, test your needs against reality. Ask yourself, *have you really not understood what you have just read, or are you merely indulging a bad habit? Is it positively essential to check up on that word, or phrase, or detail you don't feel too sure of, or can you go on notwithstanding, and with no great loss?* Try this a few times and you may be surprised to discover that regressions are seldom as vital as they may at first seem. Try building up the habit of *constantly reading forward* so long as comprehension is not totally impossible—again you may be surprised to discover, if you have the courage to take the gamble, that your understanding is better than you give it credit for and does not need frequent checking up on!

Or you might try this very effective technique:

Take any blank card large enough to cover a line of print in the average book or magazine. (A 3- by 5-inch card will do; a 4 by 6 card is better; a 5 by 8 card is ideal.)

When you start your practice in eliminating unnecessary regressions, hold the card above the top line of print; *as you read, bring the card down to conceal lines already read.*

If your brain signals a demand to regress, *consciously command your hand to disobey*—that is, do not uncover any lines that are now hidden.

Practice this technique often enough when you read, and in all likelihood you will eventually resign yourself to *pushing ever forward*, under normal circumstances, until finally regressions will no longer interfere with your speed and concentration.

(The use of a blank card to increase speed by pacing yourself at a certain rate will be explained in a later session.)

SESSION 15

PERCEPTION TRAINING II

Perception Exercise 8

Use the Fixation Card or your own homemade card, aligning the *word arrow* at the right edge of the card with the arrow on the page. Allow yourself only one split-second exposure of each word, strongly relying on your visual impression. Recognize the word, try not to "say" it or "hear" it in your mind, and then immediately conceal it by pushing your card back to cover it. Proceed in the same fashion line by line and column by column.

ankle	←	blackhearted	←
uncle	←	blackish	←
ankles	←	blackly	←

anger ←	blackness ←	→ the British have	→ found the answer
answer ←	blocker ←	→ the English know	→ loved not well
answered ←	bladder ←	→ the Germans say	→ fought the war
ants ←	bleeder ←	→ the French believe	→ the man laughed
antrum ←	bleeding ←	→ we are sure	→ the big ape
arty ←	blink ←	→ we aren't sure	→ a big dose
artist ←	blank ←	→ we weren't sure	→ in the dark
architect ←	blasted ←	→ my wife and child	→ better and faster
archer ←	bleaker ←	→ my child and wife	→ a better time
archaic ←	bleacher ←	→ my new husband	→ playing safe
architecture ←	bleeder ←	→ her new couch	→ when germs hit
arches ←	bloody ←	→ her new husband	→ exciting story
arching ←	blooded ←	→ his new mate	→ I was there
architectural ←	blend ←	→ to produce rice	→ were you there?
archives ←	blender ←	→ to produce results	→ natural result
archness ←	bland ←	→ known for value	→ important difference
black ←	blond ←	→ tears and sweat	→ the long cigarette
block ←	blonde ←	→ lost and found	→ smart window dressing
blackhead ←	blindness ←	→ pulled his leg	→ you can't miss
blockhead ←	blindly ←	→ caught his man	→ what's new
blackguard ←	blob ←	→ loved not wisely	→ key to power
blackguardly ←	bloodily ←	→ dug the grave	→ if you ever stood

Perception Exercise 9
Proceed according to instructions on page 59.

→ what's so new	→ dirty brunette	→ the man cried → the teacher said
→ that's too good	→ famous in radio	→ the little dog → as you move
→ can also provide	→ words of love	→ an awful dope → how are you?
→ beyond the walls	→ toil and trouble	→ no sooner than → in this field
→ beyond the horizon	→ taken for a ride	→ much less pain → he can figure
→ the French have	→ opened his purse	→ much less gain → richest of all
		→ far less strain → try to visualize
		→ no less rain → you have claimed

→ clean and neat

→ neat and clean

→ far and wide

→ far and near

→ near and far

→ rich or poor

→ poor and rich

→ man or boy

→ girl or boy

→ girls and boys

→ Sam and Tom

→ lost his nerve

→ lost his dog

→ will lose his cash

→ a gallant gesture

→ Sinclair Lewis

→ new Chevrolet

→ old Buick

→ beautiful blonde

→ glamorous blonde

→ skinny blonde

→ no longer alive

→ now quite dead

→ during the winter

→ during the summer

→ during the fall

→ through the spring

→ back at home

→ back in town

→ lost for years

→ when I finish

→ then I began

→ then he started

→ then we began

→ then she stopped

→ no greater sacrifice

→ happen to you

→ can happen to you

→ could happen to you

→ that violet hue

→ that violin tone

→ that violent man

SESSION 16

READ FOR ENJOYMENT!

Reading is fun!

O.K.—for you, golf, or surfing, or hang-gliding, or skiing, or watching TV, or making love, or sleeping, or swimming, or getting drunk is *more* fun.

But reading is a *special* kind of fun.

In reading you can see through another person's eyes, live another person's life, relate to another person's feelings—*at your convenience, at little if any cost, and whenever or wherever you choose, and for as long as you choose.*

Reading may seem more passive to you than surfing, skiing, swimming, etc., and no doubt it is; but if you approach reading *passively*, you will get much less enjoyment out of it than if you learn to *participate actively* in the author's thinking. If you learn to respond *actively* to the author's personality, ideas, and style of writing, and if you learn to pull out, quickly and efficiently, the *gist* of what an author wishes to communicate to you, you will find *any kind* of reading far less passive than you may now think.

Jack Smith, who writes regularly (and delightfully) for the *Los Angeles Times*, is always fun to read—and I ask you to approach two of his columns ready to read *actively*.

Smith is a humorist—like all humorists, he wraps his message (and all writing has a *message*, a *dominant theme*, a *point*—call it what you will) so subtly in his humor that you may miss it while you are chuckling.

Read the following selection quickly, *actively* looking for the subtle point that Smith is making. Enjoy his humor and funny remarks, but *actively* demand from the material, as you read, the answer to this question: What, in essence, is Jack Smith saying?

SELECTION 11

Some Editors Overcensortive
by Jack Smith

Time at start: _____ minutes _____ seconds

Start! ➡ As a friend of the women's movement I happily connive at some of their extraordinary methods, but I am alarmed at what appears to be their infiltration of the publishing world with editors whose mission is to root out "sexism" by censoring authors or rejecting manuscripts.

I am not talking about books and articles that deliberately ridicule and frustrate women in their crusade for equal rights, but books and stories in which women are innocently shown as doing the things a great many of them still do, like fixing breakfast and packing their husbands' lunch pails.

Since I never write fiction, I didn't realize how serious this infiltration of publishers' offices was until I heard from a couple of professional writers who have come up against it.

Syble Lagerquist, an established writer of children's stories, has sent me a rejection she received recently from Dillon Press in Minneapolis. It is a routine form rejection signed by Uva Dillon, politely advising Lagerquist that her manuscript does not fit the publisher's "projected publishing plans." But Ms. Dillon has added a postscript in her own handwriting:

"It sounds interesting, but we're booked for the coming year. Watch the sexism in manuscript—Mom and Jade making sandwiches, for example."

In the scene that Ms. Dillon objects to as sexist, Lagerquist explains, the family is getting ready for a picnic at the beach, and two of her women characters—Mom and Jade—are making the sandwiches.

"They call that sexism?" the author asks.

A similar experience is reported by William Gault, a man who has been writing and selling for nearly half a century. Gault was one of that school of tough but talented writers who survived during the Depression by writing for the pulps. They were good writers. Dashiel Hammett, Raymond Chandler, Ray Bradbury and James M. Cain were among them, and they gave Black Mask magazine a higher literary quality than Harper's and Atlantic Monthly.

★

"Honorable and beleaguered sir," Gault addresses me: "Rough as it must be to have women's lib readers, think of me. I have one as an editor.

"In a recent baseball book for kids," he goes on, "I had the weary old manager come in after a bad game and ask his wife: 'It's been a bad day, honey. Would you make me a cup of tea?'

"Demeaning to women, my ed said, and cut the line out, though she left the answer. Must have been confusing to readers. She is impossible.

"However, I have outlived four previous women editors (he names the publisher but I am leaving it out to protect the innocent) and hope to make it five.

"But as we know, huperson beings of their genetic structure outlive mortals of our persuasion . . . And I was 66 last week, and she is under 50.

"Oh, well," he concludes, "more important wars have been lost."

Neither Gault nor Lagerquist tells me what they have done, if anything, to make their stories acceptable, and I can't help wondering how they might solve their problems.

In the Lagerquist story, I see Father suggesting a picnic at the beach. He's had a brutal week at the office and thinks it would be fun to get away with Mom and the kids.

"Why don't you and Jade make some sandwiches?" he suggests.

"Are you kidding?" says Mom. "Make your own sandwiches, you chauvinist pig."

★

In Gault's story the old manager, stooped and weary after his bad game, shuffles into the kitchen and collapses onto a chair at the breakfast table.

"It's been a bad day, honey," he sighs. "Would you make me a cup of tea?"

"Do this, do that," grumbles his wife. "I'll make you a cup of tea, all right."

She makes a pot of tea and pours it over the old man's head. "Take that," she says, "you burned-out old jock!"

Actually, I have no such complaints as Gault and Lagerquist. A year or two ago a book of mine was published by a New York house, and it was edited by a young woman named Kelly. We worked together on the manuscript, by letter and telephone, and Kelly never made a criticism or suggestion that didn't improve the book. Not only that, but I fell in love with her, long distance and sight unseen. But perhaps that's a sexist remark.

Also, I have a woman editor here at The Times. She often saves me from myself when I misspell a name or get a fact wrong. But when I write, for example, that I came home and asked my wife to make me a cup of coffee, or that I reminded her it was Monday night and she shouldn't forget to put the trash barrels out, this woman never cuts it out or writes me a crisp little note suggesting that I "watch the sexism."

She has known me a long time, and my wife, too, and she knows that when I write something like that it isn't fiction. ◄ **Stop timing**

Time at finish: _____ minutes _____ seconds

Total time elapsed: _____ minutes _____ seconds

Comprehension Test

In your own words, finish this sentence:

Jack Smith is suggesting that editors _____

_____ _____

Compute Your Rate
(Approximate Number of Words: 840)

Time	WPM	Time	WPM
40 sec.	1260	2 min.	420
45 sec.	1120	2 min. 15 sec.	362
50 sec.	1008	2 min. 30 sec.	334
55 sec.	916	2 min. 45 sec.	304
1 min.	840	3 min.	280
1 min. 15 sec.	672	3 min. 15 sec.	258
1 min. 30 sec.	558	3 min. 30 sec.	240
1 min. 45 sec.	480	4 min.	209

Your Rate On Selection 11: _____WPM

(Record this statistic on the chart and graph on page 235)

Check Your Comprehension

Your statement, in different words, may have been somewhat as follows: . . . *are going too far in trying to remove sexism from their authors' work* . . . or: *are going to a ridiculous extreme in eliminating sexist roles in the manuscripts they edit.*

In this exercise you have been invited to take a step beyond the simple comprehension of facts and ideas—you were asked to look for the *implications* of what a writer is saying.

When you read *actively*, you get *involved*—completely involved—in a number of mental activities:

1. A clear awareness of *why* you are reading the material (*your purpose*)

2. An aggressive pursuit of a writer's ideas, organization, and structure of thinking

3. An attempt to discover the meaning *beyond* the meaning of the words and ideas

4. An awareness of a *sense of urgency* as you read

5. And a very definite feeling of pushing along rapidly (not so rapidly that you lose all comprehension, but fast enough to be conscious that you're speeding along in high gear).

This *active involvement* in what you are reading will not only improve your speed and comprehension, but will also considerably sharpen your concentration. You will be too busy to be distracted. You will be so aggressively *postured to dominate the material* that your attention will be entirely focused on what you are doing.

Such *active involvement*, such complete concentration, such awareness of urgency, speed, and *purpose*—these

are the goals your training is preparing you to reach.
You are not there yet.

But slowly, surely, methodically, you are taking steps to get there—to achieve the goals set up for you in this training program.

Pretend, for a moment, that you are training to compete in an Olympic swimming race.

Obviously, you have to practice—*in the water*—every day, perfecting your stroke, coordinating your bodily movements, etc.

Every day!

Change swimming to any other activity—becoming an expert typist, a top-flight concert pianist, a mountain climber, a chess master.

The *indispensable* requirement is *practice*—in swimming, in typing, in playing a musical instrument, etc., etc.

And in reading!

Not just practice (for one can, of course, practice all the wrong techniques until finally one has achieved perfection in doing something wrong!), but practice under expert guidance.

So you must start reading—more than you have ever read before, more than you ever thought you could find time to read.

Lots of reading (i.e., *practice*) is not enough!

You must practice efficient, productive techniques whenever you read.

As in the conquest of any high-level skill (and reading is a skill of the *highest* level), you will make errors, you will find yourself in temporary periods of nonimprovement, you may even occasionally become discouraged at slow progress or lack of progress.

Expect these static periods. They occur in all learning; they are an indication that you are adjusting, digesting, and assimilating, in preparation for the next forward movement.

So persevere!

Especially if you consider yourself a poor reader, or if the statistics and data you have gathered thus far in your training suggest that you are a poor reader, then by all means *persevere.* For your task, if such is the case, is to accomplish no less than a complete *reeducation of,* perhaps even a *revolution in,* your reading habits.

O.K. Enough pep talk!

Let's get back to work.

I ask you to read another of Jack Smith's columns.

In this column, as in so much of Smith's writing, the subsurface implication is subtle, almost elusive; and perhaps some of Smith's readers do not realize that beneath the fun and spoofing and delightful anecdotes, Smith is almost always saying something extremely serious.

Your purpose in sailing through the next selection is to catch the subtle message—to be able to put into your own words an answer to this question: In Jack Smith's view of life, what, exactly, is *class?*

The Class Menagerie
by Jack Smith

Time at start: _____minutes _____seconds

Start timing ➡ In our Newsmakers column the other morning I read that George Burns, on hearing that he had been nominated for the Academy Awards, now that he's 80, said, "I was very excited. If I win it, fine. If I don't, I was nominated."

Readers who don't remember George Burns from the old radio days with Gracie Allen might guess, from those remarks, that George Burns had a touch of class. Of course class is obsolete, and many young people might not know it ever existed, unless they had read the novels of Evelyn Waugh and P. G. Wodehouse, which I doubt.

George Burns won't remember me but years ago when I was having a hard time paying for my extravagances and my children, I took on a moonlight job as Hollywood correspondent for an English newspaper which was not, to put it in the best light, as distinguished as the *Times* of London. But it was lively, and they paid me in dollars.

Also I learned from them that money wasn't everything. The editor I worked with asked me to do impossible things; not impossible in the sense that they were hopeless enterprises, but impossible in the sense that I personally couldn't or wouldn't do them. The editor seemed to feel that an American would do things a proper Englishman wouldn't.

He phoned me once, for example, and asked me, in his tinny British accent, which managed to be arrogant and courteous at the same time, if I thought I could get Irene Dunne on the telephone and ask her if she thought the teacher in "Anna and the King of Siam" was sexually involved with the king, or was just, well, vaguely fascinated by him.

"I don't know," I said, "if I have the courage to call Irene Dunne and ask her that. The word around town is that she's quite a lady."

"Well," he said, "if you don't mind awfully."

I did mind awfully but I had to do it. I needed the money. I used some resources of mine to find Miss Dunne's phone number. When she answered I couldn't think of anything decent to say but the man from London's question, and to add, "if you don't mind, awfully."

To my surprise and relief, Miss Dunne gave me a calm, thoughtful and gracious analysis of the relationship that she imagined existed between her and the king of Siam.

The interview was so pleasing to the man in London that he wondered if I would mind awfully calling Deborah Kerr, who had played the same role in "The King and I" and who happened to be on the coast at the moment. I didn't mind awfully, because I had always adored her, and was happy to have the excuse.

Miss Kerr had never heard of me of course but she was as gracious as Miss Dunne, and said about the same thing. If I may risk misquoting her, after all these years, I believe what she said was, "How could a woman not have fallen in love with a man like that?"

That's a remark which makes me want to say, "How could a man not fall in love with a woman like that?"

There was a touch of class in Miss Dunne's answer to an impertinent question, and in Miss Kerr's. But class is indefinable. Some have so much of it, like Miss Dunne and Miss Kerr, that it comes through even though they are talking to a stranger on a phone.

Hemingway may be remembered more for his remark about courage, which is class, than for his novels. "Courage," he said, "is grace under pressure." Well, that was such a beautiful remark, so neatly put, that it almost goes unchallenged. But of course, and sadly, it is not true. Courage is hard to discover, and hard to explain.

★

Then what is class? Jack Kennedy had class, but one expected it of him. So did Harry Truman, where it was not so much expected. I saw some class when I walked down the corridor of the Biltmore Hotel with Mr. Truman, who was not in that year. "Mr. Smith," he said, after having learned my name. "how do you like the Dodgers this year?"

I call that class.

Does anyone remember Wendell Willkie? He had the courage to run against Franklin Roosevelt for President. I forget what year that was. I was working for United Press that year in Sacramento. It was the year that he lost, but he was trying again. Willkie came to visit Earl Warren, our governor, and we wondered as reporters do, why. Oddly no one met him at the airport but me and the man from International News Service. I was embarrassed that the governor had treated him so poorly though I admired the governor very much.

"We're just newspaper men," I said. "What do you mean," he said, "*just newspaper men?*"

I think that was class.

Willkie had a gift for answering questions honestly. "Why have you come to California," I asked him, "3,000 miles to visit Mr. Warren?"

"Mr. Warren," he said with utter politeness,

"invited me to breakfast, and a free meal in these days is not to be despised."

That's class. ◄ **Stop timing**

Time at finish: _____minutes _____seconds

Total time elapsed: _____minutes _____seconds

Reflect on what you have just read. There are many ways of phrasing the implication of Smith's column, and perhaps as many differently worded implications will be derived from this selection as there are people who read it. *What* your answer is will be of considerably less importance than your realization that there are meanings *behind* meanings, and that *one* purpose in reading (not, by any means, the purpose you will have in *all* your reading) is to find an *underlying* meaning.

So when you answer the comprehension question below, whatever you write will be correct *for you,* for you are practicing reading rapidly while *dominating* the material by *actively* extracting a subsurface meaning.

Comprehension Test

In Jack Smith's view of life, what, as you understood it, is *class?* _____

_____

_____

_____

Compute Your Rate
(Approximate Number of Words: 860)

Time	WPM	Time	WPM
40 sec.	1291	2 min.	430
45 sec.	1147	2 min. 10 sec.	397
50 sec.	1032	2 min. 15 sec.	382
55 sec.	938	2 min. 30 sec.	344
1 min.	860	2 min. 45 sec.	313
1 min. 10 sec.	741	3 min.	286
1 min. 20 sec.	645	3 min. 15 sec.	264
1 min. 30 sec.	573	3 min. 30 sec.	246
1 min. 40 sec.	516	3 min. 45 sec.	229
1 min. 50 sec.	470	4 min.	215

Your Rate on Selection 12: _____WPM

(Record this statistic on the chart and graph on page 235)

7

How to Get
the Gist Quickly

PREVIEW

Chapter 7 offers you practice in responding rapidly to the main ideas of 14 short selections.

You continue your training in reading more aggressively. Your practice in this chapter will help you:

• Whip through material looking for central meaning

• Eliminate from your reading habits any excessive regard for minor details

• React quickly and accurately to the *gist* of a piece of writing

THE DETAILS WILL TAKE CARE OF THEMSELVES

Let us pause, now, for a partial review.

Most untrained college students and adults, we have decided, read at speeds much slower than their innate ability to understand makes possible.

Their slowness may be caused, in part, by unnecessarily short recognition spans, so that they habitually interpret print almost word by word rather than by phrases or by thought-units of several words. Not only is their speed thus cut down—it obviously takes more time to read three or four words in separate fixations than to read them all in one fixation—but their comprehension is also likely to suffer, for their attention is focused on individual words instead of on ideas and central meaning.

Their speed may also be held back—even drastically reduced—by certain other bad habits and inefficient techniques. They may move their lips, tongue, or vocal cords in order to understand. Or they may rely excessively on auditory responses, so that they do not react as instantaneously as they should to the visual images that their eyes flash to their brain. Or they may have a psychological compulsion to *study* every word, to read and reread and then re-reread words and phrases and lines before they are convinced that they have properly understood them. Or they may dwell unnecessarily long on minor details, get lost in a patch of daydreaming stimulated by a chance idea that occurs in a paragraph, or become so easily distracted by their external environment or their internal ruminations that they continue reading without absorbing meaning, and finally have to go back to pick up the thread that their mind in effect dropped paragraphs or pages back. Any one of these characteristics can serve as a massive obstacle to efficient, aggressive, and rapid comprehension.

Or the obstacles may be of a more subtle variety.

Untrained readers may have become accustomed to reacting comfortably or lazily to the message of print at a uniformly slow and meandering rate—a rate not only slower than they need for excellent and accurate comprehension, but slower even than most types of material demand. (The rate of a trained reader, you will recall, is highly flexible, changing as the material changes, changing as the reader's purpose changes.)

Or perhaps they lack experience in differentiating between details and main ideas, and have never learned to push rapidly through the subsidiary embellishments and decorations of an author's writing to get down efficiently to the important points.

Or perhaps they do not read widely enough, maintaining little, if any, contact with the type of book or magazine that stimulates thinking and jogs the intellect. Only infrequently, if at all, are they willing to accept the challenge of a good book of nonfiction—of a deep and thoughtful novel, of the editorial page of a major newspaper—of a magazine like *Harper's, The Atlantic Monthly, Esquire, The New Yorker, Newsweek, Time, Psychology Today,* etc.

Or, they may not read *continuously* enough, often letting weeks or months slip by without doing anything more than superficially perusing the daily and Sunday papers.

(Stop and think for a moment—how many complete books have *you* read in the last few months? And how many of these were books of nonfiction, rather than novels? And if you add them up, how many hours would you say you devote on the average to leisure reading, other than newspapers, every week?)

When reading is so occasional, or so restricted in scope, a high order of skill can never be developed, let alone increased.

How long does a professional typist remain skillful and speedy after leaving a job in which typing is almost continuous to enter a field in which little or no typing is required?

How skillful can surgeons be if they do only an occasional operation, or if they restrict themselves to the simplest and least demanding type of work?

Or, finally, not to belabor the matter, how skillfully will a pianist play who only occasionally sits down at the keyboard? (The following statement, variously attributed to Paderewski, Josef Hofmann, Mendelssohn, and any number of other musicians, is very much to the point: "If I skip one day's practice, only I know it; if I skip two days, my teacher knows it; and if I skip three days, everyone in the audience knows it.")

What it all boils down to, of course, is that slow readers rarely set up for themselves those conditions that will require them to operate at the peak of efficiency, that will force them to make maximum use of their intelligence, talents, and capacities.

The kind of training you are now receiving sets up such conditions for you, shows you how to operate under them, and demands that you make every effort to draw on your latent capacities and thus increase your actual operating ability.

The basic training in this chapter, for example, will set up conditions under which you will be required to understand material at a rate substantially faster than you were accustomed to when you started this book—substantially faster than the normal, comfortable, perhaps lazy rate at which you read the first selection in Chapter 1.

The exercises you will shortly work on will continue to chip away at any tendency you may have to read more slowly than you are able to comprehend. With the perception exercises on which you practiced in previous chapters (and which will appear also in this and later chapters), you made a start at removing certain *visual* obstacles to quick comprehension; now you will begin to remove certain *psychological* obstacles.

The exercises in this chapter will give you further training in reading with a *sense of urgency;* will demand that you get into a selection without delay, get the *gist* of it quickly and correctly, and then get out without waste of time or effort, and with full assurance that you understood in essence what the author was saying to you.

In order to accomplish this, you must submit, emotionally as well as intellectually, to an important principle: *If you read for main ideas, the details will take care of themselves.*

You may be reluctant to accept this principle. You may be conditioned, because of previous habits and experience, or because of the type of reading you now do (textbook study; proofreading; editing; technical material such as contracts, legal briefs, estimates, or specifications; or medical, psychological, legal, or dental journals; etc.) to consider all details of supreme importance—and you may be emotionally opposed (whether consciously or unconsciously is of no importance) to reading for main ideas.

Or you may be a perfectionist in your daily life, a stickler for details, a person who prefers to be slow but sure.

In short, it may be a psychological wrench, because it runs so counter to your ingrained patterns and attitudes, to adjust to reading rapidly, to cruising along at a good clip with speedy comprehension of the main ideas.

I wish only to point out that you can't have your cake and eat it too.

If you wish to be a rapid, efficient reader, you must give up your excessive attention to details, your compulsive reverence for minor points, and you must be willing to develop a mind-set that concentrates on central themes.

As a college student, as an executive, or as a professional (teacher, psychologist, doctor, lawyer, chemist, etc.), you may often have to read with the careful attention to important details that your purpose requires.

As an efficient reader, however, you must develop a *variety* of speeds, a *diversity* of approaches to material, depending on the purpose for which you are reading and on the type of material you are dealing with.

In work that requires infinitely close scrutiny, that is what you will give it.

In reading for information, relaxation, or entertainment, you will be able to read swiftly for main ideas, knowing that the details will take care of themselves.

As an *efficient* reader, you will choose the tool best suited to the reading task. It would be a poor carpenter, for example, who relied on a surgical scalpel to do all the cutting of lumber which the job requires. (Indeed, it would be a poor surgeon who used only one scalpel no matter what type of tissue that was to be cut.) And so it is a poor reader who reads everything the same way, with the same careful attention to details. Good readers have a large supply of different tools, and use that tool which will best do the job. They can read carefully when their purpose requires care—that is, when details are of special importance or when they want to savor the emotional impact of every word. But they can read like the wind when they want the *ideas* of a selection, and want them quickly.

Sometimes, also (and this may at first sound paradoxical), readers who pay excessive attention to details lose a lot of the impact of the *main theme* of a piece—so that slow, finicky reading may actually not result in as good comprehension as one would logically suppose.

So you must be willing, if the practice in this chapter is to be of maximum effectiveness, to accept the validity of the principle that *if you read for main ideas, the details will take care of themselves.*

GETTING THE AUTHOR'S POINT

You will begin your practice very shortly—but, as in previous exercises, it is important that you thoroughly understand the technique under which you are to operate, and that you follow the technique exactly as directed.

I shall set down the rules clearly. Make sure you understand them, and then make sure that you apply them when you start working.

Rule 1: Do not aim to go as fast as is humanly possible—such an impatient rush to achieve in a few minutes a goal that normally requires many weeks or months will only cause fatigue and result in very great, or even total, comprehension loss.

Rule 2: *Pay no attention to fixations or eye movements as you read.* Comprehension and concentration are interfered with if part of your mind is concerned with what your eyes are doing. Aim only at understanding the author's main idea in a satisfyingly rapid manner.

Rule 3: Feel that you are going faster than you usually do. Jump into a piece, look for and follow the author's main idea (do not worry about the minor points), and finish without wasting time.

Rule 4: If you happen to lose a word, a phrase, or a minor point here or there, *do not regress*—keep reading for the main idea.

Rule 5: Get the thoughts quickly, *but don't rush.* Rushing produces tension, and tension inhibits, rather than aids, quick comprehension.

Rule 6: In a sense, you can "read" as quickly as you're able to turn pages—but you're not really reading unless you follow, with understanding, the *gist* of what an author is saying. So read quickly enough to realize you're getting the author's thoughts rapidly, but not with such reckless speed that you become confused and lose all comprehension.

Rule 7: Do not worry about auditory responses; the more conscious you are of inner speech, the more inner speech you'll have. Think only of the main ideas—the more involved you become in *main ideas*, the less you concentrate on *minor points*, and the faster you go (without rushing thoughtlessly), the better the chances are that you will become less and less aware of inner speech.

These are the seven general principles for you to follow in your training. Specific rules applying directly to the material that will be presented will be offered at the proper place.

RAPID COMPREHENSION EXERCISE 1

Your purpose is to look for the answer to the question: What type of student is now going to the typical community college?

College Enrollment of Adults on Rise

BURLINGAME (AP)—The typical community college student is no longer the teenager looking for a springboard to a four-year college. More and more, it's the part-time adult student resuming his order schooling.

That was one finding of a survey of students at California's 101 two-year community colleges. The report was presented this week to the California Postsecondary Education Commission, the state's advisory panel on colleges.

Women with grown children, unemployed workers and the elderly are enrolling at the schools in increasing numbers, the report said.

It said part-time students increased from 57 percent of the students receiving course credit in 1969 to 66 percent in 1974.

In the same period, adults 21 years and older increased from 33 to 43 percent.

The commission staff also said only 8 percent of the students in a sample survey of 32 colleges got their two-year degrees from the schools.

And only 4.1 percent—41,000 out of a total state enrollment of 1 million—transferred to a four-year school in 1974, the report said.

It said in the past five years, the colleges have been seeing new types of students.

They are "part-time students who have been out of school for several years (including women whose education was interrupted by marriage and child-rearing), skilled workers who are unemployed or underemployed, senior citizens and others whose objectives do not fit the traditional transfer and occupational categories.

"Still others . . . are the physically and otherwise handicapped; the institutionalized in prisons and hospitals; and the young who are leaving high school before the age of 18 or getting a head start on college before high school graduation," the report said.

Test Your Comprehension

Complete this sentence:

The typical community college student is no longer ____

_____

_____

but instead is _____

_____

_____

(Keys to the comprehension tests for this chapter will be found on pages 85, 86, 91. Wait until you have taken all the tests before checking your answers.)

RAPID COMPREHENSION EXERCISE 2

A clear central theme, surrounded by explanatory details, runs through the next selection. Read the piece rapidly, aiming for an accurate understanding of the author's final meaning.

Fried Foods
by Irving S. Cutter, M.D.

Fried foods have long been frowned upon. Nevertheless the skillet is about our handiest and most useful piece of kitchen equipment. Stalwart lumberjacks and others engaged in active labor requiring 4,000 calories per day or more will take approximately one-third of their rations prepared in this fashion. Meats, eggs, and French toast cooked in this way are served in millions of homes daily. Apparently the consumers are not beset with more signs of indigestion than afflict those who insist upon broiling, roasting, or boiling. Some years ago one of our most eminent physiologists investigated the digestibility of fried potatoes. He found that the pan variety was more easily broken down for assimilation than when deep fat was employed. The latter, however, dissolved within the alimentary tract more readily than the boiled type. Furthermore, he learned, by watching the progress of the contents of the stomach by means of the fluoroscope, that fat actually accelerated the rate of digestion. Now all this is quite in contrast with "authority." Volumes have been written on nutrition and everywhere the dictum has been accepted—no fried edibles of any sort for children. A few will go so far as to forbid this style of cooking wholly. Now and then an expert will be bold enough to admit that he uses them himself, the absence of discomfort being explained on the ground that he possesses a powerful gastric apparatus. We can of course sizzle perfectly good articles to death so that they will be leathery and tough. But thorough heating, in the presence of shortening, is not the awful crime that it has been labeled. Such dishes stimulate rather than retard contractions of the gall bladder. Thus it is that bile mixes with the nutriment shortly after it leaves the stomach. We don't need to allow our foodstuffs to become oil soaked, but other than that there seems to be no basis for the widely heralded prohibition against this method. But notions become fixed. The first condemnation probably arose because an "oracle" suffered from dyspepsia which he ascribed to some fried item on the menu. The theory spread. Others agreed, and after a time the doctrine became incorporated in our textbooks. The belief is now tradition rather than proved fact. It should have been refuted long since, as experience has demonstrated its falsity.

Test Your Comprehension

Complete this sentence:

It is not true that _____

_____

_____

_____

RAPID COMPREHENSION EXERCISE 3   Your Diary

Your diary, if you keep the right kind, may be a lifesaver if you turn it over to your doctor when illness strikes. He isn't interested in what Jim said under the moon, but he would like to know details of your past that can give him important information on your health history. This recommendation comes from Dr. H. E. Robertson of the Mayo Foundation. Did you turn yellow after taking that worm medicine a few years ago? There may be a clue to liver injury there. How often have those troublesome stomachaches been occurring—how many days between them? How many colds do you have a year? Were you bedridden for a day or so with a mysterious fever—and, if so, what kind of activities had you been engaging in previously? When was the last time you called a doctor and for what? This unromantic information can be very helpful indeed when you need a doctor's services.

Test Your Comprehension

Complete this sentence:

An account of your previous _____ and

_____ will help your doctor _____

_____

_____

RAPID COMPREHENSION EXERCISE 4   The Best Learning
by Cyril O. Houle

The best learning is that which occurs in adulthood. Our psychologists have demonstrated fairly conclusively that, for most people, the ability to learn is at its peak in the years from eighteen to forty-five. There is evidence to show that, even after forty-five, learning power remains high if it is exercised carefully and systematically. Adults can learn better than children; maturity is not a bar but an incentive to the person who wishes to develop his own potentialities. It is significant to recall, among other things, that virtually all the really great teachers, both religious and secular, have taught adults, not children. Naturally, the elementary school and the high school should do something more than keep children warm and dry. They can do little more, however, than prepare their pupils for the real education which maturity will bring.

Test Your Comprehension

Complete this sentence:

Adults are _____

_____

How are you doing? Do you begin to see how you can gain speed and assurance as you aim to find the gist of a selection with no loss of time, with no dawdling or minute examination of details?

Continue your practice now on the next short selection, reading with a *sense of urgency*, deliberately going a little faster than is comfortable as you search for the main point, the gist, the central meaning.

RAPID COMPREHENSION EXERCISE 5 Thought and Language

by Edward Sapir

Most people, asked if they can think without speech, would probably answer, "Yes, but it is not easy for me to do so. Still I know it can be done." ... No one believes that even the most difficult mathematical proposition is inherently dependent on an arbitrary set of symbols, but it is impossible to suppose that the human mind is capable of arriving at or holding such a proposition without the symbolism. The writer, for one, is strongly of the opinion that the feeling entertained by so many that they can think, or even reason, without language is an illusion. The illusion seems to be due to a number of factors. The simplest of these is the failure to distinguish between imagery and thought. As a matter of fact, no sooner do we try to put an image into conscious relation with another than we find ourselves slipping into a silent flow of words. Thought may be a natural domain apart from the artificial one of speech, but speech would seem to be the only road we know that leads to it.

Test Your Comprehension

Complete this sentence:

It is not true that _____

_____

You have read five fairly short pieces as a warmup. You have been interested more in your subjective awareness of going *fast* and *finding the main ideas* than in discovering your actual rate.

The next two selections are somewhat longer, and your purpose will be the same—to get in, to get the author's central idea, and to get out—but for the next two pieces you will also check your actual WPM rate.

RAPID COMPREHENSION EXERCISE 6

'Боже Мой! Моеи Фамилии В Списках Нет!'
('Oh My God! My Name's Not on Any of Those Lists!')
by Emil Draitser

Time at start: _____ minutes _____ seconds

Start timing ➡ It goes without saying that this whole incident could only have happened under circumstances totally incomprehensible to the average American. In other words, this event could only have occurred in the Soviet Union.

Chronic shortages of just about everything have created a peculiar psychosis in my former homeland. This illness manifests itself in a widespread mania that compels Soviet citizens to place their names on waiting lists for scarce goods. Just the rumor that rare merchandise is about to become available is enough to start one of these lists.

Such rosters of aspiring consumers are compiled weeks or even months before the item in question actually goes on sale. In the interim, those "lucky" enough to have their names included must return repeatedly to verify their position on the list. If they don't show up, their names are simply dropped.

Obviously, lists are no laughing matter to Soviet citizens, but until shortly before my departure even I had no idea how much a part of the national consciousness they had become. One day a friend and I were sitting in a cafe and, during a lull in the conversation, I pulled out a notebook and began to make a list of errands my wife had asked me to do for her.

"What are you writing? What list is this?" asked

my friend, trying to look over my shoulder.

"It's nothing," I replied.

"I think you're trying to put something over on me." My friend moved closer. "What's the list for?" he said, winking.

"For nothing."

"Put my name down."

"Don't be a jerk."

"Emil," he pleaded, "come on—put my name down."

"Leave me alone."

"So that's the way it is," he said furiously. "When you want something you come to me, but when I ask you to put me on your list, it's another story."

"Will you cut it out?" I snapped. "Stop bugging me about the damn list."

"What's happening, comrades?" inquired an elderly citizen who had stopped at our table. "What list is this?"

"It's not a list," I retorted.

"Understood," said the citizen coyly. "My name is Glossky. Put it down." To get rid of him I scribbled something on the page.

"Thank you," said Glossky. "When do we come in to check on our names?"

"Tomorrow morning. At 6:30." Even I was falling in step.

"Thank you," said Glossky, taking his leave.

Before he was out of sight, two more people came up and demanded that their names be added to the list. I wrote them down, then nonchalantly leaned my elbow on the open notebook.

"Emil," screamed my friend, who was turning green, "what are you doing? Why are you torturing me? Please, as a friend, please put my name down."

"No, I won't."

At that moment, a heavy-set man came up to our table and began to pull the notebook from underneath my elbow. "Give it to me," he said. "My handwriting is neater." This portly fellow sat down in a corner of the cafe and added his own name and those of two girls he knew.

Glossky appeared again. "Excuse me," he said. "Can I put my wife on the list?"

"No," I answered firmly.

"Why not? We have different last names."

"In that case, it's OK."

Glossky grinned broadly and skipped over to the heavy-set man, around whom a crowd was rapidly growing. When the pages of my small notebook were filled, someone got a piece of wrapping paper at the counter and used it to continue the list.

"I will never forgive you for this!" screamed my friend, looking back toward me as he pushed through the crowd. His perspiring face bore a tragic expression.

Just then the heavy-set man announced: "We have 200 names. No more. That's all we can take."

"Write me down," my friend begged as he finally reached the listmaker. "Somebody may drop out. . . ."

"I suppose we could keep going," the heavy-set man agreed, "but then we'll have to start checking in at 5 in the morning. There will be quite a crowd, you know."

Glossky reappeared. "Can I enter my wife's sister? She has the same last name as her husband."

"Where is she registered?"

"In Moscow."

"Go ahead," I nodded.

Soon someone started another list; then a third was begun. People argued over which list was valid.

"Could I see your palms, please?" asked an old man, pulling the stub of an indelible pencil from a toothbrush container in his pocket. "We will mark your number on the palm of your hand. Experience has shown that this is the best way to keep track of the line."

"Why there?" said Glossky, extending his palm for marking. "Sometimes palms perspire from nerves, you know."

"Because it's a good spot," said the old man, clenching his fist. "No one will see your number."

It was drizzling when I finally left the cafe. A long line of people stretched from the entrance, and continued around the corner. Among those waiting were an old woman knitting a sweater in the feeble light of the street lamp, two young men playing a serious chess game on a portable board and a substantial-looking citizen who sat on a folding chair while reading a magazine.

Smugly, I passed them by: Greed had made fools of them all. Then a terrible thought rushed through my mind. I knew that my own list was a fraud, but what of the others? What if one was for real? I asked myself. *Oh, my God! My name's not on any of those lists!*

I turned and ran down the street toward the cafe. "Citizens," I screamed, "who is last in line?" ◄ **Stop timing**

Time at finish: _____ minutes _____ seconds

Total elapsed time: _____ minutes _____ seconds

Test Your Comprehension

Complete the following:

In Russia, at the time the article was written, people were eager to get on lists because of _____

_____

the author, making a list of _____

_____

was suddenly _____

_____

_____

and then, irrationally, was himself _____

_____

_____

_____

Compute Your Rate
(Approximate Number of Words: 845)

Time	WPM	Time	WPM
45 sec.	1126	1 min. 50 sec.	462
50 sec.	1014	2 min.	423
55 sec.	922	2 min. 15 sec.	376
1 min.	845	2 min. 30 sec.	338
1 min. 10 sec.	722	2 min. 45 sec.	307
1 min. 15 sec.	676	3 min.	282
1 min. 20 sec.	634	3 min. 15 sec.	260
1 min. 30 sec.	563	3 min. 30 sec.	242
1 min. 40 sec.	507	3 min. 45 sec.	225
1 min. 45 sec.	483		

Your rate on Rapid Comprehension Ex. 6: _____ WPM

RAPID COMPREHENSION EXERCISE 7

BA '75: The Hapless Odyssey
of a Young Classicist Cum Clerk
by Michael Christie

Time at start: _____ minutes _____ seconds

Start Timing ➡ One woman who received her bachelor's degree along with me last June at Pitzer College in Claremont is currently using her hard-earned skills to serve better sodas in an ice cream parlor. Another spends her days working in an automobile repair shop. I am not significantly better off than either of them, nor, in fact, am I much better off than many others who were members of the American college class of '75.

I am a clerk in a bookstore, which is not exactly what I expected to be doing at this point in my life.

Two years ago at this time I was unconcerned as my friends worried about scores on law board exams, or nervously waited for letters from the admissions offices of medical schools, or scrambled to get into graduate business programs. They knew then what I did not know until much later: that a liberal-arts degree no longer guarantees a good job and that, given the state of the economy, college students must train for something specific if they want to be certain of winning a job they want.

I got my bachelor's degree in classics. All along I managed to persist in the study of Greek and Latin because I loved the field (still do) and because, when asked, "But what are you going to do with a classics degree?" I replied, "I can do a lot of things." I was certain that anyone confident (or crazy) enough to pursue the ultimate in liberal-arts degrees would be rewarded with interesting employment of some kind and earn at least reasonable financial remuneration.

My experience has proved otherwise. It has also shown me a lot about the plight of anybody—with or without a degree—who is seeking work in today's glutted job market. Most of all, it has made clear just how profoundly the job-seeker is at the mercy of the job-giver.

In the fall of 1974, when I decided to forgo graduate school (a decision based on lack of money, not lack of interest or aptitude), I began actively to hunt a job. I reasoned that my best opportunity would be to offer my services to private high schools where one who is able to read Cicero in his own language is still appreciated.

I failed to take into account, however, that few such openings exist in the first place. More important, I quickly found out that I was competing with a great many other individuals who not only possessed the same talents as I but also held doctorates. Not finding work at colleges, these doctors of classics had turned to the private high schools, the traditional haven of bachelor's degree holders like me. But no headmaster is going to hire a punk with a BA, when he can just as easily have a Ph.D. desperate for a job, and for only a little more money.

Ignoring this detail, I went through the process of sending out some 30 letters of inquiry to private schools. I received perhaps ten replies, with two schools saying that they might have an opening. I had the good fortune of being granted one interview.

The school was in Oakland, and since I had neither the time nor the money to make the journey in a leisurely way, I arranged to fly up and back on the same day. For my efforts I was given a 20-minute interview (during which the headmaster did most of the talking) and was taken on a brief tour of the campus. I realized I should have stayed at home when the interview opened with this question: "You're getting your MA?"

A few weeks later I was informed that the position had been filled. It was December, and I abandoned the hunt.

Simultaneous with my efforts to get work with a private school, I had been finishing work on my bachelor's degree and working in the Pitzer dining hall. The enthusiasm of the food-service director was contagious and, to my surprise, I almost enjoyed my job, in spite of its rather menial nature.

On Saturday afternoon, when I was bemoaning my dim employment prospects to my boss, he suggested that I look into what he was doing: food-service management. Since the work entailed both challenge and responsibility, things people are

supposed to thrive on, I decided to pursue his suggestion. What did I have to lose?

I had interviews with people ranging all the way from my supervisor's boss to the regional vice president of the company that ran dining halls at Pitzer and at a number of other schools. The interviews went well, and I was later told that I had nothing to worry about.

I spent last summer cleaning out produce coolers and making sandwiches in the dining hall, waiting, I thought, for my prospective bosses to decide where to send me for training. Summer ended, but I was assured a management job was being held for me, so I took a full-time job supervising student labor in the dining hall. The pay was minimal but, after all, only temporary. I never heard a further word about long-range employment, and quit my job late last fall.

So I am now working as a bookstore clerk—a job I am happy to have, since it is more closely related to my education than that of many college graduates. It is much less than I dreamed I would have, but I do not feel singled out, given my knowledge of those alumnae scooping ice cream and changing oil.

By now I suppose most members of the class of '75 are free and clear. In this post-recession period they probably have found the jobs they want, or have accepted something less, or have gotten started in graduate school, or have given up.

Just in time for the class of '76. ◄ **Stop Timing**

Time at finish: _____ minutes _____ seconds

Total time elapsed: _____ minutes _____ seconds

Test Your Comprehension

Complete the following:

A liberal-arts degree does not _____

_____

and, in the economy of 1975, college students had to __

_____

so the author, after graduation, was happy to get _____

_____

Compute Your Rate
(Approximate Number of Words: 975)

Time	WPM	Time	WPM
45 sec.	1300	55 sec.	1064
50 sec.	1170	1 min.	975

Time	WPM	Time	WPM
1 min. 10 sec.	836	2 min. 30 sec.	390
1 min. 15 sec.	780	2 min. 45 sec.	355
1 min. 20 sec.	731	3 min.	325
1 min. 30 sec.	650	3 min. 15 sec.	300
1 min. 40 sec.	585	3 min. 30 sec.	279
1 min. 50 sec.	532	3 min. 45 sec.	260
2 min.	488	4 min.	244
2 min. 15 sec.	433	4 min. 15 sec.	230

Your rate on Rapid Comprehension Ex. 7: _____WPM

Comprehension Keys

Your answers should be somewhat similar to the ideas in the italicized words below. You may have written more, but you should not have omitted any important element of the key ideas contained in these words.

Exercise 1: The typical community college student is no longer *the teenager looking for a springboard to a four-*

year college, but instead is *the part-time adult student resuming education where it was left off, or a student with special objectives who is not necessarily committed to pursuing a degree.*

Exercise 2: It is not true that *frying foods makes them indigestible.*

Exercise 3: An account of your previous *illnesses* and *physical reactions* will help your doctor *to diagnose and treat your ailments more efficiently.*

Exercise 4: Adults are *better learners than children.*

Exercise 5: It is not true that *people can think without language.*

Exercise 6: In Russia, at the time the article was written, people were eager to get on lists because of *chronic shortages of just about everything;* the author, making a list of *errands his wife had asked him to do for her* was suddenly *besieged by people eager to get on his (useless) list,* and then, irrationally, was himself *caught up in the frenzy (psychosis, illness, mob reaction, etc.).*

Exercise 7: A liberal-arts degree does not *guarantee a good job,* and, in the economy of 1975, college students had to *train for something specific if they were to be sure to get the kind of job they wanted;* so the author, after graduation, *was happy to get a job as a bookstore clerk.*

So—
How did you do?

Let us look at the statistics on your reading rates for exercises 6 and 7, comparing them with your rates for selections 1 and 2 of Chapter 1.

Exercise 6 (page 84): _____WPM
Exercise 7 (page 85): _____WPM
Selection 1, Chapter 1 (page 7): _____WPM
Selection 2, Chapter 1 (page 9): _____WPM

Can we spot a trend?

1. Were you aware that you were deliberately cruising along at a faster rate as you were reading the first seven selections in this chapter? ☐ Yes ☐ No.

2. Did your rate of reading in exercises 6 and 7 increase significantly over your rate in the two selections you read in Chapter 1? ☐ Yes ☐ No

3. As you compare your answers to those given on page 85–86, how do you evaluate your ability to grasp the central thought of a selection? ☐ excellent ☐ good ☐ fair ☐ poor

Remember this: With enough motivation, with continual practice, and with an increasing understanding of how to *dominate* material, you can gradually, surely, and permanently build your *rate and comprehension* to the point where reading is a skillful, rewarding, and enjoyable process.

PERCEPTION TRAINING III

Perception Exercise 10

Here again are words somewhat similar to each other, but not exactly alike. Follow the usual procedure with the Fixation Card or with your own homemade card, and keep your exposures infinitesimally short and your reactions as exclusively visual as possible.

bridle	←	blueberry	←
briery	←	bruiser	←
bristly	←	bruised	←
bristled	←	Brownie	←
British	←	browner	←
Britain	←	browned	←
brittle	←	brunette	←
Brittany	←	brownette	←
broccoli	←	Brunhild	←
brochette	←	brushwood	←
brochure	←	brushing	←
broken	←	blushing	←
brogan	←	blusher	←
brogue	←	Brussels	←
breakage	←	brutal	←
brokerage	←	brittle	←
broiler	←	brutish	←
broiling	←	bitterish	←
bronze	←	bitterly	←
brook	←	Brutus	←
Brooklyn	←	budding	←
Brookline	←	bulbous	←

brownish	←	Buddha	←
browser	←	buddy	←
blubbery	←	bubble	←

Perception Exercise 11

Proceed according to instructions on page 59. It is important at this point to attempt to keep your reactions more visual than auditory, even on phrase perception.

→ Mairzy Doats → read better and faster

→ we the people → How to make friends

→ for which it stands → and influence people

→ of the people → a stitch in time

→ by the people → a needle in a haystack

→ postwar plans → Buy more bonds

→ the Electoral College → in the nick of time

→ professorial dignity → a pair of Kilkenny cats

→ while the sun shines → poor cock robin

→ clutching at straws → Watch the Fords go by

→ broke the camel's back → They satisfy

→ Yanks are coming → crazy as a coot

→ old woman who → as happy as a lark

→ To be or not to be → a severe cold

→ that is the question → such unexpected promises

→ the City of New York → an unexpected provision

→ Emperor Hirohito → paralyzes Haiti's capital

→ The New York Times → British in Egypt

→ the life of Reilly → violates the cease-fire

→ a wonderful time → Egyptian sources predicted

→ Wish you were here → two college groups

→ the time of your life → vie for state aid

→ Eat and be merry → major fight brews

→ God save the king → between public schools

→ The king is dead → on missing airliner

→ Long live the king → debate is bitter

→ lived in a shoe → within a week

→ cupboard was bare → the principal provision

→ Mary had a little lamb → the Asian resolution

→ Can spring → it is what happened

→ be far behind? → tension gripped the city

→ It's toasted → most of the city

→ hickory dickory dock → police squad cars

→ Ten little Indians → during the day

→ live and let live → U.N. chief urged

→ Thomas E. Dewey → go to Moscow

→ the end of the road → to bolster reserves

→ half a loaf → has already emphasized

→ In Bed We Cry → other rights granted

→ liddle lamzee divy → begun by Dulles

→ Hungary is tense → bars tariff rise

→ phones are cut → his basic opposition

→ U.S. protests curb → rules are drafted

→ a non-Communist oath → police extend efforts

→ the criminal code → drinking law proposed

→ Home on the range → traffic accidents rise

(Some of the above phrases were excerpted from the news columns of the *New York Times*.)

SESSION 19

CONTINUED PRACTICE ON SHORT SELECTIONS

You are practicing, in these rapid comprehension exercises, to refine and sharpen an ability you already possess, an ability that every normal person possesses—the ability to understand the *central* meaning of what you read. You have this ability, believe me—if you did not, none of your reading would ever make sense to you. What I am demanding of you, as I present selection after selection, is well within your power; it is only a matter of your using that power more determinedly, more aggressively, more efficiently. And this you will learn to do through practice, through more and more and still more practice, until you have formed the reflexive habit of attacking a piece of writing with the psychological mind-set of discovering, as quickly as you can, the answer to one overriding question, namely: "What, *in essence,* is the author trying to say?

Whip through the following pieces with the conscious aim of grasping *central* meaning, of responding to the *gist* of the author's communication—don't linger on individual words, don't let yourself get sidetracked by details.

RAPID COMPREHENSION EXERCISE 8

When the individual photographs of a motion-picture film pass before our eyes at the rate of approximately twenty frames per second, we enjoy a continuous flow of meaning. But if the process slows down so that each photograph remains before us for a second or more, the movie becomes absurd, boring, and almost meaningless.

The word reader perceives isolated word pictures at a slow rate of speed. These impressions fail to blend into a meaningful pattern in exactly the same way as do the individual photographs of a slowed-down movie. The word reader sees the trees, perhaps, but the forest escapes him completely. As the psychologist puts it, "The whole is more than the sum of its parts."

Test Your Comprehension: Exercise 8

Which of the following statements best expresses the *central meaning* of this selection?

a. If the individual photographs of a motion picture are presented too slowly, the movie loses meaning.

b. The word-by-word reader does not get a continuous flow of meaning from material.

c. The faster a movie is run, the more sense it makes.

d. The whole is more than the sum of its parts.

RAPID COMPREHENSION EXERCISE 9

It is nothing new that the world is full of hate, that men destroy one another, and that our civilization has arisen from the ashes of despoiled peoples and decimated natural resources. But to relate this destructiveness, this evidence of a spiritual malignancy within us, to an instinct, and to correlate this instinct with the beneficent and fruitful instinct associated with love, this was one of the later flowers of the genius of Freud. We have come to see that just as the child must learn to love wisely, so he must learn to hate expeditiously, to turn destructive tendencies away from himself toward enemies that actually threaten him rather than toward the friendly and the defenseless, the more usual victims of destructive energy.

Test Your Comprehension: Exercise 9

Which of the following statements best expresses the *central meaning* of this selection?

a. The world is full of hate.

b. Our civilization has arisen from destruction.

c. Destructiveness is an evidence of our spiritual malignancy.

d. The child must learn to turn his destructiveness against actual enemies.

RAPID COMPREHENSION EXERCISE 10

Psychiatrists have observed that no other inadequacy creates as great a sense of frustration and failure as a reading difficulty. This is partly due to the fact that everyone is expected to be able to read adequately in order to advance in his schooling. Reading is also considered a criterion, in the cultural sense, of an individual's mental ability. If a person is deficient in some academic subject such as arithmetic or geography, he can avoid facing his inadequacy by avoiding those subjects. A reading defect cannot, however, be easily circumvented. His disability is brought to his attention, not only when he attends school, but in almost every other situation. He finds himself culturally in an inferior position because he cannot read books as ably as others, nor in some cases can he even read the newspapers with a semblance of competence. In one sense, therefore, the person with a serious reading defect finds himself in the same cultural position as the illiterate. He is reputationally classified by his fellow-men either as an inferior individual or as a queer person. As he grows older he is less able to rationalize the defect or to avoid the conflict associated with his deficiency and therefore accumulates further and further frustration.

Test Your Comprehension: Exercise 10

Which of the following statements best expresses the *central meaning* of this selection?

a. A reading difficulty creates a greater conflict and sense of frustration than any other inadequacy.

b. All people are expected to be able to read competently.

c. The ability to read is a yardstick of a person's mental ability.

d. Anyone who has difficulty in reading is considered either inferior or peculiar.

RAPID COMPREHENSION EXERCISE 11

The majority of Americans have not read a book in the last year. This is the startling conclusion from a survey by the American Institute of Public Opinion. Six out of ten adults questioned said that the last time they could remember reading a book—other than the Bible—was a year ago or more. Even among college graduates, one out of four had not read a book in the last 12 months.

Fewer books are read in the United States than in any major English-speaking democracy. In England about three times as many people are to be found reading books at any given time as in America. One survey recorded the following percentages of book readers: Great Britain, 55 percent; Australia, 34 percent; Canada, 31 percent; United States, 17 percent.

Test Your Comprehension: Exercise 11

Which of the following statements best expresses the *central meaning* of this selection?

a. Fewer books are read in the United States than in other English-speaking countries; the majority of Americans have not, according to a survey, read a book in the previous year.

b. More people read books in England than in this country.

c. Only college graduates have developed the habit of reading books.

d. We do not read enough books in this country.

RAPID COMPREHENSION EXERCISE 12

Seeing is a complex act wherein the optical system of the eye takes light emanating from the object and forms an image on a light-sensitive layer, the retina. This light energy through a photochemical process is transformed into nerve energy and passes through the visual pathways to the brain. In the broadest sense seeing is not complete until what is seen is interpreted by the observer. This interpretation is based on past experience; hence, to a considerable extent seeing is a learned skill.

Test Your Comprehension: Exercise 12

Which of the following statements best expresses the *central meaning* of this selection?

a. In seeing, the eye takes light from an object and forms an image on the retina.

b. In seeing, nerve energy is passed through visual pathways to the brain.

c. Seeing is a mental activity.

d. Seeing is, to a large extent, a learned skill.

RAPID COMPREHENSION EXERCISE 13

An early stage in learning to read is recognizing simple printed words and what they mean. With practice, recognition gradually embraces more complicated words and ideas. Then when some ideas can be understood more easily than others, a further skill is very helpful—matching speed to understanding, so that simple passages take less time to read than difficult ones. However, most people do not acquire this knack of flexibility; they maintain a constant rate regardless of its efficiency. Especially in college, where reading is the chief tool for gathering information, a student stuck in low gear is handicapped. Formulas, poems, short stories, and historical documents may all have to be understood, but understanding need not come at the same rate for all. Efficiency, therefore, implies knowing when to change speeds, and then being able to do so without undue trouble.

Test Your Comprehension: Exercise 13

Which of the following statements best expresses the *central meaning* of this selection?

a. Reading efficiency implies knowing how, and being able, to change speed in accordance with changing material.

b. Not everybody understands at the same rate.

c. College students who read slowly are handicapped.

d. To learn to read, one must be able to recognize simple words and understand what they mean.

RAPID COMPREHENSION EXERCISE 14

One does not have to learn to read. But, one does have to learn to read certain things and in more or less certain ways. The reading process is not initiated by school instruction nor does it emerge as a phenomenon of development after infancy. The reading process is comparable to other fundamental native processes such as respiration and nutrition. The innate reading process has to be developed and implemented just as do the other processes in order to make them effective for the needs of the organism.

Test Your Comprehension: Exercise 14

Which of the following statements best expresses the *central meaning* of this selection?

a. Reading is a natural process.

b. Reading has to be developed and implemented to be of greatest use to the reader.

c. Reading is not started by school instruction.

d. Reading is like respiration or nutrition.

Key:
The correct answers to the comprehension tests on the last seven exercises are as follows: Ex.8.b; Ex.9.d; Ex.10.a; Ex.11.a; Ex.12.d; Ex.13.a; Ex.14.b.

SESSION 20

A CHALLENGE TO YOUR READING HABITS

By now, since you are well into your training, there should have occurred at least a slight, and perhaps even a decided, change in your intellectual and psychological attitudes to reading. Let me catalogue, briefly, the factors in this change:

1. A realization that reading is not directly concerned with *words,* or even *phrases,* but only with *ideas.*

2. A realization that main ideas are more important than minor details.

3. A realization that the desire to get the main idea quickly will speed up your rate so appreciably that you can actually *feel* yourself going faster—and with a substantial awareness of increased comprehension skill.

4. A realization that you can significantly enlarge your recognition span and interpret more accurately and more rapidly what your eyes feed your mind in each fixation; that you can do this by the simple process of making greater demands on your perception capacities; that, in short, you can actually train and educate your vision.

As your general training continues day by day, page by page, this change in your *attitudes* will finally be translated into a change in your *habits and techniques;* with still further training and with continuous daily practice, efficient habits and aggressive techniques will become reflexive, second nature, almost automatic.

But of course you need not, and should not, rely for your practice exclusively on the material in this book—*nor, during your training, should you restrict your reading to this book.* In all your reading from now on—and the *amount* of reading you do should increase as your skill sharpens and your rate accelerates—it is important that you practice the techniques you have been learning. Read—whether it be a magazine article, a newspaper columnist, or a book of nonfiction—for the main ideas, and read to get those main ideas quickly. If you're reading a novel, follow the general lines of the plot rapidly, instead of getting bogged down in any of the details. It is true that some novels are of such depth, or stylistically so delightful, that you may wish to read for more than the plotline, but this is no justification for being poky. The important thing to keep in mind is that your *method* of reading and your *rate* of reading should be suited to the material at hand. Trained readers, you will recall, have a variety of speeds and techniques, and use whichever is required by the *type* of material they are reading, and by their *purpose* in reading it; but whatever the type, they push along at the maximum speed that the material and what they want to get out of it permit. Untrained readers, on the other hand, are likely to use the same technique and the same speed for everything. Light or heavy, easy or hard, simple or complex, all reading gets the same treatment.

You are on your way, now, toward becoming a trained reader. And so you are ready, I believe, to meet a challenge that I wish to confront you with.

Sometime today or tomorrow choose a novel of the sort that appeals to you. It can be one of the popular paperback reprints that you will find in any bookstore, supermarket, or book department of a large department store; or perhaps you've had a book lying around the house that you've meant to get to, but somehow never did; or ask the librarian at the local library to make a recommendation. Nothing heavy, no historical novel a thousand pages long; just a short, interesting, fast-paced, readable novel. Next find an evening, preferably within the next day or two, when you will have a few hours at your disposal.

Then see if you can meet this challenge: *read the entire novel through in one evening,* rapidly following the general lines of the plot, skimming or skipping where you can, but aiming to get through. You may find that you will get just as strong an emotional satisfaction from such fast cruising as from leisurely or poky reading, and you will be practicing the kind of rapid reading that you are attempting to master.*

If you can meet this challenge, you will have an experience no reader should miss. You will discover that it is possible to get the gist and the flavor of a novel in a few hours; you will learn that it is far from necessary to indulge in the slow, meticulous reading that causes untrained readers to take days or weeks before they turn the last page of a book.

And even if you do not meet the challenge completely, the effort, however short of total success it may fall, will be beneficial to you. Try it—*soon. Tonight, if possible!* You will realize that you do not have to read as slowly as you used to.

---

* When you do your reading, keep a record of the amount of actual time spent on the novel, the total number of pages, the approximate number of words in the whole book, and your average rate of reading. Instructions for gathering these statistics will be found on pages 110-111.

A SECOND TEST OF YOUR RETENTION AND RECALL

One of the chief means of increasing your retention and recall, as I pointed out at the end of chapter 4, is training in seeking out and successfully discovering the main idea of a selection.

The reason for this is obvious—one can always remember *meaningful* material with greater ease, efficiency, and clarity than material with little or no meaning. (Psychological experiments show that it takes considerably longer to memorize nonsense syllables, and that the period of retention is considerably shorter, than in the case of related words, or poetry, or running text.)

When you read to find, and follow, the main ideas of material, and when you can sense, during your reading, how the structure of a piece is built around these main ideas, you cannot fail to extract more meaning than when you passively absorb word after word, sentence after sentence.

Determine for yourself if this is not true in respect to your own reading. Below are a number of questions that explore your ability to recall the gist of the short selections that you have read in this chapter.

Answer each question as briefly as possible. Check *yes* or *no* where required.

1. Who, according to a press release, was the typical community college student in 1974? _____

_____

_____

2. Are fried foods indigestible? ☐ yes ☐ no
3. How can your diary help your doctor? _____

_____

4. Who are better learners, *adults* or *children*? _____

_____

5. Can people think without language? ☐ yes ☐ no
6. Why, in 1976, were people in Russia eager to get on lists?

_____

7a. As of 1975, did a liberal-arts degree guarantee a graduate a good job? ☐ yes ☐ no

7b. To get the kind of job they wanted, college students had to _____

_____

8. What kind of reader does *not* get a continuous flow of meaning from material? _____

9. In what direction must a child learn to turn destructive tendencies? _____

_____

10. What feeling, according to Mandel Sherman, does a reading difficulty create? _____

_____

11. Do people read as many books in this country as in other English-speaking nations? ☐ yes ☐ no
12. Is seeing to a considerable extent a *learned* skill? ☐ yes ☐ no
13. Does reading efficiency imply the ability to change speed in accordance with material? ☐ yes ☐ no
14. Must the reading process be trained in order to become effective for one's needs? ☐ yes ☐ no

Key

Here are the correct answers—your *language* may of course be different, but the *essence* should be the same.

1. *The part-time adult or other student with special objectives.*
2. *no*
3. *by giving an account of your previous illnesses and physical reactions*
4. *adults*
5. *no*
6. *chronic shortages of most things*
7a. *no*
7b. *train for something specific*
8. *the word-by-word reader*
9. *away from himself and toward actual enemies*
10. *frustration and failure*
11. *no*
12. *yes*
13. *yes*
14. *yes*

Number of Correct Responses: _____

How well did you do?

Including 7a & 7b, there were 15 questions. If you got 8 or more right at this point in your training, you did very well indeed; with such a score, permit yourself to have a feeling of triumphant success!

Effective retention of what you have read is not a matter of keenness of memory, but of the clarity of your understanding and of the sharpness of the picture painted in your mind by a page of print.

And what skills must you develop in order to attain such clarity of understanding and sharpness of mental imagery? Among others:

1. So deep an involvement in material that you are utterly

oblivious to outside distractions (in short, *complete concentration*)

2. Perception of print as *ideas, pictures, happenings—* not words or the sounds of words

3. Reflexive habits of moving along rapidly, of aggressively seeking main ideas, and of reacting to a writer's organization of these ideas

4. *Domination* of material by distinguishing between concepts and supporting details, by seeing meaning *behind* meaning, by thinking *along with* the writer, by avoiding regressions as far as possible, and by stifling vocalization

Reading efficiency is a learned activity, as one of the selections in this chapter indicated.

And efficiency comes from practice, more practice, still more practice!

SESSION 21

PERCEPTION TRAINING IV

Perception Exercise 12

Here are words somewhat similar to one another. Follow the usual procedure, aiming for *visual* recognition with decreased *auditory* response.

cabala	←	camisole	←
caballero	←	camomile	←
cabana	←	camphorate	←
cabinet	←	Canada	←
cabaret	←	Canadienne	←
cabbage	←	comedienne	←
garbage	←	Canadian	←
cablegram	←	canary	←
cabriolet	←	cancerous	←
cacoa	←	candescence	←
cocoa	←	candidly	←
cackle	←	candidature	←
cackler	←	candlenut	←

cadency	←	candler	←
cadenza	←	candlestick	←
cadenced	←	candlefoot	←
cadger	←	candied	←
cadgy	←	candled	←
cagey	←	canfield	←
cameo	←	canine	←
cameleer	←	canister	←
camellia	←	cankerous	←
camelopard	←	cannery	←
camels	←	cannonade	←
cameral	←	carom	←

Perception Exercise 13

In the material below the phrases will continue in meaningful succession.

Aim, as before, for instantaneous recognition of each line, and move the card quickly enough so that you will be able to make only one fixation for each exposure. The criterion of your success in this training will be that the selection continues to make sense.

Avoid, as much as you can, excessive auditory reactions to the *words* in the selection—try to decrease, as much as possible, your reliance on inner speech as you follow the *ideas* into which the phrases combine.

This may not be easy. If strong auditory reactions are an ingrained part of your comprehension, you will not be happy when you reduce your dependency on them. But *persevere*. If you are at all successful at this time (and eventually success is quite attainable) you will be able to shorten significantly the fraction of a second you spend on each fixation—your mind will not have to wait until the words are "heard" before it calls for more material.

→ At Saratoga	→ of trees
→ are acres and acres	→ every year.
→ of ground where	→ These trees
→ the State	→ are grown
→ of New York	→ from little seedlings
→ grows thousands	→ which are planted

→ in the ground

→ in early spring.

→ One year

→ the men

→ in charge

→ of the trees

→ became aware

→ that many seeds

→ were not

→ growing properly.

→ They soon learned

→ that the reason

→ for this

→ was that

→ fierce little

→ grub worms

→ had been feasting

→ on the tender

→ young plants.

→ It was not known

→ where the grubs

→ had come from,

→ but there they were,

→ and no one knew

→ how to get

→ rid of them.

→ Just then

→ a little skunk

→ happened by

→ —just an ordinary

→ everyday little skunk.

→ Now, there's nothing

→ a skunk

→ loves better

→ for his breakfast,

→ lunch, and supper

→ than nice fat

→ juicy grubs.

→ There were millions

→ of grubs,

→ and only

→ one skunk

→ but the skunk

→ had a

→ wonderful appetite;

→ it was not long

→ before the last

→ of the grubs

→ had disappeared

→ and the trees

→ were out

→ of peril.

→ The gardeners

→ at Saratoga

→ named the

→ skunk Eric,

→ built him

→ a warm house

→ for winter,

→ made sure

→ he always had

→ a generous supply

→ of food,

→ and, in short.

→ did their best

→ to overcome

→ any desire

→ he might have

→ to go away.

→ Eric stayed—

→ maybe he

→ knew that

→ all by himself

→ he could save

→ the lives

→ of thousands

→ of young trees

→ every year.

How was your comprehension under the conditions required? ☐ good ☐ fair ☐ poor

Perception Exercise 14

Now we shall dispense with the Fixation Card as we practice on another selection. Simply run your eyes down each column, making one fixation to a line, reducing any excessive dependency on inner speech, and yet adequately following the ideas. You have no doubt noticed that this material is on an unusually easy level of vocabulary and sentence structure. I have purposely chosen such simple material so that nothing will interfere with your efforts to decrease your reliance on auditory reactions. Later exercises of this type will be of a more difficult and more adult nature.

As in the two previous exercises, the criterion of success is that the selection continues to make sense as your eyes sweep down the columns.

↓	↓	↓
There is a man	toss its head,	mechanical ape.
in Seattle, Washington,	and stamp	Its appearance is
who has made	its foot.	so real
an ape.	It can even	and its actions
"How can anyone	grasp an accordion	so ape-like
make a real ape!"	in its	that if you
you will	hairy fingers	saw it
promptly exclaim.	and play	in a zoo
Well,	a tune.	you would
Bob Seymour's ape	What is	undoubtedly assume
is mechanical,	the explanation	that it
but it can do	of this wonderful	was alive.
so many things	life-like animal?	Mr. Seymour
that it is	It moves	has not yet
very much like	by electricity.	named his ape.
a real ape.	Mr. Seymour,	Can you think
It can sit	an expert electrician,	of an
in a cage,	spent four years	appropriate name
roll its eyes,	and $5,000	for this
move its ears,	on his	uncommon creature?

How was your comprehension under the conditions required? ☐ good ☐ fair ☐ poor

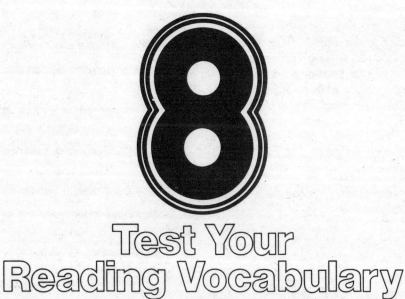

Test Your
Reading Vocabulary

PREVIEW

Chapter 8 tests the range of your vocabulary; issues a second challenge to your reading habits; offers continued training in rapid perception; and helps you distinguish "theme" from "variations."

Is a poor reading vocabulary an obstacle in your drive for quick and accurate comprehension?

In this chapter you:

• take a five-part test that determines whether your word-recognition skills are on a college-graduate, college-sophomore, high-school, or elementary-school level.

• are challenged to read *more* in order to increase your vocabulary, and to increase your vocabulary while reading.

SESSION 22

HOW GOOD IS YOUR READING VOCABULARY?

If you are a skillful reader, a page of print contains not words, but rather action, color, movement, scenery, ideas, thoughts, and feelings. Nevertheless, the vehicle on which all these things ride *is* words—individual English words or combinations of words.

The more *familiar* you are with words, then the less conscious you are of *reading* words, and the less you are aware that it is by means of words that you are reacting to the content of a sentence or paragraph or page. So, obviously, one of the factors that contribute to efficient and rapid reading is a large recognition vocabulary; conversely, and equally obviously, one of the factors that may get in the way of quick and accurate comprehension, that may even encourage regressions and vocalization, is a weak recognition vocabulary.

How about your own vocabulary? Is it as large and varied as it must be for skillful reading? Let's find out.

Take This Vocabulary Test

You may make an intelligent guess whenever you feel that you are familiar enough with a word to have an even chance of arriving at the correct answer. *Do not guess wildly.* If you have never in your life seen a particular word, or if you haven't the foggiest notion of its meaning, do not attempt an answer; baseless guessing will invalidate your score.

Part I
DIRECTIONS

To the left of each word in column A, copy the letter of the correct definition from column B.

	A		B
1.	to recline	(a)	to chew
2.	to hazard	(b)	to be sorry
3.	to munch	(c)	to make fun of
4.	to utilize	(d)	to shift one's course
5.	to saturate	(e)	to take a chance
6.	to lament	(f)	to erase
7.	to distort	(g)	to put out of focus
8.	to mock	(h)	to soak completely
9.	to veer	(i)	to use
10.	to eradicate	(j)	to lie down

Part II
DIRECTIONS

Write to the left of each number the letter of the meaning which *most clearly defines* each word.

1. egoism: (a) self-interest, (b) knowledge, (c) optimism

2. concoction: (a) refusal, (b) mixture, (c) prayer

3. pollution: (a) doing away with, (b) corruption, (c) coloring

4. candor: (a) frankness, (b) sweetness, (c) inability

5. arrogance: (a) refusal, (b) fear, (c) pride

6. extricate: (a) complicate, (b) release, (c) imprison

7. agile: (a) happy, (b) talkative, (c) spry

8. coherent: (a) powerful, (b) well-connected, (c) rambling

9. mediocre: (a) ordinary, (b) poor, (c) necessary

10. abstain: (a) ask, (b) splotch, (c) refrain

Part III
DIRECTIONS

Circle the correct answer to each question.

1. Does a *phlegmatic* person become easily excited?   yes   no

2. Do excessive eaters lead an *abstemious* life?   yes   no

3. Do *complacency* and anxiety usually go together?   yes   no

4. Is a *diffident* person self-assertive?   yes   no

5. Does *inadvertently* mean the same as *purposely*?   yes   no

6. Is a *voluble* person generally silent?   yes   no

7. Is a *panacea* a cure-all?   yes   no

8. Is a *consummate* liar a skillful liar?   yes   no

9. Does a *martinet* insist on strict obedience and discipline?   yes   no

10. Does a *misogynist* enjoy the company of women?   yes   no

Part IV
DIRECTIONS

If word and definition are nearly the *same* in meaning, circle S; if they are more nearly *opposite* in meaning, circle O.

1. *veracious:* truthful	S	O
2. *parsimonious:* generous	S	O
3. *stolid:* sluggish	S	O
4. *contrite:* sorry	S	O
5. *vitriolic:* mild	S	O
6. *pathological:* diseased	S	O
7. *disparage:* praise	S	O
8. *asceticism:* self-denial	S	O
9. *obfuscate:* clarify	S	O
10. *equivocal:* clear	S	O

Part V

DIRECTIONS

If the statement is generally true, circle T; if it is generally false, circle F.

1. Industrial *peonage* is one of the aims of American labor unions.　　　　　　　　T　F

2. Medicine has *therapeutic* value.　　　T　F

3. The automobile is an *anachronism* in America.　　　　　　　　　　　　　T　F

4. Crooked business firms try to *mulct* the public.　　　　　　　　　　　　　T　F

5. *Summary* justice is dealt out to military offenders.　　　　　　　　　　　　T　F

6. A *ukase* is commonly disobeyed.　　T　F

7. A *plethora* of money forces people to live in poverty.　　　　　　　　　　　T　F

8. A *paean* is a song of lamentation.　　T　F

9. Delight in *panoply* indicates a love of simple things.　　　　　　　　　　　T　F

10. A *truculent* person is quarrelsome.　T　F

Key

Part I: 1. j; 2. e; 3. a; 4. i; 5. h; 6. b; 7. g; 8. c; 9. d; 10. f

Part II: 1. a; 2. b; 3. b; 4. a; 5. c; 6. b; 7. c; 8. b; 9. a; 10. c

Part III: 1–6 are all *no;* 7–9 are all *yes;* 10 is *no*

Part IV: 1. S; 2. O; 3. S; 4. S; 5. O; 6. S; 7. O; 8. S; 9. O; 10. O

Part V: 1. F; 2. T; 3. F; 4. T; 5. T; 6. F; 7. F; 8. F; 9. F; 10. T

Scoring

Allow two points for each correct answer. Add up the scores you made on the five parts, and consult the chart below for a rough gauge of the present state of your recognition vocabulary.

90–100: excellent (college-graduate level)
70–88: good (college–sophomore level)
50–68: fair (high-school level)
30–48: poor (elementary-school level)

If your score was low, or lower than you had expected, then the probability is that you do not now do enough reading, or enough reading of a mature and varied kind.

During your early years, when you were learning to talk, and to comprehend the world around you, your vocabulary increased at a prodigious rate compared to later stages of your life.

After you reached late adolescence, you continued learning fewer and fewer new words each year as you grew older—*unless you did a lot of reading, and unless your reading was done on gradually higher and higher levels of maturity.*

Extensive research has turned up some startling facts about vocabulary growth in the early years, and if you are at all typical, these facts apply to you:

When you were four, you had a basic vocabulary of over 5,000 words.

By the age of seven, you were familiar with over 20,000 words.

When you were ten, you understood the meanings of close to 35,000 different words.

From ages six to ten, you were learning new words, without making any conscious effort to do so, at the rate of thousands a year.

But from your twenties on, unless you were a voracious reader, unless your learning continued, your rate of vocabulary increase slowed down to 100 new words *or less* each year of your life.

So it is reasonable to assume that, unless you are an exception to the rule, your greatest period of vocabulary growth was during the early years of your life—

The years during which the world held its greatest and freshest novelty for you, the years when *you wanted to learn,* because learning is natural to childhood, youth, and early maturity, and when words were the conveyors of thought and information, the means by which your curiosity was satisfied—

The years when you read more books (again, unless you are an exception to the general rule) than you will read all the rest of your life—*unless you consciously plan otherwise.*

Bearing in mind, then, that a large vocabulary is best achieved by wide-ranging learning and by intensive and varied reading, what can you do?

What, indeed, must you do?

You must read more—*much more.*

You may have to double, triple, even quadruple the amount of reading you have been doing in the past—assuming your vocabulary is not as extensive as it should be, assuming that your unfamiliarity with words gets in the way of rapid and accurate comprehension.

You must, furthermore, change your reading habits to include the better magazines, the more adult newspapers, a greater range of nonfiction books in a wider variety of fields.

And you must be on the alert for any new words you meet in your reading.

What is the best way to learn new words while reading?

The *seemingly* logical method is to keep a dictionary at your side.

There are some conscientious individuals who follow the practice of doggedly thumbing through their dictionaries for any word whose meaning they cannot immediately grasp. This is an excellent idea, admittedly, as far as vocabulary building is concerned. However, constant shifting from book or magazine to dictionary not only obviously slows reading to a snail's pace, but, more important, sets up numerous interruptions to complete concentration.

Here is a much more practical method:

1. Let any new word you encounter in your reading register, for a second or so, in your mind.

2. Spend a few more seconds guessing its probable or possible meaning from the context. If no clues are available, *just register the word in the back of your mind*, and continue reading.

That's all.

Just two steps.

The rest happens without any further effort on your part. Because you spend a few seconds registering a new word in your mind, and puzzling about it, the next time you meet it, it will have a stronger impact than it did the first time.

And you *will* meet it again—because you are now conscious of its existence, and are, without realizing it, on the alert for its next appearance.

Each time you meet this new word in a different context, its meaning will become a little clearer to you. Or, if you misunderstood its meaning (or failed to get any meaning) the first time, the second appearance will begin to set you straight. And the third and fourth and subsequent appearances will add a little more to the meaning.

Eventually, new words will become old friends!

Then subsequent encounters will not detract from your reading speed, and will add to the completeness of your comprehension.

Remember: unless you become *alert* to new words, your mind will skip over them, will be unaware of their existence, no matter how often you may meet them.

If you rated low on the vocabulary test in this chapter, you may wish to take more active steps toward increasing your familiarity with words.

On page 230 you will find a list of excellent vocabulary builders, all available in inexpensive paperback editions, that will considerably speed up the process of adding to your recognition vocabulary. Spend an hour several times a week with one or more of these books—you may find, to your amazement and delight, that the words you have directly studied will occur with incredible frequency in your everyday reading. What is happening is that as you learn new words, you become more keenly aware of them when you meet them; the thrill of recognition adds both to your pleasure and comprehension when you read; and even high-level, difficult material that once might have baffled and turned you off now grows increasingly easier to understand and more enjoyable to read.

Bear this important fact in mind:

A poor vocabulary is one of the major obstacles to speed and accuracy of comprehension.

SESSION 23

PERCEPTION TRAINING V

Perception Exercise 15

The instructions for this type of perception exercise are as follows:

Rely as much as possible on *visual* responses.

Once you have registered the *key* word in your mind, do not think of the *meaning* of any of the words that follow it. Try not to "hear" the words; simply snap a picture of the key word; then scan the rest of the line to find, *quickly*, any identical pictures. A line may contain one to three repetitions of the key word. With a pen or pencil check each such repetition as it occurs.

If you fail to find a repetition of the key word at your first scan, *do not go back*.

Simply go on to the next line and slow down a bit.

After you have established your time spent on the exercise, count your checked words, and compare your result with the correct answer at the end of the exercise.

Your goal: Finish in 40 seconds or less, with 90% accuracy.

Time at this moment: _____ minutes _____ seconds

Start timing!
Key Word

1. **groan**   growl   grew   grate   groan   grow   groan   green

2. **grate**   rasp   gruff   grate   grand   grail   great   grate

3. **played**   plaid   played   player   paid   played   plant   plans   played

4. **pause**   power   paws   plain   port   pause   pot   paw   pose   post

5. **beg**   bigger   beg   big   bag   beggar   bog   bog   beg

6. **catch**   thatch   hatch   catch   catch   clutch   crouch   crunch   catch

7. **dairy**   dirty   diary   dowry   dreary   dairy   fairy   dairy

8. **flame**   flume   flames   flame   flare   flair   flame   flow

9. **easter**   eater   eastern   eaten   easter   easter   each   easy

10. **joust**   just   judged   jest   joust   jump   joust   jousted

11. **harsh**   arch   starch   harsh   hard   harm   harsh   harmed

12. **cramped**   crazy   cramped   croon   crammed   cramped   crumb   cramped   crazed

13. **ganged**   gong   going   ganged   gang   growing   go   gauged   gone

14. **ideas**   ideal   ideas   idea   idiot   idle   ideas   idol

15. **kinky**   kingly   kinkier   kinky   kink   kill   key

16. **nap**   nap   net   napped   nit   nap   night   nice

17. **maker**   maker   making   masher   mashed   masker   maker   make

18. **prey**   pray   preyed   prey   prayer   prays   preys   prey

19. **queer**   queen   quilt   queer   quoit   quaint   queerer   queer

20. **gnawed**   gnu   gnaw   gnash   gnawed   gnarl   gnaws

21. **stray**   strew   strain   strap   strewn   stray   strayed   stray

22. **zeroed**   zeroes   zeros   zinc   zeroed   zest   zoom

23. **rest**   lest   most   rest   test   feast   rest   east   rest

24. **opened**   over   opal   opera   opened   open   opening

25. **loft**   loved   aloft   lofty   loft   loftier   loft   lover

Stop timing!

Time spent _____ **seconds**   **Total number of repetitions: 49**   **Number you found:** _____ (44 is 90% accuracy)

Perception Exercise 16

Ready for a slightly greater challenge? Find *two identical words* on each line. These identities may occur anywhere on the line, *but the two words will be right next to each other.*

Scan each line, snapping pictures as you go along, maintaining a high speed, and ignoring sounds and meanings. Check the two identical words as soon as you find them, and then go on to the next line.

If you fail to find the identical pair at the first scan, *do not go back.* Simply go on to the next line and try again.

Your Goal: Finish in 40 seconds with 90% accuracy.

Time at this moment: _____minutes _____seconds

Start timing!

1. art acted astral arty aster asked asked

2. dream drizzle drop drip drip drown drank

3. pill pail pall preach peachy peach peach parch

4. fled flies fed flap flees fleas fleas pleas frees

5. blown black blued blues blows blue blue belt

6. trash task task tang tangle tart tank mask tart

7. fresh flesh fish flush flash flash flat fling flow

8. kin kine dill kiss kind killed key keys keys

9. freeze froze freer freely fleas frees frees fries flies

10. cat cast cant car car curs cast catch curse

11. glide glint grant glow glance grunt grunt gnash

12. vie vane vial vest best vine vine vain veer

13. west wet wait want will will wash wish went

14. wry wry wring wrest wriggle why wiggle rest

15. extra fix nix asked axes axed axed asker

16. black back brick bock block block buck

17. crack cricket creak creak creek croak clock

18. broom brook brook brink drink brooked bracket

19. frisk frisky freak frank free flack flask flask

20. dill fill fill mill pill rill still shill will

21. goal toll mole knoll wall whole hole hole

22. sprint spring sprawl sprain spray spray string

23. quail whale wail wail bail pail stale fail

24. we're were fear near clear mere mere shear

25. bank blank blink blink plink black pink

Stop timing!

Time required: _____seconds   Number of correct choices: _____ (22-23 is 90% accuracy)

Perception Exercise 17

This type of perception exercise is extremely valuable. It sharpens your concentration; reinforces your sense of urgency; mobilizes your energy; thwarts vocalization, lip movements, and inner speech; and helps you react instantaneously to visual stimuli.

So I ask you to try once again, possibly decreasing, however slightly, the time you require to find a pair of identical words on each line.

Your goal, as before, is to finish in 40 seconds or less with 90% accuracy.

Time at this moment: _____ minutes _____ seconds

Start timing!

1. wry   why   right   tight   wine   wiry   rye   rye   while

2. tight   sight   sight   light   might   mite   site   fright

3. show   shower   slow   slower   slower   slough   showed

4. prime   line   slime   prune   tune   time   time   crime   grime

5. crash   trash   clash   clash   wash   mash   lash   hash

6. grab   grab   gab   grain   grub   groom   growl   gruel

7. drizzly   frizzy   tizzy   busy   dizzy   dizzy   cosy

8. clothes   close   clot   cloth   cloth   clear   clay   clean

9. bare   bake   bade   bide   boat   bear   bear   bride

10. dusty   dirty   dusky   duty   dreary   dreamy   dreamy

11. plover   tower   power   power   lower   shower

12. mover   drover   stove   prove   prove   love   poorer

13. shallow   bellow   below   below   pillow   shadow

14. strong   strung   strangle   straight   straight   strait

15. spring   sprung   spear   prowl   sprat   spry   spry

16. market   marked   marker   marsh   marsh   marshal

17. bull   bull   ball   bill   boll   able   about   bale

18. fling   slung   sly   flew   flu   flick   flue   flue

19. trail   train   thrust   thrush   trust   trust   thrum

20. gamble   gambol   gambol   gallon   gallop   grumble

21. hutch   hatch   hitch   hitch   teach   fetch   witch   which

22. glove   grain   gave   give   groove   groove   wave

23. milk   muck   mike   mick   match   much   much

24. clack click click cluck clock crotch crack croak

25. when why who which whether where where wear
Stop timing!

Time required: _____ **Number of correct choices:** _____ **(22-23 is 90% accuracy)**

Perception Exercise 18

Run your eyes rapidly down each column, allowing only one fixation in the center of each line, as indicated by the arrow, and with decreased reliance on inner speech. The criterion of success is clear and continuous comprehension.

↓

In the
Bronx Zoo,
New York City,
lives Jack,
a 21-foot giraffe.
You will have
no difficulty
recognizing him
—he has such
a long neck!
You can imagine
how little
he has
to exert himself
to reach
the top
of his cage
(And he
reaches it
quite often,
because he
likes to lick

↓

the paint
with his
12-inch tongue!)
Would you like
to know
what Jack eats?
Here is
his daily menu:
1¾ pails
of oats,
12 potatoes,
an apple,
3 carrots,
half a cabbage,
and 25 pounds
of hay.
That's a
considerable amount
of food,
isn't it?
But if you weighed
over 2,000 pounds

↓

(as Jack does)
you'd doubtless need
just a much
food.
Giraffes belong to
a vanishing race,
and can be found
in just
a few places
in Africa.
They are timid,
can run swiftly
and like
to feed
on the top leaves
of trees.
Do you think
perhaps
that's the way
they acquired
their long necks?

How was your comprehension under the conditions required? ☐ good ☐ fair ☐ poor

Perception Exercise 19

Continue as before.

Most of us	Harlan Major,	uncommonly rich
think of sharks	a New York	in Vitamin A
as fearful fish	fishing authority,	(something that
that chew off	stopped at	keeps people
swimmers' legs	Fort Bragg	strong and healthy).
and in other	when he made	Chemical laboratories
disagreeable ways	a fishing tour	were buying
make general nuisances	of the country.	all the soup-fin
of themselves.	He was amazed	shark livers
But the people	at the great activity	they could
of Fort Bragg,	going on there,	get hold of
California,	for Fort Bragg,	to make into
will tell you	once a sleepy little	little pills
with no uncertainty	fishing village,	for people who
that sharks are	was now experiencing	wish to avoid
their best friends—	unusual prosperity.	illnesses.
many a	Mr. Major decided	And so every day
local fisherman	to find out why.	the Fort Bragg
has become richer	He went to	fishermen
catching the huge	San Francisco	put out to sea
creatures	and learned	to look for
and selling them	that the livers	the fearful creatures
at $210 a ton	of soup-fin sharks	whose livers are
in the San Francisco	(the kind	keeping a nation
market.	around Fort Bragg)	in good health!
	had proved to be	

How was your comprehension under the conditions
required? ☐ good ☐ fair ☐ poor

SESSION 24

SENSING STRUCTURE

The final goal of all your training is rapid, accurate *comprehension*. All your work in perception, in vocabulary building, and in eliminating blocks (of whatever nature) to smooth, speedy cruising through print aims, ultimately, at *good comprehension*.

To continue your training, I offer you two selections of comparable length.

Read each one with a *sense of urgency;* be aggressively postured to get in, to get the main idea quickly and accurately, to note the structure and organization of the material, and to realize that the details exist to support, clarify, or sharpen the central point.

Read, I repeat, with a *sense of urgency,* but not so fast as to lose all comprehension.

These are *timed exercises,* followed by comprehension tests and rate charts.

SELECTION 13

The Sudden Handicap
by Kate Holliday

Time at start: _____ minutes _____ seconds

Start timing ➡ [1] Let me make it clear from the beginning that while I am physically handicapped, what has happened to me is bearable. That point is important, for there are millions of disabled people who are not so fortunate.

[2] But even that small bit of comfort cannot alter the essential fact that on the night of Oct. 26, 1973, I lost forever the use of 50% of my right shoulder. Due to the muscle deterioration that inevitably follows such an injury, I shall probably lose even more strength in the shoulder and right arm.

[3] It is, I know, almost silly to rage against misfortune. But the suddenness with which mine occurred makes it difficult to accept. I have grappled with it for more than two years, and still I cannot understand how so common an accident could have such irrevocable consequences.

[4] I know almost the exact time my mishap occurred—a few minutes after 1 a.m.—because I had just switched off the Dick Cavett show. The program had been funny, so I was still smiling as I stuffed a paper bag with the last of that day's trash and prepared to add it to the week's accumulation, which would be collected some hours later.

[5] After turning on the porch light, I descended the four steps to the front walk, and headed for the cans I had earlier placed at the curb.

[6] The next thing I knew I was staring at the stars.

[7] In shock. With not a soul around.

[8] Help finally came, and I was taken to a hospital. That moment on the walk was to change the rest of my life. Yet it was an accident that need not have happened. It was not the result of the calculated risks of war or of driving on the freeway, but of cracked, uneven cement.

[9] I shall never—ever—be whole again. The mishap has affected the way I make a living, the way I sleep, the way I hug my grandchildren, the way I shake hands, the way I drive a car, the way I write my name and, perhaps worst of all, my entire way of thinking.

[10] The fall broke my right shoulder so badly that, even after two years, the fracture has not healed. For more than four months, I have sat immobile, my arm in an orthopedic sling. I have twice undergone surgery, and my doctors talk of more. For now, there is pain.

[11] There are also challenges to the mind, and countless new situations to which I must adjust. For the first time in my life I am forced to say, *I cannot do that. I will never be able to do that again.* It is tough to accept all this without self-pity; to accept, and still keep my confidence; to accept, and get on with my job as a professional reporter.

[12] I have a friend who came down with polio while in high school and lost the use of one leg. Now he is 70. I asked him once if he had any discomfort. "No," he answered, very slowly. "But it's always there . . ."

[13] I did not know quite what he meant then. I do now. A handicap is always "there," creating its own traps.

[14] Shyness is one. When you have been isolated for months and finally go out, you find yourself talking too much about anything, just to prove you are still among the living, and you are mortified later.

[15] Finally, you come to realize that not everyone cares about your predicament. So, I now try to appear normal for as long as possible, and admit my limitations only when faced with something truly impossible.

[16] Even as a young woman, I was not particularly athletic, but I have always been active. (Odd-

ly, my best sport was swimming; now I can barely stay afloat.) As a war correspondent during the Korean conflict, I spent two weeks aboard the aircraft carrier Princeton off Wonsan, climbing up and down the ship's ladders with the swabbies. Today, I am haunted by those scenes, and I wonder a little crazily, *Could you climb a ladder with one arm?*

[17] I have long hair, worn coiled in a bun on the top of my head. But because I cannot raise my arm out to the side, let alone above the shoulder, I can do my hair each day only through a series of physical contortions.

[18] I can no longer lift anything heavier than a few pounds. This presents special problems, because I live alone, my children being grown and long gone. The crunch came last year when I had to move into a new house. Using my one good arm, I struggled with dozens of boxes of belongings, including 3000 books. Since I couldn't reach the volumes on the highest shelves, I finally paid $15 to a neighborhood teenager to get them down and boxed.

[19] Being left-handed, I was fortunate to have broken my right shoulder. My misfortune is that I was raised in the era when everyone was taught to write with the right hand. Because it was also the era of the stick shift that was how I learned to drive, too. Today I give thanks for my automatic transmission.

[20] But taking notes (my left-handed writing is illegible, even to me) is a painful ordeal, as is typing. I do both at a snail's pace, and have little sense of control. At the typewriter, I zig when I should zag. I apologize in advance to my editors in New York for typographical errors. I bless the inventor of Corrassable Bond.

[21] Time was when I could work for four or five hours at a stretch, with only an occasional ice-tea break. Now I know that my shoulder will become rigid after 30 minutes, and that when it does I must stop for a series of exercises—which may help, if the weather is not too chilly. I have a book to write, and an agent waiting for it, but I have not yet overcome the fear that I may be unable to complete such a large project.

[22] Fear is very real, in every aspect of my condition. I have a constant horror of taking another fall. I can read a medical report about "atrophy" and see it in my own mirror. How, in the years ahead, can I make ends meet? How much longer can I continue to work, even at my diminished pace? If I risk further surgery, might I lose forever what mobility I still possess?

[23] I am one of the "lucky" ones. I can do many things which others who have been suddenly handicapped cannot. But, I and those like me have been thrust into a limited world for the first time— a world of pain and fear and questions, always questions. Others ask them of us, and we desperately ask our own, both outwardly and inwardly. We can only hope to receive the right replies.

[24] In the end, there remains that elemental question, which I may never have answered, Why? Not the whining, self-pitying, Why *me*, but because there must be a reason for all this, just purely and simply, *Why?* ◄ **Stop timing!**

Time at finish _____ minutes _____ seconds

Total time elapsed: _____ minutes _____ seconds

Comprehension Test

1. To express the central thought in your own words, complete the following, as briefly as possible:

A handicap is _____

_____, creating _____

_____

and leaving the victim with that elemental question: _____

2. Where did the accident occur? _____

_____

3. What was the bodily injury caused by the accident?

_____

4. List some of the results of the handicaps caused by the accident:

_____

_____

_____

_____

_____

5. How would you describe the author's state of mind (at the time she wrote this article)? _____

Compute Your Rate
(Approximate Number of Words: 1150)

Time	WFM	Time	WPM
45 sec.	1533	2 min. 15 sec.	511
50 sec.	1380	2 min. 30 sec.	460
55 sec.	1254	2 min. 45 sec.	418
1 min.	1150	3 min.	383
1 min. 10 sec.	986	3 min. 15 sec.	354
1 min. 15 sec.	920	3 min. 30 sec.	329
1 min. 20 sec.	863	3 min. 45 sec.	307
1 min. 30 sec.	767	4 min.	288
1 min. 40 sec.	690	4 min. 15 sec.	271
1 min. 45 sec.	657	4 min. 30 sec.	255
1 min. 50 sec.	627	4 min. 45 sec.	242
2 min.	575	5 min.	230

Your rate on selection 13: _____WPM

(Record this rate on the chart and graph on page 235)

(Consider for a moment this obvious, but possibly startling, fact: If you now cruise along at 575 to 650 WPM, you take less than half as long to complete the same material—and with more dynamic comprehension—as the untrained person who reads at 250 WPM!)

Discussion of Selection 13

Paragraphs 1–3 set the stage—*this is what happened to me and this is how I feel about it*. Reading aggressively, you note these paragraphs as introductory (as most first paragraphs are, of course), and begin to look for *what happened, how it happened, and what the writer's reactions were and continue to be*. You are now *dominating* the material, making demands that may (or may not) be fulfilled, but your demands keep your concentration and comprehension sharp.

Paragraphs 4–8 describe the accident—now you know what happened, when, and where. (Answer to *Question 2* of the Comprehension Test: *On the walk in front of the porch*)

Paragraph 9 gives you some of the results of the accident—*never be whole, affects the way I make a living, sleep, etc., etc.*, thus telling you in greater detail the results of the accident; reading dynamically, you tick off in your mind, "As a result, the author is different in ways *a, b, c,* etc."

Paragraph 10 tells you, specifically, what the injury was (*Answer to Question 3: Broke her right shoulder*) and paragraphs 11–22 explore in depth the writer's reactions to the handicap. (*Answers to Question 4: shyness; fear; inability to raise arm; inability to lift; difficulty in writing,*

typing, taking notes; shoulder rigidity; worry about falling, making ends meet, continuing to work, etc.)

Paragraphs 23 and 24 are concluding statements about the author's state of mind. As you read, you are aware that Ms. Holliday is telling you how she feels—lucky that the handicap is not worse; yet angry or desperate, perhaps, because of having to live in a limited world of pain and fear and questions. Possibly there is even a subtle implication of acceptance and/or resignation (This is reading meaning *behind* meaning, as in the Jack Smith articles.) Your answer to *Question 5* might contain some of these feelings that the author states or implies.

Reading dynamically, you sense that the structure of the piece is clear and simple: *This is what happened; these are the results; this is how I feel.*

Your answer to Question 1 might be somewhat as follows, in your own words:

A handicap is *always there*, creating *its own traps*, and leaving the victim with that elemental question: *Why?*

Scoring of Comprehension Test

1: 50%; 2: 10%; 3: 20%; 4: 10% (2% for each of up to five results); 5: 10%.

Your comprehension score on Selection 13: _____%

"THEME" AND "VARIATIONS"

I ask you to read the next selection with pen or pencil in hand.

As you sweep through the content, decide which paragraphs are *"theme,"* which are *"variations."*

To put these instructions another way: *As you read, decide which paragraphs contain the "point," "message," "main idea" (call it what you will), and which paragraphs support, clarify, or flesh out the "point," etc.*

In any way that appeals to you, check, underline, bracket, or whatever, those paragraphs that play the "theme," deliberately going faster through (even partially skimming), the paragraphs that play the "variations."

Thus, you will be consciously controlling your rate while dominating the material—slowing down where the content is *central*, speeding up where the content is *marginal* or *peripheral*.

(This is an excellent, productive technique, incidentally, for college textbook study, or for going through technical or professional papers or articles that you wish to wring the main ideas out of in a minimum of time and with undistracted concentration.)

SELECTION 14

For June Graduates, a Few Words About Work
by Peter P. Bruno, Jr.

Time at start: _____ minutes _____ seconds

Start timing ➡ [1] With June and commencement fast approaching, I have some advice for all those liberal arts students who are having trouble lining up work upon graduation. Avoid whining about the paucity of comfortable and lucrative jobs; avoid desperately seeking admission to an economic system that is progressively shutting you out. Instead, let me suggest this alternative: Rather than sulk—rejoice.

[2] You have a chance to become members of an emerging class—the unemployed or menially employed liberal-arts graduate. I have personally been one for five years now, working off and on as a truck driver, and without facetiousness I can say I like it. Far from bemoaning what you may regard as an unfortunate and unfair situation, accept with excitement the new role that awaits you.

[3] It seems you have yet to perceive the grand irony: The very scholastic achievements on which you hope to capitalize are alien to the system that offers and denies jobs. You studied art, philosophy, literature, the classics and foreign languages; as a result, you became more sensitive, rational, perceptive and a little more human. Of what use are such attributes to a system in thrall to greed, acquisitiveness and surface appearance?

[4] You deceive yourselves if you think the system will leave your ideals intact. Your true calling as a liberal artist is to remain on the outer fringes, making sure that the country does not become wholly one of merchandisers and technicians.

[5] You presumably became involved in liberal arts because a few hours with James Joyce seemed inherently more meaningful than driving down the highway in a new silver Porsche. Hold onto that belief, even if that means doing a menial job.

[6] Dissatisfaction is going to come easily, but it can prove useful, for dissatisfaction foments change. It may enhance your desire to examine problems and questions that would otherwise have remained at a distance. Dissatisfaction will heighten your ability to perceive the real villains in our society and the reason there seems to be little use for you these days.

[7] Realize too that not only you but also the tradition you represent are in grave danger. In fact, if you doubt the worth of your diploma in the marketplace, that shows just how fragile the tradition is. The natural question arising from such doubt is this: Why bother at all with the liberal arts if there is no job or profession at the end of four expensive years of college?

[8] Indeed, there are those who argue that liberal arts graduates have no valid place in a modern technological society where mass-produced canvasses already pass as art and where sales potential determines what is to be published as literature and made into film. If you wholeheartedly participate in such a society, how can you express outrage to those attempting to subvert what you believe in?

[9] Be prepared for the inevitable questions that are going to slap you in the face. Pity and mockery often mix when others ask, "So what are you going to do now?" Or, "Can you do anything with that degree?"

[10] You can offer several replies:
I will practice living.

I will develop my intellect, which may incidentally contribute to the elevation of the aesthetic and cultural levels of society.

I will try to develop the noble and creative elements within me.

I will contribute very little to the grossness of the national product.

[11] Artists by the thousands are scooping ice cream. Poets are changing oil. Philosophers are driving taxicabs. The reconciliation of these apparent incongruities may be the greatest problem of all, especially for those of you who have never dirtied your hands, endured blisters or felt exhausted after eight hours of tedium. Yet there are rewards to reap.

[12] You might think that after five years of "meaningless" and "unintellectual" work, I would have become increasingly disillusioned with my liberal arts education. On the contrary, my struggle has intensified my appreciation and respect for that education. The environment in which I intermittently work is so hostile and alien to what I most cherish—literature, art and unrestrained imagination—that when opportunity comes, the intellectual rewards and satisfaction I derive from reading a brilliant novel or viewing a splendid piece of abstract art are much more exciting and vital to me.

[13] I work alongside people who attempt to secure meaning for their lives by pursuing the tawdry baubles that American industry has to offer: They grind away their lives in pursuit of junk. The kind of rote work I do has its own rewards, for it gives me a closeup look at how society victimizes people and depreciates values.

[14] I work for money only when I must; other-

wise, my time is my own. I take off when I want to, savoring a unique freedom that the 40-hour-a-week regulars regard with a certain disbelief laced with a quiet bitterness.

[15] Most have difficulty believing me when I speak of the rich experiences that my meager annual income allows. In the years since I graduated from college, I have traveled thousands of miles and visited many countries. I have seen more films, visited more museums, read more books, done more thinking and talked with more people than would have been possible had I immediately embraced a 9-to-5 job upon graduating.

[16] Above all, I have discovered the validity of some observations made by Henry Miller in "Tropic of Capricorn"—words which I probably never would have encountered had I been bogged down in work:

[17] Even if there were a job for me to fill, I couldn't accept it, because what I needed was not work but a life more abundant. I couldn't waste time being a teacher, a lawyer, a physician, a politician or anything else that society has to offer. It was easier to accept menial jobs because it left my mind free. ◄ **Stop timing!**

Time at finish: _____ minutes _____ seconds

Total time elapsed: _____ minutes _____ seconds

Comprehension Test

Indicate the numbers of the paragraphs that contain the central theme: _____

Compute Your Rate
(Approximate Number of Words: 1050)

Time	WPM	Time	WPM
45 sec.	1400	2 min.	525
50 sec.	1255	2 min. 15 sec.	467
55 sec.	1145	2 min. 30 sec.	420
1 min.	1050	2 min. 45 sec.	382
1 min. 10 sec.	900	3 min.	350
1 min. 15 sec.	840	3 min. 15 sec.	323
1 min. 20 sec.	788	3 min. 30 sec.	300
1 min. 30 sec.	700	3 min. 45 sec.	280
1 min. 40 sec.	630	4 min.	263
1 min. 45 sec.	600	4 min. 15 sec.	247
1 min. 50 sec.	573	4 min. 30 sec.	233

Your rate on selection 14: _____ WPM

(Record your rate on the chart and graph on page 235)

Answers to Comprehension Test

Important paragraphs of Selection 14: 1, 2, 12, 17.

The "theme" occurs for the first time at the end of paragraph 1—*Rather than sulk—rejoice.*

This "theme" is continued at the beginning of paragraph 2, first sentence.

The rest of the material, up to paragraph 12, plays "variations" on the "theme," with details, specifics, examples, etc.—all of it interesting and valuable as support and argument, but so clearly "variation," rather than "theme," that you can skim, or at least speed up, if the central thought is what you wish to *rip out* quickly and efficiently.

Paragraph 12 plays the "theme" in greater depth followed by elaboration (and from paragraphs 13 through 16

you can speed up). Finally, the quote from Henry Miller (paragraph 17) repeats the "theme" once again.

Notice how you can control the material, and thus vary your rate, by knowing your purpose beforehand, and by learning how to distinguish "theme" from "variations," *main ideas* from *supporting details.*

Do you wish only the gist? *Concentrate on the "theme," speed over the details.*

Do you wish to enjoy the details, while clearly aware that they *are* details in support of the main idea? *Go slower!*

You are the master. *You* can suit your rate to what you want out of material. *You* can choose the best tool for getting the job done the way *you* want it done.

Inefficient readers have *one* rate, and they read *everything* at that *one* rate.

As I have said, and it bears repeating, no workers who are skillful—whether surgeons, artists, potters, carpenters, plumbers—come to a job with only *one* tool.

No readers who are skillful approach all material in the same way, or at the same rate.

A SECOND CHALLENGE TO YOUR READING HABITS

Toward the end of chapter 7, a point you reached some time ago, I challenged you to read a complete novel in a single evening. Have you met this challenge?

If you have (and I assume that as a serious student you are following every item of your training with scrupulous care), fill in the statistics required on the chart below.

First Novel Read in One Sitting

1. Title of novel: _____

2. Author: _____

3. Total number of pages: _____

4. Total number of hours and minutes spent in reading:

_____

5. Approximate number of words in the novel: (To arrive at this statistic, turn to any full page in the book, compute the average number of words per line, and multiply by the number of lines on the page. Then multiply your last figure by the number of pages in the book): _____

6. Your average rate of reading (To arrive at this statistic, reduce the figure in item 4 to minutes (for example 3 hours, 20 minutes would be 200 minutes), and divide this into the figure in item 5. Thus, if the novel contains approximately 100,000 words, you divide 200 into 100,000 and get as a result 500 WPM.): _____

You are now ready for your second challenge. As you know, the guiding principle of this or any other training program is that as soon as you comfortably attain a certain degree of skill or excellence in your performance, the goals are set just a little higher, and you have to draw once again on your innate capacities, you have to strive once again for a new pinnacle.

To prepare you for your next pinnacle I ask you to fill out a second chart:

Novels Read and Unread

Fill in below the title (and authors, if you remember them) of *five* novels you have read in the last six months. (If you have not read five novels in that period of time—and that averages out to less than one every four weeks—write down as many as you have read.)

1. _____

2. _____

3. _____

4. _____

5. _____

Now fill in the names of *four* novels you intended to read, but somehow never got around to. (If you are not a novel-reader, and have never said to yourself, "That's a book I want to read," make a choice of four titles from the recommended list on pages 219–221, or choose four novels by the authors recommended on these pages; or, if you prefer, ask your friends or your local librarian to suggest the sort of book you would probably enjoy.)

1. _____

2. _____

3. _____

4. _____

Of the four titles listed above, obtain any *two* from a convenient source—borrow them from a friend or from your library, buy them from a bookshop, or pick them up in inexpensive reprint editions at a book or department store, supermarket, or paperback newsstand.

And then attempt to meet this second challenge to your reading habits: Within the next week, no more, read these two novels, *each in a single evening,* going fast enough to get through in three to five hours of concentrated reading, skimming or skipping wherever and whenever you wish and aiming for a quick total picture of the plot. This should not be a difficult assignment for you at this point in your training—the only obstacle you are likely to encounter is that you may not find the time.

But one doesn't *find* time for leisure reading—one *makes* the time. (You will not learn to enjoy reading, you will not become a rapid and skillful reader, if you dip into books only occasionally or at odd moments or for a few minutes before you fall off to sleep at night. Some people use books and reading purely as a sedative, as a kind of harmless sleeping pill, when they get into bed—*this is not for you if you wish to become a better reader.*) And you *can* make the time during the next week, you *can* arrange your schedule in such a way that two evenings out of the next seven will be free for reading—you can if you really want to. Possibly you are working on *this* book in the evenings—if so, allocate two of the evenings you planned to devote to your training to the reading of novels.

Before you start each book, note the total number of pages and decide, from your previous experience with reading a novel in one sitting, approximately how long it will take you to get through. Then figure how many pages you should read every hour in order to meet your self-imposed deadline—*and see to it that you meet it.* (This discipline, which is known as "pacing oneself," is, all by itself, a remarkable and effective method of developing faster reading habits.) As before, keep a record of the number of hours and minutes spent in actual reading.

If you can meet this challenge successfully (and you can if you honestly try), think what it will mean. At the rate of two novels a week, you can cover (allowing some weeks for the reading of nonfiction or of magazines) *50 to 100 novels* in the next year, whereas, in sharp contrast, you may have been unable to fill in a simple list of only *five* novels read in the last six months.

You may wonder, now, whether good readers do in fact read two full books a week. They do, indeed—*at least two.* They make the time for books, because reading books is, for them, an extremely *pleasurable and relaxing activity*—and even the busiest people, if they are at all sensible, devote some part of their 24-hour day to pleasure and relaxation.

You too can enjoy reading two or more books a week. Try it, and discover for yourself that reading is a more active, far more stimulating, and—given the present state of both arts—much more exciting activity than watching TV.

According to a survey published in the *Wall Street Journal*, the average American household spends 43 hours a week gazing at the picture tube.

Imagine how much your reading skill would improve if you spent even half that time reading books!

How to Read
with Aggressive
Comprehension

PREVIEW

Chapter 9 offers you additional practice in speeding up your comprehension; shows you how to use a new technique for increasing the usability for your peripheral vision; and asks you to make a detailed evaluation of your progress to date.

Aggressive readers *push* through material, intent on basic meaning, on main ideas.

They sense the structure and organization of writing.

They do not get enmeshed in details, but instead see details in proper perspective—as a means of giving impact, convincingness, and solidity to an author's central message.

And it is this *central message*, above all else, that aggressive readers want to grasp as quickly and as accurately as possible.

In Chapter 9, you continue training the aggressiveness of your own comprehension. For this purpose you will:

• Work on two time-checked selections, driving for the gist, the central idea, the "theme" as distinguished from the "variations"

• Become more adept at recognizing an author's pattern of thinking

• Learn more about how subordinate details serve to introduce, support, clarify, explain, or illustrate main ideas

• Develop still further your ability to speed through words and get down efficiently to central meaning

SESSION 25

RESPONDING TO CENTRAL MEANING

To read aggressively, you must get into the habit of viewing material *as a whole,* instead of passively absorbing it thought by thought, sentence by sentence, or word by word.

You have probably made a good start at developing this valuable habit. In the selections you worked on in previous chapters, you attempted to react to material as a *unit* by purposely seeking out the answer to one dominating question—namely, *What, in essence, is the author trying to say, What is the main idea of the piece, What is the central meaning that all the words and sentences add up to?* (And these are not, of course, three separate questions, but only three ways of framing the same question.)

This, no matter in what form we express it, is the important question you must force all material to answer—and you must learn to extract that answer quickly and skillfully from the mass of words and details.

But in order to find, and respond actively to, the central meaning of material, you must be able, as you read, to "touch the mind of the writer in his writing" (as John Ciardi, the eminent poet and critic, has so well phrased it); you must be able to meet the writer at least halfway; you must be able to think along with the writer. When you can do all this, when you can accurately sense how writers have organized their thinking and in what pattern they are presenting their thoughts to you, *then* you will be able— confidently, efficiently, and speedily—to strip a page down to its essentials; *then* you will be reading aggressively.

If you practice correctly and conscientiously on the two long selections in this chapter, you will find yourself moving a little closer to your goal of becoming an aggressive and rapid reader. Cruise through each selection with conscious pressure on your speed, with an awareness that you are going fast. Pay no attention to fixations or eye movements, and make no attempt to inhibit inner speech—these factors will take care of themselves if you follow the other instructions carefully. Do, however, avoid unnecessary regressions—if a word or a phrase eludes you, keep plowing ahead notwithstanding.

Keep clearly in mind that your dominating aim, as you read, is to grasp central meaning. To do this rapidly and accurately, try to sense the broad structure of the writing; try to get a feeling for the pattern the author is using in presenting material to you; try to realize how the details serve to highlight the main ideas, but don't let these details slow you up.

Skim or skip whenever you feel you can safely do so, that is, when you are pretty sure you know what a sentence or paragraph will contain. One of the overriding values of detecting the pattern of a piece is that you don't have to read every single word, or every single sentence, or every single paragraph—you know, by thinking along with the author's pattern of thinking, what is likely to come next, and whether it is important, less important, or completely unimportant to the central meaning of the selection.

You may not be able to follow these instructions with absolute success right away, even though you will try. But if you study carefully the discussion that follows each of the two pieces, you will continue learning more and more about structure and pattern, you will continue developing a keener sense for what the author is doing and of how the author is doing it.

With these selections you will keep timechecks on your reading so that you will have further statistical evidence of your continuing progress.

SELECTION 15

"Make Me a Child Again, Just for Tonight"
by Milton R. Stern

Time at start: _____ minutes _____ seconds

Start timing ➡

"Backward, turn backward, O
Time, in your flight,
Make me a child again just for
tonight."

[1] The lines above are from a poem called "Rock Me To Sleep, Mother," by Elizabeth Akers Allen, who was born in 1832 and died in 1911. By modern standards, this quotation is inexcusably sentimental and inaccurate. We moderns know better than to think of childhood as happy and carefree. We have gone to another, perhaps oversolemn, extreme. We hold that childhood is such a difficult time of life that we have child guidance associations and child study clinics and child psychologists and "child-centered" homes and a host of similar institutions in order to make childhood

endurable for the infants who have to live through it.

[2] But every age has its own kind of sentimentality, and we who have created the soap opera can scarcely afford to throw stones at the late Victorians.

[3] Sentimental as it may be, the quotation from Miss Allen's poem is worth a moment of study by people in evening classes for what it suggests about the learning process—in children and in grown-ups. If we mature adults who are studying in evening classes could be children again—just for that time we spend in class—we might be considerably surprised at how much faster and more easily we would learn.

[4] And if we cannot actually be children again, perhaps we can pick up a few helpful hints by turning backward ourselves, "just for tonight," and noticing some of the differences between the way children learn and the way grown-ups learn.

[5] Whatever the subject matter—whether it is the dates of English kings or how to pick pockets, like Oliver Twist—when it comes to learning something new, children usually learn faster than adults. A child in an unhappy situation may quickly acquire the habit of lying as a defense mechanism. But his luckier contemporaries thirstily drink in useful information of all kinds. First- and second-graders delight in the discovery of new words, new ideas, or new places on the map, African animals or the Museum of Natural History. They keep their teachers wedded to the profession by their enthusiastic curiosity, and they give their parents moments of enormous pleasure by their sudden, unexpected grasp of things.

[6] Adults, on the other hand, are by and large cautious learners. They are more timid than youngsters about asking questions. Adults have scar tissue—they are often afraid to ask questions for fear of seeming ridiculous. There are other ways in which grown-ups are handicapped as learners. They have many more demands on their time than children. They have more responsibilities—and these responsibilities cannot usually be lightly shrugged off.

[7] Furthermore, adults have often gotten more or less unconsciously into bad habits. Some adults have almost a compulsion to be "experts" on practically every subject that comes up, and others have drifted unaware into the habit of accepting whatever the "experts" say. Adults also are handicapped as students by the fact that they have largely got out of the habit of *listening*. And where first-graders are wholehearted scholars, warmly embracing the teacher as a learner, too, but equipped with more answers, the grown-ups have largely forgotten how to use their teachers, even as the bounce board of skeptical questioning.

[8] Evening college administrators say that adult experience is a priceless commodity in the classroom—for both teacher and students. And so it is. But experience is not enough. Attitude is equally important, and mature men and women need something of the enthusiasm and unself-consciousness of the child if they are to capitalize fully in the classroom on their life experience. But can grown people reacquire these qualities? Make-me-a-child-again-just-for-tonight is all very well, but is it really possible for the mature student to recapture some of the spontaneity of the six- or seven-year-old?

[9] I think it is.

[10] Perhaps a key idea to keep in mind is that of *purpose*—what educators (and the Navy) call motivation in learning. With children, motivation is easy to understand. Children literally thirst after knowledge, because they must. They have a long way to grow, and a major part of growth is the development of that subtle instrument, the mind. Actually, children have a natural or built-in motivation. They want to communicate and to be communicated with. They want to be in touch. They want mastery and power. They want to understand and to be understood.

[11] And children have sanction and approval for this almost instinctual drive. The whole society is organized to further it. Not only does the truant officer come after them if they stay away from school, but it is a rare parent who does not praise and take pride in the child's expanding knowledge.

[12] But with the adult student in evening classes, purpose does not operate in such an automatic and instinctive fashion. Nor does the adult student always come in for such complete approval and sanction in his efforts. Children, in their world, cannot afford not to know. It makes them too helpless and powerless. But adults, in their world, too often persuade themselves they can afford to be ignorant. How easy it is to find a rationalization to avoid trying to understand anything difficult. We all know how little time there is, how difficult it is to win mastery over any subject, and the omnipresent "experts" are all too eager to give us escape through the cliché of "A little knowledge is a dangerous thing" or "You can't teach an old dog new tricks." There is, too, the reality of an anti-intellectual climate of opinion. Indeed, it seems sometimes that if an adult knows enough to come in out of the rain, he may run into a certain amount of silent or open mockery when he aspires to anything further.

[13] Only when the purpose of evening study is very, very obvious can the adult student feel sure of social approval. If he does not speak English well and goes to an evening college to overcome

this handicap or if he needs more education to get into a better paying job, then he may feel fairly sure that nobody will try to dissuade him from studying in the afterschool years of life. But if his goal is not going to pay off immediately in some highly visible way, like more money or higher social prestige, then he not only has to go to school, he has to defend himself for going. Let him! He can do so boldly.

[14] "Does he propose to understand literature, music, art?"

[15] "Yes. Is there a better use of a man's time?"

[16] "Does he aspire to be an 'egghead,' then?"

[17] Let him answer, "Yes," enthusiastically. "There are thousands of us."

[18] But whatever we study, and whether we seek to overcome an obvious handicap of communication or information or technical skill, or whether we are sparked by curiosity about philosophy or chemistry, we will find such study most enjoyable and fruitful if it is approached in the way first- and second-graders approach the birth of rabbits or the circumstance that r-o-u-g-h is not pronounced the same as b-o-u-g-h.

[19] Make me a child again just for tonight? Each of us in the classroom or out, quizzing a teacher or reading a book, can be as active a learner as we were when we were six years old. We can take conscious account of our adult purposes and make them give us pleasure in learning in the same way as did our early, less conscious drives. There is the child in each of us. We have but to be aware of the fact and have the sense and courage to acknowledge it. ◀ **End timing**

Record here the time required on this selection: _____ minutes _____ seconds

Test Your Comprehension

Complete the following sentence in your own words to summarize the "theme" or central idea of selection 15: Adults would learn _____

_____

if they _____

_____

and if they _____,

_____

_____

Compute Your Rate (Approximate Number of Words: 1300)

Time	WPM	Time	WPM
45 sec.	1733	2 min. 45 sec.	480
50 sec.	1560	3 min.	435
1 min.	1300	3 min. 15 sec.	400
1 min. 15 sec.	1040	3 min. 30 sec.	370
1 min. 20 sec.	975	3 min. 45 sec.	345
1 min. 30 sec.	865	4 min.	325
1 min. 45 sec.	745	4 min. 15 sec.	305
2 min.	650	4 min. 30 sec.	290
2 min. 15 sec.	580	5 min.	260
2 min. 30 sec.	520	5 min. 30 sec.	235

Your rate on selection 15: _____ WPM

(Record this statistic on the chart and graph on page 235)

Discussion of the Selection

Glance back at the material, now, and notice the pattern Mr. Stern has followed in presenting his thinking to the reader:

Paragraphs 1 and 2 and the beginning of paragraph 3: Two lines from a poem are used as a springboard to the central theme.

Paragraph 3: The central "theme" is explicitly stated— *adults in evening classes would learn faster and more easily if they reacted the way children do.*

Paragraph 4: Transition.

Paragraphs 5 through 8: First part of the development of the central theme— *contrast between the learning attitudes, habits, and characteristics of children and of adults.* The last sentence of paragraph 8, in the form of a question, and the answer to that question in paragraph 9, serve as transition to paragraph 10.

Paragraphs 10 through 17: Second part of the development of the central theme— *adults, if they wish to learn as effectively as children do, should have the same purpose and drive that motivated their learning earlier in life.*

Paragraphs 18 and 19: Summary—the central "theme" is restated in terms of the two parts of its development, namely (1) *attitudes*, etc., and (2) *purpose and drives.*

Your answer to the comprehension test might have been phrased somewhat as follows:

Adults would *learn faster and more easily* if they *reacted the way children do*, and if they *had the same purpose and drive that motivated their own learning when they were children.*

Learning to sense structure as you read is not easy, and I am not for a moment pretending that it is. But with every selection you practice on, you will become a little surer, a little defter, in your technique. And as you study the discussion that follows each piece, you will learn to see a little more clearly how authors organize their thinking, how they develop a theme, how they use details and subordinate points to elaborate on, clarify, and drive home a main idea—in short, how they skillfully shape a mass of words into a unified and artistic *whole*. (The more skillful and lucid the writing, of course, the more clearly and easily will you be able to see all this.)

No doubt you realize that the selection you have just finished appears to contradict the paragraph on page 8, which claims that adults, not children, are the best learners. I suggest you reread that paragraph and decide whether it is possible to reconcile these seemingly opposed views. Or, if you find them unreconcilable, with which, from your own experience, do you agree?

The next selection is titled "Take It Easy to Learn Better."

Obviously, from the title, the author, Dr. Donald A. Laird, will write about *better learning*. Read with pen or pencil in hand, checking off the main points of Dr. Laird's *prescription for learning*.

Here is an instance in which the title indicates what the material will likely be concerned with. (Whenever possible, use a title, plus a subtitle, if there is one, to help you gear up for reading.)

Chapter titles, and subtitles of various parts of a chapter in a text intended for college, professional, or technical reading, indicate to you what central points to look for, and will sharpen your concentration as you aggressively look for them.

When you use titles and subtitles to develop questions in your mind that you will expect the writer to answer, *you will be thinking along with the author as these answers appear.*

One simple technique of aggressive reading is to use the cues deliberately provided by an author to prepare you for the ideas that are coming.

Use these cues to *ask questions*, then *look for answers.*

(If you are doing a study-type reading, check these answers off in pencil or marker pen as you find them. Then if you need to, you can review them quickly to tighten up your comprehension and retention.)

Try this technique as you whip through selection 16 looking for, and finding, *the principles of better learning* as Dr. Laird sees them.

SELECTION 16

Take It Easy to Learn Better
By Donald A. Laird, Sc.D.

Time at start: _____ minutes _____ seconds

I

Start timing ➡ [1] Spare-time learners are usually the best learners. Their rate of learning is helped, of course, by the fact that they want to learn and consequently try to learn. But they are also helped by circumstances—they are forced to take *their learning by easy stages*. Other work prevents them from applying themselves to learning for so long that they get dyspepsia of learning.

[2] Edgar Burchell, the janitor who became a leading medical scientist and teacher, is an example. He was one of nine children, and he had to leave school and go to work before finishing the grades. At twenty-two he was scrubbing floors twelve hours a day at the New York Eye and Ear Infirmary.

[3] But during his lunch hour he attended staff lectures, carefully pretending he was in the lecture amphitheater for janitor work, but drinking in every word that was said. When his twelve-hour stint was up he remained at the infirmary, watching the interns in the laboratory. "Teach me how you do these things," he said to them, "and I'll do them for you." Then, from his small savings, he bought a second-hand anatomy text which he studied in his other spare moments.

[4] Picking up his education in this way, Burchell made himself one of the world's authorities on bacteriology and on the anatomy of the head. Surgeons from all over the country consulted this former janitor before performing puzzling head operations. He had never been a medical student, yet he was given one of those rare honorary degrees of Doctor of Science.

[5] Such spare-time learning is especially efficient since there is time for it to soak in between learning periods. When learning complex things, there is an extra advantage in taking breathing spells. When beginning something new it also speeds up learning to have breathers. Most eager beginners push themselves too long at a time. Such crowded study or practice produces fatigue or boredom which hinders learning.

[6] You can't gain wisdom quickly, but you can

gain wisdom steadily by easy stages.

[7] Instead of practicing at the typewriter, or piano, or behind the steering wheel, for two solid hours, practice only one hour. Then take a breather before doing the second hour of practice or study. You will be fresher when you start the second lap. Such spaced practice or study is better for learning than is continuous practice of the same total length.

[8] Spaced practice not only eliminates fatigue and boredom, but also some maturation of the nerve connections which have been exercised seems to take place during the space between practice periods. Whatever the reason, however, distributed practice is better than continuous practice. Long practice periods can be safely used only after one has acquired considerable skill.

[9] The most efficient distribution of practice or study sessions varies with the kind of material being learned. Each person has to find the best distribution of practice that fits him and his task. Follow these two guides in spacing your learning periods:

1. Each practice should be long enough to warm you up and to allow the peak of your present skill to be reached.

2. It should be halted when fatigue, boredom, errors, or slowness appear.

II

[10] Learning is more efficient when it is fun, less efficient when it is drudgery. Practice periods can safely be made longer if the learner is excited about learning. Learning is often more effective in a group, since individual progress then acquires some features of a game or contest. The clever teacher, or expert job trainer, has the knack of arousing the learner's interest to the point of actual excitement. The ambitious individual often lets his ambition provide the excitement.

[11] Keeping score on oneself gives some of this game spirit to the lone learner. People usually master a sport such as golf or bowling quickly largely because they naturally keep tabs on how they're doing. Score keeping is easy for some kinds of learning, such as typing speed. These scores can be charted week after week to show one's learning curve, or rate of progress in mastering the subject.

[12] Sometimes a numerical score is not possible, but there are other ways to find an indication of one's progress. The person who is trying to improve his handwriting, for example, can keep samples of his regular Saturday morning penmanship for a period of time, pasting them side by side to observe the improvement.

[13] Don't guess at your progress if it is possible to figure some way to keep a week-by-week rec-ord. This record can give you the encouragement needed to break through a temporary slump in progress.

III

[14] Most learning shows rapid progress for the first few days; then it tapers off. After six months of practice it may take a full month of practice to make as much progress as was made the first week. This is often called the principle of diminishing returns, but that description is illusory. While the gain per week of practice may diminish, it is still a gain, bringing one closer to perfection. The jack-of-all-trades stops practice when the increases become small; so thus he never becomes king of any trade.

[15] It is when the gains slow down that you must become excited over even a slight gain.

[16] Extra practice is especially needed where the gains are small, or when the job seems to be mastered at last. Just-enough-to-learn is not enough to be satisfied. The extra practice after it is "just learned" makes the learning more permanent and easier to perform in daily life. Psychologists call this overlearning.

[17] Taxi-drivers can weave their vehicles through congested traffic with breath-taking skill because they have overlearned through months and months of practice in actual driving. Their careenings may frighten bystanders, but these overpracticed drivers have the world's best safety records.

[18] The job details which are not routinely used over and over so they become overlearned should be practiced in spare and slack times until they are overlearned.

[19] For example, when Raymond L. Ditmars was sixteen his job did not give enough practice for him to overlearn his shorthand. Consequently he practiced it by taking down the sermon in church!

[20] Much education is lost because it was not overlearned at school—and because learning stopped when school stopped. When children return to school in the fall they know about 20 percent less than they did in June. A year after graduating from high school there is a learning loss of 50 percent. This backsliding in learning is more marked among businessmen than among professional men.

[21] Keep your learning useful by rehearsing it in spare moments. Keep it growing by expanding your reading, observation, and thinking. We are what we have learned. What we have let slip is what we used to be.

IV

[22] The simplest learning is that of muscle control, as in learning to walk, swim, throw a ball, and in some of the simpler factory operations. A

higher degree of motor skill also can be learned—such as that developed by the baseball pitcher.

[23] Sensory-motor learning involves the cooperation of muscles and senses. Learning to play a musical instrument, to typewrite, and to handle many factory jobs are examples of sensory-motor learning.

[24] Ideo-motor learning combines higher thought processes with muscular actions. Learning shorthand, bookkeeping, or a foreign language are examples.

[25] Ideational learning is the highest type, in which muscular factors are not appreciably concerned. This learning is in the realm of ideas.

[26] Such a classification from muscular to ideational learning is convenient, but somewhat artificial. In practical life learning is usually a mixture of several of these levels, although one is possibly more marked than the others.

[27] The level of learning for one and the same job may also vary during the different stages of learning it. Laying bricks may be primarily a muscular task—in which case we have a "mechanical" bricklayer who is assigned to rough work. After the muscular parts of bricklaying are learned, however, ideational learning can be added—as Frank Gilbreth did when he learned to lay bricks with about one-third the conventional number of motions.

[28] The motor or mechanical aspects of a job are likely to be learned first; then the sensory and ideational aspects. When these higher aspects are neglected, the individual is no more than a mechanical worker.

[29] For individual advancement one should strive to learn not only the motions of a job, but also the sensory and ideational parts. In the practical world salary schedules run parallel to that classification of learning levels: jobs which call for mere motor learning have lowest pay scales, sensory-motor jobs a little higher pay, ideo-motor jobs still higher, and ideational the highest.

[30] Learn to use your head along with your hands; then use your head more than your hands. The ideational part of learning removes one from the wage class and promotes one into the salary class—from a job into a position, from an occupation into a profession.

V

[31] But whether simple motor learning or abstract ideational learning is involved, the laws for efficient learning are pretty much the same. The laws of efficient learning are as valuable for business as for the ambitious individual. It costs business around $100 to "break in" an employee on the simplest job; the average job has a break-in cost of $400 to $500; on some jobs the cost runs into the thousands.

[32] To the individual inefficient learning means a low earning level—and discouragement. Speed up your learning. Make it stay with you longer. Do this by:

1. Wanting to learn.
2. Taking it by easy stages at the outset.
3. Pushing yourself—but not to the point of staleness.
4. Keeping a record of your progress.
5. Getting excited about learning.
6. Keeping up practice as increases become small.
7. Using your head.

Learners come to be earners. ◄ **End timing**

Record here the time required on this selection: _____minutes _____seconds

Test Your Comprehension

What are the main principles of effective learning, according to Dr. Laird?

1. _____

_____

2. _____

_____

3. _____

_____

4. _____

_____

_____

Compute Your Rate
(Approximate Number of Words: 1825)

Time	WPM	Time	WPM
1 min.	1825	3 min. 30 sec.	522
1 min. 10 sec.	1564	3 min. 45 sec.	488
1 min. 15 sec.	1460	4 min.	456
1 min. 30 sec.	1217	4 min. 30 sec.	406
1 min. 45 sec.	1043	5 min.	365
2 min.	913	5 min. 30 sec.	332
2 min. 15 sec.	812	6 min.	304
2 min. 30 sec.	730	6 min. 30 sec.	280
2 min. 45 sec.	664	7 min.	261
3 min.	608	7 min. 30 sec.	244
3 min. 15 sec.	560	8 min.	228

Your rate on selection 16: _____WPM

(Record this statistic on the chart and graph on page 235)

Discussion of the Selection

"Here," Dr. Laird is saying to his readers, "are the principles of efficient learning. Apply them if you wish to get ahead." From beginning to end, in every sentence, in every example, in every exhortation, this "theme" is played, with the "variations" adding color, specifics, and interest.

In paragraphs 1 through 9, the author explains in elaborate detail the first of these principles—*for best results space your learning and practice,* that is, take your learning in easy stages, etc.

For the next four paragraphs (through 13), he offers, and enlarges on, his second suggestion—*keep a record of your progress.*

In paragraphs 14 through 21, he calls for *overlearning;* then, through paragraph 30, he describes four broad types of learning and suggests that you *"use your head along with . . . [or] more than your hands "*

Finally, in the last two paragraphs, he sums up, under seven headings, the four major principles around which the article is built.

ARE YOU APPLYING THE PRINCIPLES OF LEARNING?

Thirteen Significant Questions for You to Answer

Ask yourself, at this point, how you are doing in your own learning:

1. Do I really want to learn? ☐ yes ☐ no
2. Am I deliberately pushing myself, but not so fast as to become frustrated? ☐ yes ☐ no
3. Am I keeping a careful record of my progress in speed and comprehension? ☐ yes ☐ no
4. Am I moving along in high gear as I read, clearly aware of my purpose? Do I suit my rate to that purpose? ☐ yes ☐ no
5. Am I doing more outside reading now than I used to? ☐ yes ☐ no
6. Am I excited about my learning? ☐ yes ☐ no
7. Do I persevere, even when gains are small or when progress is not perceptible? ☐ yes ☐ no
8. Do I consciously make a mental note of the new words I meet in my reading? ☐ yes ☐ no
9. Do I avoid regressions? ☐ yes ☐ no
10. Do I inhibit vocalization? ☐ yes ☐ no
11. Do I ignore eye movements, focusing only on pulling the meaning out of a page of print? ☐ yes ☐ no
12. Is my concentration becoming sharper as I *think along with the writer,* seeing meaning *behind* meaning, noting *structure* and *organization,* distinguishing *main ideas* from *support,* "theme" from "variations?" ☐ yes ☐ no
13. Am I, as a result of my efforts and training, reading more *actively,* more *aggressively,* more *dominantly* (no matter by how small an increment) than I used to? ☐ yes ☐ no

Your honest answers to these 13 questions will tell you how you're doing so far.

Every person has a different rate of learning—and your own rate of learning suits your unique personality.

You are competing only with yourself; whether you reach the goal of *more efficient comprehension* and *greater speed of comprehension* with slow, methodical care, or with quick bursts and flashes of energetic progress *does not matter.*

Your aim is to reach that goal finally, and to *persevere* until you do, not to compare your progress to anyone else's.

So, if you have answered most of the 13 questions affirmatively, realize that your training is producing results.

If you checked one or more *negative* answers, pause for a moment to take stock.

In what ways are you willing to change so that your learning will be more successful, so that you will feel more successful in your learning? (Nothing spurs a person on so much as a clear *feeling of success.*)

This is an important question—please do not ignore it.

Write your answer in the space provided below.

How I must change to become, and to feel, more successful!

_____

_____

_____

_____

_____

_____

_____

SESSION 26

PERCEPTION TRAINING VI

Perception Exercise 20

Scan each line quickly, and once only, to find a pair of identical words next to each other. This exercise is similar to *perception exercise 16,* the complete directions for which can be found on page 101.

Your goal: Finish in 40 seconds or less with 90% accuracy.

Time at this moment: _____minutes _____seconds

Start timing ➡

1. fling flung flap flee flip flip flack flick

2. fool full feel file fill fill fall felt

3. grin gram grit grain grain great groat grill

4. creep crap crept crow cry crop crop croup

5. bleed bleeder bladder blip bled bled bleeding

6. break broke broke brake brook back bake

7. pluck plank poke pain pair prank prank pear

8. spread spray spray sprawl sprain spine spill

9. spill spat speck speck spoke speak spool splash

10. open over opera oval oven oven offer often offal

11. better batter butter bitter bitter baker booker

12. button broken fatten florin being bitten bitten

13. palsy flimsy clumsy cozy dizzy dizzy cleanser

14. drool drawl dull dill drill drill drop droop

15. dim dumb dumb drum dome doom dram dam

16. such touch flinch ouch much much muck

17. sadder sitter sooner soother soother slither either

18. hill harm hurt help hall hole hole hang her

19. just gem jest jell gin jist joy joy jester

20. dilly jelly hilly silly belly belly fully filly

21. park hark dark lark ark ark mark stark

22. came blame dame tame rain fame fame same

23. wave save save knave rave shave waver flavor

24. jam cram am dram ram pram ham ham

25. obey relay relay display essay gourmet convey

◄ End timing

Time required: _____seconds   Number of correct choices: _____ (22-23 is 90% accuracy)

Perception Exercise 21

Continue as before.

Time at this moment: _____ minutes _____ seconds

Start timing ➡

1. key   clay   they   tee   tree   three   tray   trey   tea   tea   wee

2. praise   braise   preys   maze   trays   flays   prays   prays

3. she   ski   ski   plea   knee   key   free   glee   skill   sky   shy

4. dry   by   cry   try   die   dye   eye   spy   fry   fry   sly

5. rich   twitch   snitch   stitch   stitch   witch   which   switch

6. star   far   spar   mar   par   par   shark   war   tar   start

7. fist   wrist   wrist   list   mist   twist   tryst   cyst   missed

8. light   fight   right   tight   tight   sight   plight   rite

9. prize   wise   size   size   rise   guise   seize   vise

10. gaze   days   ways   laze   maze   daze   daze   praise

11. white   when   which   what   wheel   where   where   whip

12. strip   strap   string   string   strong   strand   spring

13. lefty   hefty   apt   after   after   softer   swifter   dafter

14. mutter   matter   splatter   splutter   spatter   spitter   spitter

15. weather   whether   wither   wither   writhes   either   blither

16. moisten   listen   glisten   glisten   fasten   often   silken

17. trip   trap   trap   trump   tramp   troop   lamp   limp

18. little   ladle   pimple   dimple   simple   simple   waddle

19. lonely   wanly   plainly   mainly   only   only   manly

20. spackle   tickle   nickel   prickle   pickle   pickle   sickle

21. hush   wash   wish   wish   mush   mash   hash   bash

22. wind   grand   wand   wand   lend   mind   hind   gland

23. addle   paddle   ladle   riddle   middle   middle   little

24. dust   pest   pest   whist   wrist   past   fast   fussed

25. waggle   higgle   haggle   wiggle   wiggle   draggle

◀ **End timing**

Time required: _____ seconds   **Number of correct choices:** _____   (22-23 is 90% accuracy)

Perception Exercise 22

Use the Fixation Card (or your own 3 by 5 card) on the following phrases. You will notice, as soon as you start to work, that these disconnected phrases are for the most part somewhat longer than the ones you have practiced on in the past—now you must, to be successful, rely more strongly on interpreting the somewhat indistinct *peripheral* images that your eyes will photograph in the fraction of a second in which each phrase is exposed. (To refresh your memory on *peripheral* and *macular* vision, see page 53.) Keep these exposures as brief as you possibly can so that you will gradually adjust to reacting, instantaneously, to the complete phrase in one single fixation. You may not, for a time, have any realization of seeing the outer extremities of the exposed line. Or perhaps you actually may not catch the extremities at all—what you don't ''see'' you will nevertheless be able to surmise, and probably with great accuracy.

This is not going to be child's play, but with effort and practice you will soon be doing better than you may expect.

The purpose of these perception exercises is to help you develop *trained responses* that will eventually become automatic.

→ a rosy-cheeked child

→ the rosy-fingered dawn

→ with full speed ahead

→ a characteristic smile

→ a furiously speeding car

→ his happily smiling face

→ a mud-stained finger

→ an ink-stained face

→ an ink-stained wretch

→ mud-splattered fender

→ a grandstand seat

→ mud-splattered window

→ two broken windows

→ a black telephone

→ the lumbering elephant

→ a strong brew of coffee

→ a snowy landscape

→ his bulging muscles

→ furiously revolving

→ slowly revolving

→ articles of faith

→ his religious beliefs

→ principles of learning

→ his military uniform

→ their unknown beliefs

→ their threatening gestures

→ her beautiful fingernails

→ our foolish fantasies

→ a rear-view mirror

→ that clammy feeling

→ his depressed feelings

→ our early ancestors

→ his royal ancestors

→ many tall ancestors

→ a dreamlike sequence

→ in mob psychology

→ under other circumstances

→ changing circumstances

→ waves of the ocean

Perception Exercise 23

Use your Fixation Card, or a blank 3 by 5, 4 by 6, or 5 by 8 card.

Turn the Fixation Card over to the side where you will find a broad, black arrow identical to the one above each column on this page.

Hold the Fixation Card so that the arrow or the card covers the arrow on the page. If you use your own blank card, draw an arrow in the center that ends at the bottom edge. Hold the card over the first line, and when you start reading, *bring the card down line by line so that you cannot regress even if the impulse to do so is irresistible.*

Not only will you cut off regressions by this means, but also you will use the speed of your arm to govern your fixation time and your reading rate.

Do you wish to get a bit faster than is completely comfortable?

Just move your arm down the page at a brisker pace.

So using a card and your arm as a kind of pacing device, attempt to sweep down each column of print with only one fixation to the line and relying, if possible, more on visual responses than on inner speech. Soon your *trained responses* will become automatic.

You will notice, as you work through this exercise, that some of the phrases are longer than those you encountered in previous perception exercises.

Nevertheless, do not allow additional time. Instead, be confident that your peripheral vision will take in enough of both ends of the phrase to make meaning accessible to you.

Read through phrase by phrase, column by column, getting as much meaning as you can.

These phrases are taken from a short piece by C. Y. Lee, author of ''The Flower Drum Song.'' This piece in its entirety will appear in a later perception exercise (page 132.)

In places
more ancient
and, perhaps,
more civilized
than our own,
a parent has
a sacred duty
to pass on
to his children
the culture
of their people.
By culture
I do not mean
a cultivated taste
in the arts. Rather, I am speaking
of culture
as an accumulation
of the common customs
and values
a people take
from history.
But when
a contemporary American parent
attempts to discharge
this responsibility
he is likely
to find
that his children
have already
taught each other
a culture
all their own.
(Go to next column)

When the parent
is separated
from his child
not only by
a generation
but also by birth
in a different land,
as I am,
his situation is
sometimes strange, indeed.
I have thought
about this
since the Chinese New Year which
my 12-year-old daughter,
who was born
in an earlier
Year of the Dragon,
wanted to celebrate
in Los Angeles' Chinatown.
Since the other
members of our family
begged off,
I was drafted
into the role
of chaperon and chauffeur
for my daughter
and her best friend
Cathy, a Caucasian.
We started early
to avoid heavy traffic.
Although from past experience
I was prepared
for the worst,

I relaxed a bit
when the two girls
settled comfortably
in the back seat
saying they wanted
to talk.
I soon relaxed, too.
"Dad, please change the radio,"
my daughter commanded
in my ear.
She told me
the exact spot
on the dial
and as soon as
I hit it, rock music blared.
I quickly turned
the volume down.
"No, Dad," she said,
"We can't hear it."
"This is America,"
I told myself,
and dutifully turned
the radio back up.
Luckily, the music
was not too bad;
in fact, it sounded
somewhat like the country music
I used to enjoy
in my village in China—
lots of beating
of drums and gongs,
with a reed pipe
wailing in the background.

How was your comprehension? ☐ excellent ☐ good ☐ poor ☐ very poor

Perception Exercise 24

Try the same technique, using your card in the same way as in exercise 23, on another set of continuous phrases.

Read the following material, phrase by phrase, column by column, relying on your peripheral vision and surmising the left and right ends of each phrase even if you may not be aware of "seeing" them.

As before, these phrases, one after another, will make sense as continuous reading; so you may again be aware, after a possible short period of discomfort, that it is not necessary to be conscious of "seeing" every letter in a word, or every word in a phrase, in order to comprehend the entire word or phrase.

The phrases in this exercise are from a piece by Bill Weinstein that will appear in its entirety in a later perception exercise (page 127).

I used to think

that you could recognize

battered children

by their bruises.

I don't anymore.

I have known Reva

and her mother

for several years.

Now I live with them.

From 10 each night

until 8 the next morning

I sit with Reva

and in return

receive room and board.

At age 12,

Reva (not her real name)

is soft and fat.

She will not run

or take the sun.

She will not learn

skating, cycling or any sport.

She has no enthusiasms or plans.

Her fantasies originate

as though on story boards

at Hanna-Barbera.

Her conversation is of

cartoon plots and scenes

from the Six Million Dollar Man.

The tests say

that Reva is "bright,"

but she can only

read a little.

She is slow

with the simplest sums,

and her writing consists

of large, awkward characters,

painfully traced with a pencil

clenched in her fist.

Her church-sponsored school

is small and progressive,

stressing "freedom

of individual expression."

There are no formal classes

or homework assignments.

It is a school

designed to demonstrate

the parents' principles,

rather than to educate

their children.

Reva's father was a teacher,

and even when she was very young,

he treated her

as a small peer

who would toughen

into a brilliant child

of the flower children.

But Reva remained a child,

and her father found

nothing remarkable in that.

So he ignored her.

Then he died.

Reva's mother

is a nurse,

and works the graveyard shift.

When she is off duty,

she sleeps

for 12-hour stretches.

When she is awake,

she cooks gray dinners

and talks shop

on the phone.

She cares about Reva,

but has little time.

All she can do

for her daughter

is to watch with

a kind of hip cynicism.

How was your comprehension? ☐ excellent ☐ good ☐ poor ☐ very poor

Perception Exercise 25

Continue as before. These phrases are from an article by Paul Chitlik that will appear in its entirety in a later perception exercise (page 129).

Paying by check
has always been
a difficult proposition
in California,
the land of the kook,
the fly-by-nighter,
and the general all around flake.
Nowadays one routinely expects
that before a transaction
can be completed,
a driver's license
and two or more credit cards,
each bearing a number and signature,
must be produced
along with the check.
Nobody really seems to
trust the check-cashing process anymore
and apparently with good reason.
But I still wonder
whether an experience of mine
was justified
when I attempted to buy
a simple set of dishes.
Not long ago,

I went to a department store
in the Wilshire district
to purchase new dinnerware.
Actually, it was a mission
of necessity
since the only stylistic unity shared
by our existing service for 8½
was chipped edges.
I took with me
what I thought
would be sufficient cash,
but after much deliberation
chose a set whose price
would have left me
without gasoline money
for the weekend.
So I asked if
I could pay by check,
and was assured
there would be no problem.
After the sale
was rung up,
I confidently produced
my check and what

I considered adequate identification.
Then the clerk casually asked
for my thumbprint.
What for, I asked?
If the check bounced,
I was told,
the print would serve
as positive identification.
When I objected
to giving my thumbprint
to a store clerk,
I was informed that
it was "company policy"
about which nothing
could be done.
Not finding this a
particularly satisfactory explanation,
I asked to talk
to someone who could
be more explicit,
So I was sent for details
to the store manager,
who happened to
be standing nearby.

How was your comprehension? ☐ excellent ☐ good ☐ poor ☐ very poor

SESSION 27

All kinds of strange visual experiences may have resulted from attempting the last few perception exercises.

Do not be concerned if your comprehension was either spotty or consistently very poor. You are trying something new—a greater reliance on your *peripheral vision,* so that you can eventually—without any deliberate or conscious control—read with wider *eye spans.*

Perception Exercise 26

The preceding exercises, which challenged you to make greater use of your peripheral vision, were not particularly easy—this exercise, continuing the challenge, may at first be even more difficult. However, when you finally attain some degree of success in perception drills of this type, the rewards in terms of speed will amply compensate you for any initial difficulty. So follow the instructions carefully.

You will find, below, three columns of print, each one slightly narrower than those previously used for reading selections. Fixate in line with the broad black arrow, which is located at approximately the center of each column, and read down as rapidly as you can without loss of comprehension.

Concentrate on three things: (1) going fast, (2) keeping your eyes focused in the center of each line so that you will not be tempted to make more than one fixation, and (3) understanding what you read.

The more rapidly you move, the more you will have to make use of your peripheral vision, a wholly involuntary process that can be refined and perfected only through constant and unremitting practice. Some of this practice you've already had in your previous phrase-perception training—now, in the present exercise, you will move a little closer to the same goal.

A Child of Flower Children Withers Away

by Bill Weinstein

I used to think that you could recognize battered children by their bruises. I don't anymore.

I have known Reva and her mother for several years. Now I live with them. From 10 each night until 8 the next morning I sit with Reva, and in return receive room and board.

At age 12, Reva (not her real name) is soft and fat. She will not run or take the sun. She will not learn skating, cycling or any sport. She has no enthusiasms or plans. Her fantasies originate as though on story boards at Hanna-Barbera. Her conversation is of cartoon plots and scenes from the Six Million Dollar Man.

The tests say that Reva is "bright," but she can only read a little. She is slow with the simplest sums, and her writing consists of large, awkward characters, painfully traced with a pencil clenched in her fist. Her church-sponsored school is small and progressive, stressing "freedom of individual expression." There are no formal classes or homework assignments. It is a school designed to demonstrate the parents' principles rather than to educate their children.

Reva's father was a teacher, and even when she was very young, he treated her as a small peer who would toughen into a brilliant child of the flower children. But Reva remained a child, and her father found nothing remarkable in that. So, he ignored her. Then he died.

Reva's mother is a nurse, and works the graveyard shift. When she is off duty, she sleeps for 12-hour stretches. When she is awake, she cooks gray dinners and talks shop on the phone. She cares about Reva, but has little time. All she can do for her daughter is to watch with a kind of hip cynicism.

In the evenings I help cook dinner, make salads and prepare vegetables to add some color. After eating I drink beer with Reva's mother and we talk about country music. In the next room slate light and three-inch cardboard rhetoric pour from the television. Reva watches it every waking minute she is home. She even eats her meals in front of the set.

It is very simple. Reva believes that television is life, pain is slapstick, reason is manipulation, all problems are tidily solved. Cher sings to Reva. Reva cannot name the President of the United States, but she knows every character on S.W.A.T. She does not know the difference between a sentence and a paragraph, but she can recite whole commercials with every verbal nuance.

I am almost as real to her as Fred Flintstone, nearly as warm as

John-Boy Walton.

I have made gestures toward freeing her. Once I removed some tubes from the television and for a while there was a lively fuss. Reva even began to show a flicker of interest in music and books and to make honest demands on her mother. That was too much, so her mother told me to replace the tubes.

I taught her to play Monopoly, making her add up the spots each throw of the dice turned up. I borrowed a teaching machine from a psychologist, but in demonstrating it I made her miss the beginning of Little House on the Prairie. I left the machine where she might find it and do some experiments, but she never did.

Reva is a bright kid. I knew her when she was younger, and she had a quick eye. Once she drew me a picture that she said had the whole world in it. Now she is becoming so drab she frightens me. She wants affection from a TV father like Pa Ingalls. I would like to help, but I feel less for her all the time.

I began to fight with Reva's mother, demanding that she do something for her child. She responded by saying she was too exhausted to do anything herself. She knew a friend, however, who knew a doctor who would prescribe Ritalin over the phone. She gave it to Reva, who called me frantically from school. "My brain feels like it's dead," she cried. I urged that Reva be taken off the drug, and she was.

I demanded of her mother she be taken to a psychologist, a doctor, a remedial school, a family counselor, anything. I was told that my concern was appreciated, but nothing was done. So, I am leaving.

I have to go. I cannot stand to watch helplessly as Reva disintegrates. I wish she would break things, get dirty, skin her knees, have tantrums, love or scorn boys, decorate her room with garish junk, scream at me, try to cook, hit someone in anger, sing songs to herself, pick flowers or really hate school. She never does.

If only they had struck Reva, then someone would have come forward to protect her. But the sort of beating she endures leaves no physical marks. There is no law against this sort of neglect.

I hate walking away from Reva, but I don't think it will really surprise her that another adult has simply turned his back. After all, that's the story of her life—always one more bruise.

Did you get adequate comprehension from deliberately going down a narrow column fast enough to permit only one, or at most two, fixations per line?

Try answering these questions, without referring again to the selection, to discover how good your comprehension was.

Comprehension Test

1. How old is Reva? ☐ 8 years old, ☐ 10 years old, ☐ 12 years old

2. Reva ☐ does ☐ does not engage in sports.

3. Reva's tests indicate that she is mentally ☐ dull ☐ normal ☐ bright.

4. Her arithmetic and writing are ☐ good ☐ average ☐ poor.

5. Reva's school stresses formal education. ☐ true ☐ false

6. Reva's father was a ☐ doctor ☐ teacher ☐ lawyer ☐ none of these.

7. Reva's mother is a ☐ teacher ☐ cook ☐ nurse ☐ none of these.

8. According to the author, Reva is a slave to TV ☐ true ☐ false

9. How much attention does Reva's mother pay to her daughter? ☐ little ☐ a great deal

10. The author tried to wean Reva away from TV. ☐ true ☐ false

11. Check the author's message: ☐ (a) A progressive school does not fit children for life. ☐ (b) Reva is an emotionally battered child because her parents gave her so little attention, permitting TV to be her surrogate parent. ☐ (c) Reva's problems result from confusing TV programs with real life. ☐ (d) Reva became emotionally battered because her father died and her mother had to go to work.

Key

1. 12 years old; 2. does not; 3. bright; 4. poor; 5. false; 6. teacher; 7. nurse; 8. true; 9. little; 10. true; 11. b.

Count 5% for each correct answer from 1–10 and 50% for answer 11.

Your comprehension score: _____%

(You are no doubt aware that you read about one-third of this selection by Bill Weinstein in perception exercise 24, and possibly your comprehension was somewhat improved by a second reading.)

Perception Exercise 27
Continue as in the previous exercise.

The Mark of a Society That No Longer Trusts
by Paul Chitlik

Paying by check has always been a difficult proposition in California, the land of the kook, the fly-by-nighter and the general all around flake.

Nowadays one routinely expects that before a transaction can be completed a driver's license and two or more credit cards, each bearing a number and signature, must be produced along with the check. Nobody really seems to trust the check-cashing process anymore—and apparently with good reason. But I still wonder whether an experience of mine was justified when I attempted to buy a simple set of dishes.

Not long ago I went to a department store in the Wilshire district to purchase new dinnerware. Actually, it was a mission of necessity since the only stylistic unity shared by our existing service for 8½ was chipped edges. I took with me what I thought would be sufficient cash, but after much deliberation

chose a set whose price would have left me without gasoline money for the weekend. So I asked if I could pay by check, and was assured there would be no problem.

After the sale was rung up, I confidently produced my check and what I considered adequate identification. Then the clerk casually asked for my thumbprint. What for, I asked? If the check bounced, I was told, the print would serve as positive identification. When I objected to giving my thumbprint to a store clerk, I was informed that it was "company policy" about which nothing could be done. Not finding this a particularly satisfactory explanation, I asked to talk to someone who could be more explicit. So I was sent for details to the store manager, who happened to be standing nearby.

He repeated that taking thumbprints was "company policy," and that there were no exceptions. When I asked

exactly what would be done with the print, he told me that it would only be used if the check were bad. Since the thumbprint would be on the back of the check itself, the manager said, I would eventually get it back and there the matter would end.

He went on to explain that in 1975 more than $100,000 worth of merchandise had been purchased from the store with checks that bounced and have yet to be made good. Thousands of others had to be meticulously tracked down. The new thumbprint requirement, the manager told me, cut down on the number of offenses and made it easier for law-enforcement personnel to catch the bad-check passers who did slip by.

I could see the logic in that. But somewhere inside me I had a feeling my privacy was being invaded and in a certain way I was being blackmailed. In fact, I told the store manager that, in my view, only a properly authorized government agency had a right to demand my prints. The Department of Motor Vehicles, I explained, already has my thumbprint, and a full set of 10 prints is on file with the FBI because I am an instructor at a community college. While I do not object to the taking of fingerprints on principle, those others were taken by government agencies for good reason, and I had a *fairly* good idea they would not be abused. What assurance did I have that a department store would be equally sensitive to my rights?

According to the manager, the check with the print would be passed from his till to the bank via Brinks and no copy of it would be retained. He asked me to accept his word that no other use would be made of my thumbprint. I, in turn, asked him to trust my check, backed up by other identification. It was an impasse. No print, no dishes. I left the store and bought my dishes elsewhere—no thumbprint required.

I realize, of course, that this was just another case of us good guys paying for what the bad guys are doing in our new "cashless society." Precautions, I understand, are good for everybody: Fewer bad checks mean less money lost by the store and, therefore, less spent on security, which eventually could mean lower prices—or at least fewer price increases. But just as I do not give my telephone number to anyone passing on the street, so I do not give out my thumbprint to a store that "just wants to make sure my check is good."

I have been told that in the near future some stores will require identification just to get in. Perhaps some day we will have to pass through thumbprint scanners and metal detectors merely to buy groceries or go to the movies. I am not paranoid by nature, but all this seems to "positively identify" a society in which trust has diminished to the vanishing point—and without a degree of trust in one another, the very word "society" has lost its meaning.

Comprehension Test

1. The author visited a department store to buy ☐ some furniture ☐ a set of dishes ☐ a piece of clothing.

2. The author wished to pay for his purchase by check because the price would have left him without money for ☐ food ☐ entertainment ☐ beer ☐ gasoline for the weekend.

3. In addition to the identification the author produced, he was asked for ☐ his phone number ☐ his thumb print ☐ his social security number.

4. In 1975 the store had sustained losses of more than ☐ $10,000 ☐ $50,000 ☐ $100,000 ☐ $200,000 in merchandise from checks that had bounced.

5. The author finally submitted the additional identification required, and his check was accepted.
☐ true ☐ false

6. The message in this selection is (check one): ☐ (a) Checks are looked on with suspicion in California. ☐ (b) There are more passers of worthless checks in California than anywhere else in the country. ☐ (c) Paying for purchases by check is a complicated and inconvenient procedure. ☐ (d) We are living in a society in which trust seems to have diminished so greatly that "society" is hardly the right name.

Key

1. a set of dishes; 2. gasoline; 3. his thumb print; 4. $100,000 5. false; 6. d.

Count 10% for each correct answer from 1–5, and 50% for answer 6.

Your comprehension score: _____%

(This is the full selection by Paul Chitlik, about one–third of which appeared in Perception Exercise 25.)

Perception Exercise 28

Here is a third selection, to be read in the same way. Go as fast as you can without sacrificing comprehension, keeping your eyes focused on the center of the line and letting your peripheral vision bring you the two ends.

Efficiency

by Paul F. Watkins

Like most little tin gods, Efficiency is all right in its place, in the shop, the factory, the store. The trouble with efficiency is that it is a jealous god; it wants to rule our play as well as our work; it won't be content to reign in the shop, it follows us home.

And so we streamline our leisure hours for higher production; live by the clock even when time doesn't matter; standardize and mechanize our homes; speed the machinery of living so that we can go the most places, do the most things in the shortest period of time possible. We even eat, sleep, and loaf efficiently. Even on holidays and Sundays, the efficient man relaxes on schedule with one eye on the clock and the other on an appointment sheet.

To squeeze the most out of each shining hour we have streamlined the opera, condensed the classics, put energy in pellets and culture in pocket-sized packages. We make the busy bee look like an idler, the ant like a sluggard. We live sixty-miles a minute and the great God Efficiency smiles.

We wish we would return to that pleasant day when we considered time a friend instead of a competitor; when we did things spontaneously and because we wanted to; rather than because our schedule called for it. But that of course wouldn't be efficiency. And we Americans must be efficient.

Comprehension Test

Check the main idea of this selection:

1. Americans are the most efficient people in the world, both at work and at play.

2. If we are efficient, we will squeeze the most work and pleasure out of every hour.

3. It is all right to be efficient and concerned with time on the job; but outside of our working hours we ought to be less a slave to a time schedule.

4. The trouble with us is that we consider time a competitor instead of a friend.

Key

Subtract eight from ten and add one to obtain the number of the correct answer.

Perception Exercise 29

Continue as before.

A Child's Vocabulary

by Anna Perrott Rose

It was through Jimmy John that I discovered that a vocabulary is an outgrowth of experience. As fast as he learned some activity, he acquired without effort the vocabulary that went with it. From the pony he learned sad-dle, bridle, stirrup, blacksmith, and so on, although to begin with he had hidden from our pet in terror, with absolutely no words to describe anything about him. After a summer of sailing he unconsciously acquired nautical terms as a matter of course. But when we tried to increase his vocabulary by making him memorize words arbitrarily, he became confused and mixed them all up and misused them amusingly. The first time he saw a funeral procession he asked, "What's dat?" and someone said, "It's a hearse." Now it happened that Jimmy John had not been looking at the hearse when this was said. His attention had focused on an Army officer in the procession. Some time later he announced that there was a hearse in front of our house and when we peered out, rather alarmed, we saw a soldier standing there talking calmly to someone. No hearse anywhere.

I then realized that you can't make a child merely memorize words; he has to live them, and therefore many experiences are vital to the growth of a child's vocabulary. I suppose all educators know this but, when I found it out for myself, I felt as if I had discovered a new continent. I dare say a good many parents do not realize this, nor do they know that by limiting their offsprings' activities they may, to say the least, be reducing their children's chances for a good showing in those "aptitude tests" which come later and depend so much on a good vocabulary. Jimmy John educated me, I think, more than I ever educated him!

Comprehension Test
Check the central point of this selection.

1. A child with a poor vocabulary is not very intelligent.

2. Children's vocabulary comes from experience—they have to live the words they learn.

3. A child with a poor vocabulary will not pass "aptitude tests."

4. Children educate their parents more often than the other way around.

Key:
Add four and one and subtract three to determine the number of the correct answer.

Perception Exercise 30
Continue as before.

Rock 'n' Eggroll, With a Side of Coke
by C. Y. Lee

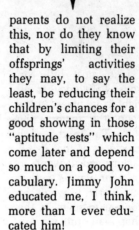

In places more ancient and, perhaps, more civilized than our own, a parent has a sacred duty to pass on to his children the culture of their people.

By culture I do not mean a cultivated taste in the arts. Rather, I am speaking of culture as an accumulation of the common customs and values a people take from history. But when a contemporary American parent attempts to discharge this responsibility, he is likely to find that his children have already taught each other a culture all their own.

When the parent is separated from his child not only by a generation but also by birth in a different land—as I am—his situation is sometimes strange, indeed. I have thought about this since the Chinese New Year, which my 12-year-old daughter, who was born in an earlier Year of the Dragon, wanted to celebrate in Los Angeles' Chinatown.

Since the other members of our family begged off, I was drafted into the role of chaperon and chauffeur for my daughter and her best friend, Cathy, a Caucasian. We started early to avoid heavy traffic. Although from past experience I was prepared for the worst, I relaxed a bit when the two girls settled comfortably in the back seat, saying they wanted to talk. I soon relaxed, too.

"Dad, please change the radio," my daughter commanded in my ear.

"Change to what?" I asked.

She told me the exact spot on the dial, and as soon as I hit it, rock music blared. I quickly turned the volume down.

"No, Dad," she said. "We can't hear it."

"This is America," I told myself, and dutifully turned the radio back up. Luckily, the music was not too bad; in fact, it sounded somewhat like the country music I used to enjoy in my village in China—lots of beating of drums and gongs with a reedpipe wailing in the background.

The girls were familiar with all the rock songs and, on occasion, interrupted their conversation and giggling to hum or sing along. I resolved to remain patient with them.

When we reached Chinatown, firecrackers were exploding everywhere. Crowds were arriving for the parade. "Kung hay fat cho!" (Happy New Year!) echoed through the air in a variety of accents. The girls wanted a Coke.

After small cups of Coke, which a sign at a temporary soft-drink stand called "large," the girls said they were hungry. A nearby restaurant advertised "family dinners," so we

went in and waited 30 minutes for a table. Seated at last, I ordered a family dinner—only to be informed by the waiter that they were not being served. Instead, he handed me a menu full of Chinese lucky sayings.

"Why aren't you ordering, Dad?" my daughter asked.

"I'm trying to figure out what they are."

"Ask the waiter," she suggested.

"I want crisp noodles," Cathy said. "I want typical Chinese food."

I tried to attract the waiter's attention, but he was too busy to respond. He had already warned me the food would be slow in coming because the kitchen was also cooking for several banquets upstairs.

Determined that our Chinese New Year would be happy, I did not want to bother anybody. So, as custom dictated, I dutifully copied the names of three dishes on a piece of paper, made another attempt to gain the waiter's attention.

"Are you ordering crisp noodles?" my daughter asked.

"I don't know," I said. "I'm specifying three dishes."

"What do you mean, you don't know?"

I told her I had picked three dishes with poetic names: "Spring Comes Back to Great Earth," "The Hall is Full of Gold and

Jade" and "The Colorful Phoenix Teases the Wandering Dragon."

"Dad, you're teasing us," my daughter said.

I explained that during the Chinese New Year some restaurants change the menu, using lucky sayings to take the place of the dishes' real names. All the same, Cathy still wanted crisp noodles, as did my daughter.

Since "The Colorful Phoenix Teases the Wandering Dragon" and the other two dishes could not possibly be crisp noodles, I decided to change plans. After all, Chinese New Year comes only once a year, and I was loath to spoil the girls' fun. Since the waiter had never come for our order, I felt free to leave for another restaurant that catered to Caucasian tourists. There, I ordered chop suey and crisp noodles. The girls were happy.

When we came out of the restaurant, Chinatown was packed with celebrators. An organ grinder was collecting a fortune on Ginling Way, and carts selling hot pretzels dipped in tomato sauce were everywhere.

Nearby, a carnival had been set up, and the girls said they would not be happy unless they took a few rides and won a doll or two at the games. They laughed and screamed as they wheeled up and down and jerked right and left in a mechanical torture chamber. Standing on my weak knees, I watched from a respectable distance. After several rides, they tried the games and lost all their quarters.

But I compensated for their losses by buying them each a hot dog. (Cathy had already quoted her own father several times: "Chinese food doesn't stay with you.")

The parade finally came. Except for the dragons, lions and fire-crackers, it was a typical American affair: The politicians and celebrities rode past in antique autos, followed by high school bands and floats bearing beauty queens and smiling princesses.

Overhead, a helicopter hovered with a big sign reading, *"Kung hay fat choy!"* For a time I lost the girls, but when the parade ended I quickly found them— eating hot pretzels dipped in tomato sauce.

On our way home I was ready to tell them a thing or two about the Chinese New Year, but the girls wanted music. I decided to concentrate on the driving and talk about Chinese culture later.

All in all, it was not an unproductive evening: The girls had taught me a lot of things. Maybe my turn will come one day, and when it does I will tell them crisp noodles are not typical Chinese food.

Comprehension Test

A. The central point of this selection is *(check one):*

☐ 1. It is quite impossible to enjoy the Chinese New Year with children brought up in an American culture.

☐ 2. The author's young guests seemed unconsciously intent on frustrating him.

☐ 3. Parents may try to pass on the culture of their people to their children, but they are likely to discover that such children have taught each other a culture of their own.

☐ 4. An older person trying to teach younger people may instead discover that he is learning from them.

B. In which part of the selection does the author express his "theme"? ☐ the beginning ☐ the middle ☐ the end

Key

A. Subtract eight from ten and add one to obtain the number of the correct answers.

B. *The beginning.* You will find C. Y. Lee's message expressed loud and clear in the last sentence of paragraph 2. All the rest is "variation," that is, the experiences Lee had with his daughter and her friend that made him realize what he expressed as his "theme."

(This is the full selection by C. Y. Lee, about one-third of which appeared in Perception Exercise 23.)

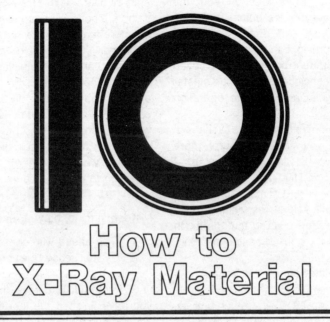

How to
X-Ray Material

PREVIEW

In Chapter 10:
• You work on four timed selections, driving rapidly and with a "sense of urgency" to grasp the structure of an author's thinking.
• You continue to refine techniques of using peripheral vision to perceive complete phrases in single fixations.
• You get additional training in sweeping down columns of print at a rapid clip and with good comprehension.
• You analyze your accomplishments thus far.

With further guided practice, you continue developing habits of aggressive comprehension that help you think along with an author as you read.

HOW TO THINK ALONG WITH AN AUTHOR

The discussion that follows each selection in this chapter is designed to show you *how to think along with the author* as you read; *how to X-ray a piece,* so to speak, in order to see clearly the inner framework that holds the ideas together; and *how to pursue the central theme* of material so that you can quickly, efficiently, and correctly distill out of a vast mass of words and sentences and paragraphs the essential meaning.

When you have learned how to do all this, when you

have learned and overlearned it so thoroughly that it has become an integral, reflexive, habitual pattern in your everyday performance, then you will be reading with aggressive comprehension, you will no longer be passively absorbing ideas and details, one after another, as they appear on a page—instead, you will understand them as parts of a unified whole, you will see them as components of a total structure, you will recognize them as related factors that work together to produce upon you, the reader, the effect or the impact that the author is striving for.

Such learning and overlearning can come only from practice, from intelligent, persistent practice on selection after selection—this is not a technique that you can master overnight, or that you can immediately put into operation simply by understanding it.

But with enough practice, mastery will be achieved. Slowly, gradually, little by little, you will become surer, more skillful, more efficient.

And as this happens, you will find that you are also becoming much more deeply involved in material, that you are taking a much more active role in responding to an author's thinking, and that you are pushing through much more rapidly and purposefully in pursuit of central meaning. Not only that.

You will discover, also, that your concentration is improved.

For concentration, in reading as in any other activity, consists of such deep, active, and purposeful involvement that inner distractions cannot occur, mind wandering is eliminated, and the external world might as well, for the time being, be completely nonexistent.

(How often has it happened to you that you find yourself reading the *words* on a page with absolutely no response to their *meaning*—suddenly you stop and realize that you've been going through all the motions of reading with none of the effect, that your mind has, for the last few minutes, been wrestling with a totally irrelevant problem, or that you have in actuality been concentrating on the sounds around you, not on the thoughts contained in the lines of print. So you go back, perhaps angry or perhaps amused that you have become so scatterbrained, and start all over again. This kind of thing is unlikely to happen if you are actively engaged in searching for the pattern and structure that underlie what a writer is saying.)

Deeper involvement in material; a more dynamic response to an author's thinking; faster and more purposeful pursuit of central meaning; better concentration—all these are rich and desirable dividends. They are dividends you can receive if your investment is great enough. And that is why I ask for continued practice, for earnest study of the discussion of every selection, and for inspired effort in applying what you learn from your work in any one selection to each subsequent selection that you read.

Keep in mind, as you read, five important rules:

1. Push ahead with conscious speed.
2. Try to sense the broad pattern of the author's thinking.
3. Purposefully pursue the *central* idea so that when you have finished the last line you will have a clear and accurate understanding of the *gist* of the author's communication to you.
4. Avoid unnecessary regressions.
5. Skim details if you wish to, and especially if such skimming makes the *structure* of the material stand out in bolder relief. (See Chapter II for techniques of skimming.)

SELECTION 17

Bangling the Language
by Norman Cousins

Time at start: _____ minutes _____ seconds

Start timing ➡ For some years, the popular impression has prevailed that the English-American language has been steadily expanding in range, variety, and color. Every so often we see impressive lists of new words which, with the blessings of the lexicographers, have passed into the bloodstream of the general vocabulary. But very little is said about the fact that many useful words are dying out each year—not because they lack value or vitality but because of increasingly lazy habits of writing and speaking.

For the fact remains that our language may actually be shrinking—despite the highly publicized stream of new recruits drawn regularly from slang, sports, entertainment, new trades, and current events. This shrinkage is represented by the loss of thousands of pithy, precise, essential words—words which, in a sort of Gresham's law applied to vocabulary, have been driven out over the years by flat, juiceless expressions. A recent edition of Shakespeare, for example, provided explanations for twenty-four hundred words which had long since passed out of general usage. True, a large number of these words deserved to die, either because they were replaced by sharper, more satisfying words, or because they were strictly a product of their times. But this still leaves a fair number of words which are as indispensable to the language today as they were when Shakespeare used them.

Could anyone think of a better word for defining someone who steals house servants out from under the unsuspecting noses of his best friends than the word *slockster*? This is not slang but a lost word from standard Anglo-Saxon English. Is there a better verb to describe the act of pushing and poking about in a crowd than the verb *to prog*? Is there any excuse for using the expression "petty liar" when the correct but forgotten word for it is *fibster*? Is there any single word in use today than can express more readily the ability of the fingers to enable the brain to recognize objects through touch alone than the lost word *felth*? And what a shorter way of referring to an unweaned infant than the old word *suckerel*? Or *taverner* for tavern-keeper? Or *nappy* for midday sleepiness?

If economy of expression is a virtue, then we have injured the language through the loss through disuse of such words as *flinders* (combining fragments and splinters: *janglesome* (combining nerve-wracking and quarrelsome); *lanken* (combining leanness and lankiness); *keek* (combining peeping with slyness); *maffle* (combining stammering and blundering); *sloomy* (combining dullness, laziness, heaviness, and sleepiness all at once).

Only sloominess in our thinking could be responsible for the fact that although we use the word "smattering" we have neglected the much more useful noun from which it is derived, *smatters*, to describe small matters or trifles. Similarly, we use the trite expression "smash it to smithereens," but overlook the word *smither*, an excellent way of describing a tiny fragment. The word "ungainly" is in common usage today but not so its affirmative opposite, *gainly*, a handy way of describing someone who is shapely, elegant, provocative. The word "same" has an equally useful variant, *samely*, which can be used instead of the phrase "always the same." We use "bereave," but what about *reave*? ("To *reave* the orphan of his patrimony"—Shakespeare's "Henry VI.")

In the matter of precision, is there any one word that describes an attitude not so strong as the word dislike but stronger than the word indifferent? Yes; the word is *mislike*. Incidentally, there is a long list of other words which, combined with the prefix *mis*, make for an effective and lucid use of English. *Misproud*—proud for the wrong reason; *misgo*—arrive at the wrong place; *misexpense*—using money for the wrong purposes; *misbelieve*—to acquire mistaken convictions; *mislive*—to lead a wasted life; *misfare*—to have things turn out poorly; etc.

If one of the proofs of a virile language is its ability to generate verbs with striking power and pithiness, then we have been enfeebling English by neglecting such trenchant verbs as *to tolter*—move with slowness and heaviness, *to strome*—walk up and down while pondering some decision; *to rax*—reach and stretch at the same time; *to bangle*—fritter away an inheritance by carelessness and stupidity; *to gowl*—weep in anger rather than sorrow; *to spuddle*—assume pompous airs in the execution of a minor mission; *to stodge*—overstuff grotesquely; *to thrump*—bump into people in a crowd; *to slorp*—eat gluttonously and with monstrous sound effects.

Picturesque, time-saving expressions we have bangled over the years would include *barrel-fever* or *jug-bitten* to describe the disease of alcoholism, or even more directly, the noun *bouse*, which combines souse and booze. *Knee-crooking* is probably the etymological ancestor of the expression "brown-nosing," so commonly used in a recent war to describe self-debasement in honeying up to a superior. *Forswat and forswunk* is a good phrase to describe someone who is grimy and sweaty after he emerges from a long day's toil in the coal pits. The word *fluttersome* could hardly be improved upon for a picture of someone gadding about at a party talking with much emotion and little sense. The victims of such flutters would aptly be termed *tirelings*. Those who can converse only by arguing and snapping and by exhibiting their tempers would be described as *toitish*.

In no branch of language is there greater need for endless reinforcements than the uncomplimentary reference. Consider these lost gems: *gowk*—an open-mouthed fool; *jabbernowle*—a slow thinker and a bore; *chuff*—a Shakespearian favorite to describe someone who converts his extra wealth into extra chins; *mome*—someone not quite arrived at, but well on his way to, the status of a blockhead; *sumph*—the same man upon becoming a blockhead; *scroil*—a slick, mean fellow; *bummel*—a small-time tramp; *dumble*—short for dumbbell.

Is it too much to hope that words such as these may be restored to the language? Far from it; we have only to consider that a large number of words which had virtually disappeared towards the end of the nineteenth century have been since rediscovered and are in common use today: *deft, blurt, gab, kindle, glower, glamor, hotfoot, grub, grip, malodorous, forbear, foreword, afterword, lush, reek, pixie, quash, runt, sheen, sag, sleuth, slick, snack, uncanny, tinsel, snarl, bolt, imp, tryste, sliver, slogan, kink, dump, croon, cleave, mole, monger.*

The value of new or rediscovered words is not that they add to the language but that they enlarge one's choice in speaking or writing with greater precision, suppleness, color. Certainly no one wants to be *word-ridden,* a lost but handy word describing a slave to words for words' sake. They used to tell the story, incidentally, about the English fishwife who looked on blandly when Daniel O'Connor accused her in court of being a perjurer, thief, strumpet, and procurer, but who put her foot down when he called her a parallelogram. ◄ **End timing**

Record here the time required on this selection: _____ minutes _____ seconds

Test Your Comprehension

In your own words, how would you express Mr. Cousins' main point? Complete this sentence:

Our language may be _____

_____

_____

_____

_____

but _____

_____

_____

Compute Your Rate
(Approximate Number of Words: 1275)

Time	WPM	Time	WPM
50 sec.	1530	2 min. 15 sec.	567
1 min.	1275	2 min. 30 sec.	510
1 min. 10 sec.	1093	3 min.	425
1 min. 20 sec.	956	3 min. 30 sec.	364
1 min. 30 sec.	850	4 min.	319
1 min. 45 sec.	730	4 min. 30 sec.	284
2 min.	638	5 min.	255

Your rate on selection 17: _____ WPM

(Record this statistic on the chart and graph on page 235)

Discussion of the Selection

The central theme of this piece is explicitly stated in *the last sentence of the first paragraph and the first sentence of the second paragraph;* and again, after rich and elaborate supporting details, in *the summarizing sentence at the beginning of the final paragraph.*

Mr. Cousins' pattern of presentation is admirably clear-cut:

1. It has been popularly thought that our language is expanding in range, variety, and color (introduction).

2. Instead, the opposite may be happening because we are lazily neglecting the older words (central theme).

3. Look at all these excellent, economical, precise, striking, pithy, and picturesque words that are now obsolete (development of the theme with specific examples).

4. But we are rediscovering many of these useful words, whose value is that they add precision, suppleness, and color to our written and spoken expression (recapitulation of central theme).

Your answer to the comprehension test should say something like the following:

Our language may be *shrinking and losing some of its force because of the thousands of old words that are no longer used;* but *we are rediscovering many of them, and we are thus able to add precision, suppleness, and color to our speaking and writing.*

SELECTION 18   It Ain't the Length, It's the Obscurity

Time at start: _____ minutes _____ seconds

Start timing ➧ [1] We hear from a friend to the following effect: "In your editorial column, you guys have now and then expressed great scorn of windy language, big $7 words, and other methods of concealing thought or lack of thought. Well, browsing through recent editorials of yours, I have come across such things as 'intolerable,' 'incompatibility,' 'vulnerable,' 'genocide,' and several other biggies. Ain't going highhat on us, be ye?"

[2] Nope, we ain't; at least, not intentionally. If now and then we let an overstuffed word fall into this column, maybe it's because our inborn culchaw and refeenment just overcome us from time to time.

[3] We do think, though, that this aspect of the use of language is not as simple as the mere difference in length between a word of four letters and one of 12, 15 or 18.

[4] For illustration, here are some shorties which we'd call real $7 words, and wouldn't use here at

this time without explanation: adit, erg, ergo, ohm, gloze, cozen, griff, modal, mure, snash, viable.

[5] Those are all perfectly good English or Scotch words (except ergo—it's Latin, meaning therefore); likewise clean. But they're $7 words or worse, as we figure it, because so few people know what they mean. When you're writing for the general public, the main object is to use language which that public can understand at a glance, without having to go grubbing into a dictionary to find out what in the blue blazes you are trying to say.

[6] But there are plenty of big, long, many-syllable words which almost everybody who can read understands. We submit that three of the four specimens listed above by our pal and critic are widely understood.

[7] Breathes there a reader who doesn't know that "intolerable" means "unbearable"?—though we must admit we prefer the latter.

[8] "Incompatibility" is a widely familiar word because of the many divorce suits brought on grounds of incompatibility—meaning two married persons just can't get along together. Bridge is a tremendously popular card game; hence "vulnerable" is a well-known word to millions of people.

[9] "Genocide" is something else again, and we'll admit we muffed a ball when we dropped that one into this column without explaining what it meant. Sorry, and we'll try not to let such a thing happen again. Here's the dope on "genocide." It's a new word, of Latin derivation, and it means murder of a whole racial or other human group. It originated, to the best of our information, at the Nurnberg trials of the German war criminals.

[10] There are whole battalions of words in common use nowadays which wouldn't have meant much, if anything, to Samuel Johnson and Noah Webster, two famous dictionary makers of generations gone by—only they called themselves lexicographers.

[11] Among these are "fission," used in connection with the atom; "blooper," when you're discussing baseball; "airborne," which is what a plane is when it gets safely off the ground; "chairborne," which is a popular word in modern wars to describe officers who never hear a shot fired in anger from start to finish of the fracas.

[12] In the gobbledygook of diplomats and bureaucrats, there are any number of big, fat blimps of words. Among these, the three that make us maddest are "quadripartite," "unilateral" and "directive." Why the boys can't just say "four-party," "onesided" and "order" is beyond us—unless, as some suspect, most present-day diplomats and bureaucrats aim with malice aforethought to confuse and befuddle the general public.

[13] To make this subject of big and little words still more fascinating, there is the fact that most people are well aware of the meaning and historical background of the very longest non-scientific word of all in current dictionaries. That one, of course, is "antidisestablishmentarianism"—and most of us know what it means simply because it has been so widely hailed as the champ. Huge though old anti-etc. is, he is in no way a $7 word.

[14] So we'd say, about this part of the technic of using the English language, that it isn't the size of a word which should rule it out of newspapers, but its obscurity. If most people know what it means, go ahead and use it, no matter how big it is; otherwise, blackball it, or be polite enough to the readers to dub in an explanation in parentheses if you feel you've got to use it.

[15] This answer the question? ◀ **End timing**

Record here the time required on this selection: _____ minutes _____ seconds

Test Your Comprehension

Write, in your own words, the central theme of this selection by completing the following sentences:

A word may be long and still be _____

_____

_____

_____

Size, by itself, _____

_____

_____

_____

Compute Your Rate
(Approximate Number of Words: 770)

Time	WPM	Time	WPM
30 sec.	1540	1 min. 30 sec.	514
40 sec.	1155	1 min. 40 sec.	462
45 sec.	1026	1 min. 50 sec.	420
50 sec.	924	2 min.	385
55 sec.	840	2 min. 15 sec.	344
1 min.	770	2 min. 30 sec.	308
1 min. 10 sec.	660	2 min. 45 sec.	280
1 min. 20 sec.	579	3 min.	257

Your rate on selection 18: _____ WPM

(Record this statistic on the chart and graph on page 235)

Discussion of the Selection

This editorial, like Mr. Cousins' article, follows a four-point organization:

1. Introduction—paragraphs 1–2: We've been asked whether, contrary to our own expressed sentiments, we're going high-hat by using $7 words. We re not.

2. Central theme—paragraphs 3–6: A word may be short and difficult to understand; or it may be long and still fully comprehensible to the general public. (A few illustrations to support the theme are included.)

3. Development of central theme, with further illustra-

tions—paragraphs 7–13: Consider these examples of big words, some commonly understood, some not.

4. Recapitulation—paragraphs 14–15: Size by itself is no criterion of understandability.

Your answer to the comprehension test may read somewhat as follows:

A word may be long and still be *fully comprehensible to the readers of the paper; or it may be short and difficult to understand.* Size by itself *is no criterion of understandabilty.*

SESSION 29

SELECTION 19

Green Light Means Danger
by William S. Dutton

Time at start: _____ minutes _____ seconds

Start timing ➡ [1] She had the green light. Confidently she drove her black sedan out onto the six-lane highway to cross. It never occurred to her to look to the left, the most likely point of danger.

[2] On the main highway a speeding driver saw, too late, the red light commanding him to stop. He jammed on his brakes, and his tires shrieked as if in horror at the impending crash. The woman was killed instantly. He died that night.

[3] Indignant witnesses blamed the man alone; he had broken a law. In grim reality she was equally to blame, for if she had but looked to the left, there would have been no accident. She had placed too much trust in a green light and in her fellow drivers.

[4] That fault today, common to most of us, is one of the largest contributors to our mounting motor casualty lists, according to two of the newest studies of how and where fatal accidents happen. The message of these studies is that a green light means not safety, but: *Beware of death!*

[5] Wilmington, Delaware, made the initial study. It embraced 15 years, 1,606 intersections and revealed that the danger ratio at light-controlled crossings, In terms of deaths, was 8.65 times higher than at unmarked and unguarded crossings in that city.

[6] Moreover, both the number and severity of accidents grew as the traffic controls moved up from none to slow signs, to stop signs, to lights. For every one death at unmarked crossings, 2.27 occurred at crossings marked slow. At stop streets, 3.51.

[7] The amazed Wilmington engineers asked the Philadelphia Bureau of Traffic Engineering to make a similar study as a check. The larger survey covered one year and 9,294 intersections of all kinds. The death ratio at light-controlled crossings as compared to those unmarked was slightly *higher* than Wilmington's.

[8] In Texas, records of the state police show that more than 80 percent of its highway deaths there are the result of motorists or others violating some traffic law or control.

[9] Only rarely are these violations deliberate. They happen every day in every community. And because to err is human, all the controls and police in the land can't put a stop to them. Each of us who drives becomes, by the law of averages, a potential if unwilling killer.

[10] What to do about it?

[11] "When you reach a corner and another car is approaching fast from a crossroad, let him cross first even if you have the right of way," warns the National Safety Council of Chicago.

[12] "We (and this means all of us) must change our thinking on traffic controls," says E. F. Koester, Wilmington's chief engineer. "Controls don't end danger. They proclaim it."

[13] No control is put up without strong reason That reason is usually a record of previous accidents at that crossing. Lights, the most arbitrary control, proclaim the greatest need for caution. The turn from yellow to green means to proceed with eyes open and wits alert, for here people have been killed and maimed—or they may be.

[14] The exact opposite attitude is assumed by most drivers toward controls, Mr. Koester says.

[15] Our mistaken notion of controls is reflected in neighborhood agitations for traffic lights as soon as a few bad accidents happen at a local corner. Mothers especially seem to think that their children will be safe if they "wait for the green light." Schools teach pupils this fallacy. The teaching is good only in part. Its emphasis is wrong, creating a false sense of security that makes the child, and later the adult, the easy victim of the first driver who didn't see that the red light was against him until too late.

[16] The feeling of safety, now induced by lights and other controls that are actually warnings, is our greatest traffic hazard of all, and it will continue to be until we change our views. ◄ **End timing**

Record here the time required on this selection: _____minutes _____seconds

Express the author's main point in your own words by completing the following sentences:
The green light _____

_____

_____

We should be just as careful _____

_____

Compute Your Rate
(Approximate Number of Words: 670)

Time	WPM	Time	WPM
30 sec.	1340	1 min. 30 sec.	448
40 sec.	1006	1 min. 45 sec.	384
45 sec.	893	2 min.	335
50 sec.	804	2 min. 15 sec.	300
1 min.	670	2 min. 30 sec.	268
1 min. 15 sec.	536	2 min. 45 sec.	244

Your rate on selection 19: _____WPM

(Record this statistic on the chart and graph on page 235)

Discussion of the Selection

Reading aggressively, as you now realize, is simply a matter of quickly and efficiently grasping *central meaning* by understanding, and reacting to, the relationship between the parts of material.

I say "simply" because it's that and no more, but do not therefore infer that this is a simple technique, or one that is simple to apply.

Seeing relationships is after all the very basis of intelligence and thinking; it is also the foundation of all comprehension. And training in aggressive reading demands of you a deeper and more active recognition of, and response to, the components of a piece of writing than you have perhaps been in the habit of using; *it demands that you think while you read.*

How clearly did you sense the pattern of Mr. Dutton's article, how successfully did you grasp his *central meaning?*

Let us go back to the selection and examine the relationship between the parts.

Paragraphs 1–3: Narrative introduction leading up to an interpretation that foreshadows the central theme—"too much trust in a green light."

Paragraph 4: More elaborate expression of the central theme, with transition to the detailed support ("according to two of the newest studies.")

Paragraphs 5–9: Support of the central theme by a description of the studies made in Wilmington and Philadelphia, plus facts from Texas.

Paragraphs 10–13: Pounding home of the central theme—how we should react to a green light.

Paragraphs 14–16: Further "variations" on the "theme"—how most of us mistakenly react to the green light, with the last paragraph concisely summing up all that has gone before. Note how the author uses paragraphs 4, 10, and 14 as transition from one section to the next:

Paragraph 4: "That fault" refers to the error of the woman who proceeded confidently when she saw the green light (paragraphs 1–3); "according to . . . studies" leads us to the content of the following five paragraphs.

Paragraph 10: "What to do" tells us what's coming in paragraphs 11–13; "about it" links those paragraphs up with the preceding information.

Paragraph 14: "The exact opposite" will be discussed in paragraph 15. The exact opposite of what? Of what was described as ideal behavior in the preceding paragraphs.

Answer to the Comprehension Test

The green light *gives us a false sense of security.* We should be just as careful *when the green light is in our favor as we are when no traffic signal governs an intersection.*

Is Traffic-Court Justice Blind?

by Albert Q. Maisel

Time at start: _____minutes _____seconds

Start timing ➡ [1] It was 2 a.m. on a hot August night. In a San Francisco suburb, a man lurched out of a bar and into his car, and roared northward at 80 miles an hour.

[2] Before police could stop the drink-crazed driver he had crashed into another car and sent six persons to the hospital. At the police station he was examined by a doctor who confirmed, by chemical test, what everyone already knew. Six people had been maimed because a madman, too drunk even to walk, had gotten behind the wheel.

[3] Is that driver now in jail? Hardly. Police charged the man with felony drunken driving (which carries a penitentiary penalty in California), reckless driving and driving on the wrong side of the highway. When he was taken to court, the felony charge was dismissed. The injured were there, ready to testify, but they weren't even called to the stand. The two lesser charges brought a fine of only $200 and a slap-on-the-wrist license suspension of 90 days.

[4] Move up the coast now to Portland, Ore., where a motorized maniac was brought into court after killing his victim and running from the scene. Did he end in the penitentiary? Not at all. A charge of negligent homicide was substituted for the original indictment, and the killer, after paying a $75 fine, walked out of court a free man.

[5] These cases are not exceptional. New York City's magistrates last year discharged nearly two-thirds of all the defendants who were tried before them for drunken driving. Of those they convicted, 91 percent were let off with either a suspended sentence or a small fine. Not a single one of the five—that's right, only five—who received jail sentences served more than 30 days.

[6] Records such as these go a long way toward explaining why we still kill some 32,000 people on our highways every year and maim 1,100,000 others. In most cities, serious offenses are all too easily written off the books in a flood of continuances, dismissals, and ridiculously small fines.

[7] But there is another shocking side to the traffic-court picture. In city after city, police and the courts have ganged up on the least dangerous of motor-law offenders—the harried salesman and the busy housewife who violate parking ordinances These motorists, guilty of little more than trying to go about their business, are being pursued with single-minded efficiency. Police are taken off their motorcycles and squad cars to spend their days ticketing parked cars.

[8] How far this has gone is demonstrated by St. Paul, Minn. In 1940 that city had 31,747 traffic cases. Last year the load on its courts had almost doubled: 63,266 cases. The entire increase is accounted for by the drive against parkers. Overtime parking cases rose from less than 22,000 in 1940 to nearly 55,000 last year.

[9] In Detroit, between 1940 and 1948, police complaints against parkers increased 65 percent while complaints against nonparking violators increased less than two percent.

[10] In Syracuse, N. Y., convictions for moving violations increased less than ten percent between 1936 and 1948 while convictions for parking violators increased more than 450 percent.

[11] Behind this urge to penalize parking lies the discovery by many tax-hungry municipal officials that there is a gold mine in parking-law enforcement. Cleveland's income from traffic fines last year was six times as great as in 1940. In Charleston, S. C., Salt Lake City, Utah, and Kalamazoo, Mich., traffic-fine revenues have jumped more than 400 percent. In Los Angeles, traffic fines and forfeitures pay the cost of operating all municipal courts and yield the city a profit of $3,220,000 besides.

[12] Throughout the country, the campaign to soak the parker has more than doubled the already overwhelming burden of traffic cases that have clogged our court machinery for years. Judges are so busy mechanically repeating the routine of "five dollars and costs" in trivial cases that they have no time to deal properly with serious violators.

[13] As the number of trivial traffic cases has grown, city after city has resorted to a new device—the cash-register or cafeteria court. More than 70 percent of all traffic tickets served by the police are now answerable in such violations bureaus. All the overtime parker has to do is to plead guilty—whether guilty or not—swallow his perhaps valid mitigating explanations and answer "Yes" to the clerk's refrain of "Yawanna pay?"

[14] True, the ticketed citizen still has the right to demand his day in court. But when he tries to exercise that right, he finds numerous pressures exerted to induce a guilty plea. I have sat in 40 courtrooms during the last six months watching this parody of justice. Typical was the performance I witnessed in a New York court last summer.

[15] The judge arrived more than an hour late

while nearly 200 accused motorists sweated and fumed. First he had his clerk call up all who were ready to plead guilty. Anyone offering a not-guilty plea or an explanation was gruffly ordered back to his seat. One woman approached the bench with a baby in her arms, to ask for special consideration. The magistrate cut her short with "Lady, if you hadn't done wrong you wouldn't be here. Now get back to your seat and take your turn like everyone else."

[16] The vast majority of the "guilty" were overtime parkers or those caught parking in restricted areas. Without discernible rhyme or reason they drew fines of from four to ten dollars.

[17] Next—an hour later—came the "guilty with an explanation" group. Many were speeders. If their stories were glib, they got off with fines which were sometimes less than those of the parkers who had pleaded guilty before them.

[18] Those who pleaded not guilty had to wait till noon before they were even called before the bench. Then the vast majority were held over for a trial at a later date. Confronted with further loss of time from work, many offered to change their pleas to guilty.

[19] Small wonder that the attitude of the average motorist tagged with a parking ticket is one of utter cynicism. As my neighbor in court, a burly truck driver, put it: "Don't be a dope. Plead guilty and get it over with."

[20] Drives against the parker do not contribute to traffic safety; often they work against it. For the last year and a half, New York City's police have been conducting a savage drive against parkers. Last year they ticketed 83,806 more parking-ordinance violators than the year before. But to accomplish this prodigy of law enforcement they had to let up elsewhere. They caught 8,270 fewer speeders, 6,807 fewer drivers who ran through red lights.

[21] As a result, New York—which has always been below the national average in street safety—has fallen into last place among the largest cities of the country. Accidents, injuries, and deaths have all increased in 1949 over the previous year.

[22] Chicago has had a different experience. Long at the bottom of the heap in traffic safety, Chicago finally called upon the Northwestern University Traffic Institute and the International Association of Chiefs of Police for a plan to cure its difficulties. Studies made early in 1948 showed

that 80 percent of all traffic tickets being issued in Chicago were for nonmoving violations. In the month of February, only three speeding tickets were issued.

[23] A new policy of selective enforcement was developed. Men were called away from the fruitless job of tagging parked cars. The number of motorcycle policemen was trebled and 54 special traffic-control autos were added. Police were instructed to give priority to violations connected with traffic accidents. Reckless and drunken driving were placed at the top of the enforcement list.

[24] The pay-off has been dramatic. In the year ending June 30, 1948 (the year before the reform), Chicago had 529 traffic deaths. In the year since, traffic deaths dropped to 435. Ninety-four lives were saved and thousands of injuries avoided.

[25] But Chicago knows this is only the first step. The process of driving shoppers and businessmen out of town by the parking-ticket route has been halted. Now the city is planning to invite more cars than ever before to park in its busiest districts—not on the streets but in municipally owned lots and garages. Nearly 30,000 parking meters are to be installed in the Loop and on outlying arteries. The revenue from these meters will finance new off-street parking spaces.

[26] Outstanding in this respect has been the achievement of White Plains, N. Y., a large shopping center, which set up the first Parking Authority in the United States in 1947. Instead of chasing parkers away with punitive fines, the city put meters on its main streets and dedicated their revenue to the improvement of parking facilities. Meter revenues have soared and the money is used by the Parking Authority.

[27] San Francisco, with one large underground municipal garage already paying for itself, is planning $19,000,000 worth of new projects to house 15,000 cars. Pittsburgh has set up a Parking Authority and is issuing $34,000,000 in bonds to be liquidated by the income from 32 big public lots and garages. Denver has a $4,500,000 program under way.

[28] These plans are impressive. Yet, there are still far too many cities which still think of parking as merely a matter for police action. Until these cities wake up, our traffic courts will continue to be swamped with petty violators and real law enforcement for safety will continue to be sacrificed. ◀ **End timing**

Record here the time required on this selection: _____minutes _____seconds

Test Your Comprehension

Complete this sentence in your own words:

Traffic accidents will decrease when _____

_____

_____

_____

_____

_____

_____

Compute Your Rate
(Approximate Number of Words: 1600)

Time	WPM	Time	WPM
1 min.	1600	3 min.	533
1 min. 10 sec.	1371	3 min. 15 sec.	492
1 min. 15 sec.	1280	3 min. 30 sec.	457
1 min. 20 sec.	1200	3 min. 45 sec.	428
1 min. 30 sec.	1067	4 min.	400
1 min. 40 sec.	960	4 min. 15 sec.	376
1 min. 45 sec.	914	4 min. 30 sec.	356
1 min. 50 sec.	873	4 min. 45 sec.	336
2 min.	800	5 min.	320
2 min. 10 sec.	738	5 min. 15 sec.	306
2 min. 15 sec.	692	5 min. 30 sec.	292
2 min. 30 sec.	640	5 min. 45 sec.	278
2 min. 45 sec.	580	6 min.	267

Your rate on selection 20: _____WPM

(Record this statistic on the chart and graph on page 235)

Discussion of the Selection

Mr. Maisel is making three important points in his article: (a) police and courts are cracking down on parking violations, rather than on serious traffic offenses; (b) as a result, safety on the road is as bad as, or worse than, ever, and shoppers and businessmen are being driven out of town; and (c) the sensible solution, followed by many cities, is to provide ample, usually off-street, parking space.

Note the clear-cut pattern of the author's presentation:

Paragraphs 1–5: Introduction, with narrative incidents to illustrate how lightly the traffic courts are punishing serious offenders.

Paragraphs 6–7: First part of the central theme—*how this attitude explains the poor safety record on our highways; and how police and courts are going after the illegal parker, rather than the reckless driver.*

Paragraphs 8–21: Statistical, illustrative, and supporting details that elaborate upon, and clarify, this part of central theme. (Paragraphs 11 and 12 contain significant details that explain the causes of the problem—the desire for revenue on the part of municipalities, and the fact that the courts are so clogged with parking cases that there is no time to deal properly with serious violations.)

Paragraphs 22–27: The second part of the central theme is elaborated upon—*the way to solve the problem is to provide more parking space.*

Paragraph 28: Recapitulation of the complete central theme.

Possible Answer to the Comprehension Question

Traffic accidents will decrease when *our cities concentrate on enforcing the law against serious traffic offenses, and on providing more parking space, rather than on detecting parking violations.* (Your language may be different—but does your summary contain the two important points in the answer above?)

Examine the chart and graph that you have been filling out for selections 15–20 (page 235).

Compare the progress you show in phase 3 with that in phases 1 and 2.

Do you begin to feel a sense of elation over your accomplishments?

SESSION 30

PERCEPTION TRAINING VII

Perception Exercise 31

Using the Fixation Card, attempt to recognize each phrase in one exceedingly brief exposure. Avoid, if possible, "hearing" the phrase as you read it.

→ a fashionable audience   → one million Japanese

→ the evening performance   → hundred million Chinese

→ frame of reference   → Union of South Africa

→ tens of thousands   → have fascinating histories

→ one of Germany's   → history of the affair

→ two or three friends   → end of the long night

→ small band of scholars   → heart of the matter

→ big commercial debt   → working on a shoestring

→ all the earmarks of

→ why this play has

→ believe in hard work

→ much greater understanding

→ few, if any, differences

→ more conservative in action

→ his many needy relatives

→ softness of flesh

→ tied to her apron strings

→ this series of words

→ brief period of exposure

→ this briefest synopsis

→ her optional accessories

→ high-octane gasoline

→ many reclining figures

→ those damn Yankees

→ preparation for disaster

→ yearns to re-establish

→ insists on his privileges

→ fraught with urgency

→ might start producing

→ conspirators in larceny

→ large combustion chamber

→ easily won the pennant

→ found to his dismay

→ return of the good life

→ for better or for worse

→ will run for office

→ Greeks bearing gifts

→ sat down for supper

Perception Exercise 32

Use your Fixation Card or your homemade card once again as a pacing device. (See perception exercise 23, page 123 for instructions.)

Read the following material phrase by phrase and column by column, relying on your peripheral vision and *trained responses*.

Govern your speed with your card, and read for comprehension, intent solely on the *meaning* of the material.

Edgar Rice Burroughs,
creator of Tarzan,
a fictional Caspar
Hauser
or ape-man,
whose jungle exploits
are known
to people
in the four corners
of the globe,
died on March 19
at the age
of 74.
About 36,000,000
copies
of his 23
Tarzan books
have been sold,
and his income
from the sale
of his books,

the Tarzan movies,
and cartoons
is estimated at
$10,000,000.
"Tarzan of the Apes"
was Mr. Burroughs'
first published book;
it was written
while the author was
a department manager
at Sears Roebuck,
and was based
on extensive research
which Mr. Burroughs
did
in his spare time
at the Chicago
Public Library.
He first sent
the manuscript
to a number of

Eastern publishers
but they all
turned it down
as being
too fantastic.
He then sent it
to *Argosy Magazine*
which promptly
accepted it
for serial publication.
After a few installments
had appeared,
the late Herbert A.
Gould,
then director
of McClurg's
retail store
on Wabash Avenue,
discovered there was
a demand
for a book

that would contain
the complete story.
Mr. Gould
talked it over
with the late
Joseph Bray,
then head of
McClurg's
publishing department,
who immediately saw
its tremendous
possibilities.
McClurg published it
in 1914
and it was

an instant success.
Mr. Burroughs
found himself famous
overnight.
Succeeding Tarzan
books
became best sellers,
too,
as soon as
they were published.
The last
Tarzan book,
"Tarzan and the
Foreign Legion,"
was published

three years ago.
Mr. Burroughs
was the author
of thirty-five
other books
of adventure stories,
and hundreds of
short stories.
He set up
his own
publishing company
in southern California
some years ago;
it is located in a town
called Tarzana.

How was your comprehension? ☐ good ☐ fair ☐ poor

Perception Exercise 33
Continue as before.

The Improvement of Eye Movements
by Ruth Strang

Good eye movements
underlie
efficient reading.
Poor eye movements
are signs of
lack of skill
in reading.
Accordingly,
we should understand
how the eyes work
and how to make them
work better.
The eyes

can be trained.
With the right kind
of training,
they become
more efficient
just as the fingers
become more skillful
with practice
on the piano
or the violin.
In order to understand
how to train the eyes,
it is first necessary

to learn how
they are used
in reading.
As you read
a line of print,
your eyes
are not moving smoothly
and steadily
across the page.
Rather,
they move
"by fits and starts"–
they make

a swift movement,
pause,
make another
swift movement,
pause again,
and so on
until they reach
the end of the line.
The movement of the
eyes along the lines
of print
is somewhat like
the movement
of an automobile
down a street
with traffic lights—
with many
stops and starts
in its progress.
During the movement
from one pause to
another, no words
are recognized.
The printed line
is a blur
because the eye moves
like a flash
between stops.
There is not time
to see the words clearly.
Only about 6 percent
of the total time
of reading
is spent in movement.
It is
during the pauses

that we comprehend
the meaning
of the printed words.
Even the pauses
are only about
one-fourth of a second
in length,
but that is long enough
to take in
an "eyeful" of words.
A good reader may pause
only four times
in reading a line
on which a poor reader
may make nine pauses.
The more pauses,
of course,
the slower is the rate
of reading.
The good reader
may be able
to recognize
four or five words
in a single pause;
the poor reader only one.
The number of pauses
per line
also depends
on the difficulty
of the material
and the purpose
for which
we are reading it.
Stories and other
easy material
which we read

just for pleasure
can be understood
with very few pauses
per line, while
mathematics problems
and other
difficult material
which we must study
require a larger number
of pauses per line.
These facts about
eye movements
were discovered
by taking
moving pictures
of the eyes of people
who were reading.
The pictures
show clearly
how many pauses
each person's eyes made
as he read,
and whether his eyes
often moved backward
along the line of print.
You can see for yourself
how one's eyes work
when he reads,
by making
the following
experiment:
Punch a small hole
in the center
of a separate page
of print.
Then ask your friend

↓

to hold the sheet
at a comfortable
reading distance
from his eyes.
Put one eye
to the little hole
in the sheet
and watch his eyes
as he reads.
Count the number
of times
his eyes pause
on each line.
See whether his eyes
sometimes move back
across the line
and how quickly
and accurately
his eyes sweep
from the end of one line
to the beginning
of the next line.
Few pauses,
no backward
movements,
and an accurate jump
from one line
to the next
are signs
of efficient reading.
Eye movements
cannot be improved
by thinking too much
about them.
To do so
might put us

↓

in the state
of the centipede
that got mixed up
as soon as it began
to think about
which leg
to move first.
The best way
to improve
eye movements
is to read
a good deal
of interesting material
with keen attention.
Such reading,
with no attention
to the mechanics
of eye movements,
trains the eyes.
For example,
in reading a paragraph,
it is better to think
of its meaning
than to wonder
how many pauses
our eyes are making.
If we eagerly
read material
that is not
too difficult for us
our eyes
naturally take in
a group of words
at each pause.
The eyes are not checked
in their

↓

forward movement
by lack of
comprehension.
Nor do they
have to go back
over the line
to pick up the meaning
of some of the words.
Reading many easy
interesting books
is the best way
to improve
eye movements.
A second way
of increasing
the number of words
we can take in
at a single pause
of the eyes
is to use
the daily newspaper
for practice material.
The newspaper column
is so narrow
that good readers
can get the meaning
of a line
by letting their eyes
rest on it
only once.
An attempt to grasp
the meaning
of this short line
by means of
only one pause
gives excellent practice

in increasing the number	may have one word	Some students
of words recognized	on each;	like to use
at each stop.	the second set,	a small notebook
A third way of learning	two words;	for this kind of drill.
to take in the meaning	and so on up to	They type
of a phrase or clause	five or six words.	a group of words
rather than	We may ask someone	on each page
of single words	to hold the cards	and practice getting
is to use	at a comfortable distance	the meaning
practice cards	from our eyes	of the words
which we can make	and uncover each card	as they quickly turn
ourselves.	for about one-fourth	each page.
These cards may be	of a second.	If we can get the meaning
three by five inches	In that short time,	of three or four words
in size.	we should try	together,
In the center	to recognize	quick as a flash,
of each card	the words on it.	we can take in
we may either type	At first,	a line of print
one or more words	we may be able	rapidly
or paste words	to recognize	and are well on our way
cut from magazines.	only one or two words	toward becoming
The first set of cards	in a quick glance.	good readers.

How was your comprehension? ☐ good ☐ fair ☐ poor

Perception Exercise 34

Use your card as a pacing device. Read the columns of solid text, going as rapidly as you can without loss of comprehension. Fixate at the broad black arrow as you sweep down each column; depend on your peripheral vision to bring you the extremities of each line.

On a Magazine Cover
by Bennett Cerf

Have you ever entertained the notion that editing a magazine would be just your dish? If so, this little piece is intended to give you pause. No job in the world offers a	surer and quicker promise of a first-class case of stomach ulcers, and if you don't believe me, you have only to take a canvass of all the dyspeptic specimens now extant.	Finding new writers and artists, and then holding onto them, avoiding libel and plagiarism suits, fighting the inroads of eager beavers in the advertising department, and

getting copy to the printer on time for every issue are only part of their problem. They must also live under the perpetual fear that something is going to happen while a number is on press or about to hit the stands that will make one of their leading articles—perhaps the one featured on the cover—look ridiculous.

Especially vulnerable, of course, are the news magazines—not to mention the motion picture "fan" periodicals, which often come out with rapturous descriptions of the idyllic home life of two famous Hollywood love-birds a day or so after said love-birds have hit the front page with a super-colossal free-for-all in a night club, and marched off to the divorce courts. . . .

Some years ago, an enterprising editor bagged a piece by a noted octogenarian which gave in details his secrets of longevity. Unfortunately, the day before the article appeared the octogenarian dropped dead. Another editor lined up eight pages of colored photographs of the accession to the throne of King Edward VIII, and a description of same by the highest-paid journalist in Britain. The editor was correcting proofs when his wife called out, "Hurry up if you want to hear Edward abdicate over the radio."

In August, 1914, a magazine featured an article about the Kaiser, calling it "The World's Greatest Peace Advocate." When it appeared, German soldiers were already tramping through the towns of Belgium. In October, 1929, a big financial digest devoted most of an issue to a widely bullish interpretation of the market. It reached the stands during the greatest Wall Street crash in history. In April 1947, another periodical printed Leo Durocher's picture on its cover, and hailed him as one of baseball's indispensables. Manager Durocher, unfortunately, had just been suspended from his job as manager of the Brooklyn Dodgers for the entire season. These were in no sense "boners" on the part of the editors involved; they simply were tough breaks, and there are dozens more like them on the records.

The great newspaper cartoonist, Jay Darling ("Ding"), made a drawing in 1935 labeled "The Fates are Funny That Way," depicting a whole series of national calamities; earthquakes, floods, and train wrecks—but in the concluding panel he showed Mr. Public complaining to his wife, "Yet nothing ever seems to happen to Huey Long!" Three days later, Long was assassinated. One Western paper, in fact, re-

ceived Ding's cartoon a bit late, and ran it and the story of Long's death in adjoining columns.

During the war, edition after edition of the big news weeklies had to be ripped apart at the last moment because of some sudden and spectacular happening. Even now, the editors of these weeklies spend the twenty-four hours before press time praying that nothing will occur to necessitate a complete reshuffling of an issue's contents. Their wives see them, if at all, by television. One of them hasn't spent a weekend away from his office since he came down with pneumonia trying to catch pictures of a fight between a flounder and a soft shell crab.

Do you still yearn to be a magazine editor? Or maybe you'd like to try your hand as a circulation manager! Listen to the sad tale of one of them.

At enormous expense, he installed a complicated machine that isolated all the index plates of patrons whose subscriptions were going to run out in five or six weeks. It automatically printed their names and addresses at the tops of one of those irresistible form letters that begin "Surely you are not going to allow yourself to miss a single issue, etc., etc." sealed and stamped the envelopes, and dropped them in a chute without human hands even so much as touching them. The circulation manager was so proud of this machine that he wrote a long article about it and hailed the company that built it as a benefactor of humanity.

Unfortunately, the machine went out of kilter one day this summer, and before the slip-up was discovered, a baffled rancher in Montana received 11,834 letters telling him his subscription was about to expire. The local postmaster had to hire a special truck to deliver them all. When the ranger succeeded in digging himself out from under, he wrote to the magazine, "I give up! A check for five dollars, renewing my subscription, is enclosed herewith."

With or without their editors, the magazines march on!

Did you follow the thinking of this selection? Then check the main idea.

1. Magazine editors are a rather scatter-brained lot.

2. Magazine editors have special and peculiar problems (largely in relation to "timing") that make their lives particularly trying.

3. A magazine editor's problems are harder than those of a circulation manager.

4. Despite the editors, magazines still manage to survive.

5. Don't become an editor.

Key

Subtract seven from eight, add one for the number of the correct answer.

Perception Exercise 35

Proceed as before.

What? You a Quiz Clansman?

by Murray Robinson

A customer walked into a neighborhood candy store in Brooklyn and said: "I want a pint of coffee ice cream."

The proprietor, a party named Max, deftly cracked a pistachio nut, spat out the shell, chewed, swallowed, and replied: "If I had coffee flavor, wouldn't I give you? What am I in business for?"

The customer, who could take a hint, said: "All right, butter pecan'll do."

Max cracked another pistachio and looked dolefully at the customer.

"Does anybody around this here neighborhood ever want butter pecan?" he answered. "Why should I keep butter pecan if I couldn't sell a pint, even, in a whole month."

The customer reared. "Who wants to hear your troubles?" he demanded. "Don't you think I have troubles of my own?"

Max looked at him with sudden interest and respect. The customer was now speaking his language— questions, nothing but questions.

You think you got troubles?" Max asked heatedly, but with evident relish. "Did you ever try THIS lousy business? Do customers want something I got in stock? Why do they always want something I ain't got?"

Max's wife, who had been arranging halvah on the counter, cracked a pistachio loudly for attention.

"Max," she said, "are you forgetting what the doctor said? Why do you have to get so excited?"

The customer departed, and, as he walked

away, he tallied the score. Max had spoken three times. Nothing but questions. His wife had spoken once—and had asked two. And the customer himself had fallen into the question habit after two affirmative statements.

Max and his wife are but two members of a strange cult spread all over New York City— the Quiz Clan. They're the people who answer questions with other questions. Under peril of losing their franchise, they never make a flat statement.

This phenomenon makes strangers blow their gaskets, but the clan members consider it a test of wit, a delicate fencing game.

Take two sportsmen of the Quiz Clan who meet at the races. Their conversation goes like this:

First Sportsman: You woikin'?

Second Sportsman: Me woikin'? You woikin'?

First Sportsman: Doin' yourself any good?

Second Sportsman: Who does any good in this here swindle?

First Sportsman: You comin' out tomorrow?

Second Sportsman: How else can I get even?

The all-quiz, no-answer system is used effectively by the girls. Here's a recent sample conversation between two subway riders who apparently hadn't seen each other in some time:

"You take the express?"

"Why should I take the express and get suffocated? The local isn't fast enough?"

"Don't you have to get in by nine?"

"Does HE get in by nine? So how will he know if I don't? Where you working now?"

"Did you forget already?"

"In the same place?"

"Is it so unusual for a girl to hold a situation for a year?"

They were still matching questions when the local's clatter drowned out the quiz bee.

Every bus rider has met the driver with a card in the Quiz Clan, whose coat of arms is a large angry-red question mark rampant on a field of smaller bilious green question marks.

This driver always has a bus whose signs are coated with a month's grime. "Does this bus go to 42nd St?" you ask him, peering futilely at the illegible sign.

And he always says: "Whatsamatter, Mac, can't you read?"

Cops guarding a parade route usually qualify for membership in the clan. Some old lady always totters up to one of them and asks: "Is there a parade?"

The cop looks at her steadily and answers: "What do YOU think, lady?"

Did you follow the thinking of this selection? Then check the main idea.

1. Some people never answer any questions.

2. In New York, members of the Quiz Clan always answer questions with other questions.

3. There is something wrong with people who never make an affirmative statement.

4. People in New York are cranky and difficult to get information from.

Key

Add one and three, subtract two, to determine the number of the correct answer.

AN ANALYSIS OF YOUR ACCOMPLISHMENTS

The many-faceted training offered in this book involves a tremendous amount of learning, of very difficult learning. It demands the acquisition and refinement of a great number of new and complex skills. It continuously challenges you to exploit your innate, but perhaps dormant, talents. It sets ever-higher (but always attainable) goals. It requires the sloughing off of inefficient (but wonderfully comfortable and long-familiar) habits of response, and the gradual development of new and more efficient responses that will, for a brief period, be somewhat uncomfortable. And, finally, it draws heavily on your time, your energy, and your capacity for self-discipline.

This is, indeed, as arduous and intensive—but also as rewarding and fruitful—a learning experience as you are ever likely to undergo.

And so, now that your formal training is more than half over, let us pause to draw up a kind of balance sheet of your progress to date, of what you have accomplished and have not yet accomplished, of your successes and your failures.

In column I of the chart below you will find a list of the goals you have been attempting to reach during your training. In column II are pertinent and searching questions that explore how successfully you have reached them—answer these questions in writing, and as honestly and objectively as you can. And in column III check the word that fairly assesses your accomplishment to date. Then, when you have filled out this chart, you will have a graphic appraisal of your progress so far—you will be able to tell at a glance where your weaknesses and strengths lie, in what areas you must invest more time and practice, where you need to devote more effort, and in what aspects of reading you have made the most improvement.

Goal	Questions	Your Evaluation of Accomplishment
1. Increase in general speed	Do you now consciously and deliberately move faster through material than you were formerly in the habit of doing? ☐ yes ☐ no How much faster do you now read than you did on selection 1? _____ WPM (See page 234) What is the percentage of your gain? _____ % (See page 235)	☐ poor ☐ fair ☐ good ☐ spectacular
2. Greater efficiency of comprehension	Do you actively distinguish supporting, clarifying, etc., details from main concepts as you read? ☐ yes ☐ no Do you alertly follow an author's central theme? ☐ yes ☐ no Do you quickly sense the framework of thinking that shapes an author's presentation? ☐ yes ☐ no	☐ poor ☐ fair ☐ good ☐ spectacular
3. Decrease of fixation time and enlargement of recognition span	Do you respond accurately to disconnected phrase units in single fixation exposures? ☐ yes ☐ no Do you feel that you can run down a column of connected phrases in single fixations and with good comprehension? ☐ yes ☐ no	☐ poor ☐ fair ☐ good ☐ spectacular
4. Greater use of your peripheral vision	Can you fixate at the center of a narrow column of continuous text and read down with good comprehension? ☐ yes ☐ no	☐ poor ☐ fair ☐ good ☐ spectacular
5. Decreased reliance on inner speech	Can you read through a selection rapidly with less awareness of the individual words than of the ideas and thoughts they add up to? ☐ yes ☐ no Do you depend less on "hearing" the words? ☐ yes ☐ no	☐ poor ☐ fair ☐ good ☐ spectacular
6. Elimination of lip movements, whispering, and other vocal or motor responses	Are your lips absolutely motionless when you read? ☐ yes ☐ no Are all other parts of your vocal apparatus completely quiet? ☐ yes ☐ no Do you ever feel hoarse after a long stretch of reading? ☐ yes ☐ no	☐ poor ☐ fair ☐ good ☐ spectacular
7. Elimination of unnecessary regressions	Do you have enough faith in your comprehension to read always forward even if you occasionally miss an unimportant point, word, or phrase? ☐ yes ☐ no Do you have to go back frequently to check on figures, punctuation, or words? ☐ yes ☐ no	☐ poor ☐ fair ☐ good ☐ spectacular
8. Deeper and more immediate concentration	Can you jump right into material with a sense of urgency and in single-minded pursuit of central meaning? ☐ yes ☐ no Do you think along with the author, actively and directly participating in the ideas presented to you? ☐ yes ☐ no	☐ poor ☐ fair ☐ good ☐ spectacular
9. Better retention	Have you made a creditable score on the two retention tests (pages 43 and 92)? ☐ yes ☐ no Is your understanding of most of what you read strong enough for you to hold it in your mind and recall it when asked to? ☐ yes ☐ no	☐ poor ☐ fair ☐ good ☐ spectacular

Goal	Questions	Your Evalutation of Accomplishment
10. More time, especially longer blocks of continuous time, spent on reading	Have you attempted to read a full novel in a single sitting? ☐ yes ☐ no	☐ poor ☐ fair ☐ good ☐ spectacular
	Do you, when you sit down with a novel, set yourself a high but reasonable goal of so many pages an hour, so many hours for the complete book? ☐ yes ☐ no	
	Have you been able to meet such goals? ☐ yes ☐ no	
	Have you read at least three novels in this way since you started your training? ☐ yes ☐ no	
	What are the titles of these novels?	

(1) _____

(2) _____

(3) _____

Goal	Questions	Your Evalutation of Accomplishment
11. Improvement of reading vocabulary	Have you directly studied a large number of new words in a vocabulary builder? ☐ yes ☐ no	☐ poor ☐ fair ☐ good ☐ spectacular
	Can you think of ten new words you've learned in this way?	

_____   _____

_____   _____

_____   _____

_____   _____

_____   _____

	Have you learned to pause, for a fraction of a second, to register in the back of your mind any new words you meet in your reading? ☐ yes ☐ no	
12. Self-discipline (The more you develop this ability, the more time you will be able to spend on reading after your training is over.)	Have you spent half an hour to an hour most days of the week, or, alternatively, one to two hours twice or three times a week, on your training? ☐ yes ☐ no	☐ poor ☐ fair ☐ good ☐ spectacular
	Do you methodically continue your training with no wide gaps, or do you pick this book up only sporadically? ☐ methodically ☐ sporadically	

Goal	Questions	Your Evalutation of Accomplishment
13. Pleasure in reading	Are you beginning to find greater enjoyment in the printed page? ☐ yes ☐ no	☐ poor ☐ fair ☐ good ☐ spectacular
	Do you get more stimulation from reading than you used to? ☐ yes ☐ no	

As you glance over your appraisals in column III you should find, if you are at all like the typical adult or college student who embarks on a long and intensive learning program, that you have checked off a few *poors,* a slightly larger number of *fairs,* a still larger number of *goods,* and an occasional *spectacular.* Let's make a graph of your self-evaluations so that we can see the results in a continuous profile:

Self-evaluation Graph

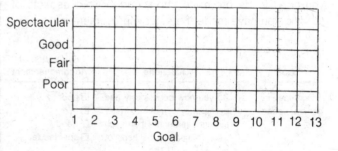

If you compare your performance six months or a year from now with your performance before you picked up this book, the overall, long-run change will be tremendous. But don't expect a revolution overnight. If you set for yourself such goals as are easily attainable, you will, on the one hand, avoid a feeling of frustration or discouragement; and, on the other, you will receive a growing sense of satisfaction, assurance, and success. Don't, for example, try to double your speed immediately; don't try to eliminate *all* vocalization, lip movements, regressions, and tendency to inner speech at one big jump; don't, in short, aim to become an expert reader in five easy lessons. Take it easy, give yourself enough time and practice, and get there by short stages. When you achieve your final goal by these small, sure steps, your achievement will be permanent; rapid reading will finally be habitual and natural.

Take your time and work for the long pull. It is impossible for people of normal intelligence, no matter what their age, *not* to show improvement in a skill if they keep practicing regularly under guidance. It is impossible for you *not* to increase your reading efficiency and speed if you apply the guiding principles in this book regularly and patiently. Be a sufficiently strict taskmaster to keep yourself at your training sessions every day, or nearly every day; but do not be so unreasonable a taskmaster as to demand immediate and spectacular success.

Be satisfied with a 25 to 100 percent increase in speed at this point in your work; be elated if you have decreased any tendencies to vocalization, motor responses, or regressions; feel triumphant if you have begun to look for main ideas and to sense structure in much of the reading you do; and so on, right down the line.

So let us catalogue the general progress you can reasonably expect to have made up to this point:

1 A new attitude to the main ideas and structure of material.

2. An awareness of a *sense of urgency* whenever you read.

3. A decrease in regressions, vocalization, lip movements, and dependence on inner speech.

4. A 25-100 percent gain in speed of general reading.

5. Greater ease in perceiving full phrases in single fixations.

6. The development of regular habits of work and practice.

7. The ability to cover an average-length novel in an evening or two of concentrated reading.

8. Freedom from word-by-word reading, from enslavement to the unimportant words and minor points of material.

9. More immediate concentration and improved retention.

10. And, finally, a growing realization that your *potential* reading ability is far better than your performance before training may have indicated.

One more point, now, before you resume your training.

Occasionally, during your work, you will find yourself on what we might call a "performance plateau." That is, you will continue to apply yourself to a problem (say speed, phrase-perception, use of peripheral vision, pursuit of central theme, response to structure, etc.) as earnestly and as enthusiastically as ever, but your performance will apparently not improve to any measurable degree.

These plateaus are temporary; they almost invariably occur in every extended learning process; they are no cause for discouragement; and they usually vanish as suddenly as they appeared. During a plateau, you are refining and integrating new learning, or are consolidating your previous gains—your mind is not quite ready to translate what it has absorbed in actual performance. It is as if you were filling your tanks with fuel while the motor idles, or as if your body were digesting the food you have eaten before transforming it into energy or assimilating it into the blood supply for growth and repair of tissues. When the fuel is all aboard (to continue the analogy), the wheels will start to turn again; when the food is broken down into its nutrients, your blood will start distributing it to the proper organs; when the learning is integrated and refined, the performance plateau will disappear. And since refinement and integration of learning and consolidation of gains are largely an unconscious process, the only thing you can do to hurry the ending of a plateau is to continue intelligent and purposeful practice while maintaining your enthusiasm and desire at a high pitch.

How to Skim

Almost all reading can be skimmed here and there; Chapter 11 tells you when and where, shows you how.

Some material must be read more or less thoroughly, some only for the overall ideas; and some can, and should be, skimmed. In this chapter:

• You get intensive instruction in skimming

• You learn how the technique is applied to specific selections, in various circumstances, and to suit certain needs and purposes

• You are challenged to read a complete issue of your favorite magazine in a single evening

REASONS FOR SKIMMING

You have now come far enough in your training, you have now sufficiently sharpened your comprehension and perception skills, to be ready to use one of the most effective weapons in the arsenal of the rapid, efficient reader.

That weapon is *skimming*.

Why should one skim? When is skimming necessary? When is it useful? When is it,.on the other hand, undesirable? What does one gain, and what does one lose, by skimming? Are there various degrees or extents of skimming?

These questions are worth exploring.

To begin with, let us understand that trained readers *always skim to a slight degree.* They do this by paying very little attention to, by practically ignoring, unimportant, linking words—words like *the, a, for, with, to, on, it, and, is, was,* etc. You yourself, if you have increased your speed by 25 percent or more and if you read over 350 WPM, frequently engage in this kind of skimming, perhaps without even being aware of doing so.

For example, let me present to you a few sentences that will sound familiar, sentences from which the unimportant, linking words have been omitted:

2 a.m. hot August night. San Francisco suburb, man lurched out of bar, into car, roared northward 80 miles hour. Before police stop drink-crazed driver, crashed another car, sent six persons hospital.

(These sentences look familiar because they are the opening lines of material you've already read—selection 20, page 142.)

Now this sentence structure may look peculiar, because ideas are not usually expressed in such telegraphic style—but you cannot deny that there is exactly as much meaning in these lines as you would get from them if the unimportant, almost meaningless words were restored:

It was 2 a.m. *on a* hot August night. *In a* San Francisco suburb, *a* man lurched out of *a* bar *and* into *his* car, *and* roared northward *at* 80 miles *an* hour. Before police *could* stop *the* drink-crazed driver *he had* crashed *into* another car *and* sent six persons *to the* hospital.

Yet 21 words out of the 54, approximately 40 percent of the content, have been eliminated! The percentage of unimportant words varies considerably, of course, from sentence to sentence and line to line in all material, but such is the nature of our language that it is rarely less than 20 to 30 percent. (In Latin, on the contrary, there are no words to correspond to *the, a* or *an,* pronouns are almost always omitted, and most other linking elements are indicated by the endings of the major words.)

So, if you read efficiently and rapidly, you skim at least 20 percent of all material without thinking further about it. In all your phrase-perception exercises you are forced to ignore unimportant words in order to respond to the meaning of a phrase in a single, split-second fixation. And in those exercises in which you attempt to train your peripheral vision, you again, perhaps without realizing it, skim through rapidly, concentrating your mental responses only on the meaningful terms, on the words that actually express thoughts and ideas.

Slight skimming, then, is no stranger to you—you've been doing it for weeks during your training, perhaps for years if you were a fairly efficient reader before you started this book. You are slightly skimming right now if you are reading this page with any skill.

But there are two other degrees of skimming—*partial skimming,* in which you go through a selection picking up mainly the central theme, the significant details that develop and clarify the theme, and only as much additional material as you want or need; and *complete skimming,* in which you read *only* for the gist or final meaning, skipping all details, all clarification and development, all illustrations, examples, and statistics, and restricting yourself largely to the opening lines and, occasionally, the closing sentence, of each paragraph.

Slight skimming is reflexive, almost automatic. *Partial* and *complete skimming,* however, are conscious and deliberate—each type is used if it suits your purpose and if the material lends itself to such skimming.

Should you skim? I cannot imagine any efficient reader going through a long article or story, or a complete novel or book of nonfiction, who does not, at least occasionally, partially skim a page, a section, or a chapter. Efficient readers do not do this in all articles or stories (although they do in most books), for sometimes the style is so delightful or the details so essential to their needs that they do not wish, or cannot afford, to skip a single meaningful word. (The unimportant, linking, words, as I have said, are skipped reflexively, except, perhaps, in the fine print of a contract or other legal document, or by a copy editor or proofreader.) And people who efficiently and skillfully do a good deal of reading, who (as I expect will eventually be true of you) go through several magazines and books a week, in addition to one or more daily newspapers, or whose profession requires them to read material most of their working day, frequently do a great deal of partial skimming—and find that they miss nothing of crucial value.

Should you skim? By all means. You should partially skim whenever you feel that the dictates of time, the structure of the material, and the needs that you are satisfying by reading make such skimming valuable, useful, or necessary. And you should skim with a clear conscience, for skillful skimming does not in any way deprive you of the essential meaning that all your reading aims at. Indeed, there are times when *partial skimming* may aid comprehension. If material is so long-drawn-out, or so overfull of minor details, illustrations, and background information, that the main idea is becoming obscured and you are in danger of losing the essence of the author's communication, then *partial skimming* is useful, even necessary, for an accurate grasp and retention of the significant points.

Complete skimming, on the other hand, is a valuable tool only under certain special circumstances. If time is absolutely of the essence, if you have no more than a few minutes to devote to a long article, story, report, textbook chapter in preparation for a test, or other piece of writing from which you wish to extract only the *central* meaning, the bare plot, or the main points, then you necessarily skim it completely. You lose the flavor, the atmosphere, the details, the explanations, the background, and many other things—but these are things that you either do not want or need or that you are willing, under the circumstances, to sacrifice.

Such skimming is useful also as a means of reviewing. When your recollection of the main points or gist of material must be refreshed some time after an original reading—perhaps for a test or for an oral report—*complete skimming* can produce efficient recall in minimum time and with minimum effort and maximum success.

As a person training to develop the greatest degree of reading skill that your capacities permit, you will want to learn how to skim successfully so that you can use this technique whenever the exigencies of time or circumstances require it, or whenever your own needs or desires dictate its use.

Possibly you will have to revise your attitudes about writing before you can happily adjust to doing a certain amount of skimming whenever you read.

Do you feel guilty if you do not read *every* word an author has written?

Do you consider every author such a consummate stylist, or so economical and concise in presentation, that every sentence, every thought, every paragraph is indispensable, supremely important?

Or are you so diffident about your ability to comprehend that you don't trust your competence in sorting chaff from wheat?

Or, finally, are you too conservative in your approach to material to take shortcuts or to rely on time- and work-saving devices?

I doubt that you would still answer any of these questions in the affirmative after the extensive practice you have had in stripping a page down to its essentials—but if you would, some successful experiences with skimming should change your feelings.

PRINCIPLES OF SKIMMING

What *is* skimming?

To skim milk, you take the cream, the richest part, off the top of the bottle.

To skim reading material, you extract the important parts—that is, the main points and the significant details; but you have to extract these where you find them, which is not necessarily at the top.

Skimming, then, is getting the *essence* of material without reading all of it—it involves judicious and selective skipping of nonessential, or of less essential, matter.

You have been invited throughout this book to do a certain amount of skimming whenever you felt so inclined; you have been asked to skim a little in novels and in a book of nonfiction in order to meet a time schedule. If you

have already attempted to skim on your own, without detailed guidance or instruction (and I hope that you have), you are psychologically and intellectually well prepared to start using the technique more extensively.

Let us go back to the article on traffic-court justice in chapter 10 and see how it might have been skimmed efficiently and successfully. Refer to selection 20, page 142, and follow along with me as we skim through the piece.

Paragraphs 1–4 contain narrative incidents showing how lightly the traffic courts are punishing serious offenders. How much of this do you actually read? Comparatively little. You know that narrative details in a nonfiction piece are not important for themselves, but serve only to illustrate a point, so you skim rapidly through the details of the crash, the arrest, the medical examination, etc., in the first two paragraphs.

You pick up the important question and answer that open paragraph 3 (*Is that driver now in jail? Hardly.*) and then skip down to the last line (*slap-on-the-wrist license suspension*) to realize what point is being illustrated (*light punishment*).

The beginning of paragraph 4 indicates further incidents, so again you skip down to the final line or two (*$75 fine, walked out . . . a free man*) to realize that the same point is being reiterated. The beginning of paragraph 5 tells you that nothing new will be added here, so you drop down to paragraph 6, where you soon recognize that the central theme is being expressed. You read this entire paragraph, and also all of paragraph 7, where you recognize further central theme material.

Now, by full reading of only two paragraphs out of seven, you have the central theme as it has been expressed thus far.

Paragraph 8 opens with *How far this has gone is demonstrated . . . ,* so you know that this paragraph will contain further supporting details.

You skip down to paragraph 9, recognize from the first two words (*In Detroit . . .*) that support is continuing, and skip the rest of that paragraph. In paragraph 10, a similar opening (*In Syracuse . . .*) shows more support, so you drop down to paragraph 11, where the first few words (*Behind this urge to penalize parking lies . . .*) indicate a shift in pattern from *examples to causes.*

You read paragraphs 11 and 12 fairly fully to pick up the causes of the problem, and then continue skimming, by reading only the opening lines or sentences, through paragraph 21, for you recognize quickly, from the beginning of each of these paragraphs, that this whole section of the material will only add support to, or substantiation of, what you have already learned.

In paragraph 22, the comprehension clue is the word *different.* If *Chicago has had a different experience* you know that something new is coming. So you read most of paragraphs 22 through 25, picking up the rest of the central theme—*the way Chicago has solved the problem.*

Paragraphs 26 and 27 are quickly recognized, from the opening lines, as elaboration on the Chicago solution, so you skip down to the last paragraph, which of course you read fully, since it is a recapitulation, in brief, of the entire article.

How much of the total piece have you read? Out of the 28 paragraphs you've given a more or less thorough reading to only 9 (paragraphs 1, 2, 11, 12, 22–25, and 28)—the rest you've skimmed, reading only the opening (or, occasionally, the closing) lines or sentences.

This was fairly *complete skimming,* yet you've extracted all the significant information—the problem, the causes of the problem, the solutions that have worked.

When you can readily distinguish main ideas from details, and when you can accurately sense the pattern of an author's thinking, you can successfully skim, to whatever extent you wish, any piece of writing that is readily skimmable.

The extent to which you skim, how much you leave out and how much you read, you yourself will determine according to what the writing contains and what you wish to get out of it. And whether or not you skim also depends on the nature, style, and content of the material and on what your purpose is in reading it.

Some writing is so meaty, so complex, so difficult, or so pleasurable that there is no point in doing any skimming at all (other than the slight, reflexive, skimming that I have mentioned).

Some material, on the contrary, has so little to say, and says it so lengthily, that it is a sheer waste not to skim.

And some material can, and should, be skimmed in certain parts, but read thoroughly, even leisurely, even somewhat slowly and carefully, in other parts.

Sometimes you will feel in the mood to skim *partially* or fairly *completely;* at other times, you will prefer, out of either need or desire, to read quite thoroughly.

Skimming, then, is a tool you use with discretion. You use it when you want to, when you have to, or when the limitation of time or the character of the material suggests it. Skimming, in short, is a kind of reserve fifth gear that you shift into whenever circumstances make it useful.

When you decide to skim, these are the principles you follow:

1. Read only as much of each paragraph as you have to in order to discover whether it contains *details* or a *main idea.* This may mean reading one or more of the opening sentences, or possibly no further than the first few words.

2. If the opening line or lines indicate that a paragraph will express or extend a *main idea,* or that it will contain other material of importance to you, read it completely.

3. If it appears, on the contrary, that a paragraph is made up only of *details* that illustrate, clarify, support, or elaborate on what you already know, skim it.

4. Sometimes the *main idea* of a piece is expressed at the *end* of one of the opening paragraphs, all the details leading up to it. So it may be necessary, at the beginning, to read also the *last* sentence or two of each paragraph.

5. Try to sense the author's pattern of thinking. What you are doing in skimming is clearing away all the padding, all the superstructure, and getting down to the basic framework—you are, in a manner of speaking, pulling off all the flesh and laying bare the skeleton. It is only the basic framework, the skeleton, that you're interested in when you do *complete skimming.* When you do *partial skimming* you read in addition any details you consider significant and anything else that interests you.

6. When you skim to any extent you often do not read complete sentences. If you are pretty sure, from your total involvement in, and accurate understanding of, what an author has been saying, that you know what the tag end of a sentence will contain, skip along to the next sentence.

7. Read thoroughly all paragraphs containing expressions of the *main idea.* The first few paragraphs usually (but not always) either set up, or lead to, the central theme; and the closing paragraphs often recapitulate the main points that the author has been making; so pay particular attention to these. And, of course, any number of paragraphs in the middle of material may be important—if you stay alert to the author's pattern you will have no difficulty in discovering *these.*

8. Follow comprehension clues to discover whether material is continuing in the same vein or whether a change of pattern is occurring.

Do the first few words indicate that more of the previous is coming? Then skip down to the next paragraph.

Do the opening words suggest, on the contrary, that the author is about to express, repeat, or extend a main idea? Or that a shift is about to occur from introduction to development, or from development to recapitulation, or from facts to conclusions, or from narrative to interpretation? Or that a whole new section is beginning, and the author is moving, say, from the cause of the problem to the solution, or from a description of a study or experiment to the results or findings? Then you will read thoroughly, skimming and skipping again when you come to paragraphs of details or of unessential information.

Skimming, I have said, is getting the essence of material without reading all of it.

To decide what parts to read and what parts to skip, you rely on two things: your ability to sense the pattern of a writer's thinking; and, through this, your recognition of what is important to the writer's basic message and what is considerably less important.

PRACTICE IN SKIMMING

Let us apply our eight principles of skimming to a number of selections.

You will notice that somewhat less than half of the material in exercise 1 is printed in boldface (heavy black) type. *Read only the boldface print—skip all the rest.*

SKIMMING EXERCISE 1

"Benefits" for Big Boys
by Sylvia F. Porter

[1] **R.A. is one of the policy-making vice presidents of a nationally known corporation which has made a lot of money in the last few years. If you saw his monthly paycheck, though, you would be surprised; you would expect the check to be much bigger considering the name of the company, the industry and his key job.**

[2] **But R.A.'s paycheck would give you a badly distorted view of the actual financial setup. For in addition to a cash salary, R.A.'s company has just in the last five years given him:**

[3] **A handsome expense account** which covers virtually all his entertaining, travel costs, etc. It also provides him with a new car every year and a beautiful vacation haven.

[4] **A retirement program** under which he's already guaranteed $21,000 a year for life and his retirement benefits are steadily increasing.

[5] **A special contract** retaining him as a **"consultant" at $14,000 a year for ten years** beginning when he's 65.

[6] **A privilege to buy a big chunk of the company's stock at a specified price** at any time between now and 1965. The stock is now quoted at $40 above the price at which R.A. can buy (or has bought) the stock and his paper profits on the stock top a quarter-million dollars.

[7] **So, if you added to R.A.'s cash salary all his "fringe benefits,"** you would find that in this era of stiff taxes on high incomes R.A. is not only building a major estate for his family; he also is in a position to move easily and comfortably in the so-called million-dollar circles of our land.

[8] **Am I making this report on R.A. because he is so exceptional? Oh no!** The point is that R.A. is becoming less and less the exception.

[9] **In corporation after corporation key officers are getting contracts and pay deals that rival or surpass the one R.A. has. As an illustration,** the magazine "Sales Management" made a survey of 50 leading corporations a short while ago, found only one in which the chief sales executive is compensated by salary alone.

[10] **In corporation after corporation, top management men are being tied to their jobs for life by a "golden cord" of fringe benefits. The deals make the executives all but immune to offers from the companies' competitors** because the men would have to give up their impressively attractive benefits if they quit.

[11] **What are some of the ways corporations are compensating key men—outside of cash? These:**

[12] **A stock option deal.** Under this plan, a key employee gets the option to buy a specified total of the company's stock at a specified price during a specified period of years. If the stock soars during the period, he still can exercise his option at the fixed price; when and as he sells his shares, his gain will be taxed only at the capital gains rate, meaning at a top of 25 percent. The profits of some men who have stock option deals run into millions of dollars!

[13] **A deferred bonus arrangement.** Under this, the company votes the officer a bonus payable in installments over a number of years, thereby cutting his year-to-year tax liability. In some cases, the executive prefers (and will get) payment of his bonus after he retires.

[14] **Handsome retirement programs.** Some contracts I've seen give executives really eye-popping incomes for life. In addition, many have contracts to remain as consultants at impressive salaries after 65.

[15] **Rich insurance policies and fat expense accounts,** special health programs, profit-sharing arrangements, many other variations of benefits.

[16] **The publicized statistics on the rate of rise in executives' salaries are meaningless unless the fringe benefits also are included.** It's becoming commonplace for top men to turn down flatly hikes in cash pay in favor of pay in forms which are subject to only moderate taxes.

[17] **The cash paycheck of an American executive is less and less the yardstick of his financial well-being and it'll continue to be less and less so as his fringe benefits multiply.**

Let us see how we apply our skimming principles to this material.

The monthly pay check of a key executive, Porter says in paragraphs 1 and 2, is surprisingly small—but his cash salary is no indication of the actual financial setup. All this is clearly central theme material, and you read most of it.

Then, from paragraphs 3 through 7, you skim by reading only opening lines, for this section of the article contains corroborating and illustrative details that support the statements made in the first two paragraphs.

The opening lines of paragraphs 8 and 9 state that R.A. is no exception; you skip to paragraph 10, in which the central theme is extended— *the fringe benefits, rather than the cash remuneration, keep executives tied to a corporation.*

Paragraph 11 is a guidepost that alerts you to coming explanatory details, and these you pick up by skimming paragraphs 12 through 15, realizing, as you read, that these details for the most part are a repetition of those found in paragraphs 3-7.

In paragraphs 16 and 17 you recognize a recapitulation of the piece, including a restatement of the central theme, and so you read more or less fully.

Thus, having read, in full, only paragraphs 1, 2, 10, 11, 16, and 17—six paragraphs out of seventeen—you have a clear understanding of what the author has said and of the pattern in which she has said it.

Fringe benefits, such as expense accounts, retirement programs, stock options, deferred bonuses, etc., are more the yardstick of remuneration to executives than their actual pay checks; and these keep the executives all but immune to offers from competitive corporations—this is the gist of the piece.

Central theme; supporting details; extension of the theme; more details; recapitulation—this is the structure of the author's thinking, a structure to which you are keenly alert as you skim through the content.

What have you lost by partial skimming? A certain richness of detail and explanation, mainly, which you must expect to sacrifice whenever you skim—and very little else. If this richness were important to you, or if you had some special interest in every bit of information, no matter how minor, that the selection contained—why, then, of course, you would not skim it.

SESSION 33

SKIMMING EXERCISE 2

DIRECTIONS:

Read, again; only the boldface print, analyzing, as you move along, why certain paragraphs are to be read more or less thoroughly, the rest only skimmed.

How to Concentrate Better
by T. E. Cochran, Ph.D.

[1] **Most of us realize the importance of concentration—that is, the giving of close attention to anything. But do we know how to improve ourselves in this connection? Also, are we willing to pay the price for this kind of improvement?**

[2] **There can be no doubt that concentration helps us to remember more accurately, more fully, and more permanently.** We have all learned from experience that when we give close attention to a sermon, a lecture, or anything we read, we can recall a rather large part of it, whereas without close attention we are able to recall but very little of what we have heard or read.

[3] **Most assuredly, it increases both the accuracy and speed of our movements.** In reading or writing, for instance, we can do either more accurately and more rapidly by increasing the degree of our concentration.

[4] **Also, concentration begets interest in, and appreciation of, the finer things of life,** such as music, painting, and literature. Without it one would never be interested in and enjoy the great music of such composers as Bach, Chopin, and Mozart, or the famous paintings of such artists as Rembrandt, Michelangelo, and Leonardo da Vinci, or the classical literature of such writers as Browning, Pope, and Shakespeare.

[5] **In fact, close attention increases our efficiency and enjoyment in everything we do.** It matters not what the activity is, whether it be reading a book, watching a sunset, listening to grand opera, learning a poem, writing an article, shooting at a target, playing golf, or making out our

income tax report; if we are to do it well, and find enjoyment in it, we must give it close attention. Without close attention, we would not only waste much time and energy but would be only partially successful and by no means happy.

[6] **"But how,"** you ask, **"can I improve myself in attentive ability?" A good question, and here are a few suggestions.**

[7] **First,** *avoid thinking of concentration, or attentive ability, as something beyond control.* To be sure, it is to some extent due to inheritance, but for the most part it is due to learning and training. For example, the artist will see things in a picture that the untrained person will miss, and the musician will notice features in a symphony that the untutored listener will overlook. If you are poor in attentive ability, it is not because you were born that way, but because you have not learned to concentrate.

[8] **Second,** *try to rate as well as you can your ability to concentrate.* If you should find yourself somewhat lacking in this ability, this would probably serve as a stimulus to improvement.

[9] **The degree of your power of concentration can be determined fairly well by the following test,** which consists of ten simple problems based upon familiar material, but of sufficient complexity to require continuous attention for quick solutions. If you can solve more than five of these correctly in eight minutes, you are above the average in concentration. Have someone time you so that you can give yourself fully to your work. Here are the problems:

1. Two different letters occur only once in the following proverb: "Be not wise in thy own eyes." Which is the second letter to occur?

2. Four different letters occur only once in the following proverb: "A drowning man will grasp at straws." Which is the third letter to occur?

3. Six different letters occur only once in this proverb: "No wind can do him good who steers for no port." Which is the fourth letter to occur?

4. Seven different letters occur only once in this proverb: "Make hay while the sun shines." Which is the middle letter to occur?

5. Write the letter that occurs the greatest number of times in this proverb: "A good name is rather to be chosen than great riches."

6. Find the number of different letters that occur only once in this proverb: "Don't judge a book by its cover."

7. What letter in *Constantinople* occurs just as far to the right of C as it does to the right of *a* in the alphabet?

8. Write the letter that is the third letter to the right of the letter that is midway between N and R in the alphabet.

9. Suppose the first and second letters of the alphabet were interchanged, also the third and fourth, the fifth and sixth, and so on. What would then be the nineteenth letter of the alphabet so formed?

10. A certain letter is the fourth letter to the left of another letter. This other letter is the seventh letter to the right of N. What is the *certain letter first mentioned?*

(The answers are as follows: 1-h; 2-m; 3-g; 4-w; 5-e; 6-12; 7-i; 8-S; 9-T; 10-Q.)

[10] **Third,** *be sure you really desire to improve.* "Quite simple," you say. No, not at all.

[11] **To illustrate, take the case of** the young woman who said that she wanted to reduce her waistline. Whenever she thought of how much better she would look and how many more dates she would probably have if her waistline were considerably reduced, she could very easily say, "Why, to be sure, I want to reduce my waistline." But whenever she thought of the many bending and stretching exercises to which she had to subject herse'f, and also the tempting foods and soft drinks she had to avoid, she could just as easily say, "I don't think I want to reduce my waistline."

[12] **What does she do?** Well, it depends solely on whether she finds it more pleasant to be more attractive with a suitably reduced wasitline or to keep to her accustomed method of eating.

[13] **So it is with** your improvement in any trait, whether it be concentration, memory, imagination, reasoning or what not. You have to consider both the pros and the cons. If you will do this in regard to concentration, I think you will be able to say with some enthusiasm, "Of course I want to improve myself in attentive ability," and this desire is imperative if you are to improve yourself in this connection.

[14] **Fourth,** *form the habit of having a definite purpose in whatever you plan to do.* Without a purpose, your mind is like a ship without a rudder, drifting hither and thither. Hence, in everything you do, try to see its value in reference to your own life.

[15] **To most of us,** I dare say, geography was a rather uninteresting subject when we were in school. But there was a vast transformation in our attitude toward it during World War II when certain of our allies and our enemies were people of whom we had learned but little, and battles were being fought in places of which we had never heard.

[16] **Similarly the encyclopedia** or the study of economics or a foreign language were uninteresting until we found some immediate need for them. In fact, the most boring material will become fascinating when it begins to serve some impelling purpose, and this makes concentration easy.

[17] **Fifth,** *keep a record of your daily im-*

provement in concentration. It has been said that "nothing succeeds like success," which is indeed true. Without such a record, you will not always be conscious of any improvement; but if you keep a record, you will be stimulated to continue trying to improve. This record should include at least two things: (1) noting the ease with which you learned to eliminate or ignore distractions; and (2) keeping track of the time that it takes you to do certain things, such as the reading of a 1,000-word passage or the typing of 100 words without an error.

[18] **Many other suggestions could be given for improving your attentive ability. But if you follow these five suggestions, you will be surprised how quickly and how well they work.**

Some kinds of material, as I have indicated, can be skimmed much more readily and successfully than others; similarly, some purposes are much better served by skimming than are others.

If you decided to skim an article with the title "How to Concentrate Better," what would you want to get out of it? Generally, of course, you want a quick and accurate understanding of the *essence* of material when you skim it. In this case, specifically, you want to know just how to go about concentrating better. With this in mind, you start to skim, clearly aware of what you expect to extract from the material.

The first paragraph, which you read completely, tells you that the article will provide what you want. The question, *But do we know how to improve ourselves in this connection?* implies a promise that the author will tell you how to concentrate better; and the following question, *Also, are we willing . . . ?* reinforces the promise, while adding that you'll have to pay a price for improvement.

Now you read the first sentence of paragraph 2 and realize that the author has begun to enlarge on the *value* of concentration, and that this ties up with the first sentence of paragraph 1.

You next skip to paragraph 3, where the opening sentence offers further information on *value;* thence to the first sentences of paragraphs 4 and 5, where still further *values* are given.

Paragraph 6 you read fully, recognizing it as a transition from *values to means* — a new section of the structure is starting, a section containing the real meat of the material.

Paragraph 7 starts off with *First . . .;* this, then, you know is the *first rule* for better concentration. You read the rule, skip the explanation and details, and drop to paragraph 8 for the *second rule,* reading only the first sentence. Now you go to paragraph 9, where the opening lines indicate further details on the second rule; skipping this mass of details in the form of a test (if you were not skimming you might be tempted to take the test), you push along to paragraph 10 for the *third rule.*

Paragraphs 11, 12, and 13 you recognize immediately as elaboration on the third rule, so you skip to the opening sentence of paragraph 14 for the *fourth rule,* omit the explanation in the rest of this paragraph and in paragraphs 15 and 16, and read the *fifth* rule in the opening sentence of paragraph 17.

Now you skip to the final paragraph, which you read completely, and in which you find a sort of recapitulation of the body of the article.

All right. By reading only three full paragraphs out of eighteen (the first, the sixth, and the last) and the opening words or sentences of the others, you have successfully skimmed the piece, extracting from it: (a) the values of concentration, and (b) five rules for better concentration. And this is all, except for details and explanations, that the article contains.

By skimming you have lost the details and explanations — but these I assume you were willing to do without, else, of course, you would not have decided to skim. You have not lost the main points, the *essence* of the material — and it is for the purpose of extracting the essence with a minimum of time and effort that skimming is used.

SKIMMING EXERCISE 3

In the following piece I shall again indicate, by the use of boldface print, the lines that must be read so that the bare essence can be quickly extracted. Read these lines plus just as much additional material as you need in order to come away with a feeling that you understand what the author is saying.

How to Make a Million
by Joseph T. Nolan

[1] **The late man-about-resorts, Alexander Phillips, bemoaning the decline of moneyed society in the United States, once complained: "The** '400' has been marked down to $3.98." Now the **Internal Revenue Service has come along with a further markdown—to 148. That, say the revenue**

officials in a report just published, is all we have left in the way of real millionaires; that is, men and women with incomes of $1,000,000 or more a year. In 1950 there were 219 in the million-dollar-a-year class, and back in 1929 before Wall Street's graphs went through the floor there were 513.

[2] **Millionaires, of course, come in all shapes and sizes.** There are the little ones who, perhaps after almost a lifetime of labor, have just barely managed to amass a million dollars worth of property, stocks and bonds, and cash. They are big wheels only in their local communities, and for them life is often a race to keep up with the Vanderbilts. Then there are those with net assets of five-to-ten million, many of whom have inherited money and invested prudently. They can live comfortably these days provided they don't splurge on things like overly fancy yachts. (J. P. Morgan told an acquaintance who inquired about the upkeep on a yacht: "If you have to ask, you can't afford one.")

[3] **Then, there are those with an annual income above a million.** Some get into this select bracket only now and then, possibly in a year when they sell an oil well or a uranium mine; others have a million dollars coming in every year and these are the big rich. **It is the million-a-year group that the Internal Revenue report discusses, statistically but namelessly, and says is getting smaller all the time.**

[4] **However, this situation is not quite so alarming as it might appear on the surface, according to financiers, investment counselors and tax specialists.** Styles change, they point out, in millionaires as in millinery. The massive fortunes of the "Pittsburgh millionaires" of the nineteenth century and the "Detroit millionaires" of the Twenties are a phenomenon not likely to be repeated. **But, say the authorities, a fellow with energy, imagination and luck can still scrape together a modest million or so in the course of a lifetime if he knows the ground rules and takes advantage of them.**

[5] **Financial experts do not see eye to eye on many things these days, but they do agree generally on these three points:**

[6] **Point 1.** *It is harder to make a million now than it was forty or fifty years ago.*

[7] Five times as hard, in the opinion of Bernard M. Baruch, who certainly qualifies as an authority. Baruch, who made his first million before he was 30, amassed a fortune once estimated at $25 million. Now 84, he has quietly given away the bulk of his money, though he told a friend not long ago that "right up to the day they put the coffin lid on me, I'll always have a dollar more than I need."

[8] Laurance S. Rockefeller, chairman of the board of Rockefeller Center and a grandson of the first John D., once remarked: "We just don't have money the way people used to have it." Actually, not many people ever had money the way Grandfather John D. used to have it. Guesses on the size of his wealth ran up to $2 billion, and one statistician figured at the turn of the century that if his money were left to accumulate at the going rate for thirty years, it would amount to $90 trillion.

[9] Statistical support for the theory that it is tougher to make a million these days is provided in a study just completed by the Tax Foundation, a private, non-profit research organization. It is a hypothetical case history of two men going into the same kind of business, with the same capital ($150,000), and the same rate of return (33⅓ percent), at two different periods. Mr. A started in 1920, Mr. B in 1955. After the first year their books looked like this:

	Mr. A.	Mr. B.
Original Investment	$150,000	$150,000
Return on Investment	50,000	50,000
Net Income (after 10 percent deduction for expenses)	45,000	45,000
Federal Taxes	7,680	16,648
Income After Taxes	37,320	28,352
Living Expenses	15,000	24,000
Profit Reinvested	22,320	4,352
Added to Original Investment Makes	172,320	154,352

[10] At this rate, Mr. A, the 1920 man, would have run up his original stake to $1,000,000 in just eleven years. Lower tax rates and a lower cost of living would have permitted him to plow back into his business a sizable portion of each year's income.

[11] On the other hand, Mr. B, the 1955 man, would have found that at the end of eleven years he had increased his investment to only $239,933. It would have taken him thirty-four years altogether, taxes and living costs being what they are, to make his million.

[12] **Point 2.** *Chances are strongly against anybody's making a million in his lifetime by depending on salary alone.*

[13] In 1900 when Andrew Carnegie earned $23,000,000 from his vast steel enterprises, he paid his chief lieutenant and golfing partner, Charles M. Schwab, a salary of $1,000,000. Not only did Schwab have no Federal income tax to pay, but his dollar went about three times as far then as it would now.

[14] "Today," says comedian Bob Hope, "the dollar goes a long way, too—all the way to Washington, D.C. But in the old days you were allowed to feel it, see it, even to use it." In the higher-income brackets the tax collector now takes up to

87 cents out of every dollar. So no companies are paying million-dollar salaries any more. Industry's highest-paid executive is Harlow H. Curtice, president of General Motors, who collected $686,000 in salary and bonuses last year. Though actual income tax returns are confidential, it is possible to figure out very roughly from a tax rate schedule that the Federal Government's claim on Curtice's income would amount to something like $595,000.

[15] A further indication of the futility of depending on salary alone to make a million is found in the Internal Revenue report on the 148 million-dollar-a-year men and women. Salaries accounted for less than 2 percent of their total incomes. They got almost half their money from dividends and another quarter from the sale of assets at a profit.

[16] **Point 3.** *A person's best bet for making a million is to take advantage of some of the "gimmicks" that are available.*

[17] **There are dozens of these "gimmicks," but here are three that the experts say have been responsible for making many of the "new" millionaires.**

[18] *Capital Gains Deals.* **Capital gains are the profits a person gets by selling stocks, bonds, land, houses or other property not a part of his stock-in-trade for more than they cost him.** Suppose a man, reading that burlesque is on its way back to New York, invests his money in a theatre. Burlesque proves to be such a hit that the man finds he can sell out six months later at a profit of $100,000. If this profit were taxed as ordinary income he would have to pay the Federal Government $66,798. But by taking advantage of the capital gains tax he can get off by paying only $25,000.

[19] This tax concession, under which assets held for at least six months can be sold and the profits taxed only 25 percent, was put on the books to induce people to risk their capital. The result has been to give many an enterprising fellow a few dollars he can call his own. For instance, Vernon Pick, the first of the successful "amateur" uranium prospectors, became a millionaire on the strength of this "gimmick." He sold his Utah uranium mine last year to an investment company called Atlas Corporation for $9,370,000 and was able to keep 75 percent of his take.

[20] *Depletion Allowances.* **These have been called "capital gains with a Texas twist." Because of the risks involved in drilling for oil—$100,000 or more to sink a well that often will turn out to be dry—the Government allows oil men to pocket 27½ percent of their gross income before paying a cent of taxes.** They can continue these deductions for the life of their oil wells and can also write off large sums as "intangible development" costs.

[21] **This tax bonanza has produced a fabulous number of Texas millionaires** (fifty, it is said, from Henderson County alone) and equally fabulous stories of their antics. Like the one about the Houston oil man who, glancing over his new six-car garage and seeing only five pairs of fishtails sticking out of the stalls, told his chauffeur matter-of-factly: "Buy me another Cadillac to plug that hole." Not long ago, one Texan brushed off a rival with the crack, "That guy never had more than forty or fifty million to his name."

[22] **Texas' best known oil millionaires are Sid Richardson** and Clint Murchison. (Of his fortune, Murchison says: "I don't know how big it is: I try to have fun out of business, make it a a hobby instead of drudgery.") Reputedly wealthier than either of them, though, is 66-year-old Haroldson Lafayette Hunt, whose estimated million-dollar-a-week income makes him, in many an expert's book, "the richest man in the United States."

[23] *Stock Option Plans.* **The story is told** of a board meeting at which the president of a large corporation was being badgered about a poor performance in one of the company's divisions. Someone suggested that the vice president in charge of the division be called on the carpet. "Hell," said the president, "I can't chew that guy out. He became a millionaire last week." During the past five or six years of the bull market, dozens of vice presidents have become millionaires—**through stock option plans.**

[24] **The plans work like this: To give a key man some additional reward that will not be grabbed up by the tax collector, a company offers him an option to buy 10,000 shares of stock at $50 a share. That is 5 percent below the market price of the stock. The executive has, say, five years to make up his mind whether he wants to buy.**

[25] A year later, the stock has gone up to $75 a share so the executive borrows money and buys it. He pays not the regular price of $75 a share but the originally agreed on price of $50. So he already has a "paper profit" of $250,000. Two years later, the stock is up to $150 a share. The company decides on a stock split of two shares for one. The executive now has 20,000 shares, each worth $75 on the market after the split.

[26] In another year, the stock is up to $125, so the executive decides to sell his 20,000 shares at this price. All told, he gets $2,500,000. Allowing for his original stake of $500,000, he has a profit of $2,000,000. On this he pays a capital gains tax of 25 percent. That leaves him $1,500,000 in the clear.

[27] **These and other "gimmicks" are helping many today to realize the American dream and ambition of "making a million." Most of them don't make it—or keep it—in a single year,** but they get it eventually. Few of them are wealthy enough to be mentioned in the same breath with

the Fords or the Woolworths or the Astors. But if they are just plain, garden-variety millionaires and not the super-millionaires of yesterday, they can perhaps take some consolation from old John Jacob Astor, who used to say: "A man who has a million dollars is as well off as if he were rich."

Before skimming Mr. Nolan's article you decided, from the title, just what you might expect from it— *suggestions, obviously, on how to make a million dollars.*

The first paragraph, which you read fully, points out that there are fewer millionaires than there used to be. You skim paragraphs 2 and 3, since these hold out little promise of anything new, the final sentence of paragraph 3 reiterating the point of paragraph 1.

The first and final sentences of paragraph 4, and the single sentence of paragraph 5, prepare you for main points to come; the first of these appears in paragraph 6, followed by several paragraphs of explanation. Point 2 occurs in paragraph 12, followed by more explanation; and point 3 occurs in paragraph 16.

Having skimmed more than half the material so far, you have found and extracted three important points— *harder now to make a million; chances are against making it out of salary; and the best bet is to take advantage of available "gimmicks."*

You are now, you realize, right at the core of the author's communication—he is going to tell you how to make your million.

Paragraph 17, which you read fully, alerts you to the three "gimmicks" that are most effective; and skimming through, you pick up the three from paragraphs 18, 20, and 24— *capital gains, depletion allowances, and stock options.* How much of the details and explanations you read depends on what you want from the material—if you need only the bare essence, you've just about finished reading, except for the opening sentence of paragraph 27, which summarizes the second half of the article.

Skimming, then, gave you the pure *gist* of the piece— the three points in the first part of the material and the three popular "gimmicks" described in the final part.

WHEN TO SKIM

We are clear, now, on how the technique of skimming operates, when it is most useful, and what advantages and disadvantages it entails. As you have discovered, you can cover, when you skim fairly completely, a tremendous amount of material in a very short time without missing anything of crucial importance—you can strip a page right down to its essence, its central meaning, without wading through paragraphs of details, support, explanation, or examples.

On the other hand, complete skimming does involve some loss, a loss you expect and are resigned to before you start. Skimmed material is deprived of a certain amount of richness, flavor, and convincingness—with everything but the main idea stripped away, a piece of writing is usually robbed of much of its sparkle and pleasurableness, the personality of the author often fails to shine through, and the reader must be content with unornamented and unclothed central meaning. And it is certainly not possible to feel a strong and satisfying emotional response to an article, a story, or a book from which only the key ideas and salient points are picked out.

So I do not, obviously, recommend that you skim everything you read— *complete skimming* is a technique to be applied when time and circumstances demand it, when the sole purpose of your reading is to pull out the *essence* as quickly as possible.

However, I do recommend that you engage in *occasional and partial skimming* whenever you feel so inclined, or whenever your needs are best met by such skimming.

Is there a longish book you have to get through within the next few days? Decide which are the most important chapters, read those, and skim the rest.

Does a long article offer more explanation and illustration than you want or need? Skim the parts you can do without.

Do you have a rough idea of what the next few paragraphs of a piece of writing are likely to say, and are you impatient to get on into new territory? Skim those paragraphs—the author might have been better advised to leave them out in the first place.

Does an otherwise excellent novel seem to be getting bogged down in superfluous detail and description? Skim along until the plot thickens again. (You'd be surprised at how long-winded some writers are, and at how immeasurably their work improves with occasional skimming!)

In doing any kind of reading, you sustain no loss of any significance if you skim intelligently here and there. And you suffer no loss whatever if you skip the tail end of a sentence or paragraph that is only repeating what you have already learned and understood.

So, to become repetitious myself, by all means skim when you read. Skim occasionally, partially, judiciously; or, at times, skim completely, if it suits your requirements; skim, in short, according to your needs and desires of the moment.

Skimming cuts the excess fat off the frame of an author's work. With the large amount of reading that you should expect to do in the next months and years (and which a later chapter will discuss in detail), intelligent and skillful skimming will prove a valuable cutting instrument.

SESSION 34

PERCEPTION TRAINING VIII

Perception Exercise 36

Scan each line, looking for a word which has essentially
the *same meaning* as the key word. Check *one synonym*
on a line.

Your goal: 100% accuracy in 40 seconds.

Time at this moment: _____minutes _____seconds

Key Word

1. **evil** harsh great going bid bed bad goat

2. **pretty** petty putty handsome pleasant handy

3. **talk** look park took spill speak spank spoke

4. **seat** stone search chair table fork some sweet

5. **floor** desk love flow flew deck devil duke

6. **have** permit leave possess prison let leave pert

7. **shove** move made bash push pray prowl

8. **clock** clever click timepiece tender chain strap

9. **clue** close catch hint hunt hate harm hill

10. **human** tiger animal person picture prison prism

11. **cat** dog canine feline man snake bat car

12. **sing** say spring wing cling singe burn chant chart

13. **foolish** boyish childish dully hilly silly finish

14. **polite** courteous rude new ragged police

15. **happy** angry calm placid content crowded sappy

16. **vain** lovely plain noisy futile smart veil

17. **stop** go hurt prevent street stuff print

18. **hold** hum him grip growl hind bold

19. **gobble** devour dress gab gabble give develop

20. **hurt** inquire inside intend injure invest inform

21. **soothe** say tooth calm irritate invent truth

22. **smell** feel hear see odor over under order

23. **rise** sit begin stand stoop stretch stray stream

24. **number** letter paper listen figure form from

25. **noise** patch crawl sound silent nutty nose

Time required: _____seconds

Key:

1. bad	6. possess	11. feline	16. futile	21. calm
2. handsome	7. push	12. chant	17. prevent	22. odor
3. speak	8. timepiece	13. silly	18. grip	23. stand
4. chair	9. hint	14. courteous	19. devour	24. figure
5. deck	10. person	15. content	20. injure	25. sound

Accuracy: _____%

Perception Exercise 37

Now scan each line fo find a word that is *essentially opposite in meaning* to the key word. Same goal: 100% accuracy in 40 seconds.

Remember: You are looking for *opposites*.

Time at this moment: _____minutes _____seconds

Key Word

1. **full** fill empty flowing free easy earthy

2. **free** happy empty bound brisk bountiful

3. **grand** great glad petty pretty graceful gruesome

4. **lovely** pretty prim press utter ugly under

5. **lovable** evil easy earnest loathsome lecherous youthful

6. **mad** angry foolish sane treacherous frolicsome

7. **gigantic** big boostful tiny tinny peppy

8. **sweet** musical selfish sour sane silly

9. **applause** removal approval disapproval interval

10. **clean** clear upper lower filthy fretful

11. **after** pursuit behind before become

12. **give** grow green take tremble trust tank

13. **clever** clear smart stupid strong weak

14. **live** let loose diet dry die done

15. **poor** afraid affair affluent pitch petty

16. **forget** forbid forbear return receive remember

17. **green** gray red blue ripe pipe riot rich

18. **dry** fry witch wet well wish drip

19. **sleep** wish dream bed nap wake weak

20. **gloomy** glum gray harmony happy healthy

21. **sow** stitch sew reap rip strip straw

22. **stout** still full thin this thing stir

23. **polite** rude rumpled riotous noisy quiet quaint

24. **silent** noisy nosy still quiet restful

25. **break** report remain return repair reach

Time required: _____ seconds

Key

1. empty	6. sane	11. before	16. remember	21. reap
2. bound	7. tiny	12. take	17. ripe	22. thin
3. petty	8. sour	13. stupid	18. wet	23. rude
4. ugly	9. disapproval	14. die	19. wake	24. noisy
5. loathsome	10. filthy	15. affluent	20. happy	25. repair

Accuracy: _____%

Perception Exercise 38

Sweep down each column, making only one fixation to the line. Go as fast as adequate comprehension permits, and be more aware of the ideas than of inner speech.

Use the reverse side of the Fixation Card or of your own homemade card to conceal lines after you've read them. (See instructions, perception exercise 23, page 123).

The Interval in Learning
by Bruno Furst

The interval between
learning and repetition
is much more important
than people
usually assume,
and it is one
of the factors
regrettably neglected
in our school education.
Almost every good book
on psychology
and learning
stresses the importance
of these intervals,
but I have not yet seen
a single schoolbook
that takes advantage
of these findings.
Ebbinghaus,
a German professor,
devoted much time
to experiments
in this particular line,
and his tests
have been checked
and double-checked
in almost every country.
You know
as well as I do
that it is entirely wrong
to assume
that any subject matter
which we once learned
and mastered

will remain
our mental property
forever.
You know
that a person
may have spoken
a foreign language
rather fluently
but,
by not using it
for several years,
may have lost
the ability
completely
and be forced
to admit
that he can neither
speak it
nor understand it
any more.
Of course,
that cannot happen
if he uses the language
constantly.
Use is repetition,
and repetition
is necessary
for everything
which we wish
to keep alive
in our minds.
So far,
the facts are known
to everyone.

What is not
so well known
is that
the spacing
of repetition
plays a very important
role
in time-saving.
Ebbinghaus
has found
that a subject
which requires
68 repetitions
if learned in one day
requires only
38 repetitions
if they are
spread out
over three days.
A more complex subject
which required
504 repetitions
in one day
could be mastered
by repeating it
158 times
the first day,
109 times
the second day,
and 75 times
the third day.
Thus repetitions
for all three
consecutive days

↓

add up to 342,

effecting a saving

of time

amounting to

approximately

30 percent

if compared

with the 504 repetitions

on a single day.

Since time is,

or should be,

of great value

to all of us,

nobody should fail

to make use of

such a

time-saving device,

especially if it is

so easy to apply

as the proper spacing

of learning

and repetition.

Whenever

you have to learn

something new,

do not try

to master it

completely

on the first day.

Be satisfied

if you acquire

a fair knowledge

of it,

allow it to

sink into your memory,

and then repeat it

on the two following days

↓

and you will see

that you can master it

better

with less effort.

It is one of

the strange phenomena

of the human mind

that memory

continues to work

even when

the actual task

of learning

has ceased

and even when

we are asleep.

It is the same

peculiar occurrence

which helps us

to solve a problem

while we are dreaming,

especially a problem

on which

we focused our attention

before going to sleep

and which proved

too tough

for solution.

The only explanation

which is possible

for both phenomena

is the fact that

our subconscious mind

continues working

and thinking

while our conscious mind

is asleep.

The same mental power

↓

which produces dreams

must be able to work

on problems

and to solve them.

It is evidently wrong

to think

of our conscious

and our subconscious

functioning

as two mental activities

which are

eternally divided.

It is much better

to think of them

as two rooms

whose separating wall

is flexible

and easily removable.

It is

figuratively accurate

to speak

of the "threshold"

between the conscious

and the

subconscious mind,

for every thought

can easily lapse

from the conscious

to the subconscious,

and we are

sometimes able

to draw a thought

from the subconscious

over this threshold

into the conscious mind.

How was your comprehension? ☐ good ☐ fair ☐ poor
Were you comparatively unaware of inner speech?
☐ yes ☐ no

Perception Exercise 39

Proceed as before with the following material. Use your card as in the previous exercise to inhibit regressions and to control speed.

Slow readers, even with good comprehension, haven't time for the extensive reading required both in and out of school. Many jobs are jeopardized by slow reading habits, and academic success is difficult unless students can compete with classmates in quantity as well as quality. Furthermore, slow reading is tedious, replete with boredom, fatigue and daydreaming. Mature readers control speed. They differentiate rates to accommodate not only material and purpose but also the various comprehension needs within a selection by varying speed from line to line, sentence to sentence, paragraph to paragraph, and chapter to chapter.

Slow reading, sometimes the result and sometimes the cause of deficiencies in other reading skills, is affected by ability to (1) read by thought units, (2) see relationships, (3) determine author-reader purpose, (4) use key ideas, (5) develop adequate sight and meaning vocabulary, and (6) eliminate inner speech. Improvement in these skills should improve rate, but such is not al-ways the case; slow reading may be a mental habit of long standing, a carry-over from earlier training. Over-emphasis on word analysis, pronunciation, phonics and oral reading tends to establish habit patterns more closely related to oral than to silent reading. Many slow readers in high school and college have not made adequate transition from oral to silent reading.

Relation of Rate to Comprehension. There is no merit in rapid or slow reading except that it meets comprehension needs. By and large, more comprehension difficulties stem from too slow, rather than from too fast, a reading rate. Theoretically, efficient reading rate should correspond to an individual's rate of thinking. Only then does the reader give full attention to the context and overcome the arch enemy of comprehension—reverie reading. Obviously, vocabulary difficulties and other deficiencies in mechanics affect concentration; however, with easy-reading materials, a reading speed which approaches thinking rate improves comprehension.

Recognizing Key Ideas. Not every word in a reading selection is important. Usually two-thirds of a sentence, paragraph, or chapter is illustrative, explanatory or repetitious. Slow readers tend to (1) confuse supplemental material with main ideas, (2) give equal emphasis to important and unimportant words, and (3) comprehend isolated ideas rather than related wholes. In slow reading, key ideas become so widely separated by intervening connectives and supplemental materials that continuity of thought is often lost.

Mature readers detect key ideas rapidly and subordinate nonessential details. Efficient rapid readers see relationships more clearly, and the induced concentration sharpens their wits for better comprehension and retention. In reporting on a selection which he has read, the slow reader tends to recount isolated details and incidents rather than to summarize key thoughts. To some extent, this may be due to over-conscientiousness;

through past experience the reader may have developed a distorted idea of careful reading. A slow reader, already lost among details, is only further confused when a teacher admonishes, "Read this again, CAREFULLY!" Rapid reading discourages the kind of "careful" reading that contributes to fragmentary thinking.

A THIRD CHALLENGE TO YOUR READING HABITS

You have already attempted, probably with reasonable success, to cover two not-too-heavy novels, each in a single stretch of continuous reading, and pacing yourself to finish each one within a few hours. (Possibly, if you were delighted with the efficiency of this type of reading, you decided to go through more than the two books required by the assignment in Chapter 8 and now find that you pick up a novel whenever you have a free evening, cruising and skimming right through from beginning to end before you put it down.)

Here, now, is another challenge for you to meet.

Within the next few days, find an evening in which you will have an hour or two at your disposal, and sit down with an issue of any magazine that you generally read—a new issue that you have not yet looked at.

Before the evening is over, finish that magazine from cover to cover.

This does not mean reading every word, nor every page, nor even every article and story.

Read those things in the magazine that interest you— it may be a total of a third, a half, three quarters, or any fraction of the issue that appeals to you. Skim whenever you feel so inclined, skip whatever you like, but stay with the magazine until you've got out of it what you want, until you've reached the point where that particular issue holds nothing else for you.

Read of course, as always, in rapid pursuit of the central theme of each article (and for the general framework of the plot of each story, if the magazine contains stories).

Have an awareness, if you can, of the structure of thinking and planning used by the writer—and think along with the writer as you read.

Try to make it a habit to read magazines through, in this way, in one sitting. If success attends your efforts, either immediately or eventually, you will discover that you can get twice as much magazine reading done as you used to—and in the same time and probably with greater enjoyment!

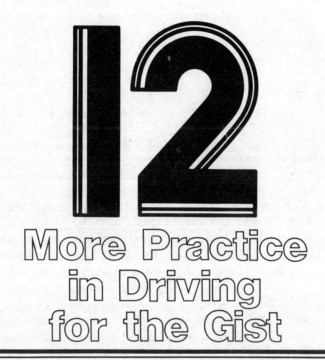

Mor Practice in Driving for the Gist

Chapter 12 challenges you to read a brief selection through quickly and then tell what it says.

You work, in this chapter, on a number of shorter selections, practicing to:

• Increase your skill and speed in driving through details to get a central picture

• Understand more clearly how details contribute to, or reinforce, a main idea

• Sharpen your response to main ideas by trying to answer, in your own words, questions on the central meaning of what you have read

CONCENTRATE ON THE GIST!

All the parts of any artistic whole are intimately related; the artist consciously and deliberately uses details in such a way as to achieve a maximum total effect.

When you look at a painting, a piece of sculpture, a building, a dress, or a beautifully furnished room—and all these are artistic compositions—what strikes you first and with the greatest impact is the overall design. The details are there, for without them there would be no design; but the painter, the sculptor, the architect, the fashion artist, or the interior decorator has so arranged and disposed the details that although each may be comparatively inconspicuous by itself, it nevertheless contributes, in one way or another, to the final result.

Indeed, if any detail is so prominent that it catches and holds the eye, thus weakening the effect of the whole, we say that the composition lacks unity and is an artistic failure.

In a landscape, for example, there may be a palm tree at the edge of a desert; or in a still life there may be some spots on a banana; but it's not the tree or the spots the artist wants you to see as much as the whole sweep of the desert or the whole bowl of fruit.

Similarly, the sculptor carves a nose and a mouth on the face of a statue, the architect strategically locates windows and doors in a structure, the designer places buttons and bows in a garment, the decorator hangs drapes and pictures in a room; but it's the effect of the *whole* statue, the *whole* building, the *whole* dress, or the *whole* room that the creative artist is striving for.

So also in a piece of writing. Like any other creative artists, authors arrange their details to achieve a total effect, a final meaning, a lasting impression; and a writer no more wants you to concentrate on isolated details than does a painter, sculptor, architect, dress designer, or interior decorator.

Unfortunately, unlike most other artistic creations, a piece of writing cannot be comprehended in a single glance. Readers have to plow through the individual details, they have to fit these details together in their own mind, they have to do a certain amount of thinking about the details before they can fully appreciate the author's central and final meaning.

As you have discovered from your own experience, *you have to work at seeing and understanding the overall meaning.*

You have to translate words into ideas, and you have to weigh the relative importance of these ideas. You have to understand details not as independent elements, but as steppingstones to, or support for, or as explanation or clarification of, the *gist* of what a writer is trying to say to you.

And, if you are a skillful reader, you do all this *rapidly, accurately,* and *intelligently.*

Rapidly, so that the words and details do not get in the way of your overall comprehension.

Accurately, so that you come away with the actual *central* meaning the author is aiming at, rather than some entirely different, irrelevant, or incorrect meaning.

And *intelligently,* so that you either accept the author's thinking as logical, well based, and in accord with truth and reality, or reject it as illogical, unfounded, or untrue.

Again I ask you, as I did in Chapter 7, to read a group of short selections, purposefully aiming at an efficient grasp of the main idea of each one. Needless to say, you are not to revert to any old habits of slow, dawdling comprehension; read, rather, with a strong *sense of urgency.*

Get into the selection quickly; grasp the author's pattern of thinking; skim to whatever extent skimming will help you x-ray the material.

Keep in mind, as you read, that your sole purpose is to look for, and find, central meaning.

In this way, you will cut down or eliminate vocal responses, motor responses, word-by-word responses, regression responses, excessive auditory responses—in fine, you'll avoid all responses but the one vital response: the intellectual and psychological response to the author's central message.

After each selection there will be a number of comprehension questions. *Answer these without, for the moment, further reference to the material.*

The first question, in each case, will test your understanding of, and your ability to recall, the *gist* of what you have read; next will come one or more questions on the important contributing elements that explain or clarify the author's central theme.

Write out all your answers. Be brief, and use your own words—do not be concerned with style or grammar, just express your thoughts in a way that is clear to yourself. (Answer all comprehension questions on the first four selections before checking with the key that follows exercise 18.)

RAPID COMPREHENSION EXERCISE 15

Self-Respect and Self-Confidence
by Douglas Remsen, M.D.

[1] No one can live with himself comfortably without self-respect; without self-confidence no one can enjoy the sense of satisfaction in accomplishment. Self-respect depends upon an emotional equilibrium in which anger, resentment, fear, and love are supports to the person's efforts and activities, not whips which drive and lacerate. Self-confidence depends upon ability, upon the adequacy to meet a situation, or to do something successfully. It incorporates also a capacity to take stock, to be honest in self-appraisal, so that one doesn't shoot at the moon and torture oneself for

missing it. It means knowing what one knows— and more important—knowing what one doesn't know and not being ashamed to say so.

[2] The standards we set unconsciously—social, puritanical, intellectual, perfectionistic—we rarely meet perfectly; but too many of us dwell upon the things we *didn't* do, the questions we *didn't* answer, to the point where the things done well are insufficient to support our self-respect and nurture our self-confidence. Then there follows self-abasement, inferiority feelings, inhibitions, and depression.

[3] This quirk of human nature frequently has its roots in the home and environmental settings. As a small child, little Willie is subjected to a constant barrage of: Don't!, Quit!, Stop It!, Why did you do that?—the equivalent of "You stupid little idiot." The parent forgets that he or she is Olympian authority in the small one's eyes. This constant equivalent of "you stupid little idiot" chokes the childish struggle for being important and for building self-confidence. There is no thought of giving any praise or approval to the fumbling successes of the child. And the final lethal dose of

poison to budding self-respect and self-confidence is "Aren't you ashamed of yourself?" administered so frequently with no thought of its stultifying effect. In later years, the fear of being shamed throws the stutterer into a dither, sends the alcoholic to have another drink, and the neurotic to hide in the cave of his inhibitions.

[4] Mr. X, a stutterer, never stutters when he issues commands as a drill sergeant at the armory. He is confident and sure. But when he meets any person who symbolizes authority, he stutters miserably. He first stuttered when he faced uniformed authority five years ago to take a test and failed. You will not be surprised to learn that his stern father, the symbol of authority, never offered him as a child a word of approval for his accomplishments, but only the belittling condemnation of "Aren't you ashamed?"

[5] Its's time for an inventory. Take stock, but with excitement; not with the doubts of an inhibited soul! What you have done and experienced can be the foundation for self-respect and self-confidence.

Comprehension Test

1. What, in brief, makes for self-respect and self-confidence? _____

_____

2. In what ways do childhood relationships frequently play a role in failing to support an adult's self-respect and self-confidence? _____

_____

RAPID COMPREHENSION EXERCISE 16 Speech Patterns

[1] Literally putting out his tongue at his audience, Dr. Cyril Darlington, a fellow of the Royal Society, a geneticist, declared that language and dialect and speech characteristics depended on heredity.

[2] He said that it now had been well established by work on blood groups—as a result of blood transfusion work in the war more than 4,000,000 persons in Britain alone had been grouped—that there was a definite connection between genetic characteristics and language. Different human groups have different tongue and throat formations that he said are transmitted by parents.

[3] To demonstrate this, he pushed out his tongue in the form of a cylinder and challenged his audience to try it. He said half of them would be able to do it and the other half would not.

[4] To support his claim of the relation of language to genetics, he took the sound "th" and showed that, far from being an Anglo-Saxon char-

acteristic as generally supposed, it extended from Iceland through Norway, Denmark, Britain, Spain, Greece, the Levant, South Arabia, South India, Burma, and Siam into China. In fact, he declared, it corresponds accurately with the geographic distribution of the O blood group.

[5] Dr. Darlington also asserted that in families, the children in learning to speak had characteristic impediments that represented individual expression of a genotype and could be identified with the parental genes.

[6] Dialects, he added, are not just acquired habits of locality but a definite expression of local or regional characteristics arising from hereditary types produced by intermarriage. Heredity, as much as local loyalties, resists the pressure of dialect change, he maintained, saying that continuing work on blood group distribution would definitely establish a connection between heredity and the character of language.

Comprehension Test

1. According to Dr. Darlington, what is the determining causative factor of people's speech patterns? _____

_____

_____

2. By what means did Dr. Darlington arrive at his conclusion? _____

_____

_____

RAPID COMPREHENSION EXERCISE 17

Retaliation Reaction
by James Sonnett Greene, M.D.

[1] An old precept admonishes us to count ten before acting in anger. I thought of that recently when someone I had liked and trusted took advantage of that trust to advance himself personally, at my expense. My first reaction was to retaliate, but having learned from sad experience the folly of acting destructively when in an emotional state, I turned my mobilized energies into a quite different channel and accomplished a task I had been trying to get to for several days.

[2] This is a type of experience that everyone goes through many times in his life, and the typical first reaction is one of retaliation. If we analyze this reaction, we find that the only thing we are really seeking at the moment, and the only thing we accomplish for ourselves by retaliation, is release of the tension that the situation has built up in us. But we accomplish this usually at the expense of erasing any feelings of guilt or remorse the other fellow may have, and thus our retaliatory reaction, far from "paying him back," actually plays into the other person's hands.

[3] We can release tension just as well by other types of action and with real reward to ourselves. The best way is to utilize the energy that has been mobilized by our anger to counteract, by some constructive action, the harm that the other person has done us. If this is impossible, the energy should be drained off in some other useful activity. But for many reasons—and if for no other, then for purely selfish ones—we should not react destructively.

[4] The important thing is to realize in our moment of anger that our adrenal glands have flooded us with energy which demands an "out," and that to play safe we should release it immediately into some constructive channel. By immediately drawing off the "charge," we avoid the danger of explosion with all its potentialities for harmful consequences to ourselves and others. In brief, when angry emotion is aroused act quickly—but not in retaliation. *War never pays!*

Comprehension Test

1. What, according to Dr. Greene, are the best ways to react when angry? _____

_____

_____

_____

2. What are we really seeking when we react with retaliation? _____

_____

_____

3. In what way does such a reaction play into the hands of the object of our anger? _____

_____

_____

4. What is the physiological result of anger? _____

_____

_____

RAPID COMPREHENSION EXERCISE 18

Chinese, Japanese, and Polynesian
by Bjorn Karlsen

[1] Of the countries in Asia whose written languages do not utilize the Roman alphabet, China has the most unusual language of them all. The teaching of reading in China, therefore, presents some unique problems. The written language consists of "characters," each of which has one sound

functioning more or less like an English syllable. Many of these characters sound alike but look different and have different meanings. This situation exists to a slight degree in English, too. The sound "too" can be spelled "to," "two," or "too," and has six different meanings. In Chinese, however, there are only about 600 different word sounds, but they cover more than 50,000 meanings. These meanings are revealed only by the characters. These characters are usually combined, forming nearly six times as many polysyllabic words as monosyllabic. Each character retains its orginal pronunciation, but the word itself takes on an entirely different meaning. (For example, the Chinese character "Tung" means east, the character "Hsi" means west, but the two characters combined mean "a thing.")

[2] It is quite obvious that this language is a very difficult one to learn to read. One Chinese scholar, Fang Chao-ying, is of the opinion that China will never become literate with this system of writing, and most Chinese will agree that the written language is one of their biggest educational problems. Three solutions for this problem have been suggested. First of all, much effort has been exerted to reduce the number of characters. These attempts have been quite successful, partly because of the existence of a great number of obsolete characters. Twenty five years ago, a Chinese unabridged dictionary could contain 45,000 characters. This number has recently been reduced to 10,000. It has been estimated by one Chinese authority that a minimum knowledge of 5000 characters is necessary for a person to manage his own affairs. The average student in China will know 5000 characters by the time he reaches twelfth grade. His word vocabulary is three times as large, however, because of his knowledge of polysyllabic words.

[3] An expert on the Chinese language, Jimmy Yen, has determined which 1000 characters are most commonly used, and has developed reading materials using nothing but these characters. Although this does simplify the processes involved in learning to read, a person is only partially literate after having learned these characters.

Comprehension Test

1. How does Dr. Karlsen account for the low literacy rate in China and Japan, and the high literacy rate in the Polynesian Islands? _____

_____

_____

2. What makes Chinese so difficult to read? _____

_____

3. What makes Polynesian so easy to read? _____

_____

[4] A second approach to this problem has been the development of 37 phonetic symbols (Juyin Fuhau), which are relatively easy to learn. Few books are printed using these symbols and they are, by most people, considered merely as stepping stones to the learning of the characters.

[5] Finally, several systems have been devised to Romanize the Chinese languages, using 22 letters. However, one syllable might have 100 meanings so that a word written with phonetic symbols or letters would not convey its exact meaning. This problem does not exist with the use of characters.

[6] The problem is a difficult one, one that is affecting many millions of people. So far, none of the solutions suggested seems to be satisfactory.

[7] Similar problems exist in Japan. Dr. Frank Freeman, who was a member of the U.S. Education Mission to Japan shortly after World War II, wrote:

Another difficulty lies in the cumbersome written language which makes it impossible for children in the elementary school to learn to read and write more than the rudiments of the language. They spend half their time in acquiring this meager command of writing and reading. They are therefore unable to learn more than a modicum of the content subjects. The mission recommended a simplification of the written language which would overcome these difficulties.

[8] There are, at the other extreme, some languages that are easy to learn. One of these is Polynesian which consists of a group of dialects spoken on the Polynesian Islands. The missionaries working on these islands have developed a written language which is probably the simplest in the world. The alphabet has only 12 letters, 5 vowels and 7 consonants. Each letter stands for one sound, making the language 100 percent phonetic. In using this system, reading can be learned in a very short time, in most instances in a couple of hours. The simplicity of this language has resulted in, except for Europe and North America, the highest literacy rate in the world today. This is a quite remarkable fact considering that many of the people on these islands were cannibals only a century ago.

Key to Exercises 15-18

(Your language will of course differ from that used in the answers below, but the thoughts should be similar. Refer to each selection when you study the discussions.)

Exercise 15 (page 176)

1. Ability, adequacy, and successes; not setting perfectionist goals that are unachievable; not constantly dwelling on one's failures; etc.

2. Criticism and abasement of the child by parents instead of approval and praise for accomplishments.

DISCUSSION

The main idea is explicitly expressed in the last half of

the first paragraph, and repeated, in the form of a personal exhortation to the reader, in the final paragraph—all else in the piece is elaboration and illustrative details. The third paragraph contains important material, since it offers an explanation of the cause for self-doubts.

Exercise 16 (page 177)

1. Heredity, that is, the different tongue and throat formations transmitted from parents to offspring.

2. By classifying people into blood groups.

DISCUSSION

As you would expect in any news item, the "lead," or main point, occurs right at the beginning, with elaboration and illustration rounding out the "story." An important detail explains by what means the conclusion was reached (paragraph 2).

Exercise 17 (page 178)

1. By counteracting damage through constructive action, or by engaging in some useful activity.

2. Release of the tension (or draining off of the excess energy) produced by anger.

3. Relieves his guilt or remorse.

4. Flooding of the body with energy by the adrenal glands.

DISCUSSION

After some introductory material, Dr. Greene foreshadows his main point toward the end of paragraph 1, expresses it completely in paragraph 3, and pounds it home again in the final paragraph. The three important details queried in the test (what we seek when we retaliate, how retaliation affects the other person, and what anger does to our physiology) all explain the reasoning behind the author's central thought.

Exercise 18 (page 178)

1. The difficulties of learning to read the complicated Chinese and Japanese written languages, and the ease of learning to read the simple Polynesian written language.

2. The large number of characters and the fact that the different word sounds combine to make up so many diverse meanings.

3. The small number of characters and the fact that the language is completely phonetic.

DISCUSSION

Here is a more complicated selection, one containing a whole mass of details that you must sort in your mind in

order to arrive neatly, efficiently, and accurately at the central point—namely *the relationship between literacy and the structure of the written language.* Note how closely the important details (*why Chinese is hard, and Polynesian easy, to read*) tie in with the main idea.

A piece of writing, we have decided, differs from true forms of visual art in that you cannot respond to the effect of the whole in a single glance. In reading, the "viewer" has to work at seeing and understanding, for a page of print, though at first apprehended by the eye, is fundamentally grasped by the mind through the powers of interpretation, reasoning, and analysis.

But just as your vision can be educated so that you respond more intelligently to a work of art, so your powers of interpretation, reasoning, and analysis can be refined so that you respond more efficiently and more rapidly to what a writer offers you on a page of print.

This process of refinement started years ago—when you first learned to read at the age of six or seven. It continued through elementary and high school and into your late adolescence. And then, possibly, it stopped, though there was still much room for improvement.

However, your training in this book has aimed at *further* refinement of all the visual and comprehension skills that efficient reading demands; and by now these skills should be sufficiently sharpened to enable you to react so quickly to the gist of an author's thinking that it might seem—to exaggerate a bit—as if you are comprehending the essence of a paragraph almost at a glance.

SESSION 36

AND STILL MORE PRACTICE

Continue this immensely valuable practice in which you attempt to respond quickly and accurately to the central point of a short selection. As before, drive straight for the gist, confident that you need not get entangled in the minor details, and aware, as you read, how the important details provide the necessary foundation for clear and full understanding.

Skim to whatever extent skimming will help you x-ray the material.

RAPID COMPREHENSION EXERCISE 19

Lengthening Longevity
by William C. FitzGibbon

[1] Although man has often been in doubt as to *how* life should be lived, he has never doubted that it should be—and for as long as possible. His efforts to prolong life (occasional lapses into wholesale homicide notwithstanding), have succeeded. Since 1900 in America, for example, he has stretched his life expectancy from 48 years to the recently announced figure of 69.8 years, an unprecedented gain of more than twenty years in little more than half a century. Thus a child born today in the United States has the bright prospect of living out the legendary (though heretofore uncommon), three score and ten.

[2] The newborn child, according to the Metropolitan Life statisticians, never had it so good. In the Bronze Age—so studies of unearthed bones reveal—an infant had a life expectancy of 18 years. Two thousand years ago a Roman urchin could count on 22 years. In the Middle Ages the figure rose to 35, with no change from then until 1838 when, in England and Wales, the expectancy hit 40.

[3] Today's increase in life expectancy is common to most Western countries. Norway, the Netherlands, Sweden, Denmark and England have rates much the same as the United States,

with other European nations close behind. Lowest life expectancy among countries on which figures are available is in India, where the rate is 32. (India is the only country where life expectancy of males is higher than that of females.) Other low rates: Egypt: 35; Mexico: 39; Puerto Rico: 46. No recent figures are available on Russia. (Scientists doubt, incidentally, that anyone has lived beyond 150 years—or that medical technique can ever extend life expectancy much over 100).

[4] Life expectancy tables had their start in the middle of the seventeenth century, one of the early innovators being the English astronomer Halley, of comet fame. Since life expectancy is a figure arrived at by averaging a population's death ages, the biggest single reason for longer expectancy has been the drop in infant mortality.

[5] When an American wakes to find that he has reached the life expectancy figure of 69.8 years, he shouldn't expect to perish before the day is up. He is one of the lucky ones who probably will live out the years at the farther end of the average. A man reaching 69.8 may expect to live 10 to 12 more years; at 75 he has about eight years; at 80 he has six. This does not, however, go on ad infinitum. Sorry.

Comprehension Test*

1. What has happened to life expectancy in most western countries since 1900? _____

_____

2. What is a main reason for the increase in life expectancy? _____

_____

RAPID COMPREHENSION EXERCISE 20

Lightning and Safety
by Dr. Theodore R. Van Dellen

[1] A flash of lightning and a deafening crash of thunder are enough to make a child scream and a dog scoot under the bed, his tail between his legs. Some adults also are frightened, particularly those who have had a close call with nature's fireworks.

[2] The child who is frightened by thunder and lightning needs comfort rather than ridicule. At night, stay in the bedroom if necessary. The majority can be calmed by a story or song. Older tots are helped by watching and discussing the flashes and roars provided the parents show no evidence of alarm.

[3] The experiments of Benjamin Franklin 200 years ago helped dispel superstitions and primitive ideas about this natural phenomenon.

[4] If a church instead of a nearby gambling joint is struck by lightning, the people no longer are amazed that a good rather than a bad place should bear the brunt. They realize the church was struck because its steeple is the highest point in the vicinity.

[5] Lightning represents a discharge of atmospheric electricity from one cloud to another or from a cloud to the earth. The best targets here

*Do exercises 19-22 before checking your answers against the key on page 184-185.

below are projections of some height. This makes the church spire more vulnerable than a low building protected by a grove of trees.

[6] On the other hand a single tree, shack, fence pole or human being becomes the best target on a prairie, more so when representing the only inlet for a bolt of lightning within a radius of miles.

[7] When an electrical charge strikes a hollow object, such as a tin box, the charge runs down the outside, not the inside. This means that when a house, metal auto or steel freight car is struck the occupants need not worry provided they are not near an open window or door.

[8] Electricity also is conducted easier through wet objects than dry. Consequently, it is poor policy to be in an open boat in the middle of a lake or under a lone wet tree on the golf course during a storm. When fishing on a lake, at the first sign of a storm, row for shore pronto. Swimmers should leave the water and seek protection.

Stay indoors during a thunderstorm but if caught outside, choose a safe shelter, preferably a large metal building or a dwelling protected against lightning.

If these are not available look for a cave, depression in the ground, valley, the foot of an overhanging cliff, or dense woods. Keep away from small exposed sheds, isolated trees, wire fences, hilltops and open spaces.

Comprehension Test

1. What should you do during a lightning storm? _____

_____

_____

2. How should you react to a child's fright over lightning?

_____

3. What kind of structures does lightning generally strike? _____

_____

4. What makes indoors safe? _____

_____

5. Why is water unsafe? _____

_____

RAPID COMPREHENSION EXERCISE 21   Quiz Kid

by Katherine V. Bishop

[1] Recently, while driving from one school to another, I heard part of a quiz program over the car radio. The MC introduced an eleven year old boy as a contestant. The youngster was well poised, and established his need for a bicycle in an admirable manner.

[2] The first question was put to the boy. The MC asked him to give a six letter word ending in *it*, the name of an animal. After a second or so of heavy silence the MC said, "Think now, I'm asking for the name of an animal, a six letter word ending in *it*, this is the name of an animal we think of at Easter." Still no answer from the boy and the MC said, "Maybe it will help you to know that the word begins with the letter *r*."

[3] "BUNNY!" shouted the boy.

[4] The studio audience roared with laughter and the boy was given full credit for a correct answer.

[5] "The next question," said the MC, "asks you to name three things we learn to do in school. In the words of a song each of these begins with the letter *r*." Since no response was forthcoming the MC said, "Give me the name of just one of the three." There was no response. In desperation, for time was running out, the MC said, "Tell me, what do you do when you open a book?"

[6] There was no hesitation now as the eleven year old boy answered, "Look at the pictures." Hilarious laughter followed this answer and the boy was awarded the prize he sought, money enough to buy a bicycle.

[7] What can this boy read from this experience with adults other than that it *is funny and lucrative to be ignorant?*

[8] To me this episode is far from laughable and far from unimportant. It is an example of the unreality that characterizes adult-child relations at home, at school, and in the community at large. In this case, I believe that the boy should have been told that he had failed to answer the questions correctly and that for that reason he had not won the money; but, that because his need was urgent the money would be loaned to him on terms that he could meet.

[9] Through such action the boy would have

gained two things more important, in my estimation, than money. He would have gained respect for the fairness of the adults in charge of the quiz, and ultimately by fulfilling his obligation, *self-respect.*

Comprehension Test

1. What, in Dr. Bishop's opinion, does this episode illustrate? _____

_____

_____

2. What has the child learned from his experience? ____

_____

_____

3. How does Dr. Bishop think the problem might better have been handled? _____

_____

4. What would have been the result of this preferable method? _____

_____

_____

RAPID COMPREHENSION EXERCISE 22

At Times I Think My Daughter Hates Me . . .
by Ruth Englund Forrest

It's almost futile to try to express deeply personal thoughts to her or to comment much about my life. Perhaps I sense that, at 17, her grasp on adulthood is too tenuous to risk infringing the realities of her mother's life on her own daily existence. Or perhaps I fear that any baring of emotion on my part—any hint of despair in this parent who has been her enemy and protector for so long—would have far too dreadful consequences for her even to contemplate.

"Come and listen to this," she says. As I do so, she watches to see whether I am as moved as she is by Cat Stevens or the Beatles or the Jefferson Starship: This much she can afford to share with me.

She reads the Bible and Nietzsche and Hesse. She has wept over "Death Be Not Proud" and reread Michener's "The Source." She studies Shakespeare's tragedies and the Classification of Insects.

She washes her hair every day.

She diets.

She's been in love. I know that, even though she's never told me in so many words. Hearing her cry, I've felt my own heart contract with remembered pain—and with pain for her. My attempts to comfort her have been met with stony face and stony eyes. Somehow, earlier, I failed to keep the door open for such exchanges, and now she seems to have no desire to help reopen it.

At times like these I think she hates me.

But on another occasion she will recount a girlfriend's troubles with her mother, as though trying to tell me I'm not all that bad.

She spends long hours in the sun, tanning her lovely torso, her long legs. I approve her purchase of this bikini, refusing to judge it with her grandparents' eyes. Yet I wonder what the boys think when they see her wearing it. Perhaps, the way girls dress now, the boys have become impervious to the display of smooth flesh. No—that simply cannot be.

Almost without thinking about it, she approves of *my* bikini. She expresses surprise that her father and I agreed to separate because we weren't happy, instead of "staying together for the kids." As she puts it, "I didn't think your generation had that much sense."

She doesn't know that I can remember—as clearly as though it were yesterday—what it is like to be 17.

We fight much too often: about her room, her frequent shampoos, her late hours, *her* attitude, *my* attitude. I say she's stubborn; she says I refuse to see her point of view.

I look at her and see myself again and again, from a thousand different angles, at a thousand different times.

As a rational person, I perceive her obstinacy and anger as an instinctive defense against my well-meant tyranny, my tendency to think of her as a little girl who must be cared for and corrected. (It's a defense I neglected to use with my parents, and I've suffered from that failure.)

Looking at her, listening to her, I try to see a young woman, not just my daughter. But looking at me and listening to me, she seems to see *only* a mother: a mother who's overprotective, too demanding, too quick to criticize, too ready to put down *her* views, *her* music, *her* desires.

Together we've built a wall with no gate. It's been slow work over many years, and is nowhere near completion. The wall is still low enough for us both to see and even step over it. Whenever I can, I knock out some of the blocks I've laid, or at least I try to. I only hope she doesn't feel the wall must be finished before she can be a grownup.

Comprehension Test

1. Why does the author believe that "it's almost futile to express deeply personal thoughts" to her daughter? _____

_____

_____

_____

_____

2. What do the author and her daughter fight about "much too often"? _____

_____

_____

_____

3. What are the author and her daughter building between them? _____

_____

_____

_____

4. In essence, the problem is that her daughter sees Mrs. Englund as _____

_____

_____

while Mrs. Englund tries to see her daughter as also _____

_____

Key to Exercise 19–22

(Your language will of course differ from that used below, but the thoughts should be similar. Refer to each selection when you study the discussions.)

Exercise 19 (page 181)

1. It has increased considerably—more than 20 years.
2. Drop in infant deaths.

DISCUSSION

We have here a mass of interesting details on life expectancy. Clearly, what the author is pointing out in total is that life expectancy has increased tremendously in recent years and that the biggest single reason is a drop in infant mortality.

I'm her mother. Perhaps, for her, that's all I can ever be allowed to be. Perhaps, for me, that will have to be enough, but over the long years ahead I do want and hope for so much more.

Exercise 20 (page 181)

1. During a lightning storm stay indoors or in a safe shelter.
2. Be comforting, soothing, calm, show no alarm, etc.
3. High, projecting, isolated, etc.
4. Lightning charge runs down the outside of a hollow object.
5. Wet objects are better conductors for electricity than dry.

DISCUSSION

Dr. Van Dellen is obviously telling his readers how to avoid being struck by lightning. Though using a large number of details and scientific facts, he is cautioning us, in essence, to remain indoors or in a safe shelter during a lightning storm, and to avoid places usually struck by lightning.

Exercise 21 (page 182)

1. The unreality of relations between adults and children.
2. That it pays to be ignorant.
3. The money loaned, rather than given to him, since he failed to answer the questions.
4. Respect by the boy for adults' fairness and for himself.

DISCUSSION

Most of this excerpt is devoted to a narrative description of the radio quiz, the MC's questions, and the child's naïve answers. Then comes an important detail ("it is funny and lucrative to be ignorant") that prepares the reader for Dr. Bishop's main idea, that adult-child relations are, as this episode shows, unrealistic. Dr. Bishop then clarifies her position with two further important details—how the boy might have been treated more realistically, and how this realistic approach would have served him better.

Exercise 22 (page 183)

1. Because the daughter, at 17, has too slight a grasp on adulthood to risk letting the mother's reality infringe on her own existence, and any awareness of her mother's personal feelings would threaten the daughter's drive to grow up and become independent.
2. The daughter's room, frequent shampoos, late hours, attitudes, etc.
3. A wall that separates them and bars open communication.
4. . . . sees Mrs. Englund as *a mother, no more than a mother, and may never view Mrs. Englund as anyone but*

her mother, while Mrs. Englund tries to see her daughter as also *a young woman.*

DISCUSSION

This selection starts with a paragraph that sets the tone and offers evidence and feelings to prepare the reader for the author's problem.

The piece goes on to show further instances of lack of communication and acceptance between mother and daughter, detailing ways in which the generation gap exists.

The author finally expresses her despair and frustration that her daughter sees her only as a mother, perhaps will always see her only as a mother, though the mother tries to see her daughter also as a young woman.

SESSION 37

PERCEPTION TRAINING IX

Perception Exercise 40

Sweep down each column, making only one fixation to the line. Go as fast as comprehension permits, and be more aware of the ideas than of inner speech. Use your card, as explained in perception exercise 23 (page 123) to inhibit regressions and to control speed.

Your eyes are muscles,	for hours	doing any great amount
and correct use	without feeling	of reading
of those muscles	the slightest fatigue.	by means of
cannot injure them.	It is generally agreed	overhead lights
If you make sure	that 75 to 100 watts	in your home;
to do	of electricity,	use a lamp,
most of your reading	in a shaded lamp—	placed to your left
in daylight,	preferably	whenever practicable,
or in artificial light	from a frosted bulb—	and see that the bulbs
so placed	coming over	are no weaker
that no shadow falls	your left shoulder,	than 75 watts.
on the page,	produces ideal,	The important things
and of sufficient strength	shadowless reading	are:
so that the act	conditions.	a sufficient intensity
of reading	Try to avoid doing	of light
causes no strain,	any considerable amount	for your type of eyes,
you can,	of reading	and the
under these	in a moving train,	complete absence
ideal conditions,	especially at night.	of shadows.
go on reading	Avoid also	

Perception Exercise 41
Continue as before.

The Best Time for Learning
by Dr. Bruno Furst and Lotte Furst

Did you ever notice
when your sleep
is deeper;
is it at night
or during
the morning hours?
Some people sleep
so much deeper
at night
that they are
not disturbed
by a noise
that would wake
them up
in the morning.
The opposite
holds true for
the morning sleeper.
That fact in itself
should not concern us
in a memory course,
but there is a
very interesting
connection
between the depth
of your sleep
and the best time
for you to learn
and memorize.
Many tests
have proven that
the person who sleeps
easily and deeply

during the early hours
of the night
is alert and
full of life
the moment
he wakes up
in the morning.
Therefore his best
learning time is
the hour
immediately
after awaking.
On the other hand,
people who sleep deeper
in the morning
usually need
several hours
after breakfast
to reach the peak
of their mental ability.
Their best learning time
is the late afternoon
and evening.
Whether or not
your job permits you
to make use
or your "best time"
for such work
as a memory course
is another question.
Frequently your
business
may require you

to spend your
"best time for learning"
on some kind
of mechanical work.
If your "best time"
is in the evening,
you may be
too tired after
a full day's work
to devote
the evening hours
to mental work.
All this can happen
in everyday life,
but it is still
important for you
to be aware of
your best learning time.
Some day
it may be possible
for you to adjust
your working hours
and to do
mental work
at such times
as are best
for you.
Doing so will
save much effort
and will
considerably shorten
the time you need
to devote to repetition

Perception Exercise 42

Scan each line quickly, checking off one word that is *essentially the same in meaning as the key word.*

Your goal: Finish in 40 seconds or less with 90% accuracy.

Remember: You are looking for *synonyms.*

Time at this moment: _____ minutes _____ seconds

Start timing!

Key Word
1. **bill** blow blush basket brush beak bring

2. **pose** predict prevent posture past push pale

3. **throw** thrum flow thrall flu flush fling fluster

4. **caution** carriage convey care close clever

5. **sure** shush shovel soothe certain curtain

6. **choice** crash chilly open oven option over

7. **ordinary** order ornery cool common clever

8. **courage** bribery bravery closer courier carriage

9. **increase** invest depend invent enlarge decrease

10. **dip** flip ship rip flunk sunk rink dunk

11. **earthly** early easy willowy winsomely worldly

12. **enter** leave stop penetrate previous precious

13. **external** eternal eventual inside outside beside

14. **fearful** faithful flowing truthful afraid aware

15. **generate** geriatric gesture brain brawl breed

16. **gather** gracious rather collect comment

17. **keep** refer remiss result retain kill king

18. **hurt** hover die due duty damage garbage

19. **jest** pest west lest poke spoke joke woke

20. **language** carriage marriage teach reach peach speech

21. **lure** fury fewer lower enjoy entice enough

22. **anger** hanger clangor entail enrage entertain enter

23. **obstinate** stubborn straitlaced overt flexible frivolous

24. **modest** proud loud humble hovel matter

25. **pleasure** measure flight treasure leisure sight delight

Time at finish: _____minutes _____seconds

Key

1. beak	6. option	11. worldly	16. collect	21. entice
2. posture	7. common	12. penetrate	17. retain	22. enrage
3. fling	8. bravery	13. outside	18. damage	23. stubborn
4. care	9. enlarge	14. afraid	19. joke	24. humble
5. certain	10. dunk	15. breed	20. speech	25. delight

Time required: _____seconds   **Number of correct responses:** _____   **(90% accuracy is 22–23)**

Perception Exercise 43

Now scan each line to discover *one word essentially opposite* in meaning to the key word. Aim for 90% accuracy in 60 seconds or less.

Remember: You are to check antonyms.

Time at this moment: _____minutes _____seconds

Key Word

1. **busy** wilder dizzy crazy idle insane

2. **external** fraternal paternal maternal tropical internal

3. **strong** heavy loud foible feeble fable string

4. **fierce** pier weird pierce feared gentle little

5. **lead** bead creed hollow follow wallow

6. **allow** bellow below shallow remit forbid

7. **empty** ugly tiny scurvy dull full bull

8. **detest** protest incest prove move love have

9. **safe** wave love prove grave tricky risky angry

10. **expose** repose impose wide ride hide glide doze

11. **untruthful** unuseful unusual modest jest honest

12. **apathetic** sympathetic empathetic responsive convulsive

13. **active** available possible previous partial passive

14. **join** disturb dissipate joust disconnect dispense

15. **lawful** awful dropful truthful illegal illegible

16. **accept** accelerate accidental refer hold refuse

17. **lucky** happy wispy unfortunate unknown unseen

18. **modern** trustful widen wooden antique angelic

19. **stay** strap strain to in with go low how

20. **large** barge urge lodge flight tight slight

21. **dark** hard park lark mark tight light

22. **pain** wane pane sane pleasure measure

23. **weak** meek seek teak great powerful sensible

24. **imaginary** ordinary stationary dull full real male

25. **reckless** helpless useless rigid timid putrid acid

Time at finish: _____ minutes _____ seconds

Key

1. idle	6. forbid	11. honest	16. refuse	21. light
2. internal	7. full	12. responsive	17. unfortunate	22. pleasure
3. feeble	8. love	13. passive	18. antique	23. powerful
4. gentle	9. risky	14. disconnect	19. go	24. real
5. follow	10. hide	15. illegal	20. slight	25. timid

Time required: _____ seconds   Number of correct responses: _____

Perception Exercise 44

Read straight down each column fixating approximately at the black arrow, and aiming for comprehension.

Although your aim is to make no more than one fixation to the line, *be totally unaware of fixations* — simply read rapidly and with a *sense of urgency,* to understand the material. Use your card, as in previous exercises, to inhibit regressions and to control speed. (see perception exercise 23, page 123.)

Bobby Returns to the Scene of the Crime

by Leon Lasken

Some months ago a black youngster was apprehended while breaking into the grocery store I own in Inglewood. The officer in charge of the case discussed the matter with me: Did I wish to press charges and have the 14-year-old boy arraigned? "Do what you think is best for Bobby," I said. "I'll trust your judgment."

He decided to seek arraignment, which required my presence at the courthouse. On the day of the proceedings, I spent four hours in the waiting room, and then the case was called to private chambers.

When I was summoned there, the pace was brisk—disposition took about 15 minutes. First, with my consent, the prosecutor reduced the felony charges to simple misdemeanors, and then the boy pleaded guilty. At that point I had played my small role, and so I rushed back to work.

If I had been permitted to speak my piece, it would have gone something like this:

"I'm sure the primary interest of all of us here is the well-being of Bobby. We know that he has everything going against him. By his own account, he doesn't even have a mother to live with him. I wonder if he even knows the meaning of the word 'love.'

"However, we owe something to ourselves and something to him. By chance and circumstance, he shares this life with us, and what happens to him will also affect us, as it will our children and our children's children.

"We must get through the layers of hate, fear and ignorance before they distort his brain and heart forever. We must give him the strong hand of understanding and concern.

"As for myself, there is little I can do. God

knows I have my hands full with the likes of Bobby at my grocery store. Existing, for me, has become a succession of everyday confrontations.

"I accept the reality of reality: that what is is because of what was. But I do not accept that tomorrow has to be the same. Perhaps it is because of my age that I am without fear or rancor, worrying little about today and even less about tomorrow.

"I would like to be Bobby's friend. I would like him to know he need never leave my store hungry and penniless. I have a broom with which he can sweep the inside, and I have a larger broom for the outside. Then, for doing either of these chores, I will give him a dollar, and for that dollar I'll give him two dollars of groceries.

"I don't know if I can ever come to understand him. I don't know if he can ever come to understand and trust me. But what do you say, Bobby? Why don't we give it a try?"

Since I never had a chance to say any of these things, I thought that was the end of it and I would never see Bobby again. But several weeks later something happened that made me wonder if Bobby had read my mind.

One day, out of the blue, he walked into the store, looking sort of sideways. "Hi, Bobby," I said, approaching

him. "How did you make out with the judge? Did you get probation?"

"Yeah."

"Have you ever been in trouble before"?

Bobby shook his head no.

"If you're hungry and don't have any money, you don't have to steal in here to get something to eat."

"Nah—I got some money."

The next morning I returned from the bank and found him waiting for me in the parking lot. He said, "I need $13 and only have $2.50. Do you have anything I can do around here to make some money?"

"What do you want the $13 for?" I asked.

"I want to get Ma a present."

"But you told the judge your mother was dead."

"I know—but she didn't want to be there, so that seemed the best thing to say."

I kept my emotions in check. "Come in tomorrow," I said, "and clean up the parking lot."

The next day he swept the parking lot. Bobby did such a good job, I gave him $2.50 worth of groceries and a bottle of pop. Yesterday he washed my car and earned $1.50.

After all these years, human behavior holds no surprises for me, and so I'll never abandon hope. If I can just bring a flash of light into Bobby's darkness . . .

How was your comprehension? ☐ excellent ☐ good
☐ fair ☐ poor

How to
Whip Through Material
with Good Comprehension

PREVIEW

SESSION 38

Chapter 13 gives you added training in aggressive and rapid comprehension.

BREAKING THROUGH THE SPEED BARRIER

Your training is winding up to a close now, and in this chapter you:

• Tackle another round of timed reading selections

• Practice to keep up your new speed even though the material will be somewhat more difficult

• Try to increase your responsiveness to an author's pattern of thinking

• Sharpen your skill in stripping a page down to its essential meaning

• Accept a fourth challenge to your reading habits

For many weeks you have been training to increase the efficiency of your reading habits by intensive practice in:

1. Consciously moving faster through material
2. Developing a *sense of urgency* whenever you read
3. Speedily pursuing the central theme of a selection while sensing the structure of the author's thinking
4. Reducing regressions, eliminating any tendency to vocalization, and decreasing your dependency on inner speech
5. Enlarging your recognition span, shortening your

fixation time, and making greater use of your peripheral vision

6. Covering a complete novel or magazine in one evening

7. Improving your reading vocabulary

8. Skimming less important parts of material

And, in general, learning to employ all the aggressive techniques that help you strip a page down to its essential meaning in the least possible time—techniques which, in a manner of speaking, permit you to break through the speed barrier that stands in the way of the inexperienced and unskillful reader.

You are now approaching the final phases of your training program. There is still a good deal of practice ahead of you—practice in refining and perfecting all the techniques of rapid and efficient comprehension that you have already learned; practice in still further speeding up your perception and in enlarging your span of recognition; practice in adding still more words to your reading vocabulary by working with a vocabulary builder; and practice in covering a complete book of nonfiction in two or three evenings.

In these final stages of your work, you will continue to extend your horizons. Are you ready to branch out some more, to spread your wings, so to speak, and fly off into new territory? Are you ready to read new magazines, new authors, new categories of books? Are you willing to react more skeptically to everything you read? (These questions will be dealt with in the next chapter.) Have you developed enough faith in your comprehension to do a certain amount of selective skimming?

And have you, by now, sufficiently sharpened your general reading skill to be able to cruise through somewhat more complex selections with a least the same speed and accuracy of comprehension that you have shown on previous selections?

This is the question you will answer in the present chapter.

By now, *whenever you read,* feel a *sense of urgency,* and be aware that you are moving along at a rapid clip—that you are understanding rapidly, that you are thinking rapidly, that you are responding rapidly.

But do even more.

Aim for a quick grasp of the main idea, the central theme, the gist, the essential meaning (call it what you will) of the material.

See the minor details as background, the important details as support, clarification, elaboration, or extension of the main idea.

Sense the pattern of the author's thinking, and think along with the author in that pattern.

Skim, without guilt or anxiety, whenever the content of the page and your purpose in reading call for, or admit of, skimming.

In short, use every technique you possess to understand quickly, accurately, and intelligently.

Sometimes, of course, you may slow up, you may reduce your rate, depending on the nature of the material and on what you want to get out of it.

You will not read all the selections of this chapter at the same speed, but will vary your pace to suit the content, to suit your purpose in reading.

However, you will never again, if your training has been successful, read as slowly as you did before you started working in this book.

A brief discussion following each comprehension test will deal with the pattern and framework of the author's thinking. Study these discussions carefully, referring to the selections as you do so, in order to continue refining your awareness and understanding of the structure of writing.

SELECTION 21

"Cures" for the Common Cold
by Harold S. Diehl, M.D.

Time at start: _____ minutes _____ seconds

Start timing ➡ Despite general skepticism about cures for the common cold, millions of dollars' worth of commercial remedies are still sold in this country every year. Old-fashioned cures like asafetida and camphor are no longer in vogue, but in their place has come a whole new arsenal of popular remedies—vitamins, vaccines, nasal medications and other drugs. Yet careful investigation shows that many of the most widely advertised remedies now on the market are utterly worthless. Some of them, in fact, may be definitely harmful.

I

In an effort to discover an effective cold remedy, a series of investigations was begun ten years ago at the University of Minnesota. The studies grew out of a chance observation which had led me to believe that morphine might be of value in relieving acute head colds. Extensive tests corroborated this observation; but morphine, because of its toxicity and the danger of habituation to it, was obviously unsuited for general use. The scope of the investigation was consequently broadened in the hope of finding a remedy that would be equally effective but less harmful. In this way, many of the most widely used cold preparations came under close study.

The investigations were carried out by the Students' Health Service of the University. Each study was specifically planned to avoid prejudice for or against any particular medication. Physicians wrote prescriptions merely for "cold medication." The pharmacist filling them used in sequence the medications being studied at the time. Neither physician nor patient knew what medication had been given. After forty-eight hours of treatment, the patients reported the results on cards prepared for this purpose. Upon the basis of these reports the effectiveness of the medication in each case was estimated. Finally, the pharmacist's record was obtained and the results tabulated according to the various medications used.

In each of these studies some of the tablets and capsules given out contained only milk sugar. These were included so that we might know what proportion of patients would recover without treatment in the forty-eight-hour period for which results were reported. In other words, the group who received sugar tablets, thinking that they contained medication, served as a "control group" for the rest of the study.

The importance of having this control was clearly shown in the very first investigations. Approximately 35 percent of the students who got the sugar tablets reported "definite improvement" or "complete cure" of their colds within forty-eight hours. Some of them experienced such prompt and remarkable improvement, in fact, that they went out of their way to praise the tablets as the most effective treatments they had ever taken. Apart from the humor of the situation, this control group showed that approximately 35 percent of patients would have recovered quickly regardless of any medication. For the purposes of our studies, therefore, we put down as of little or no value all cold medications from which less than 50 percent of our subjects reported benefit.

Virtually all of the most commonly used medications proved, on this basis, to be almost valueless. This group of remedies included aspirin, calcium and iodine, halibut liver oil (which is vitamin A), amytal, ephedrine, atropine, an aspirin-phenacetin-caffeine compound (which is sold under various names) and soda.

Although aspirin ranks at the top of this group, the results from it are very little better than from the sugar tablets. This is true regardless of the brand of aspirin used, "genuine" or otherwise.

Even less valuable were the results obtained from soda, another widely recommended cold remedy. Advertisers have emphasized the importance of "alkalization" in the treatment of colds. In

this study we gave sufficient dosages of soda to produce much more alkalization than is possible from any of the commercial preparations sold in drug stores. Yet the results of this alkalization were exactly the same as those reported from the sugar tablets.

Perhaps the most commonly used of all cold remedies are the preparations to be dropped or sprayed into the nose. In our studies we selected the most extensively advertised and widely sold brand of "nose drops."

It was transferred to unlabeled bottles, and then dispensed to the students with the directions given by the manufacturer. Only 31 percent reported benefit from it, about the same as those who used sugar tablets.

Nasal preparations not only have little value, but may do harm by interfering with the body's natural defenses. Medical research has shown that the common cold is usually initiated by a virus or by bacteria which gain entry through the upper respiratory tract. A primary stage of infection follows, whose symptoms are stuffiness of the nose, sneezing, watery nasal discharge, dryness of the throat, occasionally mild headaches, and often mild general symptoms—but with no elevation of temperature and a usual duration of four to five days. This stage may be followed by secondary infections caused by other germs that happen to be present in the nose and throat. The secondary stage is accompanied by a thick, yellow discharge, and runs a typical subacute course of two or three weeks.

Nature has provided man with remarkable local defenses against these bacterial invaders. At the entrance of the nasal passages are tiny hairs, called vibrissae, which filter out the larger particles of foreign material in the air. Next in the defense system are numerous glands located throughout the membranes of the nose. These glands constantly produce a moist, slightly sticky secretion which covers the surfaces of the membranes with a mucous film. The film is in constant movement toward the pharynx, and is renewed approximately every ten minutes. It has been estimated that 75 percent of the dust and germs present in the air are removed in this manner.

The mucous film also protects the delicate membranes of the nose from mechanical injury by particles of dust. It is extremely difficult for bacteria to find their way through this mucous covering as long as it remains intact. On the other hand, injury to this mucous coat and exposure of the underlying membranes opens a portal of entry for infection.

Last of nature's defenses are the cilia. These are microscopic, hairlike projections covering most of the mucous membranes in the nose. They are in constant wave-like motion, much like fields of grain. They pick up cells and particles of foreign matter and carry these to the pharynx, from which they are discharged or swallowed.

Nasal preparations may be harmful precisely because they can destroy or interfere with this defense system. Drying and medicated oils first slow and eventually stop the action of the cilia. Their constant use may even destroy respiratory epithelium. More important, nasal sprays or oils, though they may give temporary relief of congestion and stuffiness, frequently produce a distinct irritation of the nasal mucous membranes, in this way facilitating the path of secondary bacterial infection.

Finally, there is always the danger of a specific type of pneumonia that may result from the inhalation of oily substances into the lungs. For all of these reasons, nose and throat specialists warn against the introduction of medicinal preparations into the nose. It should be done only when definitely indicated and recommended by a physician for the treatment of some specific condition.

Equally useless are the mouth washes, gargles and antiseptics urged by advertisers upon the public. These preparations may destroy germs in test tubes if given sufficient time. But none of them acts instantaneously, nor are they effective in the weak solutions which can be tolerated by the membranes of the nose and throat. Furthermore, only a very small proportion of the membranes of the nose and throat can possibly be reached by sprays and gargles.

Several other more or less universal home remedies proved valueless in our studies. Cathartics of various kinds, for example, have long figured in home treatment of colds, and are included in many of the advertised remedies. Actually, two recent studies both show that cathartics are of no value in colds, and that patients who take them lose more time from work than those who do not.

Another popular belief stresses the value of large quantities of liquids, in the form of water, lemonade, orange juice and other drinks. The purpose of the liquids is to increase excretion. Presumably, this aids in the elimination of the supposedly toxic products produced by the infection. This sounds plausible, but unfortunately there is no evidence that it actually occurs.

Alcohol, in the form of whiskey, brandy and "hot toddies," is still another popular remedy of dubious value. Fear of increasing that popularity prevented us from using it in our series of studies. Scientifically, there may be some basis, or perhaps excuse, for the use of alcohol in colds. It causes an increase in the blood flow to the skin, with a resultant feeling of warmth if one is wet and chilled. On the other hand, alcohol itself causes nasal congestion in some people; and many reli-

able studies have shown that its continuous or excessive use lowers resistance to pneumonia, the most serious complication of colds.

II

Considerable effort has been made in recent years to discover possible measures for the prevention of colds. Two types of treatment have received particular notice. One of them is the use of dietary measures, including the taking of vitamins. The other employs the various kinds of cold vaccines.

A complete, adequate and balanced diet is necessary for the maintenance of health. But beyond this general truth, no special diet has value for either the prevention or the cure of colds. The same is true of vitamins, which have been particularly exploited as a preventive method. Studies have shown that both animals and man have a decreased resistance to infections of various kinds when suffering from vitamin deficiencies; and apparently this may be true for each of the better known vitamins. But it has not been shown that use of particular vitamins has any value for the prevention of colds. Although cod-liver oil, which contains vitamins A and D, has been reported by a number of authors to reduce the severity and the frequency of colds, most of these reports are based upon inadequately controlled studies.

To determine the value of cold vaccines, studies were made over a period of several years. These vaccines—not "cold serums" as they are commonly called—contain various mixtures of the bacteria most commonly found in the nose and throat of persons infected with colds. Our studies included two bacterial vaccines. One was administered hypodermically and the other by mouth.

Here again, we took special precautions to ensure maximum reliability. The students who volunteered for the study were assigned alternately and without selection to control groups and experimental groups. The control group received blanks instead of vaccines; but all students thought they were receiving vaccine, and so had the same attitude toward the study. Each student reported to the Health Service whenever a cold developed, and kept a record of each cold of more than twenty-four hours' duration. But even the physicians who saw these patients did not know which group they represented. The number and severity of colds experienced by these students were then tabulated according to the group—control or vaccine—to which they belonged.

First, here are the results obtained from injected bacterial vaccine, or "cold shots"—the oldest and most widely used vaccine. The students vaccinated with it reported that during the previous year they had averaged 4.7 colds per person. During the year that they were taking the vaccine they averaged only 2.1 colds per person. This is a reduction of 55 percent—apparently an excellent result. In fact, this reduction was the same as has been reported in other studies, indicating that these vaccines are of value.

Unfortunately, this report was completely neutralized by the control students who reported an average of 4.9 colds during the previous year. During the year of the study, they had only 1.9 colds, a reduction of 61 percent. In other words, the control group, which got nothing of any possible value for the prevention of colds, reported just as good results as did the group which got the vaccine. It is thus easy to see how enthusiastic recommendations may be made in good faith for particular cold remedies, and still be entirely without scientific justification.

Our results with the oral vaccine were astonishingly similar. This oral vaccine consists essentially of the same organisms contained in the vaccines for subcutaneous use. They are killed by heat and administered in capsules or tablets. In our study, the students of the experimental group received capsules containing vaccine. The control group received capsules filled only with sugar.

The reports from the vaccinated group showed a reduction of approximately 70 percent in the average number of colds per person in the year of study. This looked like an excellent result, and was again approximately the same reduction as had been reported by other investigators. But the control group, as in the previous study, also reported the same reduction in the average number of colds. Moreover, during the year of the study the vaccinated group had an average of 2.1 colds per person, which was virtually the same as the 2.0 average reported by the control group. To make the parallel even more striking, the average number of days lost per person from school work was exactly the same for the two groups!

III

Is there any remedy, then, of value in the treatment of colds?

There is no measure that is uniformly effective for the prevention of the common cold. Our studies, however, did reveal one group of medications which seemed to have distinct benefit. I have already stated that morphine, which is a derivative of opium, showed excellent results but was discarded because of its dangers. But several other derivatives of opium, which are less toxic and carry no practical danger of habituation, proved to be definitely valuable. In our first studies, codeine and papaverine both gave evidence of value in the treatment of acute colds. Neither was so effective as morphine, however, and since both are quite

different chemically it was decided to try them in combination.

The codeine-papaverine mixture proved to be, after morphine, the most valuable of all cold medications. A preparation consisting of one-quarter grain of codeine and one-quarter grain of papaverine was finally selected as the most effective dosage. Of 1,500 students who were given this preparation for the treatment of acute head colds, 72 percent reported definite improvement or complete relief within twenty-four to forty-eight hours. The chief beneficial effect was a marked decrease or complete disappearance of nasal congestion and discharge. With the relief of these symptoms, in many cases, the progress of the cold seemed to be arrested and the secondary stage of protracted nasal discharge avoided.

While taking this medication, most of the students were up and about, attending classes. Had they remained in bed while using it, it is probable that even better results might have been obtained. The earlier in the course of the cold that this preparation is used, the larger the proportion of good results. This preparation, commonly called Copavin, is not advertised to the public. But it is available through physicians, who should decide when and in what dosage it should be used.

Since these studies were made, confirmatory reports have been published by several other investigators. Dr. Russell Cecil of New York, and Dr. Fritz Hutter of Vienna, both found that the codeine-papaverine mixture was particularly beneficial if used by their patients at the very beginning of the infection. In this connection, too, it is of interest to recall the statement that opium users rarely have colds. De Quincey, in his *Confessions*, wrote that during the years in which he had taken opium he "never once caught cold, as the phrase is, nor even the slightest cough. But after discontinuing the use of opium, a violent cold attacked me, and a cough soon after." In a similar vein writes Cocteau, in his *Diary of an Addict*. "Opium," he says, "is a season. The smoker no longer suffers from changes in the weather. He never catches cold."

Less effective, but still of moderate value, were several other opium derivatives. In addition to codeine alone and papaverine alone, it was found that powdered opium and the old-fashioned Dover's powder (a combination of powdered opium and powdered ipecac) were beneficial. Quinine also came to be included in this group of moderately valuable medications. The proportion of individuals who reported "complete relief" or "definite improvement" after the use of these preparations ranged from 57 percent for powdered opium down to 50 percent for quinine.

Finally, certain general hygienic measures are

helpful in the treatment of colds. Going to bed and remaining there until recovery is good advice. The value of bed rest lies in protecting others from exposure, in increasing general resistance, and in keeping the body warm. Bed rest during the acute stages of colds, supplemented by such other treatment as is indicated, would diminish their severity, limit their spread, and reduce the frequency of complications.

Hot baths for the treatment of colds may consist of hot water, hot air or steam. The effect of these baths is to dilate the blood vessels of the skin and to increase blood flow through them. As a result,

nasal congestion and stuffiness are reduced. Similar effects may be obtained with massage or other forms of physiotherapy, with hot or cold compresses, mustard plasters and certain medicated ointments. If such treatments are followed by rest in bed with sufficient covers to prevent cooling, the effect is prolonged and the possibility of their being of more than temporary benefit is increased. Exercise, frequently utilized by athletes to "sweat out" a cold, has a similar effect. But usually the symptoms return when the body gets chilled, and then the cold may become even more severe than before. ◄ End timing

Record here the time required on this selection: _____minutes _____seconds

Test Your Comprehension

Of the following eight statements, three are *main points.* Check the *three* main points.

1. These investigations were carried on at the University of Minnesota.

2. Many widely advertised cold cures and home remedies are worthless or harmful.

3. Students treated with sugar tablets showed little or no improvement.

4. Neither vaccines, nor vitamins and other dietary measures, prevent colds.

5. Only a codeine-papaverine mixture, quinine, or certain hygienic measures were found to provide any relief or improvement in the treatment of colds.

6. Nasal oils and sprays were found to be dangerous.

7. The first type of cold remedy experimented with was hot baths.

8. Staying in bed for the duration of a cold was the only remedy that showed any results.

Compute Your Rate
(Approximate Number of Words: 3000)

Time	WPM	Time	WPM
2 min. 15 sec.	1333	5 min.	600
2 min. 30 sec.	1210	5 min. 30 sec.	545
2 min. 45 sec.	1090	6 min.	500
3 min.	1000	7 min.	429
3 min. 15 sec.	923	8 min.	375
3 min. 30 sec.	857	9 min.	333
3 min. 45 sec.	800	10 min.	300
4 min.	750	11 min.	272
4 min. 30 sec.	667	12 min.	250

Your rate on selection 21: _____WPM

(Record this statistic on the chart and graph on pages 236)

Discussion of the Selection

Paragraph 1: Dr. Diehl has three main points he wishes to make, and he states one of them at the end of his first paragraph—*many widely advertised remedies are worthless, some may be harmful.*

Section I: Here the author explains why these remedies are worthless or harmful, supporting his first point with the results of the experiment at the University of Minnesota, and with medical facts.

Section II: Now Dr. Diehl develops his second point—*colds apparently cannot be prevented either by dietary measures (including vitamins) or by vaccines.* Again he supports his statements by results of the experimental study.

Section III: Developing his third point, Dr. Diehl explains how he found a *codeine-papaverine mixture* effective in providing relief or improvement; comments on the values of *morphine* and of *quinine;* and suggests such *hygienic measures* as bedrest, massage, etc., as having some benefit in the treatment of colds.

If, as you were reading, you were able to sense the three-part structure of this article, you realized clearly that the author's central meaning was somewhat as follows: *Many advertised cold cures and home remedies are worthless or harmful; vaccines, vitamins, and dietary measures do not prevent colds; only a codeine-papaverine mixture, quinine, or certain hygienic measures were found to provide any relief or improvement.*

The statements you should have checked in the comprehension test were numbers 2, 4, and 5.

SELECTION 22

Inflation Hits the Campuses
by Milton M. Pressley

Time at start: _____ minutes _____ seconds

Start timing ➡ [1] For the past decade and a half, undergraduate grades have been steadily increasing at universities and colleges across the nation. Current undergraduate grade point averages (GPAs) would astound any university professor who retired before 1960.

[2] Recently at Yale, 42% of all undergraduate spring term grades were As (46% of the senior class graduated with honors); at American University, 75% of all undergraduate grades in the spring of 1973 were As and Bs; and at the University of Pittsburgh, the 1974 average undergraduate grade was B (up from the 1969 average of C). At Dartmouth's graduation in the spring of 1974, 41% of its seniors received As; another 40% received Bs; at Vassar 81% of all 1974 undergraduate grades were As and Bs; and at Amherst the figure was 85%.

[3] Making the assumption that grades should reflect relative achievements within a given university and then translating the current high grade levels, most of these institutions seem to be making the implausible statement: "The overwhelming majority of our undergraduate students are above average or superior when compared to our typical or average undergraduate students."

[4] To be sure, some institutions are taking corrective steps. Dartmouth recently announced that beginning with the next academic year a student to graduate summa cum laude will have to have grades as good as the top 5% of the previous year's graduating class. And for cum laude honors he or she will have to equal the top 15%. Yale last week said that it was restoring the F grade and that undergraduates, after a four year hiatus, once again will have failing grades put into their transcripts for flunked courses.

[5] But a much broader effort is called for if the evil of grade inflation, or "gradeflation" as I prefer to call it, is to be brought under control. A recent survey of 197 colleges and universities found that undergraduate grade averages increased by about one-half of a letter grade between 1960 and 1973. According to another report, the grade increase pattern applies to almost all types of colleges— large and small, public and private, urban and rural. Only in the South have colleges and universities shown a slower rate of "gradeflation."

[6] Viewing rising grades from another perspective, fewer undergraduates are flunking out or being put on academic probation. During the 1964 school year, the University of Illinois reported that 16% of its undergraduates were either expelled or put on probation for low grades. In 1971, just 3.7% fell into that category.

Declining Scores

[7] It is doubtful that today's undergraduates are really that much more intelligent than their predecessors. In fact, quite the opposite appears to be the case. The College Entrance Examination Board states that Scholastic Aptitude Test (SAT) scores began declining slowly from 1964 through 1968 and have been dropping more rapidly since then. Last year's average scores on verbal and mathematical SATs taken by college-bound high school seniors sank to the lowest level on record. Similar results are reported by the American College Testing Service (an alternate service preferred in some areas of the country). These testing services not only disclose a continuing decline in the average but that the percentage of students scoring in the upper ranges has been declining as well.

[8] In fact, according to one report from the National Assessment of Educational Progress, sponsored by the Educational Commission of the States, the mathematical skills of 17-year-olds is now so low that fewer than one in 100 is able to balance a checkbook. So much for the theory that today's undergraduates are smarter than their forerunners.

[9] It is my contention that teaching, curriculum, grading and related reforms during the past decade have lowered undergraduate academic standards and is responsible for much of the "gradeflation." Take, for example, the pass-fail system. This method of evaluation is intended to encourage students to take difficult courses in unfamiliar areas without risking a low letter grade which would bring down their grade point average. However, a study by Ohio University found that 92% of the students surveyed stated reasons other than "to explore an unfamiliar academic area" for exercising the pass-fail option. Russell Simpson, dean of Harvard Law School, believes that pass-fail is really "pass-pass" and that no one fails. Mr. Simpson cites figures for the fall of 1971 at Harvard to substantiate his opinion. During that term, when 1,320 undergraduates took pass-fail courses, only 12 (less than 1%) received a failing grade.

[10] Some hold the view that professors often give higher grades to win both popularity and promotion, on the dubious evidence that high grades are an indicator of effective teaching. It has also been observed that there is a tendency among

teachers to compensate for poorly prepared minority students. This tends to drive up their grades and also raises the grades given to other students.

[11] College administrations themselves may be adding to the problem as they try to keep enrollments up during economically difficult times. A student suspended from college represents quite a few dollars lost and, according to A. L. Addington, chairman of the Department of Business at Valdosta State, most colleges are doing everything possible to hold on to even marginal students, with high grades as one incentive.

[12] Mr. Addington also singles out five other "reforms" that have served to lower academic standards:

—Many colleges are moving to fewer and fewer required courses. If, for example, a language course is changed from being required (a monopoly position) to being an elective (a competitive position), the price of an A could be expected to go down as departments and professors compete for enrollment.

—With formalized student evaluations of faculty now a standard practice, teachers may be tempted to use easy grading as a means of buying high student evaluations. The concept of "judge not, that you be not judged" is bound to build a little compassion into the judgment.

—A new idea in grading, accepted by some professors in the last few years, is that students should not experience failure. That is, they must be "positively reinforced" regardless of effort or performance. Grade inflation is a natural result.

—Coupled with the concept of positive reinforcement is the view that grades should reflect the student's accomplishment in relationship to his native ability. That means an A student is doing the best he can, regardless of how poor it is in absolute terms.

—Finally, some professors point to the general loss in values reflected by society. This view holds that everything is of equal value in education, that a knowledge of Shakespeare, for example, is no more important than a knowledge of comic books.

[13] Who are the victims of "gradeflation"? The first victims are the truly superior students who are unable to receive due recognition. "I've worked hard to achieve good grades and I thought they would help when I was ready for grad school," said one typical student. "Now I find out everybody has good grades."

[14] Mediocre students are the second victims, with delusions of excellence—delusions which the world will painfully destroy in due time. But truly inept students may suffer the most, staying on in college for four wasted years when they would be much better off spending that time preparing themselves for a career in which they could adequately perform.

[15] "Gradeflation" is also costly to parents. Few would argue that it now takes a bachelor's degree to qualify one to be considered for many jobs which, just a decade or so ago, required only a high school degree. Thus parents are often required to incur the extra expense of four years of college in order that their children may acquire these jobs.

[16] Taxpayers are burdened by "gradeflation" to the extent that it unnecessarily increases enrollment in tax supported institutions of higher education. Graduate and professional school administrators are being snowed under by the horde of applicants. Many law and medical students are beginning to judge applicants largely by their scores on admission exams, having lost faith in the ability of grades to discriminate among the candidates.

'Mismarked Merchandise'

[17] Employers have a stake as well. Rightly or wrongly, they often like to use grades as a selection criterion. To the extent that "gradeflation" has resulted in "mismarked merchandise," professors are depriving them of this selection information. Perhaps more important, employers count on institutions of higher learning to supply them with individuals who know how to learn and how to solve problems. To the extent that the institutions have failed, employers will be forced to spend even more than they do to train their employes.

[18] "Gradeflation" also poses dilemmas for many faculty members. For those of us who still believe in high academic standards, it is becoming increasingly difficult in terms of time and mental anguish to maintain such standards.

[19] Scattered cries for grade deflation are being heard. Surprisingly, there is a move among some students to return to conventional grading methods. At Oberlin, for example, the proportion of freshmen taking ungraded courses dropped from 63% in 1970 to below 16% in 1974. Princeton students, now leaning toward the traditional grading system, believe they learn more, work closer to their capacity and are motivated to work in conventionally graded courses. At Stanford, where a system of A-B-C-pass was adopted in 1970, the faculty senate voted to restore D grades beginning last fall.

[20] However, such changes are still few in number. If the current easy grading, no grading (pass-pass) and related systems continues, it may soon take a master's degree to qualify for a secretary's position. What will happen in the following decade?

[21] Quite simply, what's needed is a return to the old, more rigorous standards. Realistically, however, it's not quite that simple. It will, in fact, take concerted efforts from many individuals and

institutions to correct the problem. Primary and secondary schools not only need to return to teaching the three Rs, but should begin grading realistically as well. Parents need to stop insisting that their children go to college. State legislators and others charged with allocating scarce resources at the highest levels need to closely review the situation in terms of society's needs and wants. In some cases this may call for putting an end to what some college administrators often strive for—growth for growth itself.

[22] Students can help by understanding that easy grades lead to easy degrees which often turn out to be of much less value than the four years and thousands of dollars they invested in obtaining them. And, finally, each faculty member should look at the grades he is assigning. If the "average" is approaching the incongruent "above average" level, he should ask himself "Is this really an honest evaluation?" ◄ **End timing**

Record here the time required on this selection: _____minutes _____seconds

Test Your Comprehension

I. First, take this true - false test to determine whether you have accurately followed the writer's argument. Check T or F, according to the material.

1. Undergraduate grades in college today are about the same as they were 15 years ago.   T. F.

2. It is to be assumed that grades should indicate relative achievement within an institution.   T. F.

3. Some institutions are attempting to bring "gradeflation" under control.   T. F.

4. Today's undergraduates are more intelligent than their predecessors.   T. F.

5. Scores on verbal and mathematical SATs achieved by college-bound high school seniors have been steadily rising.   T. F.

6. Undergraduate academic standards have been reduced in the past ten years by "reforms" in teaching, curriculum, and grading.   T. F.

7. Professors tend to give high grades, according to some views, to win popularity and prove that they are teaching effectively.   T. F.

8. But college administrations are bringing pressure to reduce "gradeflation."   T. F.

9. Offering fewer "required" courses tends to counteract "gradeflation" because only those students truly interested in a course enroll for it.   T. F.

10. Formalized student evaluations of instructors tempt instructors to raise the grades they give.   T. F.

11. Some professors in the last few years have accepted the philosophy that students should experience failing grades in order to be better equipped to deal with the reality that the world will reward only actual achievement.   T. F.

12. The victims of "gradeflation" are superior students, parents, taxpayers, and employers; but mediocre or poor students, and professors, benefit from the trend to higher grades.   T. F.

13. There is a move among some students to return to conventional grading methods.   T. F.

14. The solution is quite simple, and can quite easily be achieved: we must return to the old, more rigorous standards.   T. F.

15. Such a solution will require the efforts of many groups: primary and secondary schools, parents, legislators, administrators, and students.   T. F.

II. Now go back over the selection, scanning it quickly to see how the author has divided his material into three parts. Indicate which numbered paragraphs deal with each part.

Part I. *The problem, its extent, and its causes:* Paragraphs _____ through _____.

Part II. *Results of the problem:* Paragraphs _____ through _____.

Part III. *Solution to the problem and a call to action:* Paragraphs _____ through _____.

III. Check the statement that most accurately expresses the *main idea* of this selection.

1. Undergraduate students in college today are not as intelligent as their predecessors, but they earn higher grades.

2. Grades in college should reflect the relative achievement of students within the institution.

3. Teaching is more effective in college today, and professors are more popular; nevertheless, academic standards are falling.

4. Students as well as teachers are the victims of "gradeflation."

5. Easy grades lead to easy degrees.

6. "Gradeflation" is a serious problem in today's col-

leges, with wide-ranging causes; there must, as a solution, be a return to more rigorous standards, and cooperation among many groups of people will be required.

Compute Your Rate
(Approximate Number of Words: 1850)

Time	WPM	Time	WPM
1 min. 15 sec.	1480	3 min. 15 sec.	569
1 min. 30 sec.	1233	3 min. 30 sec.	529
1 min. 40 sec.	1110	3 min. 45 sec.	493
1 min. 45 sec.	1057	4 min.	463
1 min. 50 sec.	1009	4 min. 15 sec.	435
2 min.	925	4 min. 30 sec.	411
2 min. 10 sec.	854	4 min. 45 sec.	390
2 min. 15 sec.	822	5 min.	370
2 min. 20 sec.	793	5 min. 15 sec.	352
2 min. 30 sec.	740	5 min. 30 sec.	336
2 min. 40 sec.	694	5 min. 45 sec.	322
2 min. 45 sec.	673	6 min.	308
3 min	617	6 min. 30 sec.	285

Your rate on selection 22: _____ WPM

(Record this statistic on the chart and graph on page 236)

Answers to Comprehension Test

I. 1. F; 2. T; 3. T; 4. F; 5. F; 6. T; 7. T; 8. F; 9. F; 10. T; 11. F; 12. F; 13. T; 14. F; 15. T.

II. Part I: paragraphs 1–12. Part II: paragraphs 13–18. Part III. paragraphs 21–22.

III. The main idea is most accurately expressed in statement 6.

Discussion of the Selection

Mr. Pressley introduces the problem in paragraph 1: "For the past decade and a half, undergraduate grades have been steadily increasing . . ."

Paragraph 2 backs up the writer's statement with statistical evidence.

Paragraph 3, accepting the assumption that "grades should reflect relative achievement . . . ," shows that this evidence indicates, implausibly, that "The overwhelming majority . . . are above average or superior . . ."

In paragraphs 4, 5, and 6, the writer admits that "some institutions are taking corrective steps" to cure grade inflation, but calls for a "much broader effort."

Paragraphs 7–8 suggest, with evidence from Scholastic Aptitude Test scores, that today's undergraduates are likely not as intelligent academically as their predecessors, despite the higher grades they are given.

The author contends, in paragraphs 9–12, that changes in the past ten years in college have reduced academic standards in a number of specific ways and that high grades are given for reasons not related to achievement.

In paragraphs 13 through 18, Mr. Pressley explains that the *victims* of "gradeflation" are truly superior students; mediocre students; parents who pay the costs of their children's college education; taxpayers; employers; and faculty members.

Paragraphs 19–20 admit that "scattered cries for grade deflation are being heard" and that "there is a move among some students and instructors for a return to conventional grading methods," but claim that "such changes are still few in number."

Finally, in paragraphs 21 and 22, the author offers the solution to the problem: "A return to the old, more rigorous standards." He then calls for action from primary and secondary schools, parents, state legislators, and college students themselves.

So this selection can be quickly determined to be a "problem-solution—call-for-action" piece, and once so recognized, can be read much more speedily and with a clear and accurate understanding of the author's thinking and method of presentation:

Part I, paragraphs 1–12: *The problem, its extent, and its causes.*

Part II, paragraphs 13–18: *The unfortunate results of the problem.*

Part III, paragraphs 21–22: *The solution and a call to action to put the solution into effect.*

As expected, occasional paragraphs throughout the piece (numbers 4–6 and 19–20) admit that something is being done, but not enough.

SESSION 39

SELECTION 23

Diet and Die
by Carlton Fredericks

Time at start: _____ minutes _____ seconds

I

Start timing ➡ [1] Most Americans love to diet. Men and women, old and young, plump and fat, rich and poor, sooner or later are tempted to try some "miracle diet" that promises to shed weight easily, quickly, and painlessly. Yet in their eagerness to outwit the laws of nature and medicine, they forget that improper dieting can lead to grim and inexorable death.

[2] But wait a minute, you protest. Isn't that statement about death extreme? Intelligent people don't go in for lethal diets and deadly food fads. They cut out fats and starches, to be sure; perhaps they try mineral-oil salad dressings or some of the other widely publicized tricks. But can such dietary shortcuts lead directly to the grave?

[3] Well, it is true that death certificates never read "Reducing Diet." Yet science has taught us that a human body lacking in a full ratio of proteins and vitamins stands little chance in a fight against disease. So no matter how the certificates may read, if death comes on the heels of a reducing diet, who is the real culprit? The disease germ itself, or the inadequate diet that weakened the body?

[4] First, let's glance at some case histories in Hollywood, where the camera makes everyone look ten pounds heavier. Thanks to this phenomenon of the lens, the calory is the god of movie stars. And because the waistline is the lifeline of film society, the calory has driven some studio notables to gastronomic suicide.

[5] Remember Laird Cregar, brilliant but bulky screen villain? Villains don't make romantic stars, so he decided to reduce. In a few months he starved away 100 pounds. As delighted as his tailor, he looked forward to more glamorous roles.

[6] The end of the story was no beat of publicity drums for the "new" Cregar, but a muffled roll for his death. Actually it occurred on the operating table, yet everyone knows that operations are more often successful if the patient is strong and in good condition. Was this precipitous loss of weight and the untimely loss of life merely a strange coincidence?

[7] And how about bent-nosed, beloved Louis Wolheim? Months and pounds passed away as he dieted. Then the wire services flashed the stark words: "Louis Wolheim, ex-professor of mathematics, star of *What Price Glory*, died suddenly tonight." Wolheim's death certificate didn't read "starvation." But did he decide to juggle calories with waistline and forget to hold on to health? . . .

[8] Now for the case of a third Hollywood star. By the grace of her physician's intervention she is still on the screen, so let's call her plain Mary. She was another who found herself losing in the endless fight against the fattening camera, so she condemned herself to breakfasts of black coffee and butterless toast, luncheons of skimpy salads and almost vitamin-free Melba toast, dinners of one lamb chop, vegetable and coffee. Yet even this diet, pittance for a hard-working body, failed to bring her weight down.

[9] Whereupon Mary shifted from skimpiness to starvation. This did the trick—yet scarcely had she remodeled her wardrobe when she was rushed to a sanitarium.

[10] The studio said: "Mary has been overworking. She must guard against a nervous breakdown."

[11] The truth was, Mary's reducing diet lacked everything the human body needs to sustain life. *Everything*: proteins, calories, fats, vitamins, minerals, and bulk.

[12] Unfortunately, you don't have to be a movie star to find the die in diet. Furthermore, for the unknown ordinary thousands who learn too late, there are countless others who escape the grave, only to fall victim to influenza, pneumonia, insanity, prolonged invalidism, and pregnancy complications.

[13] If you embark on a dolt's diet—which they all are unless tailored by an expert to your own specifications—any of these disasters can occur. According to the Mayo Clinic, a group of volunteer subjects traveled to the edge of insanity on what seemed to be a nourishing diet. It was adequate indeed as to calories, but far below the danger point in a vitamin essential to the nervous system. After a few months every "guinea pig" reported insomnia, forgetfulness, confusion, apathy, and "an inescapable sense" that some misfortune awaited him.

[14] Further proof that proper nutrition involves far more than a minimum number of calories is

offered by the case of Miss S.R. Proud of her figure, this young Manhattan woman fought the battle of the bulge successfully until she underwent an operation. Then inactivity and a forced diet caused her to gain twenty pounds. Her doctor wisely refused to help, saying: "Plenty of time for that when you're completely well again."

[15] So S.R. walked out on him and into the hands of a "specialist"—"naturopath," to be precise. This gentleman was happy to take her currency in return for placing her on a two-month diet of nothing but mashed potatoes and fruit juices. As the pounds slipped away, S.R. was happy too. Delighted, in fact—until they began slipping too fast.

[16] Fright then set in, changing to terror when her face erupted with boils, her ankles swelled, her nails grew dry and brittle, and her hair fell out by the handful. Sensibly she dropped the diet. But it was too late; the symptoms continued. So back to her doctor she went—pale, sallow, anemic.

[17] He found her deficient in everything essential to minimum nutrition. Like many people, she didn't realize the nutritional deficiencies can become irreversible. In other words, human cells too long deprived of essential substances reach a point where they cannot assimilate those substances, no matter how the concentrations are administered.

[18] S.R. happened to be lucky. A high protein diet, ample in calories, rich in vitamins and minerals, brought her slowly back to normal. And today she has a stock reply to everyone who mentions the subject of reducing: "Narrow coffins cost as much as wide ones."

[19] Because we are civilized people, we like our meat "fractionated"—that is, the muscle meats separated from the organ meats, just as we prefer grains stripped of the vitamin-rich bran and germ. While we attempt partially to replace natural vitamins lost in baker's bread with synthetic ones, we do not replace the food values lost in eating muscle meats without the organs.

[20] The Eskimos forestall this danger intuitively. They gobble their animals from nose to tail, including bone marrow, with the result that pernicious anemia and prematurely gray hair are rare in the Arctic. When white explorers contract scurvy up there, the Eskimos cure them with animals' adrenal glands containing high concentrations of vitamin C.

[21] Suppose your "commonsense" low-starch muscle-meat diet happens to lack pantothenic acid, the vitamin which affects the endocrine gland. Dogs deficient in it look well and even eat well, right up to the moment when, without warning, they drop dead.

[22] We have much to learn about the effects of pantothenic acid on human beings, yet we know that a lack of it produces an unhealthy mouth and tongue. It also slows down peristalsis of the colon, a phenomenon which contributes to the $100,000,000-a-year laxative business—and to nothing else.

[23] Yes—the fact that people don't die from their diets is a testimonial not to the diet but to the adaptability of the human body. For example, the wiseacres who substitute mineral oil for salad dressings are making, in one step, more mistakes than their instinct for error should permit.

[24] Mineral oil hinders the body in absorbing the fat-soluble vitamins A, D, E and K. Vitamin A prevents colds and skin trouble; D helps the skin to assimilate oxygen; E wards off miscarriage and other pregnancy complications; K is the blood-clotting vitamin that slows down or averts hemorrhages. Mineral oil also interferes with the absorption of C, the anti-tooth-decay vitamin. I have actually seen scurvy in children fed plenty of orange juice—and too much mineral oil. The oil washes the vitamin out of the body.

[25] But there's still more to the grim story. Mineral oil forms a coating in the digestive tract which sneers at the vitally important vitamin-B complex—the B complex which serves many functions, such as helping digestion. Americans who contracted heart weakness as prisoners of war and were released before the muscle failure had become irreversible responded successfully to B complex treatment.

[26] Some scientists suspect that the human embryo itself is affected by B complex deficiency. We know it causes harelips, cleft palates, and bone derangements in animals. It has not yet been proved that human harelips are similarly caused, but the implication is enough to warn against toying with vitamin-B complex.

II

[27] If I have persuaded you that there is a die in diet, so much the better. Yet reducing can be safe and successful. All you need do is follow a few simple rules.

[28] First, if you are too fat you must discover the cause. It may be plain overeating, a glandular defect, or even nerves.

[29] Actually, a neurotic frustration is a common cause, as in the case of T.W., a 35-year-old Brooklyn housewife. Five feet six inches tall, she weighed 245 pounds—all of it acquired on a diet of penny candy, coffee, meat, cigarettes, laxatives and indigestion remedies. She complained that the skimpy meals merely added more weight. Her dietitian soon discovered she had never been popular with men, and that food proved a happy substitute. Even her small amount was always there, always pleasing and soothing.

[30] The dietitian persuaded her to toss the can-

dy overboard, while the skimpy meals were replaced by three balanced ones, low only in calories. She felt she was eating more, but she lost 115 pounds in 18 months.

[31] When she reached her proper weight she became pregnant for the first time in seven years of married life. Her grateful glands had finally responded, a frequent result once fatness has been overcome by a balanced diet.

[32] Glandular obesity is as rare as a hen's tooth. Only one case of overweight in a thousand, say the specialists, can be traced to the glands. Yet glands serve as scapegoats for droves of fat females.

[33] Of course thyroid and pituitary obesity do exist. But the rare case of thyroid overweight is not necessarily corrected by administering extract, for the gland may have become underactive for quite another reason: a deficiency of vitamin B_1 or thiamine.

[34] Hydrated individuals, people whose tissues store abnormal quantities of water, sometimes lose weight under a diet of restricted salt and fluids. And occasionally effective treatment is given for pituitary disturbance. But whether obesity is normal or otherwise, diet is the first step that must be taken. Everything else is secondary.

[35] Once you have discovered why you are fat, it is time to start shedding the pounds. And a good way to begin is to get rid of all your food superstitions.

[36] No phase of nutrition has provoked more folklore than reducing. Often you hear people say: "Don't eat that. It's fattening." Just ignore them. No food is fattening in itself, any more than an extra shovel of coal is necessarily too much for the furnace.

[37] Like coal, food makes energy. Like the furnace, your body needs food to burn into energy. Without knowing how much fuel has already been fed to the furnace, how do you know which shovelful is too much? The same thing is true of food. The kind and quantity must be determined in exact relation to the body's needs.

[38] A particularly vicious superstition is the one which says, "Don't take vitamins when reducing. They make you gain." Only calories make you gain. Vitamins have no calories. They do, however, perform the vital job of protecting you against the deficiences of a reducing diet. That is why nutritionists supplement diets with vitamin prescriptions.

[39] In addition to getting rid of superstitions and guarding against nutritional deficiencies, avoid drugs. The magic road to sylphdom was never traveled with a suitcase of pills and potions. At best they are useless. At worst they pack a terrible wallop of misery. Let those who tried excess doses of various phenol products show you the cataracts on their eyes.

[40] Psyllium-seed laxatives, touted because they form bulk and thus create an illusion of fullness in the stomach, are of no value unless taken under careful medical guidance. Most other "reducing aids" are merely powerful laxatives— and nothing more. Concocted of salts, leaves or herbs, they rush foods through the system so fast that the calories vanish along with the food. So do the vitamins, minerals, and proteins. If this is your choice of how to lose weight, why bother to eat at all?

[41] But you still think there is a magic road to reducing? Exercise, for example, or massage or nine-day diets? Exercise will not do it. Look at the charts to see how many miles of walking is necessary to dispose of the calories in one lamb chop and an apple.

[42] Massage is a wonderful reducer—for the massager. Try to pound the fat out of a piece of meat. Even a sledge hammer won't do it, and surely you are not going to put that kind of a weapon in the hefty arms of your masseur.

[43] As to most of the nine-day wonder diets, the wonder is that you survive. Many nutrition specialists warn against them because their caloric restrictions are too severe or because they lack vitamins. Yet this imbalance is a minor drawback compared to the one they share with all mass-production diets. Whether a reducing regimen includes starvation, drugs, psychoanalysis, deficiencies, and nine- or even 90-day schedules, it is never suitable for all cases of obesity. Every diet must be individually planned.

[44] A physician may order a 1,200-calorie diet to take 40 pounds off a 160-pounder, and he may prescribe the same number of calories from a totally different diet to remove the same weight from a 200-pounder. This is because the two people have different requirements, and indulge in different activities. These and other variables must be carefully considered when one is prescribing a diet tailored precisely to each individual's needs.

[45] C.K. found this out to her eventual joy. At 16, she carried 178 pounds on a five-foot chassis. Yet she, a growing girl, lived on a cruel diet of 800 calories a day, supplemented by baneful drugs and thyroid tablets. And to make matters worse, she kept gaining!

[46] Vitamin-B complex, multiple vitamin and mineral capsules were substituted for the drugs she had been taking, and a 1,200-calorie diet was ordered, well balanced but not too high in proteins. For the first ten days she was restricted in salt and fluid intake. The youngster proceeded to lose 12 pounds in 40 days. Today she weighs 110 pounds. Her complexion, hair and nails are proof enough of her excellent health.

III

[47] Whoever you are and whatever your individual requirements, remember that a reducing diet should not be fantastic, distorted, unbalanced, or deficient in anything essential to health. It should be supplemented with the calory-free elements it lacks. Except that it is low in calories, it should be a miniature of an unrestricted diet.

[48] The acid test of a perfect reducing diet is this: *Can you expand the size of the portions and live happily ever after?* If not, think of those deceptive death certificates and, with the help of a competent doctor, work out a diet which will meet every nutritional test. ◂ **End timing**

Record here the time required on this selection: _____ minutes _____ seconds

Test Your Comprehension

Check the main idea:

1. Unwise dieting will mean a sure and quick trip to the cemetery.

2. The advice of a physician is not necessary in selecting a proper diet if we just use common sense.

3. Improper dieting can be extremely harmful or even fatal; the safe and successful diet is made by a physician to fit your individual needs, is low in total calories, and is nutritionally balanced.

4. A number of well-known Hollywood stars died because the strain of dieting as well as acting proved too much for their constitutions.

5. Nutritional deficiencies, if unduly prolonged, can always be overcome by skillful doctoring.

6. In preparing a diet, the expert nutritionist mainly has to select fattening foods to be avoided.

Compute your Rate
(Approximate Number of Words: 2850)

Time	WPM	Time	WPM
2 min.	1425	5 min. 30 sec.	518
2 min. 15 sec.	1267	6 min.	475
2 min. 30 sec.	1140	6 min. 30 sec.	436
2 min. 45 sec.	1036	7 min.	407
3 min.	950	7 min. 30 sec.	380
3 min. 30 sec.	814	8 min.	353
4 min.	706	8 min. 30 sec.	336
4 min. 30 sec.	634	9 min.	317
5 min.	570	10 min.	285

Your rate on selection 22: _____ WPM

(Record this statistic on the chart and graph on page 235)

Discussion of the Selection

As you read this long selection, you may have been aware that Mr. Fredericks organized his presentation into three divisions. Let's look at the piece together to see what these divisions are and what each contains.

PART 1

Paragraph 1: First part of central theme—*improper dieting can be fatal.*

Paragraphs 2–26: Elaborate development of this part of the theme, full of examples, illustrations, case histories, and explanations that bad diets can be extremely harmful, even indirectly cause death.

PART 2

Paragraph 27: Transition from part 1 ("a die in diet") to part 2 ("simple rules" for "safe and successful" dieting).

Paragraphs 28–34: The rules for safe and successful dieting. First, discover the cause of stoutness—is it neurotic, glandular (rare), or plain overeating?

Paragraphs 35–38: Next, get rid of food superstitions, and guard against nutritional deficiencies.

Paragraphs 39–40: Avoid drugs.

Paragraphs 41–43: No magic road—not exercise, nor massage, nor wonder diets.

Praragraphs 43 (last sentence)–46: Diets must be individually planned.

PART 3

Paragraphs 47–48: Summary—expression of the second part of the central theme as detailed and supported in part 2, plus recapitulation of first part (diets can be fatal).

Part 1, then, elaborated on the main point that *improper dieting can be harmful or fatal;* part 2 gave the *rules for safe and successful dieting;* and part 3 summarized the entire article.

Correct choice on the comprehension test is statement 3.

SELECTION 24	Coexisting with Teen-Agers

Coexisting with Teen-Agers
by Eda J. LeShan

Time at start: _____ minutes _____ seconds

I

Start timing ➡ In any discussion among parents of adolescents, sooner or later one question is almost certain to arise: What shall we do when we know our children are doing things we don't approve of? Shall we voice our objections? Or shall we accept the behavior on the theory that in this way at least we avoid secrecy and deceit?

Do we, because a 16-year-old insists that "it's done," serve cocktails to youngsters at a birthday dance? ("Otherwise," the adolescent may insist, "somebody's liable to spike the punch!") Do we buy cigarettes for a 12-year-old and sit by while he smokes them? ("I can get them for 2 cents apiece from a guy at school. You wouldn't want me smoking in the street, would you?") Do we, to prove our broad-mindedness, laugh at—and thus encourage—the 14-year-old's off-color stories or ignore his locker-room language just because we know it is commonplace among other youngsters his age?

For many parents the course is never in doubt. No child of theirs will do thus and so! Others, however, may have been confused by warnings against "indoctrinating" their children with their own thinking, or attempting to "mold them in their own image." These are the ones who suffer doubts when questions like the above arise.

Methods of control that worked in earlier years are useless now. (The 12-year-old who wants to try smoking will not be "distracted" for long by a lollipop!) By this time, too, youngsters have learned to hide what they are doing. Or they may not even resort to subterfuge but will announce, "If I can't do this in front of you, I'll just do it behind your back!"

Parents who want urgently to keep their youngsters' confidence by acting as "pals" might consider the experience reported recently by a young social worker. On his first job as recreation leader in a community centre, wanting very much to be accepted by the neighborhood adolescents, he decided to gain their confidence by "meeting them at their level."

He began spending a good deal of time at their local hang-outs. Then after several months, thinking he had been accepted almost as a member of the gang, he joined a crap game one night and rolled the dice like a veteran. He noticed a stiffening in the group around him, an uneasiness later as they all walked home. Finally, one boy said:

"You know, Doc, you get more and more like us instead of us getting more like you!"

In their attempts to be "modern" some mothers and fathers may run the risk of a reaction similar to the social worker's experience. Yet parents want to keep up-to-date. They've been cautioned against making their youngsters "different" from their friends. The adult wish to get a clear picture of the youngster's social scene today has prompted an increasing number of surveys among parents and students of various schools on such matters as clothing considered appropriate for school and parties, use of makeup, smoking, dating behavior. (One recent survey included a question on whether or not lights should be left on during parties.)

II

Interestingly enough, the results of a recent questionnaire given to 2,000 parents and students in a big city junior high school indicated that the students were just as uncertain about standards and limits as their parents. While the youngsters demonstrated a wish for many signs of increasing freedom (such as being permitted to earn money and have full responsibility for handling allowances), they also showed a strong desire for parental controls in matters where they seemed aware that their own impulses might get the best of them.

These youngsters said they thought parties should be planned, should have adult supervision; felt their parents should know where they were and with whom. Two-thirds of the students thought they ought to be home by midnight on weekends and holidays, and seemed to want help in scheduling homework and keeping to a reasonable bedtime during the week.

The results of such a questionnaire suggest that, useful as such surveys may be in giving parents a picture of the social scene today, youngsters in the complicated business of growing up need more than the statistical analysis of a questionnaire to guide them. It is important for children of all ages to have direct guidance and a clear understanding of what their parents expect of them, even though they cannot live up to parental standards all the time.

Often mothers and fathers can help youngsters understand what behavior is appropriate and acceptable merely by their own steady example of maturity and good judgment. At other times they may have to point out in no uncertain terms the hazards of certain conduct, and suggest more acceptable ways of doing.

But growing up is slow. Even with the best of adult guidance, youngsters will experiment with new forms of behavior in ways that parents may not like. There will be times when their self-control will fail, when they will feel they must challenge parental authority, when they must satisfy special needs whether their conduct has parental approval or not. Adult sanction for inappropriate behavior, however, may just add to adolescent confusion.

It is certainly true that young people must learn to think for themselves. In a time of rapid social change they will inevitably face situations requiring new judgments that we cannot make for them. But it is quite possible to encourage individual thinking, while still keeping in mind the inexperience and immaturity of youngsters which make them need a strong foundation from which to move forward. We must give them both "roots and wings."

Young people gain strength in controlling their impulses when we hold to our point of view with firmness, accepting the fact that behind-the-back experimentation may be the price we will pay occasionally for sticking to the validity and worth of our standards. ◆ **End timing**

Record here the time required on this selection: _____minutes _____seconds

Test Your Comprehension
Check the main idea.

1. Parents of adolescents are constantly beset with the problem of the best way to handle their children, and should learn to find out what the adolescents themselves want.

2. Those parents who insist on rigid discipline and see that their standards are lived up to will produce the most secure adolescents.

3. Parents who act as "pals" to their youngsters will help adolescents fit into the community pattern.

4. Adolescents want parental control in certain areas; they need guidance and clear understanding of parental expectations although they may not always to able to live up to these expectations.

5. Adolescence is a period of conflict and insecurity, for parents as well as children. The best rule to follow in this troublesome period is to teach young people to think for themselves.

Compute Your Rate
(Approximate Number of Words: 1010)

Time	WPM	Time	WPM
40 sec.	1515	1 min. 40 sec.	605
45 sec.	1346	1 min. 50 sec.	550
50 sec.	1102	2 min.	505
1 min.	1010	2 min. 15 sec.	450
1 min. 5 sec.	932	2 min. 30 sec.	405
1 min. 10 sec.	865	2 min. 45 sec.	370
1 min. 15 sec.	810	3 min.	340
1 min. 20 sec.	760	3 min. 15 sec.	310
1 min. 30 sec.	675	3 min. 30 sec.	290

Your rate on selection 24: _____WPM

(Record this statistic on the chart and graph on page 236)

Discussion of the Selection
This piece divides nicely into two parts:

SECTION I—THE PROBLEM

The first paragraph expresses the problem: How should parents react when adolescents do things parents don't approve of—with acceptance or with objections?

The rest of the section then elaborates on the problem, with emphasis on the doubts of parents who fear to be too controlling and on the possible negative results of being too accepting.

SECTION II—THE SOLUTION

Now the central idea of the piece, as summarized in statement 4 of the comprehension test, is developed, with a kind of recapitulation in the final paragraph.

The selection first poses the problem; next shows why it is so complex; finally indicates a solution that arises out of the adolescents' own desires and needs.

Correct choice on the comprehension test is statement 4.

Examine the statistics you have recorded on the chart and graph for Chapter 13, phase 4 (page 236).

Compare your average rate for phase 3 (Chapters 9 and 10) with your average rate for this chapter.

You may possibly have made no appreciable percentage gain in this chapter; or your gain may be small; or, possibly, you may show a 25–50 percent gain or more.

Your gain may depend, in part, on how great an increase in speed Chapters 5, 6, and 8 represented over Chapters 1, 3, and 4. Normally, the biggest jump is expected in the second series of timed selections, with relatively smaller increases showing up after that as new skills become integrated and refined, and as new habits and techniques become less self-conscious, more nearly reflexive or automatic.

On the other hand, it is possible that you had so well

integrated your new skills of comprehension, perception, and use of peripheral vision before you started working on the selections of this chapter that your speed has taken another healthy jump. If this is so, your training has been signally successful; and while future gains may for a time be small, there is no reason why you cannot eventually still further improve the skill and speed of your comprehension.

The important thing, at this point, is for you to feel—subjectively—that you move along much faster, much more competently, much more self-confidently, much more aggressively, than you used to in the past; that you are no longer intimidated by a page, an article, a chapter, or even an entire book; that you look forward to every reading experience as a pleasure, as something you cannot wait to enjoy; and that you find you have much more time for reading because you willingly, indeed eagerly, make the time.

A FOURTH CHALLENGE
TO YOUR READING HABITS

Which brings us to the fourth challenge to your reading habits. You have already tried, I expect with some measure of success, to read novels through at one sitting and to cover a complete magazine in one evening. Now let us see how successfully you can read a whole book of nonfiction in a strictly limited time.

The secret of meeting this challenge lies in your choice of the book to be read, and the determining factor in that choice is your field of interest.

What area of human knowledge, information, or living can you get most excited about? Science, art, music, psychology, mathematics, history, religion, economics, politics, sports, criminology? In which of these, or any other, subjects can a book most easily, most successfully stimulate you, hold your attention and interest, keep you engrossed?

Your first step, then, is to choose a book to which you will be able to make a rapid and happy emotional adjustment. Find a book that is not overly long, that is written for popular consumption rather than for specialists or experts, that is simple, readable, and interesting. Ask for a recommendation at your local library, from your friends, or at a bookstore. (Many excellent nonfiction titles are published in inexpensive paper-covered editions.) Or make your choice from the books suggested on pages 218–220. Or, if you are a college student, choose a title in some field that you are currently studying, a field in which you are, preferably, vitally interested.

Once you have the physical book in hand, sit down with it when you have two to three hours at your disposal. Read the table of contents carefully so that you can make a quick orientation to the type of material you will be reading. Then arbitrarily divide the book into either two or three approximately equal parts, depending on how long a book

you are tackling, and determine that you are going to finish *one* of those parts before you stop reading.

Now start reading—and read rapidly, for an over-all perspective. *Do not study.* Do not read every sentence, nor every paragraph, nor every page. Skim here and there. Read largely for central theme, for main ideas, for essential meaning, without becoming unduly concerned about the masses of details (which, of course, every book possesses in abundance). And go through either one-half or one-third of the material in a single sitting of no more than three hours. (If you happen to get more than one part done in that time, so much the better.)

If you become really absorbed in what you're reading (and if your choice of title is a wise one, you'll become absorbed quickly), you will have no trouble staying with the book at least until you have finished the first portion that you decided to cover.

Your next step, of course, is to return to the book as soon as possible within the following days in order to complete the remaining portion or portions. In any case, determine to turn the last page of the book within no more than a week from the day you started it, and in no more than three sessions of continuous reading. That allows you up to nine hours, in total—no book of less than five or six hundred pages, if you skim selectively, should take any longer.

This challenge, if you can meet it with any degree of success, may open for you a whole new approach to nonfiction reading—may make it possible for you to say three months from now, "In the last few months I have read almost a dozen solid, informative books that I would not have wanted to miss!"

And keep a record of your accomplishment with the book you're going to work on this week.

1. Title: _____

2. Author: _____

3. Area of Knowledge, Information, Etc. _____

4. Number of Pages: _____

5. Number of sittings: ☐ 2   ☐ 3

6. Date begun: _____   Date finished: _____

7. Number of hours spent: _____

8. Approximate number of pages read per hour: _____

9. Approximate number of words per page: _____

10. Average rate of reading: _____WPM

SESSION 40

PERCEPTION TRAINING X

Perception Exercise 45

Sweep down each column, feeling that you are making only one fixation to the line. Go as fast as comprehension permits, and be more aware of ideas than of inner speech.

Use your card, as in previous exercises, to inhibit your regressions and control your speed. (See perception exercise 23, page 123, if necessary, for instructions.)

The oral trends may,	if they do	or turn on
and they usually do,	independent work,	the radio.
manifest themselves	they concentrate best	Such individuals
in a manner	when there are	may concentrate so well
that has outwardly	people around	that they can write
nothing to do	and when there is even	with utmost
with the mouth	a little noise.	concentration
at all.	Such people	literally in the middle
Instead, they may,	are frequently admired	of the street—
and they usually do,	for their extraordinary	like Marcel Proust,
appear in the form	powers of concentration	who wrote a part
of the individual's	despite the rattle	of his
being rather a	and din around them.	Remembrance of
sociable person who	Yet it is	Things Past
does not like to be	exactly this rattle	in the glass-covered
and does not tolerate	and din	booth
being alone,	that makes it possible	of the porter
even as the little baby	for them to concentrate;	of the Ritz Hotel
when awake	as soon as	in Paris.
is never left alone.	quiet sets in	Such people are also
Such people	and there is	given to moods,
are not only	a real chance	mostly depressive
very sociable,	to concentrate	in nature,
but some of them	without interference,	but they may
do not like	such people are apt	just as easily
to work alone;	to become restless,	swing into a state
they either always	and they either	of great cheer.
have collaborators or,	drop their work	They are self-centered

in a charming way,	a great deal	of concentration.
and they are apt	despite the apparent	
to procrastinate	push and powers	

Perception Exercise 46
Continue as before.

By calling attention	to understand meanings.	school;
to the importance	Present methods	other readers
of larger	of teaching reading	let their reading habits
perceptual units	attempt to produce	crystallize at a point
in reading,	as wide a span	where a narrow span
psychology has	of recognition	of recognition
contributed	as possible.	becomes a permanent
a new methodology	The curves of growth	characteristic.
to its teaching.	for this factor	A narrow span
Under the old	have been plotted	not only necessitates
word method,	objectively	slow reading
for which oral reading	and are well known.	but emphasizes
was largely responsible,	Good readers	attention
children developed	have attained	to the form of words
an ability	a broad span	and sentences,
to pronounce words	of recognition	a rapid acquisition
but often failed	by the end of	of meaning
to develop	the sixth grade	being thereby blocked.
equal ability	of the elementary	

Perception Exercise 47
Continue as before.

It would seem correct	*whenever he is not able*	*of his environment.*
to say	*to read well enough*	Since environments
that *an individual*	*to meet the*	differ
has a reading disability	requirements	a great deal,

↓ | ↓ | ↓

a reading level | this is true | to carry on

that would represent | in connection with | a successful law

a disability in | vocational adjustment | practice,

one environment | where an individual | while he might

might be | with, | be able to adjust

entirely satisfactory | let us say, | very well

for successful | sixth-grade reading | to the reading

adjustment | ability | requirements

in another environment. | could never do | of a skilled trade.

We know that | the reading necessary |

Perception Exercise 48

Sweep down the columns, intent only on comprehension, and relying on your new-found skill in absorbing each line in very few fixations (possibly only one). Do not think of fixations, eye movements, vocalization, *or anything except comprehension of what the author in essence is saying.* Use your card to inhibit regressions and to control speed.

The Gull Who Came to Dinner—and Stayed On
by Nick B. Williams

LAGUNA BEACH—A ceramicist friend of mine, Adam Meklar, has learned the hard way that the milk of human kindness often becomes a strain.

Adam's primary devotion probably is to art, but he has other enthusiasms and among them is an occasional solitary stroll along the beach, where he communes with sea and sand and limitless horizons.

"It's a kick," he says. "Just me in all that space, not quite like ownership but certainly on loan. Out there I'm back to fundamentals, eye to eye with the universe. Sort of soothes the breast."

But not invariably. For not too long ago,

ambling along, he came upon a seagull huddled on the strand. Nothing unusual in that, except this seagull did not do what seagulls usually prefer when humans get too close. It just stood there, its beady eye fixed balefully on his.

"Defiant," Adam says. "And obviously obsessed with hate."

Adam is not the pushy sort but he does have this yearning to be loved and he could not quite understand why any gull—and certainly a gull he's never met before—should hate him so. He took another placatory stride toward it, making what he believed were pacifying sounds. The gull let out a squawk, scur-

ried away and finally attempted to take off.

"Heart-rending," Adam says. "Its left wing was broken. That desperate attempt to fly away must have been agony."

So Adam scooped it up; losing sufficient skin to sour most Good Samaritans—a gull can be more of a handful than you might suppose—and took it to a veterinarian he knew.

"Infection's spreading rapidly," the vet explained. "It'll die unless we amputate that wing."

"But won't a one-winged gull die anyway?" Adam inquired.

"Left on the beach, it wouldn't have a chance. Too many predators—dogs, cats, people. Even other gulls. But if you kept it at your home and could supply it with a proper diet..."

"What's a proper diet?" Adam asked.

"Fish. Small fresh fish. And quite a lot of them."

And so, being the kind of man he is, Adam was saddled with a one-winged gull, bad-tempered and a misanthrope to boot, that would require, daily of course, a lot of fresh, small fish.

The fresh, small fish became a strain, Adam admits. For here he was, not only a married man and a committed ceramicist, as well as putting in five days a week at La Cienega's Jody Scully Gallery, but also, now that he was harboring a bad-tempered gull, spending all of his spare time—"Actually, I had no spare time at all," he says—going pier-fishing with a jig line for the small kinds of stuff his one-winged seagull deigned to gulp.

"I knew I couldn't keep it up," he says. "And for a while there, desperate for time, I tried to wean him with small bits of halibut. I'd buy a slab of it and whack it up, nice little bite-size hunks that should have been okay for him—I guess it was a him, no female could have been so utterly malevolent—but he would take one peck at it, then drop it and stare evilly at me, the way he did when I first met him on the beach. You would have

thought that it was me who broke his wing—I even had a sense of guilt myself. That gull had me. He owned me. And he knew it."

More and more Adam became a Sunday jig-line fisherman. A jig line features a series of small hooks, each with a tiny feather that attracts the eyes of smelt and herring that swim near a pier. You jiggle the line, which flaps the feather on each hook, and if you're very lucky you keep hauling up these tiny smelt and herring, which are very suitable for gulls. The trouble was that Adam couldn't make it every day, and so on weekends he was putting in more hours at it than he now likes remembering, building up a week's supply of fish which he wrapped in plastic and kept in the refrigerator at his home.

But complications soon set in. His wife was less than fond of fishy smells, and certainly not those of smelt and herring which percolated readily through the plastic.

"I didn't care too much for them myself," Adam admits. "When the milk starts smelling like a herring you've got problems, haven't you? But what the heck could I do? That gull's life was at stake, and miserable as he was I couldn't bring myself to cast him back upon the beach to perish there."

The gull owned him, as he realizes now, this gull who came to dinner and stayed on. And

as you might expect it soon came up with yet another bit of surliness, for just as it had once refused to eat chopped halibut it now began refusing all the herring Adam caught for it. Nothing would do but smelt. Fresh smelt. The herring it let lie there in its backyard pen.

An all-smelt diet meant that Adam had to double the amount of time that he spent on the pier. Each time he'd feel a tugging on his jig line, he says, he'd breathe a prayer, "Oh, Lord, let it be smelt— let it be smelt!" He was beginning to feel paranoid and could not quite contain his rage when he pulled up another herring that he knew his seagull would disdain.

"I'd reached the breaking point," he says. "My ceramics, my wife, and in fact my entire existence all were disoriented by my compassion for that bad-tempered gull. And finally, one night, I told myself, 'Damn him, let him adjust—let him eat herring like the rest of us.'"

The next morning Adam took six of his hoarded herring to the seagull's pen, dropped them there and left at once. The herring were still lying there, untouched, on the next morning, and the next, when Adam added six more herring to the pile. But on the fourth day, luckily a Sunday, when Adam returned from the pier he did have two small smelt, which he dropped where the gull could gobble them. But two were all he had, and so he added the remainder of his catch, a double handful of herring.

The gull, Adam says, inspected each of them, flapping its single wing in rage, and then let out a shrill accusing squawk and fell down dead.

"A coronary," Adam says, "or a cerebral hemorrhage. Poor creature, may it rest in peace at last. I know we will."

How was your comprehension? ☐ excellent ☐ good ☐ fair ☐ poor

Are you willing to take a quick test to see if your comprehension was as *excellent, good, fair,* or *poor* as you subjectively decided it was?

Comprehension Test

Do not guess; leave an answer blank if you do not recall the pertinent material. If a later question implies the correct answer to a previous question *do not go back.*

1. When Adam approached the seagull, it flew away, as "seagulls usually prefer to do when humans get too close." ☐ true ☐ false

2. The seagull had a broken wing. ☐ true ☐ false

3. The gull was friendly, affectionate, and quiet when Adam took it to a veterinarian. ☐ true ☐ false

4. The veterinarian suggested amputating the broken wing and then returning the gull to its natural habitat. ☐ true ☐ false

5. Adam decided to take the gull home. ☐ true ☐ false

6. The gull enjoyed the pieces of halibut that Adam offered him. ☐ true ☐ false

7. Adam spent many hours on weekends fishing for food for the gull. ☐ true ☐ false

8. The gull enjoyed herring more than smelts. ☐ true ☐ false

9. Adam's existence was disoriented by his compassion for the gull. ☐ true ☐ false

10. The gull died from overfeeding. ☐ true ☐ false

11. The main point of the article occurred in ☐ the first paragraph ☐ the middle ☐ the final two paragraphs

Key

1. false; 2. true; 3. false; 4. false; 5. true; 6. false; 7. true; 8. false; 9. true; 10. false; 11. the first paragraph.

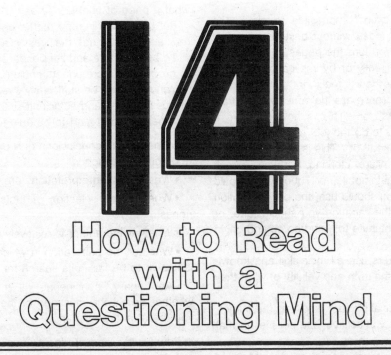

How to Read with a Questioning Mind

PREVIEW

Chapter 14 offers you a list of lively books in various fields of human knowledge, plus a number of worthwhile novels and novelists, to guide your future reading; and challenges you to follow a long-range plan that will help you become an alert, well-rounded reader.

Now, as you near the end of your training, we discuss the importance of:

- Reading critically
- Resisting the "mesmerism which is resident in print"
- Traveling widely among books in order to form "a background for opinion and a touchstone for judgment"

THE IMPORTANCE OF SKEPTICISM

Whatever you read—a book, an article, a poem, a short story, a news item, an editorial, a column of opinion, criticism, or comment, even a road sign—tries to tell you something, tries to get a message across to you, tries to make you believe.

All authors, no matter what their medium of communication, aim to convince you, their reader, that what they have to say is true and should be accepted as truth.

Even writers of fiction attempt, consciously or otherwise, to persuade you that their characters can conceivably exist; that the conflicts these characters find themselves in are important; and that the action makes sense within the framework of the time and place in which the story occurs.

If the novelists and short-story writers succeed, they get you to accept and even to share—at least momentarily—their philosophy of life, their attitude to people and events, and the point of view from which they look at the world. In a broad sense, then, even though they are writing fiction, they are special pleaders.

And of course, it is almost impossible to pick up a magazine or newspaper today without being bombarded by special pleading. As you turn the pages, almost every writer is saying to you, directly or by implication, "This is what I think" or "This is how I feel" or "This is how I interpret a situation" or "These are the conclusions I draw from the (selected) facts" or "This is how to solve a problem" or "This is how to do the job" or "This is how I react to what has happened" or "This is how you should react" or "This is the furniture, clothing, perfume, cereal, book, soap, cigarette, automobile, or liquor you should buy, the transportation you should use, the play or motion picture you should see, the vacation you should take, or the charity you should contribute to;" and so on and on, in endless, infinite variety.

And in every case writers use all their skill and knowledge to convince you of the truth and validity of what they are saying.

Even this book is a special pleader, and I, as the author, bend every effort to make you believe, and believe in, what I say.

I strive constantly, by every means at my command, to persuade you to do certain things and to do them in certain ways—I promise, I cajole, I threaten, I appeal to reason or emotion, I present evidence, and I draw on other authorities in the field, all for the purpose of eliciting as strong a positive response from you as I can possibly get.

And most, if not all, of the selections that we have used as reading exercises also ask you to believe.

For example, in previous chapters each of the selections was, in a sense, engaged in a form of special pleading:

In "Traffic Court Justice," that most communities are handling the traffic problem all wrong, and that a better solution is being tried by Chicago, San Francisco, White Plains, etc.

In " . . . the Common Cold," that most advertised remedies are valueless.

In "Inflation Hits the Campuses," that "gradeflation" is a serious problem that must be solved in certain ways.

In "Diet and Die," that improper dieting may be harmful, that there are proper ways to diet.

In "Coexisting with Teen-Agers," that there is an effective way to handle adolescents.

If you come right down to it, only a mathematical equation, a chemical formula, a page in the telephone directory, or something equally neutral can be considered totally free of every vestige of an effort by a writer to influence the reader's thinking and/or belief.

Most of your work in this program has been devoted to developing greater skill and efficiency in *understanding* what a page of print has to say.

But understanding, no matter how skillful, how clear, or how accurate, is not, manifestly, enough.

To be a mature and intelligent reader, you must be able to go beyond mere understanding.

You must also be sufficiently *skeptical* to be in the habit of questioning—and sufficiently informed, knowledgeable, experienced, and alert to be able to decide:

• Whether the conclusions of a piece of writing are valid and soundly reasoned

• Whether the interpretations are trustworthy

• Whether the selection of facts or so-called facts is honest

• Whether the author is relatively unbiased

• Whether the publication in which the material appears is known to be fair in its search for truth

• And finally, considering all the previous *whethers,* whether or not the message of the piece is deserving of your belief and acceptance

People who read intelligently approach all material with a questioning, even a *skeptical,* mind. They read critically as well as accurately; they evaluate what the author says; they test the truth of the writing against their own knowledge and experience of reality; they do not accept statements and conclusions simply because they appear in print. As J. Donald Adams once wrote in the *New York Times Book Review:*

All our lives most of us, and perhaps most of all those in whom the habit of reading is ingrained, have to guard and fight against that strange mesmerism which is resident in print. Statements that have the peculiar sanction of type, and which, if orally made, we would brush away like a buzzing fly, often receive our respectful attention merely because they have achieved the spurious dignity of print. Sometimes I think the best we can get from a formal education is the inflexible habit of examining every new fact and every new conclusion drawn from fact, warily from top to toe. An education, however conducted, that neglects the skeptical approach is no education at all. And if the wisdom of the world is in books, so, too, is a vast amount of nonsense.

The ability to approach material critically can best be developed through wide reading. To judge, you must have a touchstone for judgment. To be skeptical of opinions expressed in writing, you must have tentative opinions of your own on a subject, opinions based either on personal experience or on knowledge. Few people can be directly experienced in more than a very limited number of areas, but people who know how to read can acquire as much of the world's knowledge as they are willing to absorb. In one of the best books in its field, *Teaching Every Child to Read*, Kathleen B. Hester makes somewhat the same point:

The type of reading required for critical evaluation is a complex form of comprehension in which the reader develops the habit of appraising the material against certain criteria. It is evident that the broader and richer the background of the reader, the more able he will be to judge the reasonableness, the worth-whileness, the relevancy, and the accuracy of what is read; the more tolerant he will be of material about which he possesses insufficient background. He will criticize in light of what he knows about the subject.

To gain the broad and rich background of which Ms. Hester speaks you cannot, of course, restrict your reading to just one daily newspaper, a few light magazines, and an occasional novel.

How long have you been reading a single newspaper, and how much of an influence does this newspaper exercise on your political and social thinking? If a paper of a different political or social complexion is available in your town, or can be bought by mail, try changing for a while—you may discover that some of your beliefs are prejudiced, that some of your attitudes come from not having heard both sides of the story.

Do you keep up with the outside world by reading only one or two periodicals consistently? And is your thinking in politics or economics or world affairs subtly shaped, week after week and month after month, by the viewpoint of the one or two newspapers or magazines that you read exclusively? Then try switching to a newspaper or magazine with a different viewpoint, and come to an independent decision after hearing opposing opinions on current problems.

Are you, by background, culture, or intuition, politically and/or economically liberal or ultraliberal in your attitudes? Then open your mind to the arguments of the more conservative periodicals.

Do you lean more to the conservative side? Then open your mind to what writers who are more or less liberal have to say.

You need not be sympathetic to, let alone believe, what writers of political or economic thought antagonistic to your own say—but at least discover what they *are* saying, so that you yourself can come to an informed judgment.

The truth does not lie at any extreme, but somewhere—shiftingly—in between.

Much more to the point for someone like yourself who aims at increased skill in reading, are these questions:

Do you, at this time in your life, get much, or most, of your information and entertainment from TV?

Are your attitudes and your concepts of reality being subtly shaped by the picture tube? (A recent *Wall Street Journal Survey*, as I have said, indicated that the TV set is turned on 43 hours a week in the average American household!)

If so, discover the world of print, where controversy rages; where opposing philosophies are in a continuous state of conflict; where every shade of opinion—from deepest reactionary to wildest radical—vies for your attention; where *you* are in control by being able to choose not among a mere half dozen channels, but from thousands of books of the present and past, and from scores of magazines and newspapers. Then *you* can decide *where, when, what, why* and *how* you are going to read.

In short, and to reiterate my own special pleading:

To sharpen your critical faculties, to develop habits of reacting skeptically to what you read, and to broaden and enrich your background of knowledge—read widely.

Read books in fields with which you are at present unacquainted; read newspapers with differing political and social viewpoints; read as great a variety of magazines as you can lay your hands on.

Go out of your way to hear, and to understand, the other side of an issue. Read opinion, lots of it, that is opposed to your own intuitive prejudices, fears, likes, and dislikes. But *read*.

And when you read, keep an open mind. Do not accept passively or blindly; demand evidence, insist on all the facts, test whatever an author is saying against what you know, against what you have read in other sources.

Above all, don't succumb to the "mesmerism which is resident in print." Be alert to detect the "vast amount of nonsense," much of it probably sincere, but nonsense nonetheless, that you will find in many books, magazines, and newspapers.

WHAT TO READ

You have come a long way since the first day you started your training. If you have worked hard and faithfully, you have not only developed considerable skill as a reader, you have also begun to build habits that will help you *increase* your skill every time you tackle a page of print.

Learning to read, as you know, is a continuous, never-ending process. If, after you finish this book, you do very little additional reading, or if you read only material that offers no challenge to your comprehension, your training will be of little use to you.

Too many adults, once they reach a certain age, or once their formal schooling is completed, become so restricted in their choice of reading that they shy away from any new type of reading experience. They are reluctant to try anything beyond the level of a detective story or light novel, as if no other kind of book ever published could possibly interest them. Or they read only books in their professional or business field. Or only inspirational books. Or only their one favorite newspaper every morning. Or only one magazine for which they have developed a liking.

It is the *only* that causes the trouble. You do not read for entertainment *only,* nor for information *only.* You read also for intellectual growth, for mental stimulation, for enriching your background of knowledge, for increased wisdom, and for a broader outlook and a maturer understanding.

Let me quote from an editorial printed over forty years ago in the *Saturday Review* (it was then called the *Saturday Review of Literature*) to impress upon you the importance of reading as an influence on intellectual growth. The editors were addressing the new graduates of the nation's colleges in the year 1935, but what they had to say is as pertinent and as true today as it was then:

At this moment, when the universities are again sending forth their eager thousands into a world distraught by gigantic problems, a fresh tide of energy is about to be let loose upon the country. The country, heaven knows, has need of all that it can get of vigor and idealism and ideas. But what it needs not at all is half-baked theorists and ill-buttressed opinions. It needs a youth full of generous enthusiasm and ranging curiosity, versatile in its interests but not overweening in its self-reliance, a youth that spurns, as is its prerogative, those mistakes of the past which the present has thrown into focus, but that has sufficient balance not to cry anathema on all that is because part of it is bad. It needs a youth that is versatile in the sense that it has aptitude for new tasks, but whose versatility smacks nothing of superficiality. It demands young men and young women who do not believe that education ends with college, but who carry away from the university an abiding delight in books as the source of entertainment and invigoration and guidance.

For the man who reads well is the man who thinks well, who has a background for opinion and a touchstone for judgment. He may be a Lincoln who derives wisdom from a few books or a Roosevelt who ranges from Icelandic sagas to "Penrod." But reading makes him a full man, and out of his fullness he draws that example and precept which stand him in good stead when confronted with the problems which beset a chaotic universe. Mere reading, of course, is nothing. It is but the veneer of education. But wise reading is a help to action. American versatility is too frequently dilettantism, but reinforced by knowledge it becomes motive power. "Learning," as Mr. James L. Mursell, writing of it in a current periodical, remarks, "cashes the blank check of native versatility." And learning is a process not to be concluded with the formal teaching of college days or to be enriched only by the active experience of later years, but to be broadened and deepened by persistent and judicious reading. "The true University of these days is a Collection of Books," said Carlyle. If that is not the whole of the truth it is enough of it for every graduate to hug to his bosom.

What kind of books should your read to continue your intellectual growth, to gain "a background for opinion and a touchstone for judgment"?

The answer is a simple one: *Read books in fields you have little or no acquaintance with, books that will open for you new horizons of learning, books that will help you explore new areas of knowledge and experience, books that will make the world and people more understandable to you, books you can really sink your teeth into.*

Visit your local library, and browse among the nonfiction shelves. Does some title offer an introduction to a field that you have never previously explored? Take a few books home; spend an evening discovering whether there are adventures in reading and learning that you may now be unaware of.

If you prefer a few specific recommendations, here is a random list of 25 books that I myself have thoroughly enjoyed and that may possibly open up new worlds of information and experience for you.

ANTHROPOLOGY

Male and Female, by Margaret Mead

ARCHAEOLOGY

Gods, Graves, and Scholars, by C. W. Ceram

BIOGRAPHY
(Starred titles are autobiographical)

The Cry and the Covenant, by Morton Thompson
*The Story of San Michele, by Axel Munthe
*Black Boy, by Richard Wright

MEDICAL SCIENCE

Rats, Lice, and History, by Hans Zinnser
The Human Body, by Logan Clendening

CONSERVATION

Our Plundered Planet, by Fairfield Osborn
Road to Survival, by William Vogt
Silent Spring, by Rachel Carson

GENETICS

The New You and Heredity, by Amram Scheinfeld

HISTORY

Fantastic Interim, by Henry Morton Robinson
Only Yesterday, by Frederick Lewis Allen
The Tragic Era, by Claude G. Bowers

MATHEMATICS

One, Two, Three, Infinity, by George Gamow

PHILOSOPHY

Man Against Myth, by Barrows Dunham

PHYSICS

The Birth and Death of the Sun, by George Gamow

PSYCHOLOGY

The Human Mind, by Karl A. Menninger
The Three Faces of Eve, by Corbett H. Thigpen and Hervey M. Cleckley
Mind and Body, by Flanders Dunbar
Emotional Problems of Living, by O. Spurgeon English and G. H. J. Pearson

SEMANTICS

Language in Thought and Action, by S. I. Hayakawa
People in Quandaries, by Wendell Johnson

SOCIOLOGY

The Lonely Crowd, by David Riesman
The Crack in the Picture Window, by John Keats

While you're at the library, you might wish to pick up a couple of novels that you can get completely absorbed in, that you'll be able to read at a rapid clip in one or two sittings.

Here again is an entirely personal list:

Of Human Bondage, by W. Somerset Maugham
The Store, by T. S. Stribling
Captain Horatio Hornblower, by C. S. Forester
Hold Autumn in Your Hand, by George Sessions Perry
Hunger, by Knut Hamsun
H.M. Pulham, Esq., by John P. Marquand
Compulsion, by Meyer Levin
The Caine Mutiny, by Herman Wouk
Mottke the Thief, by Sholem Asch
Two Adolescents, by Alberto Moravia
The Lost Weekend, by Charles Jackson
The Grapes of Wrath, by John Steinbeck
The Good Earth, by Pearl Buck
Night and the City, Song of the Flea, and **The Thousand Deaths of Mr. Small,** by Gerald Kersh
Butterfield 8, Appointment in Samarra, and **A Rage to Live,** by John O'Hara

From Here to Eternity, by James Jones
A Tree Grows in Brooklyn, by Betty Smith
The Fountainhead, by Ayn Rand
Animal Farm and **1984** by George Orwell
The Last Detail, Cinderella Liberty, and **The Accomplice** by Darryl Ponicsan
Portnoy's Complaint, by Philip Roth

Taste in novels is a highly personal thing, but I think you will find most of these books exciting experiences. They are books you can practice on to increase your speed, books that will grab your interest from the very first page and thus make complete concentration easier to achieve.

They are not necessarily "great" novels, nor are they recommended as such, but every one is superbly enjoyable, many are deeply moving, quite a few will vastly increase your understanding of people, and some of them will provide you with the richest kind of emotional experience. And these, after all, are the reasons for reading novels—to enjoy, to be moved, to develop a mature understanding, to experience vicariously.

If you're willing to buy books in inexpensive soft-cover editions, go into any paperback bookstore and browse among the shelves. Many such stores are immense, containing thousands of books to choose from.

Perhaps you'd like some specific suggestions? The following list of paperbacks is made up of titles available at the present time and likely to be so for many years. Here are a number of random categories in no particular order:

EDUCATION AND LEARNING

The Soft Revolution, by Neil Postman and Charles Weingartner
How to Survive in Your Native Land, by James Herndon
Education and the Endangered Individual, by Brian V. Hill
Open Education, edited by Ewald B. Nyquist and Gene R. Hawes
How Children Fail and **What Do I Do Monday?,** by John Holt
Teaching Human Beings, by Jeffrey Schrank
Teaching for a Change, by John Anthony Scott
Education and Ecstasy, by George B. Leonard
Human Teaching for Human Learning, by George Issac Brown

PSYCHOLOGY

Biofeedback, by Marvin Karlins and Lewis M. Andrews
I Ain't Well—but I Sure Am Better, by Jess Lair, Ph.D.
The Disowned Self, by Nathaniel Brandon
The Third Force, by Frank G. Goble
A Primer of Behavioral Psychology, by Adelaide Bry
I'm OK—You're OK, by Thomas A. Harris, M.D.
Fully Human, Fully Alive, By John Powell
Freedom To Be, and **Man the Manipulator,** by Everett L. Shostrum
Games People Play, by Eric Berne, M.D.

Games Alcoholics Play and Scripts People Live, by Claude Steiner, Ph.D.

Love and Orgasm, Pleasure, and The Language of the Body, by Alexander Lowen, M.D.

The Transparent Self, by Sydney M. Jourard

Don't Say Yes When You Want to Say No, by Herbert Fensterheim and Jean Baer

Gestalt Therapy Verbatim, by Frederick S. Perls

The Gestalt Therapy Primer, by Daniel Rosenblatt

Born to Win, by Muriel James and Dorothy Jongeward

Joy and Here Comes Everybody, by William C. Schutz

The Fifty-Minute Hour, by Robert Lindner

The Heart of Man, and The Ability to Love, by Erich Fromm

SEX, LOVE, MARRIAGE

Couple Therapy, by Gerald Walker Smith and Alice I. Phillips

Your Fear of Love, by Marshall Bryant Hodge

Sexual Suicide, by George F. Gilder

Intimacy, by Gina Allen and Clement G. Martin, M.D.

How to Live with Another Person, by David Viscott, M.D.

Pairing, by George R. Bach and Ronald M. Deutsch

The Intimate Enemy, by George R. Bach and Peter Wyden

The Rape of the Ape, by Allan Sherman (Humor)

The Hite Report, by Shere Hite

Sex in Human Loving, by Eric Berne, M.D.

WOMEN, FEMINISM, ETC.

Rebirth of Feminism, by Judith Hole and Ellen Levine

The Way of All Women, by M. Esther Harding

Knowing Woman, by Irene Claremont de Castillejo

Sexist Justice, by Karen De Crow

Our Bodies, Our Selves, by The Boston Women's Health Book Collective

How to Be an Assertive Woman in Life, in Love, and on the Job, by Jean Baer

CHILDREN, CHILD-RAISING, ETC.

Between Parent and Child and Between Parent and Teenager, by Dr. Haim Ginott

Children Who Hate, by Fritz Redl and David Wineman

Parent Effectiveness Training, by Dr. Thomas Gordon

Dare to Discipline, by Dr. James Dobson

How to Parent, by Dr. Fitzhugh Dodson

The Me Nobody Knows, edited by Stephen M. Joseph

Escape from Childhood, by John Holt

One Little Boy, by Dorothy W. Baruch

HEALTH

Save Your Life Diet Book, by David Reuben, M.D.

Folk Medicine, by D. C. Jarvis, M.D.

Get Well Naturally, by Linda Clark

Let's Eat Right to Keep Fit, by Adelle Davis

PHILOSOPHY

The Way of Zen and What Does It Matter?, by Alan W. Watts

Love's Body, by Norman O. Brown

BUSINESS, ECONOMICS, FINANCE

The Affluent Society, by John Kenneth Galbraith

Financial Success, by Wallace D. Wattles

Parkinson's Law, by C. Northcote Parkinson

The Peter Principle, by Laurence J. Peter

Up the Organization, by Robert Townsend

The Money Game and Super-Money, by "Adam Smith"

SOCIOLOGY

Passages, by Gail Sheehy

Future Shock, by Alvin Toffler

Hard Times, by Studs Terkel

Roots, by Alex Haley

BIOGRAPHY

Your best introduction to this area is any of the books by Irving Stone, who has written fascinating works on Sigmund Freud, Mary Todd and Abraham Lincoln, Clarence Darrow, Michelangelo, and Vincent Van Gogh.

DEATH AND DYING

Life After Life, by Raymond A. Moody, Jr., M.D.

On Death and Dying, by Elisabeth Kiubler-Ross

MISCELLANEOUS

Books by Edgar Cayce will serve as an excellent introduction to a kind of mysticism; and if you think you might become interested in the theory of visitors from other planets or from outer space, try any book by Erich Von Daniken or the excellent In Search of Ancient Mysteries, by Alan and Sally Landsburg.

FANTASY

Watership Down, by Richard Adams

The Wind in the Willows, by Kenneth Grahame

The Hobbit, and the Lord of the Rings, by J. R. R. Tolkien

Charlotte's Web, by E. B. White

The Little Prince, by Antoine de Sainte Exupery

The Last Unicorn, by Peter S. Beagle

NOVELS

Here you will find an absolute treasure-trove to choose from. Let me list some of my favorite novelists instead of titles, for each author has written a number of books, all worth reading, and most of them available in paperback.

William Goldman	Irving Wallace
Earl Thompson	Meyer Levin
Robert Wilder	Frank Yerby
Ira Levin	Herman Wouk
Philip Roth	Rumer Godden
Arthur Hailey	Saul Bellow
Ayn Rand	John Updike
Evan Hunter	James A. Michener
Gore Vidal	John Gardner
Norman Mailer	Taylor Caldwell
James Clavell	Norah Lofts
Gail Parent	Jerzy Kosinski

If you enjoy (or think you might enjoy) suspense, detective, or mystery novels, or science-fiction novels, read them without guilt, without the slightest feeling that you are "wasting time."

Such books are an excellent means by which you can keep improving your rate, practice your skimming techniques, and improve your concentration. You will be able to get completely involved, you will learn to speed along following the thread of the plot, and you will have no difficulty starting and finishing this type of novel at one sitting of less than two to three hours.

MYSTERIES, SUSPENSE, ETC.

Some or all of the following authors may appeal to you.

Dashiell Hammett	Alfred Harris
Dick Francis	Donald Westgate
Raymond Chandler	Nero Wolfe
Rex Stout	Richard Stark
Eric Ambler	Josephine Tey
Ellery Queen	Ross McDonald
Samuel·A. Taylor	John D. MacDonald
Alistair MacLean	Agatha Christie
Francis Iles	Ed McBain
Raymond Postgate	Joseph Wambaugh
Hilda Lawrence	Maj Sjowall and Per Whahloo
Johy Godey	Helen MacInnes
"Trevanian"	

SCIENCE FICTION

Recommended authors:
Kurt Vonnegut, Jr.
Robert A. Heinlein
Harlan Ellison
Samuel R. Delany
Issac Asimov
Larry Niven
Ray Bradbury

The list of stimulating books catalogued in this chapter makes no pretense at completeness, but if you read a number of them you will be taking a long step forward in becoming an informed, well-rounded person. If you have not had a liberal college education, these books will provide you with its equivalent; if you are a college student or graduate, they will continue and extend your education.

But do not restrict yourself either to the suggested categories or to the recommended individual titles. Between the time these pages are written and the time you read them, many new and excellent books will be published in a wide variety of fields, and once you develop a broad range of interests you will want to keep up with the latest thinking and discoveries in many areas of life, you will want to keep abreast of what's new in the world.

Learn to make your own choices.

You will quickly discover the types of book that can delight and stimulate you; you will find certain authors to whom you make such an immediate and strong attachment that you will search out, and gobble up, everything they have written. When this happens, you will have no problem making time for reading, and you will wonder how you ever survived on a slim diet of half a dozen or so books a year.

MAKE A LONG-RANGE READING PROGRAM

Now is the time to make some definite plans for wide and continuous reading of as many types of books as you can become interested in. Decide on a *minimum* program of fifty books in the next year, at least one book a week. Once you have started, you will discover this goal so easy to reach that you may eventually find yourself reading two or more books each week, with several books piled up near your favorite chair waiting their turn.

You have possibly already checked off a number of nonfiction titles in fields that appeal to you; now pick some titles or names from among the suggested novels and novelists, and make yourself a list of the books you intend to read in the next few months.

You will be surprised at the psychological motivation there is in having *physical possession* of the books you plan to read.

Get the books you want, or reasonable substitutes for them, into your home.

Then decide which of the books you're going to start your reading program with, and *exactly when* you're going to get started. Make a date with one of the books on your list, and *keep your date* —keep it as faithfully as if you had purchased tickets to the theater or to a concert.

If you decide to start with a book of nonfiction, follow the procedure outlined in the fourth challenge to your reading habits, page 209. Read rapidly, skim when you wish to, skip chapters or parts that are repetitive or that do not interest you, and get an overall view of the subject matter of the book.

If you decide to start with a work of fiction, bear in mind that only a very long novel should require more than one or two evenings of continuous reading. With the training you have had, indeed, you are prepared to cover a comparatively short novel in a few hours if you push yourself.

However you start, keep reading—complete at least one book a week, preferably two or three. Vary your diet with occasional magazines of the more challenging types. And, to avoid losing momentum, always have a few unread books around the house—books you plan to get to, and do get to, as soon as you've finished whatever book you're working on.

If you have been laboring under the delusion that you aren't the type of person who can do much leisure reading, let me disabuse you. I have found that most adults restrict their reading unnecessarily. They claim a lack of time, the wrong kind of temperament, or an inability to relate to, or enjoy, books, but, as a matter of fact, what holds them back is that they don't know *what* to read; or they haven't yet discovered the *kind of reading* they can thoroughly

enjoy; or they just don't keep enough good books at hand to get into the habit of spending their leisure time in the pleasant and stimulating relaxation that continuous reading provides more conveniently and more satisfyingly than perhaps any other recreational activity.

The success of your own future reading program will depend on your discovering what kinds of books you personally will find enjoyable and rewarding; on going out and getting those books; and on actually reading them, at a rate of no less than one a week, starting either immediately or as soon as you can after you finish your training with this book.

Once you get started, the pleasure and stimulation you derive will provide all the further motivation you'll need.

If you put this plan into effect, and keep to it, you will find that the amount and range of your reading over the next twelve months may well dwarf your accomplishments of the last five, even ten, years.

Final Training
in Rapid
Comprehension

PREVIEW

Chapter 15 reminds you, as the book comes to a close, that this need not be the end of your training, and that you can go on by yourself making still further gains; for learning to read is a continuous, never-ending process.

In this chapter, you:

• Tackle a final round of two fairly complex timed selections

• Continue to aim for a quick and accurate grasp of main ideas by responding aggressively to the structure of writing

• Evaluate your total progress

FINAL PRACTICE TESTS IN FASTER READING

You are now coming to the end of months of hard practice in the techniques of rapid and efficient reading. During this time you have gradually increased your speed of comprehension, you have developed greater competence and aggressiveness in attacking a page of print, you have begun to form habits of cruising through material with sharper awareness not only of *essential meaning* but also of the *pattern* in which this meaning is presented. In short, if your training has been at all successful, you have become a better and much faster reader than you were when you started your work.

Now you will have your last chance (in this book, but of course not in your outside reading) to measure the speed of your performance. In reading the long and fairly difficult selections in this chapter, observe all the rules that have constantly been emphasized and reemphasized throughout your training: Mobilize yourself so that you are aware of a *sense of urgency* as you read; *dominate* the material rather than letting the material dominate you; consciously push yourself, so that you have a feeling of comprehending rapidly; sense the broad outlines of structure; find and follow the main ideas, the central theme, without losing time on unimportant details; and skim whenever the character of the material makes skimming desirable and useful.

Time your reading of each piece, and keep a record of your statistics on the new chart and graph on page 236.

Ready for your final tests?

SELECTION 25

Beware the Psychos
by Fred Dickenson

Time at start: _____ minutes _____ seconds

Start timing ➡ [1] That pretty girl who just sold you the wrong pack of cigarets; that rude man who shoved ahead of you to grab the subway seat; the smiling fellow in the office who "forgot" to pay back the loan as he had promised so faithfully to do—watch out for them!

[2] They're psychopathic personalities and they're as dangerous as a package of dynamite with fuse attached and ready to go.

[3] Scandal, disgrace, grief, and even death await the unwary who are drawn too deeply into their erratic orbit. They walk the streets by the millions, sit beside you in the gay glitter of the theatre and in the calm sanctity of the church. They're at the wheel of the car bearing down on you.

[4] Are they insane? Not in a legal sense. Nor do they exhibit any of the common symptoms we have come to associate with "crazy" people. They do not babble or burst into bizarre song, effect weird costumes or think they are Napoleon.

[5] Because to the casual eye they can appear as normal as the sturdiest, they pack a double peril. When their unstable world collapses, they pull down with them anyone within reach. It can be you.

[6] Police officers come into contact daily with psychopathic personalities, who are born "trouble makers." To guide officers in this work, the National Association for Mental Health has issued a manual called "How to Recognize and Handle Abnormal People," by Robert A. Matthews, M.D., head of the Department of Psychiatry and Neurology, Louisiana State University School of Medicine, and Lloyd W. Rowland, Ph.D., director of the Louisiana Association for Mental Health.

[7] Their tips also form a valuable guide for the average person who may unwittingly become involved with a psychopathic personality unless he can spot and interpret flying danger signals.

[8] Since the disorder shows up in many forms and degrees, one or several of the warning signs may be seen in a person by a trained observer. Crediting Hervey Cleckly's book, "The Mask of Sanity," as their source, Drs. Matthews and Rowland list in modified form the characteristic points which can alert you to the possibility that a person is a psychopath. They are:

1. Shallow, on the surface charm, often seems rather bright.
2. Lack of symptoms one would observe in a person who is mentally ill.
3. Lack of nervousness of the sort commonly seen in a neurotic patient.
4. Unreliability—you can't depend on him.
5. Untruthfulness and insincerity.
6. Selfishness—thinks only in terms of how things affect him personally; has no capacity to really love another person.
7. Antisocial behavior.
8. Poor judgment and failure to learn from experience.
9. Lack of any feeling of shame, after he has done something wrong.
10. Lack of feeling for the rights of others.
11. Lack of realization that there is something wrong with him. It is always somebody else's fault.
12. Callousness and lack of ability to work harmoniously in a team with others.
13. Foolish behavior with drink or even without it.
14. Threats of suicide when in trouble—seldom carried out.
15. Sex life—superficial, often promiscuous.
16. Failure to follow a life plan.

[9] "It is easy to see how persons with such character traits become vagrants and try all shorts of schemes to make money," say Drs. Matthews and Rowland. "They do foolhardy things that en-

danger their own lives and the lives of others, and they may eventually drift into crime.

[10] "Many drug addicts are psychopaths and a large proportion of our criminal population belongs in this category. Sometimes the psychopath does well in a wartime army but is a troublemaker in a peacetime military unit when he cannot find a way to get rid of his hostile impulses."

[11] The psychopath (unlike the truly insane) is held responsible by society for his behavior and is punished for his misdemeanors and crimes. Invariably, the doctors say, this punishment does no good but makes the person worse.

[12] "He makes solemn promises to turn over a new leaf only to repeat some wrong act immediately upon release from custody. It almost seems that he feels a need to be punished because he lacks a conscience that will punish him."

[13] What makes a psychopath—these persons whom an English physician long ago called "moral imbeciles" because they are often intelligent but have no sense of right or wrong?

[14] Drs. Matthews and Rowland state that the psychiatric concensus today is that most persons with character defects get that way because of unfortunate childhood experiences. "As children, nobody wanted them or loved them. Many came from broken homes or homes where there were no sturdy parents to provide a pattern for growth.

[15] "Sometimes they come from wealthy homes which are long on comfort but short on love. Feeling insecure, unwanted, even hated as a child, they can hardly have much faith in their future."

[16] The psychopathic personality, they add, is angry at the world and gets even by doing things which are wrong. He feels he must seize his pleasure at the moment, and does so regardless of consequences. Punishment usually follows, and the cycle proceeds relentlessly until a delinquent or a criminal is created.

[17] Since punishment does not seem to help, can anything else be done for them? In a London hospital today, a hundred persons with various character disorders are being treated in what is called a "therapeutic community." A sincere attempt is made to understand the psychopath, and with medical help the patients try to understand one another.

[18] The feeling that people are for them and not against them seems to aid about half of the patients, doctors report. Why the treatment does not work with the other 50 percent is still a mystery.

[19] The fact that medical science cannot yet straighten the character kinks of so many psycho-pathic personalities is added warning to the layman to avoid their clutches. Giving children genuine love to prevent creation of new cases is the duty and responsibility of every parent. In the presence of a full-blown character disorder, however, the layman's wisest course to protect himself and society is to try to get the afflicted person to see a doctor.

[20] How many psychopathic personalities are there? How many people steal, skip out on debts, start unfounded and malicious gossip, repeatedly walk out on jobs, wreak, deliberate mischief, are constantly getting injured, or take physical revenge to the point of murder?

[21] Their numbers dwarf the 750,000 persons now under the care of mental hospitals in this country. Of the latter, suffering recognized mental disorders such as schizophrenia, manic depression, involutional melancholia, etc., relatively few come from the ranks of the psychopathic personality.

[22] Occasionally, a judge will recommend psychiatric care for an habitual thief and a person will cross the bridge between the two groups. A drug addict may wind up in a hospital and do the same thing. But all too often, say officials of the Mental Health Association, the psychopathic personality merely goes his weird way taking a frightful toll in blighted lives, and costing the public untold millions for the upkeep of jails, reformatories and various other institutions.

[23] The enormity of the problem can be highlighted by the fact that already there are more people hospitalized in this country for *recognized mental illness* than for polio, cancer, heart disease and all other diseases combined. The chance of your being hospitalized for a severe mental illness today is one in 10, whereas in 1934 it was one in 20.

[24] Of the $180,000,000 spent each year on all medical research, only about $6,000,000—or 3 percent—goes toward conquering the more than 100 different kinds of mental disorders.

[25] Thus, the community must still grapple, somehow, with the vast number of psychopathic personalities about us who are not being treated and for whose problem virtually no research is being carried on.

[26] They must wait until the more recognizable forms of mental illness are brought under control. Then, doctors say, the truly Herculean task of salvaging psychopathic personalities can begin. Meanwhile, the best the average citizen can do is be on his guard among them. ◆ **End Timing**

Test Your Comprehension

Which one of the following statements best summarizes the essential meaning of this selection?

1. Psychopathic personalities are not insane, in the legal sense of the word.

2. Be on guard against psychopathic personalities—they are dangerous.

3. Psychopathic personalities are charming, intelligent, and unusually calm.

4. Punishment does not cure the psychopathic personality.

Compute Your Rate
(Approximate Number of Words: 1520)

Time	WPM	Time	WPM
1 min.	1520	2 min. 40 sec.	570
1 min. 10 sec.	1303	2 min. 45 sec.	550
1 min. 20 sec.	1140	3 min.	505
1 min. 30 sec.	1013	3 min. 15 sec.	470
1 min. 40 sec.	912	3 min. 30 sec.	435
1 min. 45 sec.	869	3 min. 45 sec.	405
1 min. 50 sec.	829	4 min.	380
2 min.	760	4 min. 15 sec.	360
2 min. 10 sec.	700	4 min. 30 sec.	340
2 min. 15 sec.	675	4 min. 45 sec.	320
2 min. 20 sec.	660	5 min.	305
2 min. 30 sec.	610	5 min. 30 sec.	275

Your rate on selection 25: _____ WPM

(Record this statistic on the chart and graph on page 236)

Discussion of the Selection

Mr. Dickenson is saying one main thing to his readers. This point is mentioned in the title, is expressed clearly in paragraphs 1 and 2, and is fully developed and often repeated throughout the selection. He is saying, in brief: *Watch out for psychopathic personalities—they're dangerous.*

Let us examine together the pattern Mr. Dickenson follows in developing his central theme.

Paragraphs 1-2: Expression of central theme.

Paragraphs 3-5: Explanation of the danger.

Paragraphs 6-12: Description of the psychopathic personality.

Paragraphs 13-16: Causes of the psychopathic personality (lack of love in childhood, hence angry at the world).

Paragraphs 17-19: Treatment and prevention of the psychopathic personality—show people are not against him (works for 50 percent of those treated); give love to children; get the afflicted person to see a doctor.

Paragraphs 20-26: Further description of the psychopathic personality, statistics as to his prevalence, etc., supporting the author's theme that the best thing we can do at present is be on our guard against him.

Mr. Dickenson uses every detail in his piece to bolster his main idea. *Watch out*, he says, *for psychopathic personalities—they're dangerous.* Then he goes on, point by point:

1. This is the danger they present.

2. This is how to recognize them.

3. This is what causes their affliction.

4. This is how to treat them, but treatment is effective in only half the cases.

5. Their numbers are vast, most of them are not treated, and there is virtually no research on their illness. So be on your guard!

Correct choice on the comprehension test is statement 2.

SELECTION 26   ## Why Do Accidents Happen?

Time at start: _____ minutes _____ seconds

Start timing ➡ [1] Before we can develop a really effective program to prevent auto accidents, we will have to learn far more than we now know about why such accidents happen.

[2] The National Safety Council, while pointing out that most accidents result from a combination of causes, and that "few accidents are investigated carefully enough to determine exactly what their underlying causes were," estimates that in about 80% of accidents, the most important single factor is the driver himself.

[3] Bad weather, poor road conditions, and defects in cars do cause some accidents, but, generally, speaking, such circumstances appear to be of minor significance compared with the mental and physical condition of the driver. And recent research indicates that the driver's physical condition is of less importance than his personality and his emotional state. Many, if not most, accidents, this research suggests, are the result of wayward impulses and motivations, of faulty judgments and attitudes, of poorly controlled aggressiveness and

competitiveness. Further study of personality and emotions in relation to driving probably would contribute much to the understanding and prevention of accidents.

[4] Nearly two-thirds of the drivers involved in fatal accidents in 1954 were speeding, driving while under the influence of alcohol, disregarding stop lights or signs, or otherwise violating the law, according to the Safety Council. The pertinent question is *why* do people drive too fast, drive after drinking, take risks in passing, or, in general, commit dangerous, careless, illegal, impulsive, or unfriendly acts when they get behind the wheel?

[5] A small beginning has been made toward finding answers to this question. Several studies comprehensively described by Dr. Ross McFarland and his associates at Harvard's School of Public Health have probed the personality and emotional characteristics of so-called accident-prone drivers and discovered such traits as emotional instability, impulsiveness, suggestibility, excitability, lack of a proper sense of social responsibility, aggressiveness, and intolerance of authority. Although fault may be found with the quality of this research in terms of controls and other safeguards, it may prove provocative enough to lead to sounder efforts.

[6] "A man drives as he lives," say Drs. Tillman and Hobbs in an article in the *American Journal of Psychiatry*. "If his personal life is marked by caution, tolerance, foresight, considerations for others, then he will drive in the same way. If his personal life is devoid of these desirable characteristics, then his driving will be characterized by aggressiveness, and over a long period of time, he will have a higher accident rate than his more stable companions."

[7] The trouble with the first part of this statement is that no human being is, at all times, cautious, tolerant, foresighted, and considerate of others. Even though we may be exemplary persons most of the time, there are certain moments, or longer periods, in the lives of all of us when we become temporarily impulsive, aggressive, or otherwise emotionally off balance. If we happen to be driving during one of these episodes—and if external circumstances favor an accident—then an accident is likely to occur.

[8] As Dr. Edward Press, of the University of Illinois, puts it: "Just as almost all of us will respond with a neurosis or other nervous disorder to a sufficiently strong or repeated stress, so most average people under certain combinations of circumstances that occur frequently in our current civilization can become temporarily accident prone." Excessive fatigue, fear, worry, sleeplessness, irritability, preoccupation, headache, too much alcohol or other drugs—all may have this effect.

[9] While the study of behavior and conscious mental activities by way of aptitude, intelligence, and psychologic tests and by clinical scrutiny of life histories and attitudes will increase our understanding of accident causes, our knowledge will be incomplete without more information about the unconscious and its influence on drivers. More than 40 years ago, Freud said, "Psychoanalysis has concluded from a study of dreams and mental slips of normal people as well as from the symptoms of neurotics, that . . . primitive [and] savage . . . impulses of mankind have not vanished in any individual, but continue their existence, although in a repressed state in the unconscious, and that they wait for opportunities to display their activity." For many people, the automobile apparently provides some of the most irresistible of such opportunities—especially with the current glorification of the high-speed car with its formidable horsepower, and fast-starting and quick-passing ability.

[10] While, admittedly, the evidence for the great importance of psychological factors in auto accidents rests on a fragile statistical framework, the same is true of the evidence on physical defects of drivers responsible for auto accidents. The National Safety Council says that "only one out of 14 drivers involved in fatal accidents had a physical condition that could have been a contributing factor in the accident." Such statistics mean very little unless we know what is meant by a "physical condition"; and psychosomatic medicine has taught us that even major "physical" disorders often have important emotional components.

[11] Some test of visual acuity is a standard device in almost all states for helping to determine the fitness of drivers. Such a test is of value in detecting impairment of ability to see far objects, and it undoubtedly deprives the near-blind of the freedom of killing themselves and others on the road. However, Dr. Leon Brody, of New York University, has been stressing for years the scant relationship between a driver's visual fitness, as measured by a conventional driver's license test, and his safety record.

[12] To be more meaningful, tests of driver vision, should include peripheral vision, or ability to see objects on the sides while looking straight ahead; dark adaptation, or night vision; glare recovery; and ability to "accommodate," or shift from a far focus to a near focus (such as on a speedometer) and back. Color-blindness tests are of little importance, since even a person color-blind to red and green can readily learn to distinguish between red and green lights. Dark adaptation and glare recovery are particularly important in view of the fact that the fatal-accident rate per mile of travel is three times as high during the night as during the day. Dark adaptation is im-

paired by alcohol, carbon monoxide and lack of vitamin A or oxygen. After age 45 or 50, there is a gradual decline in all visual functions, but what effect this decline has on auto-accident rates is unknown. Probably most older drivers compensate for it by more conservative driving practices.

[13] Hearing acuteness also declines with age, but, again, there are no statistics to suggest a connection between hearing defects and auto accidents. Obviously, though, a deaf driver—or a driver with normal hearing who keeps his radio on full blast—has one less physical sense on guard to warn him of danger.

[14] Driving skill by itself does not insure safety in driving, according to a study made by Dr. Brody in 1941. Many drivers repeatedly involved in accidents are skilled drivers, as determined by controlled driving tests. Some of these may get into trouble because they are convinced that they can safely take more risks than less-skilled drivers.

[15] Although people with an organic disease or disability—epilepsy, heart disease, or high blood pressure, for example—may be more prone to disabling symptoms while driving than healthy persons, this very fact may act as an incentive to more cautious driving on their part. At any rate, statistical evidence of a connection between such disorders and a high rate of auto accidents is lacking. Certainly, the emotional stresses associated with contemporary auto driving are not likely to be beneficial for a person with coronary artery disease or high blood pressure. No one knows how many heart attacks in innocent pedestrians and drivers have been caused by the foolish behavior of "healthy" drivers.

[16] "Carotid sinus syncope" is a disorder caused by oversensitivity of certain nerve tissue in the carotid arteries of the neck. A tight collar could conceivably produce faintness, dizziness, or even loss of consciousness in a driver suffering from this condition.

[17] Other organic ailments—such as uncontrolled diabetes, kidney trouble, and neurological disorders—also can cause impairment of driving fitness. Undoubtedly, more study of this problem is needed, and other states might well follow the lead of New York in requiring a doctor's certification of the fitness of persons with mental and certain physical disorders to receive a license to drive. At the same time, physicians should warn their patients with such disorders of the potential danger to themselves and others in driving.

[18] Safe driving does not require hard muscular effort, but it does call for skill and mental concentration, both of which involve faculties that are subject to fatigue after several hours at the wheel. Visual fatigue also may be of considerable importance as an accident factor. It is good driving practice to take a rest or brief exercise after two hours or so at the wheel. This can also help to relieve road monotony and prevent the driver's falling asleep at the wheel—two frequently cited causes of auto accidents. Heavy meals, which dispose to sleepiness and fatigue, should be avoided by drivers.

[19] The exhaust gas from auto engines contains carbon monoxide in percentages ranging from about 1% to 7%, and a car idling in a closed garage can produce enough of the gas in a few minutes to render the atmosphere deadly. Tests of passenger cars on the road have shown that carbon monoxide concentrations within the car can reach dangerous levels. The gas can come from leaks in the car's own exhaust system—such as blown-out gaskets, loose manifold and exhaust pipe connections, and holes in mufflers and exhaust pipes—and, in heavy traffic, from the exhaust of other cars. In streets where traffic is heavy, the concentration of carbon monoxide rises to about a hundred parts per million parts of air, enough to cause headaches, dizziness, faintness, weakness, and other toxic symptoms in many persons after an exposure of several hours.

[20] Carbon monoxide also is one of the important toxic ingredients of tobacco smoke, and a person who smokes 20 to 30 cigarettes a day has from 4% to 8% of his hemoglobin blocked by this gas. There is little doubt that the carbon monoxide from other cars, your car, and smoking can combine to interfere seriously with driving efficiency.

[21] Not long ago, Dr. Frank Dutra, the chief medical examiner for Cincinnati, urged that the carbon monoxide concentration in the blood of any driver involved in an accident be measured, predicting that such tests would pinpoint carbon monoxide as the cause of some otherwise unexplained fatal accidents.

[22] Widely used sedatives, tranquilizers, stimulants, hormones (such as ACTH and cortisone) and antihistamine drugs may cause disturbing side effects that impair driving skill, judgment, and attention. The disabling effects of some of these drugs were brought out at the last highway safety research conference sponsored by the National Academy of Science and the National Research Council in 1954. Even ordinary doses of sedatives or stimulant drugs can evoke hostile and aggressive practices. Such barbiturate drugs as phenobarbital, *Nembutal,* and *Seconal,* when taken by order of a physician, are valuable for relieving nervous tension and promoting sleep, but taken at the wrong time or in uncontrolled amounts, they can cause physical and mental symptoms that interfere with driving ability.

[23] The stimulants—*Benzedrine, Dexedrine,* and similar amphetamine drugs—are frequently misused by drivers who do not realize that there is no substitute for rest and adequate sleep to assure

effective exercise of their faculties. If misused, these drugs may cause irritability, excitement, and impairment of timing, coordination, and judgment. Abuse of the newer tranquilizing drugs, such as *Miltown, Noludar, Thorazine*, and reserpine, now frequently prescribed for common nervous disorders, can have equally harmful effects. The caffeine in cola drinks, coffee, and tea has a mild stimulant action which may improve driving alertness, but in excess or in sensitive persons, can impair muscular coordination and timing.

[24] Since some antihistamine drugs are freely available without a doctor's prescription, many people take them indiscriminately for colds, grippe, coughs, and other acute respiratory infections. Other antihistamine drugs (*Dramamine* and *Boramine*, for example) are taken to control motion sickness. Among the more important possible side effects of these drugs are dizziness, difficulty in focusing the eyes, sleepiness, impaired reflex and reaction time, and disturbance of coordination and judgment—any of which obviously would be dangerous in a driver.

[25] In the whole array of drugs capable of seriously interfering with driving skill and judgment, alcohol undoubtedly is the outstanding culprit. From the viewpoint of auto safety, the most important aspect of alcohol is its effect on the central nervous system. It is not a stimulant, as many people believe, but a depressant of the nervous system, sharing the characteristic actions of the general anesthetics. In small amounts, alcohol may improve mood and sociability, but, as Drs. Goodman and Gilman say in "The Pharmacological Basis of Therapeutics": "Carefully controlled experiments have shown that alcohol increases neither mental nor physical ability; although the individual estimates his own performance as greatly improved, in reality, actual measurements show it to be inferior."

[26] To a certain extent, man can use his intelligence to overcome his physical and emotional shortcomings as a driver and the other threats to his safety on the road. He can make cars and roads safer, enforce traffic laws more rigorously, improve driving education, encourage training of visual and other skills useful in driving, and probably most important, apply psychiatric, psychologic, and psychoanalytic research to the auto-accident problem. While Colorado has made a good start in this latter direction by requiring a psychiatric examination for persistent violators of driving laws, it obviously would be impractical to make such an examination a routine part of driver's-license tests.

[27] Until we find a way to screen out potentially dangerous drivers or to get more people to practice common sense and consideration for others on the road, it would be wise for each of us to assume that other drivers, will behave discourteously, carelessly, aggressively, illegally, or stupidly—and to try to maintain a safety margin adequate to compensate for such behavior. ◄ **End timing**

Record here the time required on this selection: _____minutes _____seconds

Test Your Comprehension

Which one of the following statements best summarizes the total and final meaning of this selection?

1. If we ever hope to prevent or reduce automobile accidents, we must set up machinery to investigate the exact causes of accidents.

2. Most accidents are caused by bad weather, poor road conditions, and car defects, but the mental and physical condition of the driver is often a contributing factor.

3. Human beings must learn to be more cautious, tolerant, and considerate when they drive if we are going to reduce the toll of lives taken by automobile accidents.

4. Only those people who are physically and mentally fit—possessed of good vision and hearing, free of organic disease, well-balanced in personality—and who are really skillful at the wheel, should be licensed to drive.

5. Most important single cause of most automobile accidents is the driver himself, that is, his mental and physical condition and his personality type and emotional state.

Compute Your Rate
(Approximate Number of Words: 2400)

Time	WPM	Time	WPM
1 min. 30 sec.	1600	3 min. 45 sec.	640
1 min. 40 sec.	1440	4 min.	600
1 min. 50 sec.	1309	4 min. 15 sec.	565
2 min.	1200	4 min. 30 sec.	535
2 min. 10 sec.	1108	4 min. 45 sec.	510
2 min. 15 sec.	1067	5 min.	480
2 min. 20 sec.	1029	5 min. 30 sec.	440
2 min. 30 sec.	960	6 min	400
2 min. 40 sec.	900	6 min. 30 sec.	370
2 min. 45 sec.	873	7 min.	345
2 min. 50 sec.	847	7 min. 30 sec.	320
3 min.	800	8 min.	300
3 min. 15 sec.	740	8 min. 30 sec.	280
3 min. 30 sec.	685	9 min.	270

Your rate on selection 26: _____WPM

(Record this statistic on the chart and graph on page 236)

Discussion of the Selection

This piece, a model of clear organization, divides neatly into three parts. Let us look at the material together.

PART 1—STATEMENT OF CENTRAL THEME

Paragraphs 1–3: Direct answer to the question in the title and a statement of the central theme—*most important single cause of most accidents is the driver himself*, according to estimates of the National Safety Council. Bad weather, road conditions, and car defects cause some accidents, but the important thing is *the mental and physical condition of the driver, especially his personality type and emotional state.*

PART 2—DEVELOPMENT OF CENTRAL THEME

Paragraphs 4–9: How the personality and the emotional state of the driver cause accidents.

Paragraphs 10–18: Physical condition of the driver as a cause of accidents—vision, hearing, disease, fatigue, disabilities, etc.

Paragraphs 19–21: Carbon monoxide as a deterrent to driving efficiency and a reducer of physical fitness.

Paragraphs 22–25: The wide use of drugs, sedatives, alcohol, etc. as a cause of reducing mental and physical fitness and efficiency.

PART 3—RECAPITULATION

Paragraphs 26–27: How to reduce accidents—a kind of recapitulation of the central theme. The causes have been stated and explained, and obviously the best solution is to remove the causes.

Correct choice on the comprehension test is statement 5.

Referring to the charts you have been keeping on pages 234–236, fill in, below, the chart of your progress throughout your training.

Progress Chart

Initial Rate (Selection 1)	_____WPM
Average Rate:	
Chapters 1, 3, 4 (Phase 1)	_____WPM
Chapters 5, 6, 8 (Phase 2)	_____WPM
Chapters 9, 10 (Phase 3)	_____WPM
Chapter 13 (Phase 4)	_____WPM
Chapter 15 (Phase 5)	_____WPM

LAST WORDS—A PLAN FOR THE FUTURE

This is not necessarily the end of your training, even though you have faithfully covered every page in the book, have worked hard for months, and have noted an increase in your general reading speed of anywhere from 50 to 100 percent or more.

What you have learned, and what you have accomplished so far, should represent for you no more than a broad base, a strong foundation, on which to continue building. This was *basic* training; this provided you with a good initial push, a fast start, and excellent momentum.

Now you can, and should, go on by yourself—for, as I have said in the past, *learning to read is a continuous, never-ending process.*

Put your training to use. With the increased skill and speed you now possess, you can do up to twice or three or four times the amount of reading you used to do in any given period of time. You can do this, that is, if you form the *habit* of reading—if you make reading of magazines, novels, and books of nonfiction as much a regular part of your life as eating, or sleeping, or going to the movies, or visiting your friends, or watching television.

Set yourself the kind of goal I have suggested—let no week go by in which you haven't read at least one book, of whatever nature. And if you can manage to read two or three or more books most weeks, so much the better.

You will make no dent in the available reading material. But what a change you will effect in your own intellectual equipment, in your store of knowledge and ideas, in your alertness to what is going on in the world! How much more efficiently, if you are a student, you will get your assignments read; how much more accurately you will respond to your reading; how much better you will retain what you have studied!

Or I can give you a far more potent and convincing reason—*you'll enjoy it, you'll have a wonderful time.* Reading, you will discover (you have probably already made this discovery), is one of the great and satisfying pleasures of human living.

Continue building your reading vocabulary.

Get yourself a good vocabulary-building manual. Here are a number of top-notch aids in the field, listed alphabetically:

HOW TO BUILD A BETTER VOCABULARY, by Maxwell Nurnberg and Morris Rosenblum
INSTANT VOCABULARY, by Ida Ehrlich
NEW WAYS TO GREATER WORD POWER, by Roger B. Goodman and David Lewin
POWER WITH WORDS, by Norman Lewis
RAPID VOCABULARY BUILDER, by Norman Lewis
SIX WEEKS TO WORDS OF POWER, by Wilfred Funk
30 DAYS TO A MORE POWERFUL VOCABULARY, by Wilfred Funk and Norman Lewis
2300 STEPS TO WORD POWER, by Edward C. Gruber
WORD POWER MADE EASY, by Norman Lewis

Continue, in your everyday reading, your practice in occasional or partial skimming, or even in total skimming if the material and the circumstances warrant it. Continue sharpening your comprehension skill by keeping alert to the broad structure of whatever you read, by finding and following central themes, and by occasionally writing out, in your own words, the gist of what you have just read.

Continue pushing yourself, quickly and with a *sense of urgency,* through material. Read with the feeling that you are comprehending fast, that you are thinking along with the author, that you are reacting critically to what the author is saying.

Continue training your peripheral vision by sweeping down a narrow newspaper column as fast as comprehension permits and making, as far as possible, only one fixation to the line.

And test yourself periodically. Take a magazine article or a chapter in a book and time your reading. Count or estimate the number of words, and compute your rate. You may be surprised and gratified to discover that you can increase your present speed by as much as 10–50 percent within the next six months if you keep up your training.

All these suggestions, as you realize, only ask you to continue, on your own, the kind of practice this book has provided.

The dividends of increased speed, understanding, and satisfaction that you have received from your formal training program have been in direct proportion to the amount of time and creative effort that you have invested in your work.

Continue your investment and the dividends will continue to build up.

Appendix:
Improvement Charts

PHASE 1

Chapters 1, 3, 4

SELECTION 1: _____WPM
SELECTION 2: __ _____WPM
SELECTION 3: _____WPM
SELECTION 4: _____WPM
SELECTION 5: _____WPM
SELECTION 6: _____WPM
SELECTION 7: _____WPM
SELECTION 8: _____WPM
SELECTION 9: _____WPM

Average rate, selections 2-9: _____WPM
 (*add selections 2-9, divide by 8.*)

Average gain over selection 1: _____WPM
 (*Subtract selection 1 from average rate.*)

Percentage gain over selection 1: _____%
 (*Divide average gain by selection 1; change fraction to decimal, move decimal point two places right to read percentage. With calculator, divide average gain by selection 1, move decimal two places to the right.*)

IMPROVEMENT GRAPH—PHASE 1

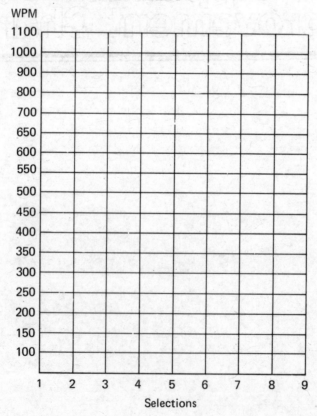

Fig. A-1

Draw a straight horizontal line on the graph to indicate your average rate, phase 1.

PHASE 2

Chapters 5, 6, 8

SELECTION 10: _____WPM
SELECTION 11: _____WPM
SELECTION 12: _____WPM
SELECTION 13: _____WPM
SELECTION 14: _____WPM

Average rate, selections 10-14: _____WPM
Average gain over selection 1: _____WPM
Percentage gain over selection 1: _____%
   (See instructions, phase 1.)

PHASE 3

Chapters 9, 10

SELECTION 15: _____WPM
SELECTION 16: _____WPM
SELECTION 17: _____WPM
SELECTION 18: _____WPM
SELECTION 19: _____WPM
SELECTION 20: _____WPM

Average rate, selections 15-20: _____WPM
Average gain over selection 1: _____WPM
Percentage gain over selection 1: _____%
   (See instructions, phase 1.)

IMPROVEMENT GRAPH—PHASE 2

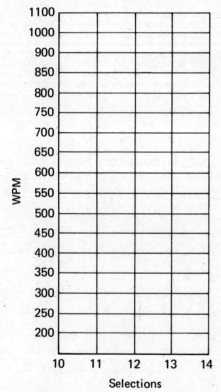

Fig. A-2

Draw a straight horizontal line on the graph to indicate your average rate, phase 2.

IMPROVEMENT GRAPH—PHASE 3

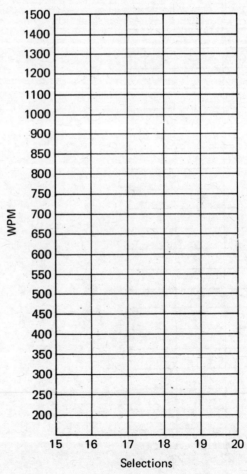

Fig. A-3

Draw a straight horizontal line on the graph to indicate your average rate, phase 3.

PHASE 4

Chapter 13
SELECTION 21: _____ WPM
SELECTION 22: _____ WPM
SELECTION 23: _____ WPM
SELECTION 24: _____ WPM

Average rate, selections 21-24: _____ WPM
Average gain over selection 1: _____ WPM
Percentage gain over selection 1: _____ %
(See instructions, phase 1.)

IMPROVEMENT GRAPH—PHASE 4

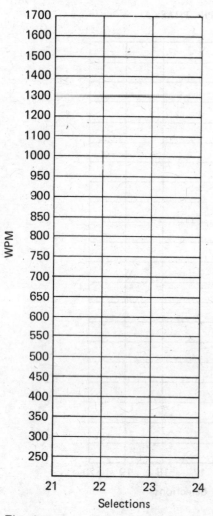

Fig. A-4

Draw a straight horizontal line on the graph to indicate your average rate, phase 4.

PHASE 5

Chapter 15
SELECTION 25: _____ WPM
SELECTION 26: _____ WPM

Average rate, selections 25-26: _____ WPM
Average gain over selection 1: _____ WPM
Percentage gain over selection 1: _____ %
(See instructions, phase 1.)

IMPROVEMENT GRAPH—PHASE 5

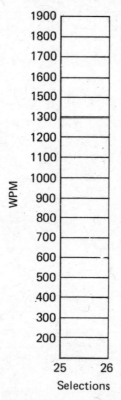

Fig. A-5

Draw a straight horizontal line on the graph to indicate your average rate, phase 5.

Index

Index to Excerpts and Selections